McGraw Hill Education create™

Course Norco College

Course Number **COM-1**

McGraw Hill Education create™

http://create.mheducation.com

ISBN-10: 1308827601   ISBN-13: 9781308827605

Contents

Credits

The Art of Public Speaking

TWELFTH EDITION

Stephen E. Lucas
University of Wisconsin—Madison

Mc Graw Hill Education

THE ART OF PUBLIC SPEAKING, TWELFTH EDITION

Published by McGraw-Hill Education, 2 Penn Plaza, New York, NY 10121.

This book is printed on acid-free paper.

1 2 3 4 5 6 7 8 9 0 RMN/RMN 1 0 9 8 7 6 5 4

ISBN 978-0-07-352391-0 *(Student Edition)*
MHID 0-07-352391-7 *(Student Edition)*

ISBN 978-0-07-779752-2 *(Instructor's Edition)*
MHID 0-07-779752-3 *(Instructor's Edition)*

Senior Vice President, Products & Markets: *Kurt L. Strand*
Vice President, General Manager, Products & Markets: *Michael Ryan*
Vice President, Content Design & Delivery: *Kimberly Meriwether David*
Managing Director: *David Patterson*
Director: *Susan Gouijnstook*
Director, Product Development: *Meghan Campbell*
Marketing Manager: *Laura Kennedy*
Director of Development: *Elissa Pinto*
Digital Product Analyst: *Janet Byrne Smith*
Director, Content Design & Delivery: *Terri Schiesl*
Program Manager: *Jennifer Gehl*
Content Project Managers: *Jennifer Gehl*
Buyer: *Laura M. Fuller*
Design: *Keith McPherson*
Content Licensing Specialists: *Shawntel Schmitt*
Cover Image: *Getty, Royalty Free, Rainbow soundwave backgrounds, By: Jamie Farrant*
Compositor: *Aptara®, Inc.*
Printer: *R. R. Donnelley*

All credits appearing on page or at the end of the book are considered to be an extension of the copyright page.

Library of Congress Cataloging-in-Publication Data

Lucas, Stephen, 1946–
The art of public speaking / Stephen E. Lucas, University of Wisconsin–Madison—Twelfth edition.
pages cm
ISBN 978-0-07-352391-0 (paperback)
1. Public speaking. I. Title.
PN4129.15.L83 2015
808.5'1—dc23 2014027557

About the Author

Stephen E. Lucas is Professor of Communication Arts and Evjue-Bascom Professor in the Humanities at the University of Wisconsin–Madison. He received his bachelor's degree from the University of California, Santa Barbara, and his master's and doctorate degrees from Penn State University.

Professor Lucas has been recognized for his work as both a scholar and a teacher. His first book, *Portents of Rebellion: Rhetoric and Revolution in Philadelphia, 1765–1776,* received the Golden Anniversary Award of the National Communication Association and was nominated for a Pulitzer Prize. His major articles include "The Schism in Rhetorical Scholarship" (1981), "The Renaissance of American Public Address: Text and Context in Rhetorical Criticism" (1988), "The Stylistic Artistry of the Declaration of Independence" (1990), and "The Rhetorical Ancestry of the Declaration of Independence" (1998), for which he received the Golden Anniversary Monograph Award of the National Communication Association. His most recent book is *Words of a Century: The Top 100 American Speeches, 1900–1999* (2009).

Professor Lucas has received a number of teaching awards, including the Chancellor's Award for Excellence in Teaching at the University of Wisconsin and the National Communication Association's Donald Ecroyd Award for Outstanding Teaching in Higher Education. He is featured in the Educational Video Group's program on the history of American public address, and he appeared on the History Channel's documentary on the Declaration of Independence.

Professor Lucas has directed the introductory public speaking course at the University of Wisconsin–Madison since 1973. Over the years he has been responsible for numerous teaching innovations and has supervised the training of hundreds of graduate assistants. He has also served as a judge for the major national English-language public speaking competitions in China, has lectured at numerous Chinese universities, has conducted workshops for Chinese instructors on teaching public speaking, and has been instrumental in the development of public speaking as a dedicated course in the English curriculum of Chinese universities. *The Art of Public Speaking* has been translated into several languages, including Chinese, Portuguese, Korean, and Romanian.

Stephen Lucas and his wife, Patty, live in Madison, Wisconsin, and have two sons, Jeff and Ryan. His interests include travel, sports, art, and photography.

Brief Contents

Contents

Chapter 10 Beginning and Ending the Speech 184

Chapter 11 Outlining the Speech 204

PART FOUR PRESENTING THE SPEECH

Chapter 12 Using Language 220

Chapter 13 **Delivery** 238

Chapter 14 **Using Visual Aids** 264

Chapter 19 Speaking in Small Groups 370

Appendix Speeches for Analysis and Discussion A1

SPEECHES

SPEECHES BY GENRE

INTRODUCTORY SPEECHES

INFORMATIVE SPEECHES

PERSUASIVE SPEECHES

SPEECHES OF PRESENTATION

SPEECHES OF ACCEPTANCE

COMMEMORATIVE SPEECHES

A Note from the Author

When I wrote the first edition of *The Art of Public Speaking,* I could not have imagined the extraordinary response the book would receive. I am deeply appreciative of the students and teachers who have made it the leading work on its subject at colleges and universities across the United States and around the world.

In preparing this edition, I have retained what readers have identified as the main strengths of the book. *The Art of Public Speaking* is informed by classical and contemporary theories of rhetoric, but it does not present theory for its own sake. Keeping a steady eye on the practical skills of public speaking, it offers full coverage of all major aspects of speech preparation and presentation.

It also follows David Hume's advice that one "who would teach eloquence must do it chiefly by examples." Whenever possible, I have tried to *show* the principles of public speaking in action in addition to describing them. Thus you will find in the book a large number of narratives, speech excerpts, and full sample speeches that illustrate the principles of effective public speaking.

Because the immediate task facing students is to present speeches in the classroom, I rely heavily on examples that relate directly to students' classroom needs and experiences. The speech classroom, however, is a training ground where students develop skills that will serve them throughout life. Therefore, I also include a large number of illustrations drawn from the kinds of speaking experiences students will face after they graduate from college.

Because speeches are performative acts, students need to be able to view speakers in action as well as read their words on the printed page. *The Art of Public Speaking* has an extensive video program that is available both on DVD and on *Connect,* McGraw-Hill's innovative online learning platform. The video program includes 36 full student speeches, plus more than 60 speech excerpts. Ten of the full speeches and 15 of the excerpts are new to this edition.

Connect also provides a wide range of teaching and learning resources in addition to the speech videos. These resources include SmartBook Achieve, hands-on study tools, critical-thinking exercises, speech analysis questions, worksheets, assessment forms, and more. Taken together, *The Art of Public Speaking* and the digital resources available on *Connect* provide an interactive public speaking program that meets the needs of students and teachers alike.

The Art of Public Speaking has changed over the years in response to changes in technology, student demographics, and instructional needs. But it has never lost sight of the fact that the most important part of speaking is thinking. The ability to think critically is vital to a world in which personality and image too often substitute for thought and substance. While helping students become capable, responsible speakers, *The Art of Public Speaking* also seeks to help them become capable, responsible thinkers.

Instructor's Guide to McGraw-Hill Connect

When you assign Connect you can be confident—and have data to demonstrate—that your students, however diverse, are acquiring the skills, principles, and critical processes that constitute effective communication. This leaves you to focus on your highest course expectations.

TAILORED TO YOU. Connect offers on-demand, single sign-on access to learners—wherever they are and whenever they have time. With a single, one-time registration, learners receive access to McGraw-Hill's trusted content. **Learners also have access to a *two-week courtesy access* period during registration.**

EASY TO USE. Connect seamlessly supports all major learning management systems with content, assignments, performance data, and LearnSmart, the leading adaptive learning system. With these tools you can quickly make assignments, produce reports, focus discussions, intervene on problem topics, and help at-risk learners—as you need to and when you need to.

SmartBook Achieve

SmartBook Achieve is the first and only adaptive reading and study experience designed to change the way students read and master key course concepts. As a student engages with SmartBook Achieve, the program creates a personalized learning path by highlighting the most impactful concepts the student needs to learn at that moment in time. The learning path continuously adapts by delivering just-in-time learning resources—videos, animations, and other interactivities—catered to each student's needs. These rich, dynamic resources help students learn the material, retain more knowledge, and get better grades.

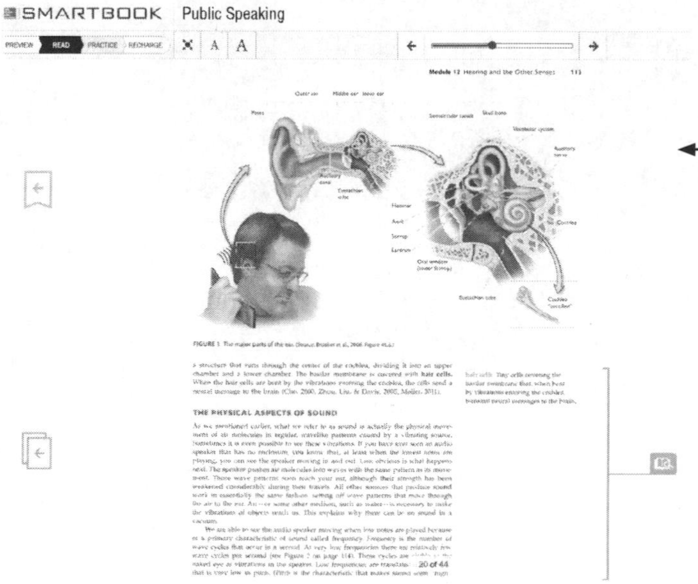

SmartBook Achieve highlights the key concepts of every chapter, offering students a high-impact learning experience. Here, highlighted text and an illustration together explain the physical aspects of sound.

Insight Analytics

Mobile-ready Connect Insight provides at-a-glance analysis on five key insights, available at a moment's notice from your tablet device. The first and only analytics tool of its kind, Insight will tell you, in real time, how individual students or sections are doing (or how well your assignments have been received) so you can take action early and keep struggling students from falling behind.

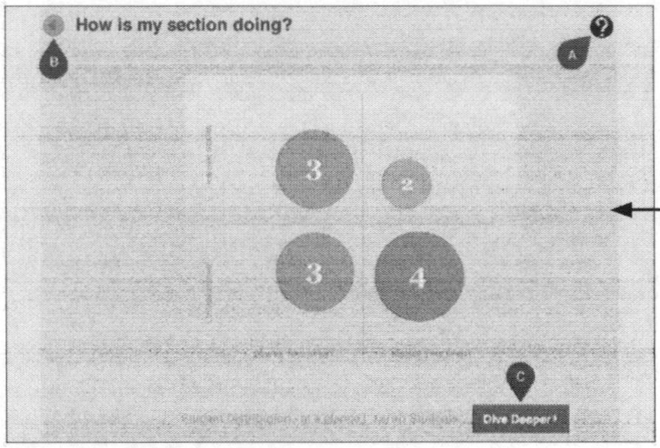

Connect Insight shows instructors how many students have completed an assignment, how long they spent on the task, and how they scored.

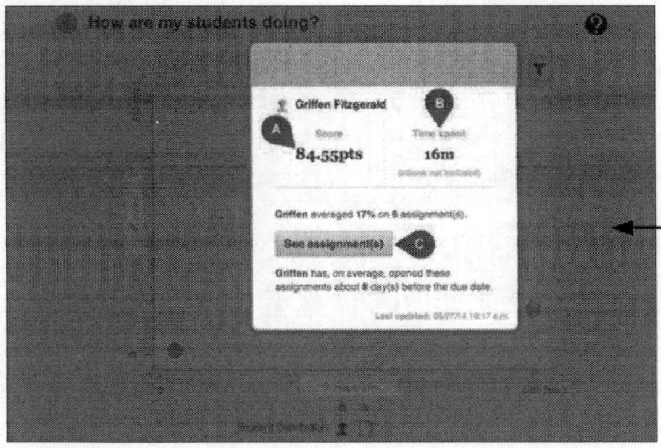

With Connect Insight, instructors can see, at a glance, individual student performance: analytics showing student investment in assignments, and success at completing them, help instructors identify, and aid, those who are at risk.

Connect LearnSmart Reports

LearnSmart Instructor Reports allow instructors to quickly monitor student activity, making it easy to identify which students are struggling and to provide immediate help to ensure those students stay enrolled in the course and improve their performance. The Instructor Reports also highlight the concepts and learning objectives that the class as a whole is having difficulty grasping. This essential information lets you know exactly which areas to target for review during your limited class time.

Some key LearnSmart reports include:

Progress Overview report—View student progress for all LearnSmart modules, including how long students have spent working in the module, which modules they have used outside of any that were assigned, and individual student progress through LearnSmart.

Missed Questions report—Identify specific LearnSmart probes, organized by chapter, that are problematic for students.

Most Challenging Learning Objectives report—Identify the specific topic areas that are challenging for your students; these reports are organized by chapter and include specific page references. Use this information to tailor your lecture time and assignments to cover areas that require additional remediation and practice.

Metacognitive Skills report—View statistics showing how knowledgeable your students are about their own comprehension and learning.

Speech Capture

Designed for use in face-to-face, real-time classrooms, as well as online courses, Speech Capture allows you to evaluate your students' speeches using fully customizable rubrics. You can also create and manage peer review assignments and upload videos on behalf of students for optimal flexibility.

Students can access rubrics and leave comments when preparing self-reviews and peer reviews. They can easily upload a video of their speech from their hard drive or use Connect's built-in video recorder. Students can even attach and upload additional files or documents, such as a works-cited page or a PowerPoint presentation.

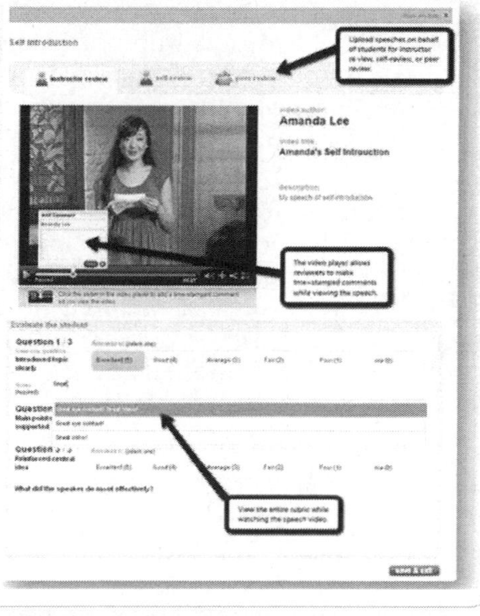

PEER REVIEW

Peer review assignments are easier than ever. Create and manage peer review assignments and customize privacy settings.

SPEECH ASSESSMENT

Connect Speech Capture lets you customize the assignments, including self-reviews and peer reviews.

Connect saves your frequently used comments, simplifying your efforts to provide feedback.

Support to Ensure Success

- **Digital Success Academy**—The Digital Success Academy on Connect offers a wealth of training and course creation guidance for instructors and students alike. Instructor support is presented in easy-to-navigate, easy-to-complete sections. It includes the popular ***Connect*** video shorts, step-by-step ***Click through Guides***, and ***First Day of Class*** materials that explain how to use both the Connect platform and its course-specific tools and features. http://create.mcgraw-hill.com/wordpress-mu/success-academy

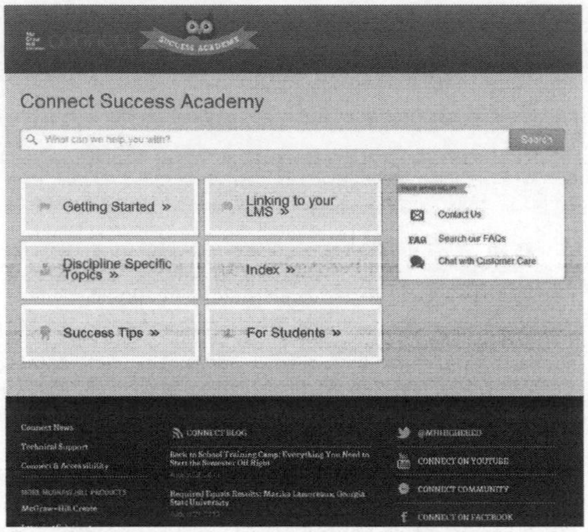

- **Digital Success Team**—The Digital Success Team is a group of specialists dedicated to working online with instructors—one-on-one—to demonstrate how the Connect platform works and to help incorporate Connect into a customer's specific course design and syllabus. Contact your digital learning consultant to learn more.
- **Digital Learning Consultants**—Digital Learning Consultants are local resources who work closely with your McGraw-Hill learning technology consultants. They can provide face-to-face faculty support and training. http://catalogs.mhhe.com/mhhe/findRep.do
- **Digital Faculty Consultants**—Digital Faculty Consultants are experienced instructors who use Connect in their classroom. These instructors are available to offer suggestions, advice, and training about how best to use Connect in your class. To request a Digital Faculty Consultant to speak with, please e-mail your McGraw-Hill learning technology consultant. http://connect.customer.mcgraw-hill.com/dfc/
- **National Training Webinars**—McGraw-Hill offers an ongoing series of webinars for instructors to learn and master the Connect platform as well as its course-specific tools and features. We hope you will refer to our online schedule of national training webinars and sign up to learn more about Connect! http://webinars.mhhe.com/

CONTACT OUR CUSTOMER SUPPORT TEAM

McGraw-Hill is dedicated to supporting instructors and students. To contact our customer support team, please call us at 800-331-5094 or visit us online at http://mpss.mhhe.com/contact.php

New to the Twelfth Edition of *The Art of Public Speaking*

- **A personalized and adaptive learning experience with Smartbook Achieve.** As a student engages with SmartBook Achieve, the program creates a personalized learning path by highlighting the most impactful concepts a student needs to learn at that moment in time. The learning path continuously adapts by delivering just-in-time learning resources—videos, animations, and other interactivities—catered to each student's needs. These rich, dynamic resources help students learn the material, retain more knowledge, and get better grades.

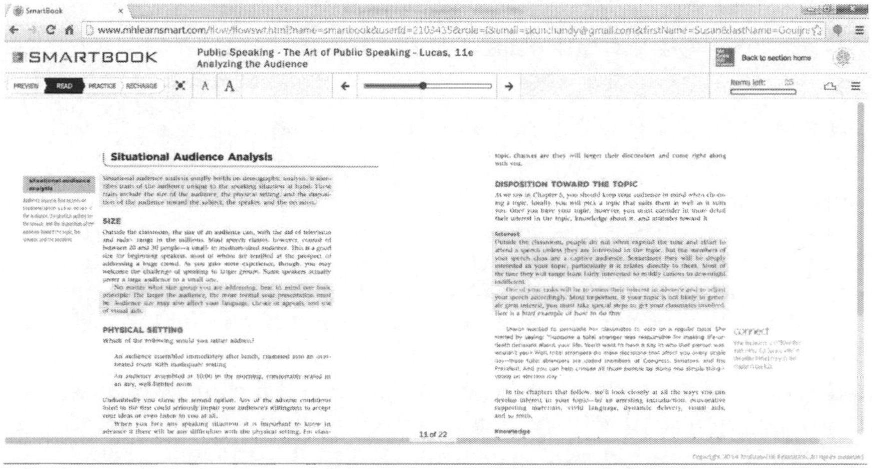

- **Student performance analytics with Connect Insight.** Mobile ready for students, Insight will also be available for students. Students will be able to track their performance throughout the course.
- **New and expanded coverage of presenting online.** Chapter 13, on speech delivery, explores the appropriate technology and specialized skills needed to present professional, compelling speeches in a digital environment. The chapter has been updated with an extensive discussion of the special nature of the online milieu. Professor Lucas explains the importance of mastering today's technology and controlling the visual environment, and offers tips on lighting, camera technique, appropriate onscreen atmosphere, and personal appearance. The discussion also explores how speakers can adapt their nonverbal communication, adjust their pacing, and manage Q&A when speaking online.
- **Fresh real-world examples.** Every chapter of *The Art of Public Speaking* opens with an engaging and relevant model, and dozens of additional examples appear throughout the chapters, each demonstrating the importance—and art—of public speaking in school, business, and social settings.

- **New checklist.** Chapter 13 includes an important, 8-point checklist to help students successfully prepare and deliver an online speech.

checklist

Presenting an Online Speech

YES	NO	
☐	☐	1. Have I considered the special nature of the online speech environment?
☐	☐	2. Do I understand the capabilities and limitations of my presentation software?
☐	☐	3. Do I control the visual environment of my presentation so it will work to my advantage?
☐	☐	4. Have I adapted my nonverbal communication so it will be effective when viewed online?
☐	☐	5. Will the pacing of my speech keep the audience focused on my message?
☐	☐	6. Have I considered how best to handle questions and answers?
☐	☐	7. Have I taken all the steps necessary to rehearse my speech for online presentation?
☐	☐	8. Do I have a backup plan in case I run into technical problems?

- **New compelling student speeches.** Ten full speeches, plus 15 excerpts and six "needs improvement" versions, are new to this edition, augmenting the robust Lucas video program, which now includes 36 full student speeches and more than 60 speech excerpts. Whether a full speech or an excerpt, each video illustrates specific skills and concepts from the text and models the unique features of a variety of speech genres.
- **Updated MLA and APA citation models.** Chapter 7, on gathering materials, presents all-new sample bibliography entries, reflecting the latest MLA and APA citation formats to help students correctly cite academic, digital, and other sources.
- **Expanded coverage of outlining and revised model outlines.** Chapter 11, on outlining the speech, features updated models that illustrate the features of a good speech outline. The chapter also features additional discussion of the principles of outlining to help students better understand how to arrange their thoughts clearly and effectively.
- **Updated discussion of presentation technology.** Guidance on the use of visual aids and presentation technology is enhanced to explore best practices when using PowerPoint, Keynote, Prezi, Google Docs, Zoho Show, and other tools that aid the public speaking experience.

Resources for Instructors

- **Instructors' Guide to Connect.** An overview of Connect and information to get you started can be found on pages xvii–xx.
- **Annotated Instructor's Edition.** The Annotated Instructor's Edition provides a wealth of teaching aids for each chapter in the book. It is also cross-referenced with *Connect*, the *Instructor's Manual*, the *Instructor's Resource CD*, and other supplements that accompany *The Art of Public Speaking*.
- **Resources within Connect:**
    - **Connect Insight.** This powerful analytics tool displays a range of visual data—framed by an intuitive question—to provide instructors at-a-glance information regarding how their classes are doing.
    - **Connect Reports.** Assignments and activities on Connect allow instructors and departments to gauge students' grasp of public speaking skills with exercises and assessment built around learning outcomes. Detailed reports support formative assessment and improve efficacy at the student, section, and program levels.
    - **Instructors' Manual.** This comprehensive guide to teaching from *The Art of Public Speaking* contains suggested course outlines and speaking assignments; chapter outlines; supplementary exercises and classroom activities; and teaching tips for all exercises and activities.
    - **Test Bank.** The Lucas Test Bank furnishes 2,782 examination questions based on *The Art of Public Speaking;* more than 300 of the questions are new or revised for this edition.
    - **PowerPoint Slides with Video Clips.** The PowerPoint presentations for *The Art of Public Speaking* provide chapter highlights that help instructors create focused yet individualized lesson plans.
    - **Teaching Public Speaking Online.** Fully revised for the twelfth edition, the *Teaching Public Speaking Online* manual includes new and revised chapter exercises and discusses performance analytics and approaches to the flipped classroom.
- **Instructor's Online Resource Center.** Augment the planning and teaching experience with the help of a full suite of Lucas instructional tools, including speech transcripts, professional resources, speech evaluation forms, and speech-preparation worksheets.
- **Instructor's Resources CD.** Captured on a single disc for maximum convenience, access the Instructor's Manual, Test Bank, PowerPoint Slides, *Teaching Public Speaking Online* manual, *Selections from the Communication Teacher,* and the *Handbook for Teachers of Non-Native Speakers of English.*

Acknowledgments

"'Tis the good reader," said Ralph Waldo Emerson, "that makes the good book." I have been fortunate to have very good readers indeed, and I would like to thank the reviewers and other contributors whose names appear on pages xxv–xxvii for their expertise and recommendations.

In addition, I would like to express my gratitude to the students at the University of Wisconsin whose speeches provided the material for many of the examples in the book—especially to Shannon Huberty, Rebecca Miller, Heidi Voelker, and Su Hyun (Sarah) Yim. I am grateful as well to the teaching staff of Communication Arts 100 at Wisconsin and to Sarah Jedd, assistant course director, for her splendid work in that capacity and for her insights about the book and its pedagogy.

Thanks go as well to Margaret Procario for her work on the *Instructor's Manual* and the *Test Bank;* to Jennifer Cochrane for her many contributions, including her supplement on using *The Art of Public Speaking* in an online course; and to Jeff Przybylo and Tim Pierce for their activities on behalf of the book's digital program. Above all, I am indebted to Paul Stob, who has worked with me on four editions, including this one. In addition to taking on primary responsibility for the *Instructor's Manual,* he has collaborated on multiple aspects of the book and the entire *Art of Public Speaking* program. To say that he has been indispensable is an understatement.

I also owe much to the *Art of Public Speaking* team at McGraw-Hill. Susan Gouijnstook provided superb overall direction; I have been fortunate to have top-notch editors over the years, but Susan takes a back seat to none of them. Program manager Jennifer Gehl kept everything on track notwithstanding an exacting schedule and the inevitable obstacles that arise in any large and complex publishing project. After a hiatus of several years, Keith McPherson returned to McGraw-Hill and proved once again why he is a superior designer. Jennifer Blankenship was unflagging in finding the best photographs to give visual resonance to the principles discussed in the book.

Many other people at McGraw-Hill made their mark on this edition. Michael O'Loughlin dealt with a host of matters, large and small. Laura Kennedy oversaw the marketing effort. Shawntel Schmitt coordinated the image licensing. Meghan Campbell and Janet Byrne Smith spearheaded the book's innovative digital program. They were assisted by John Francis, Irina Blokh-Reznik, Jonathan Genkin, Srinivas Nathani, Navaneetha Krishan, Srini Mogalipuvuu, Sarah Hegarty, Andrea Pasquarelli, and Adina Lonn. Finally, but certainly not least, Kurt Strand, Michael Ryan, Kim David, David Patterson, and Lisa Pinto lent executive direction to the entire project.

As always, my biggest debt is to my wife, Patty, whose love and support have sustained me through the years.

Stephen E. Lucas
Madison, Wisconsin

Reviewers; Contributors; Symposium, Focus Group, and Survey Participants

Clark Adams, *Randolph Community College*
Ruth Aipperspach, *Texas A&M University–Corpus Christi*
Jayson Akridge, *Augusta Technical College*
Kasim Alimahomed, *California State Polytechnic University–Pomona*
Karen Allbee, *Chaffey College–Rancho Cucamonga*
Lisa Athearn, *University of Maine–Machias*
Bill Bachman, *Penn State University–Wilkes-Barre*
Ruth Baldrige, *Central Piedmont Community College–Levine and Queens University of Charlotte*
Christina Ballard, *Madison Area Technical College*
Andrew Barnes, *James Madison University*
Kris Barton, *Dalton State College*
Arlen Baumhoefner, *Concordia University–St. Paul*
Susanne Bentley, *Great Basin College*
Annette Bever, *Midwestern State University*
Margaret Bilos, *Harper College*
Erica Bobby, *Black Hills State University–Rapid City*
John Bourhis, *Missouri State University*
Jeff Boyd, *New Mexico Military Institute*
Ellen Bremen, *Highline Community College*
Aaron Brown, *Hibbing Community College*
Ferald Bryan, *Northern Illinois University*
Amy Bryant, *Nashville State Community College*
Karen Buchanan, *Regis University–College for Professional Studies*
Paige Bukowski, *University of Houston*
Kenisha Burke, *Austin Peay State University*
Crystal Burnett, *Wayne Community College*
M. Lee Buxton, *Bellevue College*
Dennis Cali, *University of Texas–Tyler*
Christy N. Carter, *Harper College*
Jeff Carter, *Azusa Pacific University*
Shera Carter, *San Jacinto College–Central*
Isaac E. Catt, *Penn State University–York*
Victoria Chai, *Nassau Community College*
Kimberly J. Chandler, *Xavier University of Louisiana*
Thomas Chester, *Ivy Tech Community College–Muncie*
Jeanne Christie, *Western Connecticut State University*
Helen Chronis, *Moraine Valley Community College*
Ruth Cimperman, *Milwaukee Area Technical College*
Karen Clark, *Mitchell Technical Institute*
Terrell Clark, *Owensboro Community and Technical College*
Vernon Clarke, *Clayton State University*
Jennifer Cochrane, *Indiana University–Purdue University Indianapolis*
Paula Cohen, *Ohio State University–Mansfield*
Ronald E. Compton, *McHenry County College*
Adrienne Hacker Daniels, *Illinois College*
Elaine Davies, *Chapman University*
Patti Deak, *College of Southern Nevada*
Cynthia Dewar, *City College of San Francisco*
Martha Dumas, *University of New Haven*
Barbara DuMont, *Moraine Valley Community College*
Jessica Ebert, *Northern Illinois University*
Tim Echternach, *Moberly Area Community College*
Khristi Edmonds, *Mississippi State University*
Thomas Eisemann, *Palomar College–San Marcos*
Denise Elmer, *Southeast Community College–Beatrice*
Liz Emmert, *Kutztown University of Pennsylvania*
Steve Epstein, *Suffolk Community College*
Kathy Espy, *Palm Beach Atlantic University*
Gail Felker, *Embry-Riddle Aeronautical University*
Josef Fioretta, *Nassau Community College*
Glynis Fitzgerald, *Central Connecticut State University*
Nikole Ford, *Henry Ford Community College*
Paul Forester, *Southcentral Kentucky Community and Technical College–Bowling Green*
Richard Forney, *Drexel University–University City*
David Fotopulos, *Ozarks Technical Community College*
Amy Fountain, *Mississippi State University*
Rebecca Franko, *California State Polytechnic University–Pomona*
Bonnie Gabel, *McHenry County College*
Laura Garcia, *Washington State Community College*
Kim Gatz, *Northern Illinois University*
Jan Geyer, *Hudson Valley Community College*
Charles T. Gilbert, *Kendall College of Art and Design*
Melissa Gomez, *Harper College*
Donna Goodwin, *Tulsa Community College–Northeast*
Michelle Gorthy, *City College of San Francisco*
Donna Gotch, *California State University–San Bernardino*
Matthew Grindstaff, *Ozarks Technical College*
Jackie Grogan, *St. John's University*
Alyce Grover, *Somerset Community College*
Jill Hall, *Jefferson Community and Technical College–Downtown*
Beth Hallquist, *Palm Beach Atlantic University*
Carole J. Hannon, *College of Southern Nevada*

Lisa Hebert, *Louisiana State University*
Cynthia Y. Hill, *Newbridge Cleveland Center*
Ronald Hochstatter, *McLennan Community College*
Vernon Humphrey, *Columbus State University*
Marilyn Hunt, *Missouri Western State University*
Patti Interrante, *Oakton Community College*
Kedra James, *North Carolina Wesleyan College*
Charles Jerred, *Bryant & Stratton College*
Joseph J. Jewusiak, *Penn State University–Abington*
Deborah Johnson, *Metropolitan State University*
Shay Jones, *Penn State University–Harrisburg*
Russell Kahn, *State University of New York Institute of Technology*
Kelly Soczka Kaiser, *Mid-State Faculty Association–Stevens Point*
Verna Kerans, *Northern Virginia Community College–Alexandria*
Lori Kerrigan, *Digital Media Arts College*
Gregory M. Kielmeyer, *Bob Jones University*
Susan Kilgard, *Anne Arundel Community College*
Ben Kilpatrick, *Southwest Baptist University*
Sandy King, *Anne Arundel Community College*
Stephanie Klatzke, *Northern Kentucky University*
Keith Klein, *Ivy Tech–Bloomington*
Margaret Knapp, *Oakton Community College*
Maria Kossakowski, *Malcolm X Junior College*
David Lane, *Muscatine Community College*
Bailey Lathem, *Austin Community College District*
Dianna Laurent, *Southeastern Louisiana University*
Melanie A. Lea, *Bossier Parish Community College*
Kenneth S. Lee, *Antelope Valley College*
Maxine LeGall, *University of the District of Columbia–Van Ness*
Gail Lewis, *Nassau Community College*
Jason Lucas, *Ohio University–Ironton*
Rebecca Luck, *Minot State University–Minot Air Force Base*
Maria Luskay, *Pace University*
Krista MacDonald, *Doña Ana Community College*
Ron Mace, *Somerset Community College*
Jessica Mankey, *Ivy Tech Community College–Marion*
Lori Manship, *University of Texas of the Permian Basin*
Thomas Mapes, *Luther Rice University*
Lauretta Maslanka, *Bridgewater State University*
Sujanet Mason, *Luzerne County Community College*
Brenda DeVore Marshall, *Linfield College–McMinnville*
Peg McCree, *Middle Tennessee State University*
Laura McDavitt, *Jackson State University*
Bonny McDonald, *Louisiana State University*
Georgia McGill, *Queensborough Community College, City University of New York*
Terence McGiver, *State University of New York–Cobleskill*
Jan McKissick, *Butte Community College*
Christopher Medjesky, *Defiance College*
Beth Merry, *Waynesburg University*
Shellie Michael, *Volunteer State Community College*
Patricia Milford, *California University of Pennsylvania*
Miranda Miller, *Gillette College*
Joe Mirando, *Southeastern Louisiana University*
John Morgan, *East Mississippi Community College*
Gregory L. Morley, *North Central College*
Tom Moseley, *Austin Peay State University*
J.D. Mota, *San Jacinto College*
Daryle Nagano, *Los Angeles Harbor College*
Diana Karol Nagy, *University of Florida*
John Nash, *Moraine Valley Community College*
Cheritha Nelson, *College of Southern Nevada*
Jennifer Neumann, *Southeastern Community College*
Tuong Nguyen, *State University of New York–Broome*
Angela Niedermyer, *Austin Community College Northridge*
Ronn Norfleet, *Jefferson Community and Technical College*
Matthew S. Novak, *Embry-Riddle Aeronautical University*
Travice Baldwin Obas, *Georgia Highlands College–Cartersville*
P. Maureen Olguin, *Eastern New Mexico University–Roswell*
Patricia Smith Ollry, *Concordia University–Irvine*
Emma O'Neal, *Wilberforce University*
Sonja Osborne, *Fayetteville Technical Community College*
Jeff Ousborne, *Suffolk University*
Kathryn Paluscio, *Mercer County Community College*
Kate Pantinas, *Ivy Tech Community College*
Martie Parsley, *Riverside Community College*
Jennifer Patterson, *Ulster County Community College*
Ivo Ray Peterson, *Snow College Ephraim*
Matthew Petrunia, *Fashion Institute of Technology, State University of New York*
Amanda Pettigrew, *Moraine Valley Community College*
Jeremy Pettitt, *Trinity International University*
Tim Pierce, *Northern Illinois University*
Elisabeth Pitts, *James Sprunt Community College*
Andrew Plaks, *Colorado Mountain College–Alpine*
Marti Plemons, *Middle Tennessee State University*

Timi Poeppelman, *California State University–Sacramento*
Jan Poppenga, *Southeast Community College–Lincoln*
Amy Powell, *Central Michigan University*
Jean Powers, *Holmes Community College–Ridgeland*
Jeff Przybylo, *Harper College*
Thomas Rapp, *Oakton Community College*
Sharaf Rehman, *University of Texas–Brownsville*
Nancy Reynolds, *Angelina College*
Marilyn Ribble, *California State University–San Marcos*
Mary Richardson, *Hendrix College*
William Richter, *Lenoir-Rhyne University*
Amy Ritchart, *Austin Peay State University*
Kellie Roberts, *University of Florida*
Tim Roe, *Eastern Washington University*
Alisa Roost, *Hostos Community College*
Tedro R. Rouse, *South Carolina State University*
Ronald Edward Ruland, *State University of New York–Cobleskill*
Tim Rumbough, *Bloomsburg University*
Mark Ryan, *Hawkeye Community College*
Thomas Sabetta, *University of Kentucky*
Felicia Sanders, *The College of Southern Nevada*
Gina Santoro, *Community College of Rhode Island–Flanagan*
Lisa Sayles, *College of the Redwoods*
Lori Schroeder, *Metropolitan State University*
Eugenia Scott, *Southcentral Kentucky Community and Technical College–Bowling Green*
Dr. Mike Searcy, *Somerset Community College*
Jonathan Segol, *Hudson Valley Community College*
Michelle Selk, *San Jacinto College–Central*
Helene Serewis, *Oregon State University*
Michael Shannon, *Moraine Valley Community College*
Jeff Shires, *Purdue University–North Central*
Mary Shortridge, *Ashland Community and Technical College*
Elizabeth Simas, *Santa Rosa Junior College–Petaluma*
Dorothy Simpson, *Luna Community College*
Ann Marie Smith, *Southeastern Community College–West Burlington*
Susan Smyth, *Harper College*
Paula Spugnardi, *Bellarmine University*
Mallory Sribanditmongkol, *Ohio Christian University*
Roberta Steinberg, *Mount Ida College*
Jim Stenerson, *Pace University*
L'Oreal Stephens, *Middle Tennessee State University*
Darcy Heller Sternberg, *Borough of Manhattan Community College*
David Stevenson, *College of the Canyons*
Kelly Stockstad, *Austin Community College*
Carla Stout, *Mississippi Gulf Coast Community College*
Heather Strafaccia, *Park University–Minot Air Force Base*
Harry Strine, *Susquehanna University*
Jacob Stutzman, *Oklahoma City University*
Tammy Swenson-Lepper, *Winona State University*
Ileana Torres, *Florida National University*
Dawn Trickett, *Cerritos College*
Kathryn Trombley, *Minnesota State Community and Technical College–Wadena*
Billie A. Unger, *Blue Ridge Community and Technical College*
Nancy Vagim, *Willow International Center–Reedley College*
Sam Vegter, *Western Piedmont Community College*
Maria Verardo, *College of Southern Nevada–West Charleston*
Rosanne Vogel, *Queensborough Community College*
Mark Wadleigh, *Washington State University*
James Waldron, *Fullerton College*
Ardith Weiss, *Jarvis Christian College*
Edward Whitelock, *Gordon State College*
Brandi Wilkins, *Kaskaskia College*
Julie Williams, *San Jacinto College–Central*
Alan Winson, *John Jay College*
Emily Workman, *Guilford Technical Community College*
Angela Wright, *Patrick Henry Community College*
Min Wu, *Louisiana State University–Alexandria*
Carleen Yokotake, *Leeward Community College*
Donna K. Young, *Ivy Tech Community College–Bloomington*
Robert Zetocha, *Southeast Community College–Lincoln*
Jennifer Zimmerman, *Rock Valley College*

The Art of Public Speaking

Speaking and Listening

1

Speaking in Public

- The Power of Public Speaking
- The Tradition of Public Speaking
- Similarities Between Public Speaking and Conversation
- Differences Between Public Speaking and Conversation
- Developing Confidence: Your Speech Class
- Public Speaking and Critical Thinking
- The Speech Communication Process
- Public Speaking in a Multicultural World

Growing up in the mountain town of Mingora, Pakistan, Malala Yousafzai had no idea how far her voice would travel. A bright and outspoken student, she dreamed of being a doctor. But her passion for education flew in the face of the Taliban regime that controlled her town. When Malala was 15 years old, two armed gunmen boarded her school bus and shot her at close range in the head and neck.

Miraculously, Malala survived. Since that time, she has become a symbol of the struggle for the rights of girls and women across the globe. She has established her own nonprofit organization, has met with leaders from many nations, and has turned her story of survival into a lesson on the importance of education. At age 16, she became the youngest person ever nominated for a Nobel Peace Prize.

How has Malala achieved all this? Partly through her bravery, partly through her commitment to education, and partly through her unyielding hope for a better world. But also important is her ability to communicate with people through public speaking, which has become a primary medium for spreading her message.

Best known is the speech Malala gave to the United Nations General Assembly on July 12, 2013, her 16th birthday. In addition to describing the attack on her school bus and the compassion she now felt for her attackers, she made her experience part of a larger struggle for human rights. "I speak not for myself," she told world leaders, "but so those without a voice can be heard."

If you had asked Malala several years ago, "Do you see yourself as an important international speaker?" she would probably have laughed at the idea. Yet today she gives at least one presentation in almost every city she visits. In addition to speaking at the United Nations, she has addressed Amnesty International, the World Bank, and the European Parliament. Her speeches have captivated audiences the world over.

The Power of Public Speaking

Throughout history people have used public speaking as a vital means of communication. What the Greek leader Pericles said more than 2,500 years ago is still true today: "One who forms a judgment on any point but cannot explain" it clearly "might as well never have thought at all on the subject."[1] Public speaking, as its name implies, is a way of making your ideas public—of sharing them with other people and of influencing other people.

During modern times, many women and men around the globe have spread their ideas and influence through public speaking. In the United States, the list includes Franklin Roosevelt, Billy Graham, Cesar Chavez, Barbara Jordan, Martin Luther King, Ronald Reagan, Hillary Clinton, and Barack Obama. In other countries, we have seen the power of public speaking employed by people such as Margaret Thatcher, Nelson Mandela, and Aung San Suu Kyi.

As you read these names, you may think to yourself, "That's fine. Good for them. But what does that have to do with me? I don't plan to be a president or a preacher or a crusader for any cause." Nevertheless, the need for public speaking will almost certainly touch you sometime in your life—maybe tomorrow, maybe not for five years. Can you imagine yourself in any of these situations?

> You are one of seven management trainees in a large corporation. One of you will get the lower-management job that has just opened. There is to be a large staff meeting at which each of the trainees will discuss the project he or she has been developing. One by one your colleagues make their presentations. They have no experience in public speaking and are intimidated by the higher-ranking managers present. Their speeches are stumbling and awkward. You, however, call upon all the skills you learned in your public speaking course. You deliver an informative talk that is clear, well reasoned, and articulate. You get the job.

> One of your children has a learning disability. You hear that your local school board has decided, for budget reasons, to eliminate the special teacher who has been helping your child. At an open meeting of the school board, you stand up and deliver a thoughtful, compelling speech on the necessity for keeping the special teacher. The school board changes its mind.

> You are the assistant manager in a branch office of a national company. Your immediate superior, the branch manager, is about to retire, and there will be a

retirement dinner. All the executives from the home office will attend. As his close working associate, you are asked to give a farewell toast at the party. You prepare and deliver a speech that is both witty and touching—a perfect tribute to your boss. After the speech, everyone applauds enthusiastically, and a few people have tears in their eyes. The following week you are named branch manager.

Fantasies? Not really. Any of these situations could occur. In a recent survey of more than 300 employers, 93 percent stated that the ability to think critically and communicate clearly is more important for career success than is a job candidate's undergraduate major. In another survey, the American Management Association asked 768 executives and managers to rank the skills most essential to today's workplace. What was at the top of their list? Communication skills.[2]

The importance of such skills is true across the board—for accountants and architects, teachers and technicians, scientists and stockbrokers. Even in highly specialized fields such as civil and mechanical engineering, employers consistently rank the ability to communicate above technical knowledge when deciding whom to hire and whom to promote.

Businesses are also asking people to give more speeches in the early stages of their careers, and many young professionals are using public speaking as a way to stand out in today's highly competitive job market.[3] In fact, the ability to speak effectively is so prized that college graduates are increasingly being asked to give a presentation as part of their job interview.

Nor has the growth of the Internet and other new technologies reduced the need for public speaking. In this age of Instagram and Twitter, businesses are concerned that college graduates are losing the ability to talk in a professional way. As career expert Lindsey Pollak states, "It's so rare to find somebody who has that combination of really good technical skills and really good verbal communication skills. You will be head and shoulders above your colleagues if you can combine those two."[4]

The same is true in community life. Public speaking is a vital means of civic engagement. It is a way to express your ideas and to have an impact on issues that matter in society. As a form of empowerment, it can—and often does—make a difference in things people care about very much. The key phrase here is "make a difference." This is what most of us want to do in life—to make a difference, to change the world in some small way. Public speaking offers you an opportunity to make a difference in something you care about very much.

The Tradition of Public Speaking

Given the importance of public speaking, it's not surprising that it has been taught and studied around the globe for thousands of years. Almost all cultures have an equivalent of the English word "orator" to designate someone with special skills in public speaking. The oldest known handbook on effective speech was written on papyrus in Egypt some 4,500 years ago. Eloquence was highly prized in ancient India, Africa, and China, as well as among the Aztecs and other pre-European cultures of North and South America.[5]

In classical Greece and Rome, public speaking played a central role in education and civic life. It was also studied extensively. Aristotle's *Rhetoric,* composed during the third century B.C., is still considered the most important work on its subject, and many of its principles are followed by speakers (and writers) today. The great Roman leader Cicero used his speeches to defend liberty and wrote several works about oratory in general.

Over the centuries, many other notable thinkers have dealt with issues of rhetoric, speech, and language—including the Roman educator Quintilian, the Christian preacher St. Augustine, the medieval writer Christine de Pizan, the British philosopher Francis Bacon, and the American critic Kenneth Burke. In recent years, communication researchers have provided an increasingly scientific basis for understanding the methods and strategies of effective speech.

Your immediate objective is to apply those methods and strategies in your classroom speeches. What you learn, however, will be applicable long after you leave college. The principles of public speaking are derived from a long tradition and have been confirmed by a substantial body of research. The more you know about those principles, the more effective you will be in your own speeches—and the more effective you will be in listening to the speeches of other people.

Similarities Between Public Speaking and Conversation

How much time do you spend each day talking to other people? The average adult spends about 30 percent of her or his waking hours in conversation. By the time you read this book, you will have spent much of your life perfecting the art of conversation. You may not realize it, but you already employ a wide range of skills when talking to people. These skills include the following:

1. *Organizing your thoughts logically.* Suppose you were giving someone directions to get to your house. You wouldn't do it this way:

> When you turn off the highway, you'll see a big diner on the left. But before that, stay on the highway to Exit 67. Usually a couple of the neighbors' dogs are in the street, so go slow after you turn at the blinking light. Coming from your house you get on the highway through Maple Street. If you pass the taco stand, you've gone too far. The house is blue.

Instead, you would take your listener systematically, step by step, from his or her house to your house. You would organize your message.

2. *Tailoring your message to your audience.* You are a geology major. Two people ask you how pearls are formed. One is your roommate; the other is your nine-year-old niece. You answer as follows:

> To your roommate: "When any irritant, say a grain of sand, gets inside the oyster's shell, the oyster automatically secretes a substance called nacre, which is principally calcium carbonate and is the same material that lines the oyster's shell. The nacre accumulates in layers around the irritant core to form the pearl."
>
> To your niece: "Imagine you're an oyster on the ocean floor. A grain of sand gets inside your shell and makes you uncomfortable. So you decide to cover it up. You cover it with a material called mother-of-pearl. The covering builds up around the grain of sand to make a pearl."

Many skills used in conversation also apply in public speaking. As you learn to speak more effectively, you may also learn to communicate more effectively in other situations.

3. *Telling a story for maximum impact.* Suppose you are telling a friend about a funny incident at last week's football game. You don't begin with the punch line ("Keisha fell out of the stands right onto the field. Here's how it started. . . ."). Instead, you carefully build up your story, adjusting your words and tone of voice to get the best effect.

4. *Adapting to listener feedback.* Whenever you talk with someone, you are aware of that person's verbal, facial, and physical reactions. For example:

> You are explaining an interesting point that came up in biology class. Your listener begins to look confused, puts up a hand as though to stop you, and says "Huh?" You go back and explain more clearly.
>
> A friend has asked you to listen while she practices a speech. At the end you tell her, "There's just one part I really don't like—that quotation from the attorney general." Your friend looks very hurt and says, "That was my favorite part!" So you say, "But if you just worked the quotation in a little differently, it would be wonderful."

Each day, in casual conversation, you do all these things many times without thinking about them. You already possess these communication skills. And these are among the most important skills you will need for public speaking.

To illustrate, let's return briefly to one of the hypothetical situations at the beginning of this chapter. When addressing the school board about the need for a special teacher:

- You *organize* your ideas to present them in the most persuasive manner. You steadily build up a compelling case about how the teacher benefits the school.
- You *tailor your message* to your audience. This is no time to launch an impassioned defense of special education in the United States. You must show how the issue is important to the people in that very room—to their children and to the school.

- You *tell your story* for maximum impact. Perhaps you relate an anecdote to demonstrate how much your child has improved. You also have statistics to show how many other children have been helped.
- You *adapt to listener feedback.* When you mention the cost of the special teacher, you notice sour looks on the faces of the school board members. So you patiently explain how small that cost is in relation to the overall school budget.

In many ways, then, public speaking requires the same skills used in ordinary conversation. Most people who communicate well in daily talk can learn to communicate just as well in public speaking. By the same token, training in public speaking can make you a more adept communicator in a variety of situations, such as conversations, classroom discussions, business meetings, and interviews.

Differences Between Public Speaking and Conversation

Despite their similarities, public speaking and everyday conversation are not identical. Imagine that you are telling a story to a friend. Then imagine yourself telling the story to a group of seven or eight friends. Now imagine telling the same story to 20 or 30 people. As the size of your audience grows, you will find yourself adapting to three major differences between conversation and public speaking:

1. *Public speaking is more highly structured.* It usually imposes strict time limitations on the speaker. In most cases, the situation does not allow listeners to interrupt with questions or commentary. The speaker must accomplish her or his purpose in the speech itself. In preparing the speech, the speaker must anticipate questions that might arise in the minds of listeners and answer them. Consequently, public speaking demands much more detailed planning and preparation than ordinary conversation.

2. *Public speaking requires more formal language.* Slang, jargon, and bad grammar have little place in public speeches. When Malala Yousafzai addressed the United Nations, she didn't say, "We've got to stop Taliban creeps from going after innocent people." Listeners usually react negatively to speakers who do not elevate and polish their language when addressing an audience. A speech should be "special."

3. *Public speaking requires a different method of delivery.* When conversing informally, most people talk quietly, interject stock phrases such as "like" and "you know," adopt a casual posture, and use what are called vocalized pauses ("uh," "er," "um"). Effective public speakers, however, adjust their voices to be heard clearly throughout the audience. They assume a more erect posture. They avoid distracting mannerisms and verbal habits.

With study and practice, you will be able to master these differences and expand your conversational skills into speechmaking. Your speech class will provide the opportunity for this study and practice.

Developing Confidence: Your Speech Class

One of the major concerns of students in any speech class is stage fright. We may as well face the issue squarely. Many people who converse easily in all kinds of everyday situations become frightened at the idea of standing up before a group to make a speech.

If you are worried about stage fright, you may feel better knowing that you are not alone. A 2001 Gallup Poll asked Americans to list their greatest fears. Forty percent identified speaking before a group as their top fear, exceeded only by the 51 percent who said they were afraid of snakes. A 2005 survey produced similar results, with 42 percent of respondents being terrified by the prospect of speaking in public. In comparison, only 28 percent said they were afraid of dying.[6]

stage fright

Anxiety over the prospect of giving a speech in front of an audience.

In a different study, researchers concentrated on social situations and, again, asked their subjects to list their greatest fears. More than 9,000 people were interviewed. Here is the ranking of their answers:[7]

Greatest Fear

Public speaking

Speaking up in a meeting or class

Meeting new people

Talking to people in authority

Important examination or interview

Going to parties

Talking with strangers

Again, speechmaking is at the top in provoking anxiety.

NERVOUSNESS IS NORMAL

If you feel nervous about giving a speech, you are in very good company. Some of the greatest public speakers in history have suffered from stage fright, including Abraham Lincoln, Margaret Sanger, and Winston Churchill. The famous Roman orator Cicero said, "I turn pale at the outset of a speech and quake in every limb and in my soul."[8]

Jennifer Lawrence, Conan O'Brien, and Oprah Winfrey all report being anxious about speaking in public. Early in his career, Leonardo DiCaprio was so nervous about giving an acceptance speech that he hoped he would not win the Academy Award for which he had been nominated. Eighty-one percent of business executives say public speaking is the most nerve-wracking experience they face.[9] What comedian Jerry Seinfeld said in jest sometimes seems literally true: "Given a choice, at a funeral most of us would rather be the one in the coffin than the one giving the eulogy."

Actually, most people tend to be anxious before doing something important in public. Actors are nervous before a play, politicians are nervous before a campaign speech, athletes are nervous before a big game. The ones who succeed have learned to use their nervousness to their advantage. Listen to tennis star Andy Murray speaking after his 2013 Wimbledon title match against Novak Djokovic: "If I'm feeling butterflies in the stomach, I know I'm ready, focused on what I'm going to try and accomplish. If you aren't nervous before playing on Centre Court at Wimbledon, maybe you're doing the wrong job." Putting his butterflies to good use, Murray beat Djokovic in straight sets to become the first British man to capture Wimbledon in 77 years.

Much the same thing happens in speechmaking. Most experienced speakers have stage fright before taking the floor, but their nervousness is a healthy sign that they are getting "psyched up" for a good effort. Novelist and lecturer I. A. R. Wylie once said: "I rarely rise to my feet without a throat constricted with terror and a furiously thumping heart. When, for some reason, I *am* cool and self-assured, the speech is always a failure."

adrenaline

A hormone released into the bloodstream in response to physical or mental stress.

In other words, it is perfectly normal—even desirable—to be nervous at the start of a speech. Your body is responding as it would to any stressful situation—by producing extra *adrenaline.*

This sudden shot of adrenaline is what makes your heart race, your hands shake, your knees knock, and your skin perspire. Every public speaker experiences all these reactions to some extent. The question is: How can you control your nervousness and make it work for you rather than against you?

DEALING WITH NERVOUSNESS

positive nervousness

Controlled nervousness that helps energize a speaker for her or his presentation.

Rather than trying to eliminate every trace of stage fright, you should aim at transforming it from a negative force into what one expert calls *positive nervousness*—"a zesty, enthusiastic, lively feeling with a slight edge to it. . . . It's still nervousness, but it feels different. You're no longer victimized by it; instead, you're vitalized by it. You're in control of it."[10]

Don't think of yourself as having stage fright. Instead, think of it as "stage excitement" or "stage enthusiasm."[11] It can help you get focused and energized in the same way that it helps athletes, musicians, and others get primed for a game or a concert. Actress Jane Lynch, talking about her gig hosting *Saturday Night Live*, said that she got through it with "that perfect cocktail of nervousness and excitement." Think of that cocktail as a normal part of giving a successful speech.

Here are six time-tested ways you can turn your nervousness from a negative force into a positive one.

Acquire Speaking Experience

You have already taken the first step. You are enrolled in a public speaking course, where you will learn about speechmaking and gain speaking experience. Think back to your first day at kindergarten, your first date, your first day at a new job. You were probably nervous in each situation because you were facing something new and unknown. Once you became accustomed to the situation, it was no longer threatening. So it is with public speaking. For most students, the biggest part of stage fright is fear of the unknown. The more you learn about public speaking and the more speeches you give, the less threatening speechmaking will become.

Of course, the road to confidence will sometimes be bumpy. Learning to give a speech is not much different from learning any other skill—it proceeds by trial and error. The purpose of your speech class is to shorten the process, to minimize the errors, to give you a nonthreatening arena—a sort of laboratory—in which to undertake the "trial."

The need for public speaking arises in many situations. Here United Nations Commissioner Pierre Krähenbühl speaks at a news conference in Gaza City.

Your instructor recognizes that you are a novice and is trained to give the kind of guidance you need to get started. In your fellow students you have a highly sympathetic audience who will provide valuable feedback to help you improve your speaking skills. As the class goes on, your fears about public speaking will gradually recede until they are replaced by only a healthy nervousness before you rise to speak.[12]

Prepare, Prepare, Prepare

Another key to gaining confidence is to pick speech topics you truly care about—and then to prepare your speeches so thoroughly that you cannot help but be successful. Here's how one student combined enthusiasm for his topic with thorough preparation to score a triumph in speech class:

> Jesse Young was concerned about taking a speech class. Not having any experience as a public speaker, he got butterflies in his stomach just thinking about talking in front of an audience. But when the time came for Jesse's first speech, he was determined to make it a success.
>
> Jesse chose Habitat for Humanity as the topic for his speech. He had been a volunteer for three years, and he believed deeply in the organization and its mission. The purpose of his speech was to explain the origins, philosophy, and activities of Habitat for Humanity.
>
> As Jesse spoke, it became clear that he was enthusiastic about his subject and genuinely wanted his classmates to share his enthusiasm. Because he was intent on communicating with his audience, he forgot to be nervous. He spoke clearly, fluently, and dynamically. Soon the entire class was engrossed in his speech.
>
> Afterward, Jesse admitted that he had surprised even himself. "It was amazing," he said. "Once I passed the first minute or so, all I thought about were those people out there listening. I could tell that I was really getting through to them."

How much time should you devote to preparing your speeches? A standard rule of thumb is that each minute of speaking time requires one to two hours of preparation time—perhaps more, depending on the amount of research needed for the speech. This may seem like a lot of time, but the rewards are well worth it. One professional speech consultant estimates that proper preparation can reduce stage fright by up to 75 percent.[13]

If you follow the techniques suggested by your instructor and in the rest of this book, you will stand up for every speech fully prepared. Imagine that the day for your first speech has arrived. You have studied your audience and selected a topic you know will interest them. You have researched the speech thoroughly and practiced it several times until it feels absolutely comfortable. You have even tried it out before two or three trusted friends. How can you help but be confident of success?

Think Positively

Confidence is mostly the well-known power of positive thinking. If you think you can do it, you usually can. On the other hand, if you predict disaster and doom, that is almost always what you will get. This is especially true when it comes to public speaking. Speakers who think negatively about themselves and the speech experience are much more likely to be overcome by stage fright than are speakers who think positively. Here are some ways you can transform negative thoughts into positive ones as you work on your speeches:

Negative Thought	Positive Thought
I wish I didn't have to give this speech.	This speech is a chance for me to share my ideas and gain experience as a speaker.
I'm not a great public speaker.	No one's perfect, but I'm getting better with each speech I give.
I'm always nervous when I give a speech.	Everyone's nervous. If other people can handle it, I can too.
No one will be interested in what I have to say.	I have a good topic and I'm fully prepared. Of course they'll be interested.

Many psychologists believe that the ratio of positive to negative thoughts in regard to stressful activities such as speechmaking should be at least five to one. That is, for each negative thought, you should counter with a minimum of five positive ones. Doing so will not make your nerves go away completely, but it will help keep them under control so you can concentrate on communicating your ideas rather than on brooding about your fears and anxieties.

Use the Power of Visualization

Visualization is closely related to positive thinking. It is used by athletes, musicians, actors, speakers, and others to enhance their performance in stressful situations. How does it work? Listen to Jamie Anderson, who, during the 2014 Winter Olympics, won the first-ever gold medal in the women's Slopestyle event. Afterward, she talked about how she used visualization to settle her nerves before the winning ride:

> There was so much anticipation leading up to this event, I just had to calm my mind and have the trust and faith that I was capable of doing what I really

> wanted to do. At the top of the course, I took a moment, took a deep breath, and saw everything I wanted to see happen. . . . I was visualizing it, seeing it to the end, and knowing that I was going to land everything perfectly with as much style as possible.

Of course, visualization doesn't mean that Anderson wins every competition she enters. But research has shown that the kind of mental imaging she describes can significantly increase athletic performance.[14] It has also shown that visualization can help speakers control their stage fright.[15]

The key to visualization is creating a vivid mental blueprint in which you see yourself succeeding in your speech. Picture yourself in your classroom rising to speak. See yourself at the lectern, poised and self-assured, making eye contact with your audience and delivering your introduction in a firm, clear voice. Feel your confidence growing as your listeners get more and more caught up in what you are saying. Imagine your sense of achievement as you conclude the speech knowing you have done your very best.

visualization

Mental imaging in which a speaker vividly pictures himself or herself giving a successful presentation.

As you create these images in your mind's eye, be realistic but stay focused on the positive aspects of your speech. Don't allow negative images to eclipse the positive ones. Acknowledge your nervousness, but picture yourself overcoming it to give a vibrant, articulate presentation. If one part of the speech always seems to give you trouble, visualize yourself getting through it without any hitches. And be specific. The more lucid your mental pictures, the more successful you are likely to be.

As with your physical rehearsal of the speech, this kind of mental rehearsal should be repeated several times in the days before you speak. It doesn't guarantee that every speech will turn out exactly the way you envision it—and it certainly is no substitute for thorough preparation. But used in conjunction with the other methods of combating stage fright, it is a proven way to help control your nerves and to craft a successful presentation.

Know That Most Nervousness Is Not Visible

Many novice speakers are worried about appearing nervous to the audience. It's hard to speak with poise and assurance if you think you look tense and insecure. One of the most valuable lessons you will learn as your speech class proceeds is that only a fraction of the turmoil you feel inside is visible on the outside. "Your nervous system may be giving you a thousand shocks," says one experienced speaker, "but the viewer can see only a few of them."[16]

Even though your palms are sweating and your heart is pounding, your listeners probably won't realize how tense you are—especially if you do your best to act cool and confident on the outside. Most of the time when students confess after a speech, "I was so nervous I thought I was going to die," their classmates are surprised. To them the speaker looked calm and assured.

Knowing this should make it easier for you to face your listeners with confidence. As one student stated after watching a videotape of her first classroom speech, "I was amazed at how calm I looked. I assumed everyone would be able to see how scared I was, but now that I know they can't, I won't be nearly so nervous in the future. It really helps to know that you look in control even though you may not feel that way."

Don't Expect Perfection

It may also help to know that there is no such thing as a perfect speech. At some point in every presentation, every speaker says or does something that

Like many well-known public figures, Jennifer Lawrence often experiences stage fright before a speech. Most speakers report that their nervousness drops significantly after the first 30 to 60 seconds of a presentation.

does not come across exactly as he or she had planned. Fortunately, such moments are usually not evident to the audience. Why? Because the audience does not know what the speaker *plans* to say. It hears only what the speaker *does* say. If you momentarily lose your place, reverse the order of a couple of statements, or forget to pause at a certain spot, no one need be the wiser. When such moments occur, just proceed as if nothing happened.

Even if you do make an obvious mistake during a speech, that is no catastrophe. If you have ever listened to Martin Luther King's "I Have a Dream," you may recall that he stumbles twice during the speech. Most likely, however, you don't remember. Why? Because you were focusing on King's message, rather than on the fine points of his delivery.

One of the biggest reasons people are concerned about making a mistake in a speech is that they view speechmaking as a performance rather than an act of communication. They feel the audience is judging them against a scale of absolute perfection in which every misstated word or awkward gesture will count against them. But speech audiences are not like judges in a violin recital or an ice-skating contest. They are not looking for a virtuoso performance, but for a well-thought-out address that communicates the speaker's ideas clearly and directly. Sometimes an error or two can actually enhance a speaker's appeal by making her or him seem more human.[17]

As you work on your speeches, make sure you prepare thoroughly and do all you can to get your message across to your listeners. But don't panic about being perfect or about what will happen if you make a mistake. Once you free your mind of these burdens, you will find it much easier to approach your speeches with confidence and even with enthusiasm.

Besides stressing the six points just discussed, your instructor will probably give you several tips for dealing with nervousness in your first speeches. They may include:

- Be at your best physically and mentally. It's not a good idea to stay up until 3:00 A.M. partying with friends or cramming for an exam the night before your speech. A good night's sleep will serve you better.
- As you are waiting to speak, quietly tighten and relax your leg muscles, or squeeze your hands together and then release them. Such actions help reduce tension by providing an outlet for your extra adrenaline.
- Take a couple of slow, deep breaths before you start to speak. When they are tense, most people take short, shallow breaths, which only reinforces their anxiety. Deep breathing breaks this cycle of tension and helps calm your nerves.
- Work especially hard on your introduction. Research has shown that a speaker's anxiety level begins to drop significantly after the first 30 to 60 seconds of a presentation.[18] Once you get through the introduction, you should find smoother sailing the rest of the way.
- Make eye contact with members of your audience. Remember that they are individual people, not a blur of faces. And they are your friends.
- Concentrate on communicating with your audience rather than on worrying about your stage fright. If you get caught up in your speech, your audience will too.
- Use visual aids. They create interest, draw attention away from you, and make you feel less self-conscious.

checklist

Speaking with Confidence

YES	NO	
☐	☐	1. Am I enthusiastic about my speech topic?
☐	☐	2. Have I thoroughly developed the content of my speech?
☐	☐	3. Have I worked on the introduction so my speech will get off to a good start?
☐	☐	4. Have I worked on the conclusion so my speech will end on a strong note?
☐	☐	5. Have I rehearsed my speech orally until I am confident about its delivery?
☐	☐	6. Have I worked on turning negative thoughts about my speech into positive ones?
☐	☐	7. Do I realize that nervousness is normal, even among experienced speakers?
☐	☐	8. Do I understand that most nervousness is not visible to the audience?
☐	☐	9. Am I focused on communicating with my audience, rather than on worrying about my nerves?
☐	☐	10. Have I visualized myself speaking confidently and getting a positive response from the audience?

If you are like most students, you will find your speech class to be a very positive experience. As one student wrote on her course evaluation at the end of the class:

> I was really dreading this class. The idea of giving all those speeches scared me half to death. But I'm glad now that I stuck with it. It's a small class, and I got to know a lot of the students. Besides, this is one class in which I got to express *my* ideas, instead of spending the whole time listening to the teacher talk. I even came to enjoy giving the speeches. I could tell at times that the audience was really with me, and that's a great feeling.

Over the years, thousands of students have developed confidence in their speechmaking abilities. As your confidence grows, you will be better able to stand before other people and tell them what you think and feel and know—and to make them think and feel and know those same things. The best part about confidence is that it nurtures itself. After you score your first triumph, you will be that much more confident the next time. And as you become a more confident public speaker, you will likely become more confident in other areas of your life as well.

Public Speaking and Critical Thinking

> That guy at the party last night really owned me when we were talking about the economy. I know my information is right, and I'm sure his argument didn't make sense, but I can't put my finger on the problem.
>
> I worked really hard on my term paper, but it's just not right. It doesn't seem to hang together, and I can't figure out what's wrong.
>
> Political speeches are so one-sided. The candidates sound good, but they all talk in slogans and generalities. It's really hard to decide who has the best stands on the issues.

critical thinking

Focused, organized thinking about such things as the logical relationships among ideas, the soundness of evidence, and the differences between fact and opinion.

Have you ever found yourself in similar situations? If so, you may find help in your speech class. Besides building confidence, a course in public speaking can develop your skills as a critical thinker. Those skills can make the difference between the articulate debater and the pushover, the A student and the C student, the thoughtful voter and the coin tosser.

What is critical thinking? To some extent, it's a matter of logic—of being able to spot weaknesses in other people's arguments and to avoid them in your own. It also involves related skills such as distinguishing fact from opinion, judging the credibility of statements, and assessing the soundness of evidence. In the broadest sense, critical thinking is focused, organized thinking—the ability to see clearly the relationships among ideas.[19]

If you are wondering what this has to do with your public speaking class, the answer is quite a lot. As the class proceeds, you will probably spend a good deal of time organizing your speeches. While this may seem like a purely mechanical exercise, it is closely interwoven with critical thinking. If the structure of your speech is disjointed and confused, odds are that your thinking is also disjointed and confused. If, on the other hand, the structure is clear and cohesive, there is a good chance your thinking is too. Organizing a speech is not just a matter of arranging the ideas you already have. Rather, it is an important part of shaping the ideas themselves.

What is true of organization is true of many aspects of public speaking. The skills you learn in your speech class can help you become a more effective thinker in a number of ways. As you work on expressing your ideas in clear, accurate language, you will enhance your ability to think clearly and accurately. As you study the role of evidence and reasoning in speechmaking, you will see how they can be used in other forms of communication as well. As you learn to listen critically to speeches in class, you will be better able to assess the ideas of speakers (and writers) in a variety of situations.

To return to the examples at the beginning of this section:

> The guy at the party last night—would well-honed critical thinking skills help you find the holes in his argument?
>
> The term paper—would better organization and a clear outline help pull it together?
>
> Political speeches—once you get past the slogans, are the candidates drawing valid conclusions from sound evidence?

If you take full advantage of your speech class, you will be able to enhance your skills as a critical thinker in many circumstances. This is one reason public speaking has been regarded as a vital part of education since the days of ancient Greece.

Using public speaking in your CAREER

It's been three years since you graduated from college, and one year since you and your friends launched a mobile app development company. The app, a note-taking and collaboration tool for college students, has taken a while to create, but now you're ready to unveil it at a regional technology conference. Although you have given a few brief talks since your speech class in college, the conference will be your first major presentation to a large audience.

The closer you get to the day of the speech, the harder it is to control the butterflies in your stomach. There will be approximately 200 people in your audience, including potential investors, rival development companies, and members of the press. All eyes will be on you. It's important that you come across as confident and well informed, but you're afraid your stage fright will send the opposite message. What strategies will you use to control your nerves and make them work for you?

The Speech Communication Process

As you begin your first speeches, you may find it helpful to understand what goes on when one person talks to another. Regardless of the kind of speech communication involved, there are seven elements—speaker, message, channel, listener, feedback, interference, and situation. Here we focus on how these elements interact when a public speaker addresses an audience.

SPEAKER

speaker

The person who is presenting an oral message to a listener.

Speech communication begins with a speaker. If you pick up the telephone and call a friend, you are acting as a speaker. (Of course, you will also act as a listener when your friend is talking.) In public speaking, you will usually present your entire speech without interruption.

Your success as a speaker depends on *you*—on your personal credibility, your knowledge of the subject, your preparation of the speech, your manner of speaking, your sensitivity to the audience and the occasion. But successful speaking also requires enthusiasm.

You can't expect people to be interested in what you say unless you are interested yourself. If you are truly excited about your subject, your audience is almost sure to get excited along with you. You can learn all the techniques of effective speechmaking, but before they can be of much use, you must first have something to say—something that sparks your own enthusiasm.

MESSAGE

message

Whatever a speaker communicates to someone else.

The message is whatever a speaker communicates to someone else. If you are calling a friend, you might say, "I'll be a little late picking you up tonight." That is the message. But it may not be the only message. Perhaps there is a certain tone in your voice that suggests reluctance, hesitation. The underlying message might be "I really don't want to go to that party. You talked me into it, but I'm going to put it off as long as I can."

Your goal in public speaking is to have your *intended* message be the message that is *actually* communicated. Achieving this depends both on what you say (the verbal message) and on how you say it (the nonverbal message).

Getting the verbal message just right requires work. You must narrow your topic down to something you can discuss adequately in the time allowed for the speech. You must do research and choose supporting details to make your ideas clear and convincing. You must organize your ideas so listeners can follow them without getting lost. And you must express your message in words that are accurate, clear, vivid, and appropriate.

Besides the message you send with words, you send a message with your tone of voice, appearance, gestures, facial expression, and eye contact. Imagine that one of your classmates gets up to speak about student loans. Throughout her speech she slumps behind the lectern, takes long pauses to remember what she wants to say, stares at the ceiling, and fumbles with her visual aids.

Her intended message is "We must make more money available for student loans." But the message she actually communicates is "I haven't

The powers of critical thinking you develop in researching and organizing your speeches can be applied in many forms of communication, including meetings and group projects.

prepared very well for this speech." One of your jobs as a speaker is to make sure your nonverbal message does not distract from your verbal message.

CHANNEL

The channel is the means by which a message is communicated. When you pick up the phone to call a friend, the telephone is the channel. Public speakers may use one or more of several channels, each of which will affect the message received by the audience.

Consider a speech to Congress by the President of the United States. The speech is carried to the nation by the channels of radio and television. For the radio audience the message is conveyed entirely by the President's voice. For the television audience the message is conveyed by both the President's voice and the televised image. The people in Congress have a more direct channel. They not only hear the President's voice as amplified through a microphone, but they also see him and the setting firsthand.

channel

The means by which a message is communicated.

In a public speaking class, your channel is the most direct of all. Your classmates will see you and hear you without any electronic intervention.

LISTENER

The listener is the person who receives the communicated message. Without a listener, there is no communication. When you talk to a friend on the phone, you have one listener. In public speaking you will have many listeners.

listener

The person who receives the speaker's message.

Everything a speaker says is filtered through a listener's *frame of reference*—the total of his or her knowledge, experience, goals, values, and attitudes. Because a speaker and a listener are different people, they can never have

frame of reference

The sum of a person's knowledge, experience, goals, values, and attitudes. No two people can have exactly the same frame of reference.

exactly the same frame of reference. And because a listener's frame of reference can never be exactly the same as a speaker's, the meaning of a message will never be exactly the same to a listener as to a speaker.

You can easily test the impact of different frames of reference. Ask each of your classmates to describe a chair. If you have 20 classmates, you'll probably get 20 different descriptions. One student might picture a large, overstuffed easy chair, another an elegant straight-backed chair, yet another an office chair, a fourth a rocking chair, and so on.

Even if two or more envision the same general type—say, a rocking chair—their mental images of the chair could still be different. One might be thinking of an early American rocker, another of a modern Scandinavian rocker—the possibilities are unlimited. And "chair" is a fairly simple concept. What about "patriotism" or "freedom"?

Because people have different frames of reference, a public speaker must take great care to adapt the message to the particular audience being addressed. To be an effective speaker, you must be *audience-centered*. You will quickly lose your listeners' attention if your presentation is either too basic or too sophisticated. You will also lose your audience if you do not relate to their experience, interests, knowledge, and values. When you make a speech that causes listeners to say "That is important to *me,*" you will almost always be successful.

FEEDBACK

feedback

The messages, usually nonverbal, sent from a listener to a speaker.

When the President addresses the nation on television, he is engaged in one-way communication. You can talk back to the television set, but the President won't hear you. Most situations, however, involve *two-way* communication. Your listeners don't simply absorb your message like human sponges. They send back messages of their own. These messages are called feedback.

In public speaking there is plenty of feedback to let you know how your message is being received. Do your listeners lean forward in their seats, as if paying close attention? Do they have quizzical looks on their faces? Do they shuffle their feet and gaze at the clock? The message sent by these reactions could be "I am fascinated," "I am bored," "I agree with you," "I don't agree with you," or any number of others. As a speaker, you need to be alert to these reactions and adjust your message accordingly.

Like any kind of communication, feedback is affected by one's frame of reference. How would you feel if, immediately after your speech, all your classmates started to rap their knuckles on the desks? Would you run out of the room in despair? Not if you were in a European university. In many parts of Europe, students rap their knuckles on their desks to show admiration for a classroom lecture. You must understand the feedback to be able to deal with it.

INTERFERENCE

Interference is anything that impedes the communication of a message. When you talk on the telephone, sometimes there is static, or wires get crossed so that two different conversations are going on at once. That is a kind of interference.

In public speaking there are two kinds of interference. One, like the static or crossed wires in a phone conversation, is *external* to the audience. Many classrooms are subject to this kind of interference—from traffic outside the building, the clatter of a radiator, students conversing in the hall, a room that is stifling hot or freezing cold. Any of these can distract listeners from what you are saying.

interference

Anything that impedes the communication of a message. Interference can be external or internal to listeners.

A second kind of interference is *internal* and comes from within your audience. Perhaps one of your listeners has a toothache. She may be so distracted by the pain that she doesn't pay attention to your speech. Another listener could be worrying about a test in the next class period. Yet another could be brooding about an argument with his girlfriend.

As a speaker, you must try to hold your listeners' attention despite these various kinds of interference. In the chapters that follow you will find many ways to do this.

SITUATION

The situation is the time and place in which speech communication occurs. Conversation always takes place in a certain situation. Sometimes the situation helps—as when you propose marriage over an intimate candlelight dinner. Other times it may hurt—as when you try to speak words of love in competition with blaring music. When you have to talk with someone about a touchy issue, you usually wait until the situation is just right.

situation

The time and place in which speech communication occurs.

Public speakers must also be alert to the situation. Certain occasions—funerals, church services, graduation ceremonies—require certain kinds of speeches. Physical setting is also important. It makes a great deal of difference whether a speech is presented indoors or out, in a small classroom or in a gymnasium, to a densely packed crowd or to a handful of scattered souls. When you adjust to the situation of a public speech, you are only doing on a larger scale what you do every day in conversation.

For a complete model of the speech communication process, see Figure 1.1 below.[20]

FIGURE 1.1

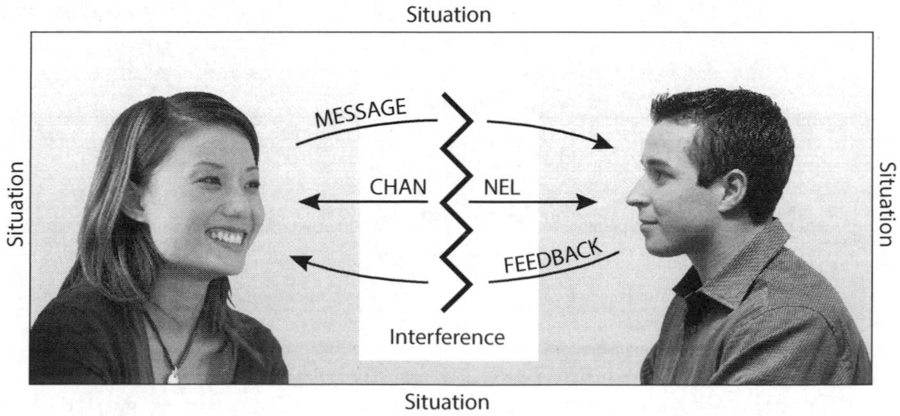

THE SPEECH COMMUNICATION PROCESS: EXAMPLE WITH COMMENTARY

The following example shows how the various components of the speech communication process interact:

Situation	It was 5:15 P.M., and the Midwest Food Festival and Expo had been going on all day. Gourmet food vendors from across the Great Lakes region were presenting their products to distributors and restaurant owners, but the presentations had taken much longer than expected.
Speaker	Jason Cruz, owner and operator of a gourmet salsa company, was worried. As the last speaker of the day, he knew he faced a tough situation. He had been allotted 30 minutes, but the festival was scheduled to end in 15 minutes, and the success of his products depended in large part on his presentation.
Channel	Jason stepped to the microphone and began to speak. He could see members of the audience looking at their watches, and he knew they were eager to get to dinner after a long day of meetings.
Adapting to Interference	"Good afternoon," Jason said, "and thanks for your attention. I know everyone is ready to relax after a long day—I certainly am. I was given 30 minutes to tell you about my salsa, but I'll do my best to finish in 15. I think you'll find the time well worth your while, because your customers are going to love my products." Jason was relieved to see people smiling as they settled back in their seats.
Message	Now that he had the audience's attention, Jason presented each of his products as briefly as he could. He streamlined his planned remarks to emphasize the salsas that would be most appealing to grocery shoppers and restaurant diners. He ended by handing out samples of two new salsas that had won awards in recent food shows.
Feedback	As promised, Jason finished in 15 minutes. "So, that's it!" he concluded. "Thanks for your attention after such a long day." The festival organizer came up to Jason after his presentation. "Great stuff—both the talk and the salsa," she said. "Next year I think we'll try to make all the presentations as concise and efficient as yours."

Public Speaking in a Multicultural World

CULTURAL DIVERSITY IN THE MODERN WORLD

The United States has always been a diverse society. By the middle of the 19th century, it contained so many people from so many lands that novelist Herman Melville exclaimed, "You cannot spill a drop of American blood without spilling the blood of the whole world."[21]

One can only imagine what Melville would say today! The United States is the most diverse society on earth. That diversity can be seen in cities and towns, schools and businesses, community groups, and houses of worship all across the land.

Globally, we live in an age of international multiculturalism. The Internet allows for instant communication. CNN is broadcast to more than 1 billion people around the world. Social media connect people across ancient boundaries. Despite political, social, and religious differences, all nations are becoming part of a vast global network. For example:

- There are 82,000 transnational corporations around the world, and they account for one-third of the world's economic output.
- McDonald's sells twice as many hamburgers and French fries abroad than it does in the United States; Nike makes 63 percent of its sales through exports.
- France has more Muslims than practicing Catholics; radio CHIN in Toronto, Canada, broadcasts in over 30 languages.

CULTURAL DIVERSITY AND PUBLIC SPEAKING

Speechmaking becomes more complex as cultural diversity increases. Part of the complexity stems from the differences in language from culture to culture. Nothing separates one culture from another more than language. Language and culture are so closely bound that "we communicate the way we do because we are raised in a particular culture and learn its language, rules, and norms."[22]

The meanings attached to gestures, facial expressions, and other nonverbal signals also vary from culture to culture. Even the gestures for such basic messages as "hello" and "goodbye" are culturally based. The North American

Public speaking is a vital mode of communication in cultures around the world. Indian President Narendra Modi addresses an audience at the Gujarat Training Academy in Ahmedabad.

"goodbye" wave is interpreted in many parts of Europe and South America as the motion for "no," while the Italian and Greek gesture for "goodbye" is the same as the U.S. signal for "come here."[23]

Many stories have been told about the fate of public speakers who fail to take into account cultural differences between themselves and their audiences. Consider the following scenario:[24]

> The sales manager of a U.S. electronics firm is in Brazil to negotiate a large purchase of computers by a South American corporation. After three days of negotiations, the sales manager holds a gala reception for all the major executives to build goodwill between the companies.
>
> As is the custom on such occasions, time is set aside during the reception for an exchange of toasts. When it is the sales manager's turn to speak, he praises the Brazilian firm for its many achievements and talks eloquently of his respect for its president and other executives. The words are perfect, and the sales manager can see his audience smiling in approval.
>
> And then—disaster. As the sales manager closes his speech, he raises his hand and flashes the classic U.S. "OK" sign to signal his pleasure at the progress of the negotiations. Instantly the festive mood is replaced with stony silence; smiles turn to icy stares. The sales manager has given his Brazilian audience a gesture with roughly the same meaning as an extended middle finger in the United States.
>
> The next day, the Brazilian firm announces that it will buy its computers from another company.

As this story illustrates, public speakers can ill afford to overlook their listeners' cultural values and customs. The methods of effective speech explained throughout this book will be helpful to you when addressing culturally diverse audiences. Here we need to stress the importance of avoiding the ethnocentrism that often blocks communication between speakers and listeners of different cultural backgrounds.

AVOIDING ETHNOCENTRISM

ethnocentrism

The belief that one's own group or culture is superior to all other groups or cultures.

Ethnocentrism is the belief that our own group or culture—whatever it may be—is superior to all other groups or cultures. Because of ethnocentrism, we identify with our group or culture and see its values, beliefs, and customs as "right" or "natural"—in comparison to the values, beliefs, and customs of other groups or cultures, which we tend to think of as "wrong" or "unnatural."[25]

Ethnocentrism is part of every culture, and it can play a positive role in creating group pride and loyalty. But it can also lead to prejudice and hostility toward different racial, ethnic, religious, or cultural groups. To be an effective public speaker in a multicultural world, you need to keep in mind that all people have their special beliefs and customs.

Avoiding ethnocentrism does not mean that you must agree with the values and practices of all groups and cultures. At times you might try to convince people of different cultures to change their traditional ways of doing things—as speakers from the United Nations seek to persuade farmers in Africa to adopt more productive methods of agriculture, or as delegates from the United States and China attempt to influence the other country's trade policies.

If such speakers are to be successful, however, they must show respect for the cultures of the people they address. They need to adapt their messages to the values and expectations of their listeners.

When you work on your speeches, be alert to how cultural factors might affect how listeners respond. Try to put yourself in their place and to hear your message through their ears. If there is a language difference, avoid words or phrases that might cause misunderstanding. When researching the speech, keep an eye out for visual aids and other materials that will relate to a wide range of listeners. When delivering the speech, be alert to feedback that might indicate the audience is having trouble grasping your ideas.

It is also important to avoid ethnocentrism when listening to speeches. When you listen to a speaker from a different cultural background, be on guard against the temptation to judge the speaker on the basis of his or her appearance or manner of delivery. No matter what the cultural background of the speaker, you should listen to her or him as attentively as you would want your audience to listen to you.[26]

Summary

Public speaking has been a vital means of personal empowerment and civic engagement throughout history. The need for effective public speaking will almost certainly touch you sometime in your life. Your speech class will give you training in researching topics, organizing your ideas, and presenting yourself skillfully. This training is invaluable for every type of communication.

There are many similarities between public speaking and daily conversation, but public speaking is also different from conversation. First, it usually imposes strict time limitations and requires more detailed preparation than does ordinary conversation. Second, it requires more formal language. Listeners react negatively to speeches loaded with slang, jargon, and bad grammar. Third, public speaking demands a different method of delivery. Effective speakers adjust their voices to the larger audience and work at avoiding distracting physical mannerisms and verbal habits.

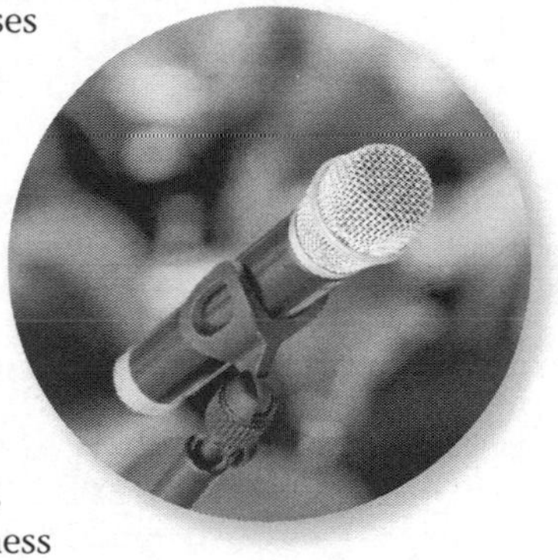

One of the major concerns of students in any speech class is stage fright. Your class will give you an opportunity to gain confidence and make your nervousness work for you rather than against you. You will take a big step toward overcoming stage fright if you think positively, prepare thoroughly, visualize yourself giving a successful speech, keep in mind that most nervousness is not visible to the audience, and think of your speech as communication rather than as a performance in which you must do everything perfectly.

A course in public speaking can also help develop your skills as a critical thinker. Critical thinking helps you organize your ideas, spot weaknesses in other people's reasoning, and avoid them in your own.

The speech communication process includes seven elements—speaker, message, channel, listener, feedback, interference, and situation. The speaker is the person who initiates a speech transaction. Whatever the speaker communicates is the message, which is sent by means of a particular channel. The listener receives the communicated message and provides feedback to the speaker. Interference is anything that impedes the communication of a message, and the situation is the time and place in which speech communication occurs. The interaction of these seven elements determines the outcome in any instance of speech communication.

Because of the diversity of modern life, many—perhaps most—of the audiences you address will include people of different cultural backgrounds. When you work on your speeches, be alert to how such factors might affect the responses of your listeners and adapt your message accordingly. Above all, avoid the ethnocentric belief that your own culture or group is superior to all others. Also keep in mind the importance of avoiding ethnocentrism when listening to speeches. Accord every speaker the same courtesy and attentiveness you would want from your listeners.

Key Terms

stage fright (9)
adrenaline (10)
positive nervousness (10)
visualization (13)
critical thinking (16)
speaker (18)
message (18)
channel (19)
listener (19)
frame of reference (20)
feedback (20)
interference (21)
situation (21)
ethnocentrism (24)

Review Questions

After reading this chapter, you should be able to answer the following questions:

1. In what ways is public speaking likely to make a difference in your life?
2. How is public speaking similar to everyday conversation?
3. How is public speaking different from everyday conversation?
4. Why is it normal—even desirable—to be nervous at the start of a speech?
5. How can you control your nervousness and make it work for you in your speeches?
6. What are the seven elements of the speech communication process? How do they interact to determine the success or failure of a speech?
7. What is ethnocentrism? Why do public speakers need to avoid ethnocentrism when addressing audiences with diverse cultural, racial, or ethnic backgrounds?

connect

For further review, go to the LearnSmart study module for this chapter.

Exercises for Critical Thinking

1. Think back on an important conversation you had recently in which you wanted to achieve a particular result. (*Examples:* asking your employer to change your work schedule; explaining to a friend how to change the oil and filter in a car; attempting to talk your spouse or partner into buying the computer you like rather than the one he or she prefers.) Work up a brief analysis of the conversation.

   In your analysis, explain the following: (1) your purpose in the conversation and the message strategy you chose to achieve your purpose; (2) the communication channels used during the conversation and how they affected the outcome; (3) the interference—internal or external—you encountered during the conversation; (4) the steps you took to adjust to feedback; (5) the strategic changes you would make in preparing for and carrying out the conversation if you had it to do over again.

2. Divide a sheet of paper into two columns. Label one column "Characteristics of an Effective Public Speaker." Label the other column "Characteristics of an Ineffective Public Speaker." In the columns, list and briefly explain what you believe to be the five most important characteristics of effective and ineffective speakers. Be prepared to discuss your ideas in class.
3. On the basis of the lists you developed for Exercise 2, candidly evaluate your own strengths and weaknesses as a speaker. Identify the three primary aspects of speechmaking you most want to improve.

2

Ethics and Public Speaking

- The Importance of Ethics
- Guidelines for Ethical Speaking
- Plagiarism
- Guidelines for Ethical Listening

When the rumors started, Brian Pertzborn, chief financial officer for a prominent charity in the southwest United States, called a press conference. Dozens of reporters showed up. Brian looked directly into the cameras and said, "I assure you that no one at this charity has taken money away from the children and families we work so hard to serve. Embezzlement is illegal and a serious breach of trust. I would never let either happen."

Brian's presentation was highly convincing, and for a time it quieted the rumors. Unfortunately, his statements were false. Two months later, he was indicted by the federal government for stealing more than $2.5 million from the charity.

At the trial, it became clear that Brian was guilty as charged. It also came out that on the very day of his press conference, he had tried to cover his tracks by transferring some of the embezzled money to an overseas bank account.

When the judge sentenced Brian to a stiff prison sentence, she made clear that she was influenced partly by Brian's lies at the press conference. Had he told the truth, his pleas for leniency might have been better received.

This is not a happy story, but it shows why public speaking needs to be guided by a strong sense of integrity. Brian Pertzborn was persuasive when speaking to the press, but he was unethical in lying to cover his illegal activities. As a result, he hurt people who relied on the charity, destroyed his reputation, and ended up with a long jail sentence. Perhaps if he had confessed before the cameras that day, he would have received a fine and a reprimand instead of the harshest sentence the judge could impose.

The goal of public speaking is to gain a desired response from listeners—but not at any cost. Speechmaking is a form of power and therefore carries with it heavy ethical responsibilities. As the Roman rhetorician Quintilian stated 2,000 years ago, the ideal of speechmaking is the good person speaking well. In this chapter, we explore that ideal by looking at the importance of ethics in public speaking, the ethical obligations of speakers and listeners, and the practical problem of plagiarism and how to avoid it.

The Importance of Ethics

ethics

The branch of philosophy that deals with issues of right and wrong in human affairs.

Ethics is the branch of philosophy that deals with issues of right and wrong in human affairs. Questions of ethics arise whenever we ask whether a course of action is moral or immoral, fair or unfair, just or unjust, honest or dishonest.

We face such questions daily in almost every part of our lives. The parent must decide how to deal with a child who has been sent home from school for unruly behavior. The researcher must decide whether to shade her data "just a bit" in order to gain credit for an important scientific breakthrough. The shopper must decide what to do with the $5 extra change mistakenly given by the clerk at the grocery store. The student must decide whether to say anything about a friend he has seen cheating on a final exam.

Questions of ethics also come into play whenever a public speaker faces an audience. In an ideal world, as the Greek philosopher Plato noted, all public speakers would be truthful and devoted to the good of society. Yet history tells us that the power of speech is often abused—sometimes with disastrous results. Adolf Hitler was unquestionably a persuasive speaker. His oratory galvanized the German people, but his aims were horrifying and his tactics despicable. He remains to this day the ultimate example of why the power of the spoken word needs to be guided by a strong sense of ethical integrity.

As a public speaker, you will face ethical issues at every stage of the speechmaking process—from the initial decision to speak through the final presentation of the message. And the answers will not always be easy. Consider the following example:

> Felicia Robinson is running for school board in a large eastern city. Her opponent is conducting what Felicia regards as a highly unethical campaign. In addition to twisting the facts about school taxes, the opponent is pandering to racial prejudice by raising resentment against African Americans and recently arrived immigrants.
>
> Five days before the election, Felicia, who is slightly behind in the polls, learns that the district attorney is preparing to indict her opponent for shady business practices. But the indictment will not be formally issued until after the election.

Nor can it be taken as evidence that her opponent is guilty—like all citizens, he has the right to be presumed innocent until proven otherwise.

Still, news of the indictment could be enough to throw the election Felicia's way, and her advisers urge her to make it an issue in her remaining campaign speeches. Should Felicia follow their advice?

There are creditable arguments to be made on both sides of the ethical dilemma faced by Felicia Robinson. She has tried to run an honest campaign, and she is troubled by the possibility of unfairly attacking her opponent—despite the fact that he has shown no such scruples himself. Yet she knows that the impending indictment may be her last chance to win the election, and she is convinced that a victory for her opponent will spell disaster for the city's school system. Torn between her commitment to fair play, her desire to be elected, and her concern for the good of the community, she faces the age-old ethical dilemma of whether the ends justify the means.

"So," you may be asking yourself, "what is the answer to Felicia Robinson's dilemma?" But in complex cases such as hers there are no cut-and-dried answers. As the leading book on communication ethics states, "We should formulate meaningful ethical guidelines, not inflexible rules."[1] Your ethical decisions will be guided by your values, your conscience, your sense of right and wrong.

ethical decisions

Sound ethical decisions involve weighing a potential course of action against a set of ethical standards or guidelines.

But this does not mean such decisions are simply a matter of personal whim or fancy. Sound ethical decisions involve weighing a potential course of action against a set of ethical standards or guidelines. Just as there are guidelines for ethical behavior in other areas of life, so there are guidelines for ethical conduct in public speaking. These guidelines will not automatically solve every ethical quandary you face as a speaker, but knowing them will provide a reliable compass to help you find your way.

Guidelines for Ethical Speaking

MAKE SURE YOUR GOALS ARE ETHICALLY SOUND

Several years ago, I spoke with a former student—we'll call her Melissa—who had turned down a job in the public relations department of the American Tobacco Institute. Why? Because the job would have required her to lobby on behalf of the cigarette industry. Melissa did not believe she could ethically promote a product that she saw as responsible for thousands of deaths and illnesses each year.

Given Melissa's view of the dangers of cigarette smoking, there can be no doubt that she made an ethically informed decision. On the other side of the coin, someone with a different view of cigarette smoking could make an ethically informed decision to *take* the job. The point of this example is not to judge the rightness or wrongness of Melissa's decision (or of cigarette smoking), but to illustrate how ethical considerations can affect a speaker's choice of goals.

Your first responsibility as a speaker is to ask whether your goals are ethically sound. During World War II, Hitler stirred the German people to condone war, invasion, and genocide. More recently, we have seen politicians who betray the public trust for personal gain, business leaders who defraud investors of millions of dollars, preachers who lead lavish lifestyles at the expense of their religious duties. There can be no doubt that these are not worthy goals.

But think back for a moment to the examples of speechmaking given in Chapter 1. What do the speakers hope to accomplish? Improve the quality of education. Report on a business project. Pay tribute to a fellow worker. Support Habitat for Humanity. Few people would question that these goals are ethically sound.

As with other ethical issues, there can be gray areas when it comes to assessing a speaker's goals—areas in which reasonable people with well-defined standards of right and wrong can legitimately disagree. But this is not a reason to avoid asking ethical questions. If you are to be a responsible public speaker, you cannot escape assessing the ethical soundness of your goals.

BE FULLY PREPARED FOR EACH SPEECH

"A speech," as Jenkin Lloyd Jones stated, "is a solemn responsibility." You have an obligation—to yourself and to your listeners—to prepare fully every time you stand in front of an audience. The obligation to yourself is obvious: The better you prepare, the better your speech will be. But the obligation to your listeners is no less important. Think of it this way: The person who makes a bad 30-minute speech to an audience of 200 people wastes only a half hour of her or his own time. But that same speaker wastes 100 hours of the audience's time—more than four full days. This, Jones exclaimed, "should be a hanging offense!"

At this stage of your speaking career, of course, you will probably not be facing many audiences of 200 people. And you will probably not be giving many speeches in which the audience has come for the sole purpose of listening to you. But neither the size nor the composition of your audience changes your ethical responsibility to be fully prepared. Your speech classmates are as worthy of your best effort as if you were addressing a jury or a business meeting, a union conference or a church congregation, the local city council or even the United States Senate.

Being prepared for a speech involves everything from analyzing your audience to creating visual aids, organizing your ideas to rehearsing your delivery. Most crucial from an ethical standpoint, though, is being fully informed about your subject. Why is this so important? Consider the following story:

> Victoria Nuñez, a student at a large state university, gave a classroom speech on suicide prevention. Victoria had learned about the topic from her mother, a volunteer on a suicide-prevention hotline, but she also consulted her psychology textbook, read several magazine articles on the warning signs of suicide, and interviewed a crisis-intervention counselor at the campus health service.
>
> In addition to her research, Victoria gave a lot of thought to planning and delivering her speech. She created a handout for the class listing signs that a person might attempt suicide and providing contact information for local mental-health resources. On the day of her speech, Victoria was thoroughly prepared—and she gave an excellent presentation.
>
> Only a few days later, one of Victoria's classmates, Paul Nichols, had a conversation with his roommate that raised a warning flag about whether the roommate might be depressed and in danger of suicide. Based on the information in Victoria's speech, Paul spoke to his roommate, got him to talk about his worries, and convinced him to seek counseling. Paul might have saved his roommate's life, thanks to Victoria's speech.

Among current public speakers, Nobel Peace Prize recipient Leymah Gbowee is well regarded for her ethically sound goals and public speaking skills.

This is an especially dramatic case, but it demonstrates how your speeches can have a genuine impact on your listeners. As a speaker, you have an ethical responsibility to consider that impact and to make sure you prepare fully so as not to communicate erroneous information or misleading advice. If Victoria had not done such a thorough job researching her speech, she might have given her classmates faulty information—information that might have had tragic results.

No matter what the topic, no matter who the audience, you need to explore your speech topic as thoroughly as possible. Investigate the whole story; learn about all sides of an issue; seek out competing viewpoints; get the facts right. Not only will you give a better speech, you will also fulfill one of your major ethical obligations.

BE HONEST IN WHAT YOU SAY

Nothing is more important to ethical speechmaking than honesty. Public speaking rests on the unspoken assumption that "words can be trusted and people will be truthful."[2] Without this assumption, there is no basis for communication, no reason for one person to believe anything that another person says.

Does this mean *every* speaker must *always* tell "the truth, the whole truth, and nothing but the truth"? We can all think of situations in which this is impossible (because we do not know the whole truth) or inadvisable (because it would be tactless or imprudent). Consider a parent who tells his two-year-old daughter that her screeching violin solo is "beautiful." Or a speaker who tells a falsehood in circumstances when disclosing the truth might touch off mob violence. Few people would find these actions unethical.[3]

In contrast, think back to the case of Brian Pertzborn at the start of this chapter. Brian knew he had embezzled money from the charity. Yet he denied that he had done so, even as he was profiting at the expense of people who depended on the charity's services. There is no way to excuse Brian's behavior.

Such blatant contempt for the truth is one kind of dishonesty in public speaking. But more subtle forms of dishonesty are just as unethical. They include juggling statistics, quoting out of context, misrepresenting sources, painting tentative findings as firm conclusions, citing unusual cases as typical examples, and substituting innuendo and half-truths for evidence and proof. All of these violate the speaker's duty to be accurate and fair in presenting information.

While on the subject of honesty in speechmaking, we should also note that ethically responsible speakers do not present other people's words as their own. They do not plagiarize their speeches. This subject is so important that we devote a separate section to it later in this chapter.

AVOID NAME-CALLING AND OTHER FORMS OF ABUSIVE LANGUAGE

name-calling

The use of language to defame, demean, or degrade individuals or groups.

"Sticks and stones can break my bones, but words can never hurt me." This popular children's chant could not be more wrong. Words may not literally break people's bones, but they can leave psychological scars as surely as sticks and stones can leave physical scars. As one writer explains, "Our identities, who and what we are, how others see us, are greatly affected by the names we are called and the words with which we are labeled."[4] This is why communication ethicists warn public speakers to avoid name-calling and other forms of abusive language.

Name-calling is the use of language to defame, demean, or degrade individuals or groups. When applied to various groups in America, it includes such epithets as "redskin," "fag," "kike," "nigger," "honkey," "wop," "jap," "chink," and "spic" that have been used to label people because of their sexual orientation, religious beliefs, or ethnic background. Such terms are ethically suspect because they stereotype and devalue the people in question.

Name-calling is also a destructive social force. When used repeatedly and systematically over time, it helps reinforce attitudes that encourage prejudice, hate crimes, and civil rights violations.[5] The issue is not one of political correctness, but of respecting the dignity of the diverse groups in contemporary society.

In addition, name-calling and abusive language pose ethical problems in public speaking when they are used to silence opposing voices. A democratic society depends upon the free and open expression of ideas. In the United States, all citizens have the right to join in the never-ending dialogue of democracy. As a public speaker, you have an ethical obligation to help preserve that right. This obligation is the same regardless of whether you are black or white, Christian or Muslim, male or female, gay or straight, liberal or conservative.

Bill of Rights

The first 10 amendments to the United States Constitution.

Like other ethical questions in public speaking, name-calling raises some thorny issues. Although name-calling can be hazardous to free speech, it is still protected under the free-speech clause of the Bill of Rights. This is why broadly worded codes against hate speech on college campuses—and in society at large—have not survived legal challenges.[6]

Questions of ethics arise whenever a speaker addresses an audience. Here Shannon Watts, founder of Moms Demand Action, speaks at a rally after the school shootings in Newtown, Connecticut

But regardless of the legal issues, they do not alter the ethical responsibility of public speakers to avoid name-calling and abusive language. Legality and ethics, though related, are not identical. There is nothing illegal about falsifying statistics in a speech, but there is no doubt that it is unethical. The same is true of name-calling. It may not be illegal to cast racial, religious, sexual, or religious slurs at people in a speech, but it is still unethical. Not only does it demean the dignity of the groups or individuals being attacked, but it undermines the right of all groups in the United States to be fairly heard.

PUT ETHICAL PRINCIPLES INTO PRACTICE

It is easy to pay lip service to the importance of ethics. It is much harder to act ethically. Yet that is just what a responsible public speaker must do. As one popular book on ethics states, "Being ethical means behaving ethically *all the time*—not only when it's convenient."[7]

As you work on your speeches, you will ask yourself such questions as "Is my choice of topic suitable for the audience?" "Are my supporting materials clear and convincing?" "How can I phrase my ideas to give them more punch?" These are *strategic* questions. As you answer them, you will try to make your speech as informative, as persuasive, or as entertaining as possible.

But you will also face moments of *ethical* decision—similar, perhaps, to those faced by Brian Pertzborn, Felicia Robinson, and other speakers in this chapter. When those moments arrive, don't simply brush them aside and go on your way. Keep in mind the guidelines for ethical speechmaking we have discussed and do your best to follow them through thick and thin. Make sure you can answer yes to all the questions on the Checklist for Ethical Public Speaking on page 36.[8]

checklist

Ethical Public Speaking

YES	NO	
☐	☐	1. Have I examined my goals to make sure they are ethically sound? a. Can I defend my goals on ethical grounds if they are questioned or challenged? b. Would I want other people to know my true motives in presenting this speech?
☐	☐	2. Have I fulfilled my ethical obligation to prepare fully for the speech? a. Have I done a thorough job of studying and researching the topic? b. Have I prepared diligently so as not to communicate erroneous or misleading information to my listeners?
☐	☐	3. Is the speech free of plagiarism? a. Can I vouch that the speech represents my own work, my own thinking, my own language? b. Do I cite the sources of all quotations and paraphrases?
☐	☐	4. Am I honest in what I say in the speech? a. Is the speech free of any false or deliberately deceptive statements? b. Does the speech present statistics, testimony, and other kinds of evidence fairly and accurately? c. Does the speech contain valid reasoning? d. If the speech includes visual aids, do they present facts honestly and reliably?
☐	☐	5. Do I use the power of language ethically? a. Do I avoid name-calling and other forms of abusive language? b. Does my language show respect for the right of free speech and expression?
☐	☐	6. All in all, have I made a conscious effort to put ethical principles into practice in preparing my speech?

Plagiarism

plagiarism

Presenting another person's language or ideas as one's own.

"Plagiarism" comes from *plagiarius,* the Latin word for kidnapper. To plagiarize means to present another person's language or ideas as your own—to give the impression you have written or thought something yourself when you have actually taken it from someone else.[9] We often think of plagiarism as an ethical issue in the classroom, but it can have repercussions in other situations:

Chris Spence became director of education for the Toronto School Board in July 2009. As the chief educator for Canada's largest school district, he gave numerous speeches, in addition to writing newspaper articles and blog posts about his thoughts on education. Many people called him inspiring and his personality larger-than-life.

Then reporters discovered that portions of Spence's speeches and writings were lifted word-for-word from other people. They also noticed that passages of his doctoral dissertation at the University of Toronto lacked proper attribution. One newspaper referred to him as a "serial plagiarist" who repeatedly published "inspirational columns and blogs and speeches that were moving and thought-provoking—but not at all his own."

As the revelations mounted, Spence faced severe criticism within the school district. By January 2013, he had little choice but to resign as education director, putting an end to his once stellar career. "There are no excuses for what I did," he said. "I didn't give credit where credit was due."[10]

As this story shows, plagiarism is a serious matter. If you are caught plagiarizing a speech in class, the punishment can range from a failing grade to expulsion from school. If you are caught plagiarizing outside the classroom, you stand to forfeit your good name, to damage your career, or, if you are sued, to lose a large amount of money. It is worth your while, then, to make sure you know what plagiarism is and how to avoid it.

GLOBAL PLAGIARISM

Global plagiarism is stealing your speech entirely from another source and passing it off as your own. The most blatant—and unforgivable—kind of plagiarism, it is grossly unethical.

global plagiarism

Stealing a speech entirely from a single source and passing it off as one's own.

Global plagiarism in a college classroom usually occurs because a student puts off the assignment until the last minute. Then, in an act of desperation, the student downloads a speech from the Internet or gets one written by a friend and delivers it as his or her own.

The best way to avoid this, of course, is not to leave your speech until the last minute. Most instructors explain speech assignments far enough in advance that you should have no trouble getting an early start. By starting early, you will give yourself plenty of time to prepare a first-rate speech—a speech of your own.

If, for some reason, you fail to get your speech ready on time, do not succumb to the lure of plagiarism. Whatever penalty you suffer from being late will pale in comparison with the consequences if you are caught plagiarizing.

PATCHWORK PLAGIARISM

Unlike global plagiarism, in which a speaker pirates an entire speech from a single source, patchwork plagiarism occurs when a speaker pilfers from two or three sources. Here's an example:

patchwork plagiarism

Stealing ideas or language from two or three sources and passing them off as one's own.

Craig Lemark chose "The Benefits and Drawbacks of Natural Gas" as the topic for his informative speech. In his research, Craig found three especially helpful sources. The first was a recent article in the journal *Energy Policy* on America's clean-energy programs. The second was Wikipedia, and the third was the Web site of the University of Texas Energy Institute.

Unfortunately, instead of using these materials creatively to write a speech in his own words, Craig lifted long passages from the article, from Wikipedia, and from the university Web site and patched them together with a few transitions. When he was finished, he had a speech that was composed almost entirely of other people's words.

When Craig's teacher read his speech outline, it did not sound authentic to her. So she plugged several phrases from the outline into Google. In less than a minute, she had found both the Wikipedia article and the University of Texas Web site. After searching on Google Scholar, she also found the journal article. Craig was caught red-handed.

This story illustrates an important point about plagiarism. Craig did not take his speech from a single source. He even did a little research. But copying from a few sources is no less plagiarism than is copying from a single source. When you give a speech, you declare that it is your work—the product of your thinking, your beliefs, your language. Craig's speech did not contain any of these. Instead, it was cut and pasted wholly from other people's words.

"But," you may be thinking, "not many students are experts on their speech topics. Why should they be expected to come up with new ideas that even the experts haven't thought of?"

The answer is they aren't. The key is not whether you have something absolutely original to say, but whether you do enough research and thinking to come up with your own slant on the topic.

As with global plagiarism, one key to averting patchwork plagiarism is to start working on your speech as soon as possible. The longer you work on it, the more apt you are to come up with your own approach. It is also vital to consult a large number of sources in your research. If you have only two or three sources, you are far more likely to fall into the trap of patchwork plagiarism than if you consult a wide range of research materials.

INCREMENTAL PLAGIARISM

incremental plagiarism

Failing to give credit for particular parts of a speech that are borrowed from other people.

In global plagiarism and patchwork plagiarism, the entire speech is cribbed more or less verbatim from a single source or a few sources. But plagiarism can exist even when the speech as a whole is not pirated. This is called incremental plagiarism. It occurs when the speaker fails to give credit for particular parts—increments—of the speech that are borrowed from other people. The most important of these increments are quotations and paraphrases.

Quotations

Whenever you quote someone directly, you must attribute the words to that person. Suppose you are giving a speech on Malcolm X, the famous African-American leader of the 1960s. While doing your research, you run across the following passage from Bruce Perry's acclaimed biography, *Malcolm: The Life of the Man Who Changed Black America:*

> Malcolm X fathered no legislation. He engineered no stunning Supreme Court victories or political campaigns. He scored no major electoral triumphs. Yet because of the way he articulated his followers' grievances and anger, the impact he had upon the body politic was enormous.[11]

Speakers who begin work on their speeches early and consult a wide range of sources are less likely to fall into the trap of plagiarism than are speakers who procrastinate and rely on a limited number of sources.

This is a fine quotation that summarizes the nature and importance of Malcolm's impact on American politics. It would make a strong addition to your speech—as long as you acknowledge Perry as the author. The way to avoid plagiarism in this instance is to introduce Perry's statement by saying something like:

> In *Malcolm: The Life of the Man Who Changed Black America,* historian Bruce Perry says the following about Malcolm's impact on American politics: . . .

Or,

> According to historian Bruce Perry in his book *Malcolm: The Life of the Man Who Changed Black America,* . . .

Now you have clearly identified Perry and given him credit for his words rather than presenting them as your own.

Paraphrases

When you paraphrase an author, you restate or summarize her or his ideas in your own words. Suppose, once again, that your topic is Malcolm X. But this time you decide to paraphrase the statement from Bruce Perry's biography rather than quoting it. You might say:

paraphrase

To restate or summarize an author's ideas in one's own words.

> Malcolm X was not a politician. He did not pass any laws, or win any Supreme Court victories, or get elected to any office. But he stated the grievances and anger of his followers so powerfully that the whole nation took notice.

Even though you do not quote Perry directly, you still appropriate the structure of his ideas and a fair amount of his language. Thus you still need to give him credit—just as if you were repeating his words verbatim.

It is especially important in this case to acknowledge Perry because you are borrowing his opinion—his judgment—about Malcolm X. If you simply recount basic facts about Malcolm's life—he was born in Omaha, Nebraska, converted to the Nation of Islam while in prison, traveled to Mecca toward the end of his life, was assassinated in February 1965—you do not have to report the source of your information. These facts are well known and can be found in any standard reference work.

On the other hand, there is still considerable debate about Malcolm's views of other African-American leaders, the circumstances surrounding his death, and what he might have done had he lived. If you were to cite Perry's views on any of these matters—regardless of whether you quoted or paraphrased—you would need to acknowledge him as your source.

As more than one speaker (and writer) has discovered, it is possible to commit incremental plagiarism quite by accident. This is less offensive than deliberate plagiarism, but it is plagiarism nonetheless. There are two ways to guard against incremental plagiarism. The first is to be careful when taking research notes to distinguish among direct quotations, paraphrased material, and your own comments. (See Chapter 7 for a full discussion of research methods.) The second way to avoid incremental plagiarism is to err on the side of caution. In other words, when in doubt, cite your source.

PLAGIARISM AND THE INTERNET

When it comes to plagiarism, no subject poses more confusion—or more temptation—than the Internet. Because it's so easy to copy information from the Web, many people are not aware of the need to cite sources when they use Internet materials in their speeches. If you don't cite Internet sources, you are just as guilty of plagiarism as if you take information from print sources without proper citation.

One way to avoid patchwork plagiarism or incremental plagiarism when working with the Internet is to take careful research notes. Make sure you keep a record of the following: (1) the title of the Internet document, (2) the author or organization responsible for the document, (3) the date on which the document was last updated, (4) the date on which you accessed the site. You will need all this information for your speech bibliography.

You will also need to identify your Internet sources when you present the speech. It's not enough to say "As I found on the Web" or "According to the Internet." You need to specify the author and the Web site. In Chapter 8, we'll look more closely at how to cite Internet documents. For now, keep in mind that providing such citations is one of your ethical responsibilities as a public speaker.

Another problem with regard to the Internet is the large number of Web sites that sell entire speeches or papers. In addition to being highly unethical, using material from one of these sites is extremely risky. The same technology that makes it easy to plagiarize from the Web makes it easy for instructors to locate material that has been plagiarized and the exact source from which it has been taken.

Using public speaking in your CAREER

Having graduated with a degree in public administration and hoping to pursue a career in politics, you have been fortunate to receive a staff position with one of the leading senators in your state legislature. Since your arrival two months ago, you have answered phones, ordered lunch, made copies, stapled mailings, and stuffed envelopes. Finally you have been asked to look over a speech the senator will deliver at your alma mater. Surely, you think, this will be the first of many important assignments once your value is recognized.

After reading the speech, however, your enthusiasm is dampened. You agree wholeheartedly with its support of a bill to fund scholarships for low-income students, but you're dismayed by its attack on opponents of the bill as "elitist bigots who would deny a college education to those who need it most." You haven't been asked to comment on the ethics of the speech, and you certainly don't want to jeopardize your position on the senator's staff. At the same time, you think his use of name-calling may actually arouse sympathy for the opposition.

The senator would like your comments in two hours. What will you tell him?

You should also know that almost all the speeches (and papers) offered for sale on the Web are of very low quality. If you are ever tempted to purchase one, keep in mind there is a good chance you will waste your money and get caught in the process. Here, as in other aspects of life, honesty is the best policy.

Guidelines for Ethical Listening

So far in this chapter we have focused on the ethical duties of public speakers. But speechmaking is not a one-way street. Listeners also have ethical obligations. They are (1) to listen courteously and attentively; (2) to avoid prejudging the speaker; and (3) to maintain the free and open expression of ideas. Let us look at each.

BE COURTEOUS AND ATTENTIVE

Imagine that you are giving your first classroom speech. You have put a great deal of time into writing the speech, and you have practiced your delivery until you are confident you can do well—especially once you get over the initial rush of stage fright.

You have worked hard on your introduction, and your speech gets off to a fine start. Most of your classmates are paying close attention, but some are not. One appears to be doing homework for another class. Another keeps sneaking glances at his cell phone. Two or three are gazing out the window, and one is leaning back in his chair with his eyes shut!

> You try to block them out of your mind—especially since the rest of the class seems interested in what you are saying—but the longer you speak, the more concerned you become. "What am I doing wrong?" you wonder to yourself. "How can I get these people to pay attention?" The more you think about this, the more your confidence and concentration waver.
>
> When you momentarily lose your place halfway through the speech, you start to panic. Your nerves, which you have held in check so far, take the upper hand. Your major thought now becomes "How can I get this over as fast as possible?" Flustered and distracted, you rush through the rest of your speech and sit down.

Just as public speakers have an ethical obligation to prepare fully for each speech, so listeners have a responsibility to be courteous and attentive during the speech. This responsibility—which is a matter of civility in any circumstance—is especially important in speech class. You and your classmates are in a learning situation in which you need to support one another.

When you listen to speeches in class, give your fellow students the same courtesy and attention you want from them. Come to class prepared to listen to—and to learn from—your classmates' speeches. As you listen, be conscious of the feedback you are sending the speaker. Sit up in your chair rather than slouching; maintain eye contact with the speaker; show support and encouragement in your facial expressions. Keep in mind the power you have as a listener over the speaker's confidence and composure, and exercise that power with a strong sense of ethical responsibility.

AVOID PREJUDGING THE SPEAKER

We have all heard that you can't judge a book by its cover. The same is true of speeches. You can't judge a speech by the name, race, lifestyle, appearance, or reputation of the speaker. As the National Communication Association states in its Credo for Ethical Communication, listeners should "strive to understand and respect" speakers "before evaluating and responding to their messages."[12]

This does not mean you must agree with every speaker you hear. Your aim is to listen carefully to the speaker's ideas, to assess the evidence and reasoning offered in support of those ideas, and to reach an intelligent judgment about the speech. In Chapter 3, we will discuss specific steps you can take to improve your listening skills. For now, it is enough to know that if you prejudge a speaker—either positively or negatively—you will fail in one of your ethical responsibilities as a listener.

MAINTAIN THE FREE AND OPEN EXPRESSION OF IDEAS

As we saw earlier in this chapter, a democratic society depends on the free and open expression of ideas. The right of free expression is so important that it is protected by the First Amendment to the U.S. Constitution, which declares, in part, that "Congress shall make no law . . . abridging the freedom of speech." Just as public speakers need to avoid name-calling and other tactics that can undermine free speech, so listeners have an obligation to maintain the right of speakers to be heard.

It is vital for a democratic society to maintain the free and open expression of ideas. Here former Baltimore Ravens linebacker Brendon Ayanbadejo speaks on the subject of marriage equality.

As with other ethical issues, the extent of this obligation is open to debate. Disputes over the meaning and scope of the First Amendment arise almost daily in connection with issues such as terrorism, surveillance, and hate speech. The question underlying such disputes is whether *all* speakers have a right to be heard.

There are some kinds of speech that are not protected under the First Amendment—including defamatory falsehoods that destroy a person's reputation, threats against the life of the President, and inciting an audience to illegal action in circumstances where the audience is likely to carry out the action. Otherwise, the Supreme Court has held—and most experts in communication ethics have agreed—that public speakers have an almost unlimited right of free expression.

In contrast to this view, it has been argued that some ideas are so dangerous, so misguided, or so offensive that society has a duty to suppress them. But who is to determine which ideas are too dangerous, misguided, or offensive to be uttered? Who is to decide which speakers are to be heard and which are to be silenced?

No matter how well intentioned they may be, efforts to "protect" society by restricting free speech usually end up repressing minority viewpoints and unpopular opinions. In U.S. history, such efforts were used to keep women off the public platform until the 1840s, to muzzle labor organizers during the 1890s, and to impede civil rights leaders in the 1960s. Imagine what American society might be like if these speakers had been silenced!

It is important to keep in mind that ensuring a person's freedom to express her or his ideas does not imply agreement with those ideas. You can disagree entirely with the message but still support the speaker's right to express it. As the National Communication Association states in its Credo for Ethical Communication, "freedom of expression, diversity of perspective, and tolerance of dissent" are vital to "the informed decision making fundamental to a civil society."[13]

Summary

Because public speaking is a form of power, it carries with it heavy ethical responsibilities. Today, as for the past 2,000 years, the good person speaking well remains the ideal of commendable speechmaking.

There are five basic guidelines for ethical public speaking. The first is to make sure your goals are ethically sound—that they are consistent with the welfare of society and your audience. The second is to be fully prepared for each speech. The third is to be honest in what you say. The fourth is to avoid name-calling and other forms of abusive language. The final guideline is to put ethical principles into practice at all times.

Of all the ethical lapses a speaker can commit, few are more serious than plagiarism. Global plagiarism is lifting a speech entirely from a single source. Patchwork plagiarism involves stitching a speech together by copying from a few sources. Incremental plagiarism occurs when a speaker fails to give credit for specific quotations and paraphrases that are borrowed from other people.

In addition to your ethical responsibilities as a speaker, you have ethical obligations as a listener. The first is to listen courteously and attentively. The second is to avoid prejudging the speaker. The third is to support the free and open expression of ideas. In all these ways, your speech class will offer a good testing ground for questions of ethical responsibility.

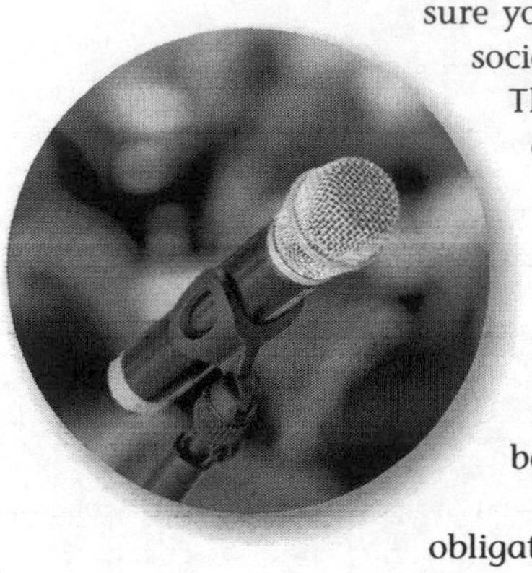

Key Terms

ethics (30)
ethical decisions (31)
name-calling (34)
Bill of Rights (34)
plagiarism (36)
global plagiarism (37)
patchwork plagiarism (37)
incremental plagiarism (38)
paraphrase (39)

Review Questions

After reading this chapter, you should be able to answer the following questions:

connect

For further review, go to the LearnSmart study module for this chapter.

1. What is ethics? Why is a strong sense of ethical responsibility vital for public speakers?
2. What are the five guidelines for ethical speechmaking discussed in this chapter?
3. What is the difference between global plagiarism and patchwork plagiarism? What are the best ways to avoid these two kinds of plagiarism?
4. What is incremental plagiarism? How can you steer clear of it when dealing with quotations and paraphrases?
5. What are the three guidelines for ethical listening discussed in this chapter?

Exercises for Critical Thinking

1. Look back at the story of Felicia Robinson on pages 30–31. Evaluate her dilemma in light of the guidelines for ethical speechmaking presented in this chapter. Explain what you believe would be the most ethical course of action in her case.
2. The issue of insulting and abusive speech—especially slurs directed against people on the basis of race, religion, gender, or sexual orientation—is extremely controversial. Do you believe society should punish such speech with criminal penalties? To what degree are colleges and universities justified in trying to discipline students who engage in such speech? Do you feel it is proper to place any boundaries on free expression in order to prohibit insulting and abusive speech? Why or why not? Be prepared to explain your ideas in class.
3. All of the following situations could arise in your speech class. Identify the ethical issues in each and explain what, as a responsible speaker or listener, your course of action would be.
   a. You are speaking on the topic of prison reform. In your research, you run across two public opinion polls. One of them, an independent survey by the Gallup Organization, shows that a majority of people in your state oppose your position. The other poll, suspect in its methods and conducted by a partisan organization, says a majority of people in your state support your position. Which poll do you cite in your speech? If you cite the second poll, do you point out its shortcomings?
   b. When listening to an informative speech by one of your classmates, you realize that much of it is plagiarized from a Web site you visited a couple of weeks earlier. What do you do? Do you say something when your instructor asks for comments about the speech? Do you mention your concern to the instructor after class? Do you talk with the speaker? Do you remain silent?
   c. While researching your persuasive speech, you find a quotation from an article by a highly respected expert that will nail down one of your most important points. But as you read the rest of the article, you realize that the author does not in fact support the policy you are advocating. Do you still include the quotation in your speech?

3

Listening

Rose Finnegan burst through the front door of her condo ready to share the good news: She had just been promoted to operations manager at the FedEx distribution center where she works. Bubbling with excitement, she found her husband on the couch staring into his laptop. "Guess what?" she asked.

"What?" he replied, his eyes never leaving the computer screen.

"I got the promotion at work!"

"That's great," he murmured.

"Let's go out to dinner to celebrate," she said, heading into the bedroom to change clothes.

Fifteen minutes later, Rose emerged from the bedroom and saw her husband in the same position on the couch, his eyes still glued to the screen. Finally looking up, he noticed his wife's clothes. "You look nice!" he exclaimed. "Where are you going?"

This story illustrates what one research study after another has revealed—most people are shockingly poor listeners. We fake paying attention. We can look right at someone, appear interested in what that person says, even nod our head or smile at the appropriate moments—all without really listening.

hearing

The vibration of sound waves on the eardrums and the firing of electrochemical impulses in the brain.

Not listening doesn't mean we don't hear. *Hearing* is a physiological process, involving the vibration of sound waves on our eardrums and the firing of electrochemical impulses from the inner ear to the central auditory system of the brain. But *listening* involves paying close attention to, and making sense of, what we hear. Even when we think we are listening carefully, we usually grasp only 50 percent of what we hear. After 24 hours we can remember only 10 percent of the original message.[1] It's little wonder that listening has been called a lost art.[2]

Listening Is Important

listening

Paying close attention to, and making sense of, what we hear.

Although most people listen poorly, there are exceptions. Top-flight business executives, successful politicians, brilliant teachers—nearly all are excellent listeners.[3] So much of what they do depends on absorbing information that is given verbally—and absorbing it quickly and accurately. If you had an interview with the president of a major corporation, you might be shocked (and flattered) to see how closely that person listened to your words.

In our communication-oriented age, listening is more important than ever. According to one study, more than 60 percent of errors made in business come from poor listening.[4] Replacing poor listening with good listening improves efficiency, sales, customer satisfaction, and employee morale. This is why, in most companies, effective listeners hold higher positions and are promoted more often than ineffective listeners. When business managers are asked to rank-order the communication skills most crucial to their jobs, they usually rank listening number one.[5]

Even if you don't plan to be a corporate executive, the art of listening can be helpful in almost every part of your life. This is not surprising when you realize that people spend more time listening than in any other communicative activity—more than reading, more than writing, more even than speaking.

Think for a moment about your own life as a college student. Most class time in U.S. colleges and universities is spent listening to discussions and lectures. A number of studies have shown a strong correlation between listening and academic success. Students with the highest grades are usually those with the strongest listening skills. The reverse is also true—students with the lowest grades are usually those with the weakest listening skills.[6]

There is plenty of reason, then, to take listening seriously. Employers and employees, parents and children, wives and husbands, doctors and patients, students and teachers—all depend on the apparently simple skill of listening. Regardless of your profession or walk of life, you never escape the need for a well-trained ear.

Listening is also important to you as a speaker. It is probably the way you get most of your ideas and information—from television, radio, conversation, and lectures. If you do not listen well, you will not understand what you hear and may pass along your misunderstanding to others.

Besides, in class—as in life—you will listen to many more speeches than you give. It is only fair to pay close attention to your classmates' speeches; after all, you want them to listen carefully to *your* speeches. An excellent way to improve your own speeches is to listen attentively to the speeches of other people. Over and over, instructors find that the best speakers are usually the best listeners.

A side benefit of your speech class is that it offers an ideal opportunity to work on the art of listening. During the 95 percent of the time when you are not speaking, you have nothing else to do but listen and learn. You can sit there like a stone—or you can use the time profitably to master a skill that will serve you in a thousand ways.

Listening and Critical Thinking

One of the ways listening can serve you is by enhancing your skills as a critical thinker. We can identify four kinds of listening:[7]

- *Appreciative listening*—listening for pleasure or enjoyment, as when we listen to music, to a comedy routine, or to an entertaining speech.
- *Empathic listening*—listening to provide emotional support for the speaker, as when a psychiatrist listens to a patient or when we lend a sympathetic ear to a friend in distress.
- *Comprehensive listening*—listening to understand the message of a speaker, as when we attend a classroom lecture or listen to directions for finding a friend's house.
- *Critical listening*—listening to evaluate a message for purposes of accepting or rejecting it, as when we listen to the sales pitch of a car salesperson or the campaign speech of a political candidate.

appreciative listening

Listening for pleasure or enjoyment.

empathic listening

Listening to provide emotional support for a speaker.

comprehensive listening

Listening to understand the message of a speaker.

critical listening

Listening to evaluate a message for purposes of accepting or rejecting it.

Although all four kinds of listening are important, this chapter deals primarily with comprehensive listening and critical listening. They are the kinds of listening you will use most often when listening to speeches in class, when taking lecture notes in other courses, when communicating at work, and when responding to the barrage of commercials, political messages, and other persuasive appeals you face every day. They are also the kinds of listening that are most closely tied to critical thinking.

As we saw in Chapter 1, critical thinking involves a number of skills. Some of those skills—summarizing information, recalling facts, distinguishing main points from minor points—are central to comprehensive listening. Other skills of critical thinking—separating fact from opinion, spotting weaknesses in reasoning, judging the soundness of evidence—are especially important in critical listening.

When you engage in comprehensive listening or critical listening, you must use your mind as well as your ears. When your mind is not actively involved, you may be hearing, but you are not *listening.* In fact, listening and critical thinking are so closely allied that training in listening is also training in how to think.

At the end of this chapter, we'll discuss steps you can take to improve your skills in comprehensive and critical listening. If you follow these steps, you may also become a better critical thinker.

Four Causes of Poor Listening

NOT CONCENTRATING

The brain is incredibly efficient. Although we talk at a rate of 120 to 150 words a minute, the brain can process 400 to 800 words a minute.[8] This would seem to make listening very easy, but actually it has the opposite effect. Because we can process a speaker's words and still have plenty of spare "brain time," we are tempted to interrupt our listening by thinking about other things. Here's what happens:

spare "brain time"

The difference between the rate at which most people talk (120 to 150 words a minute) and the rate at which the brain can process language (400 to 800 words a minute).

> A senior majoring in kinesiology, Jessica Chen is excited to be wrapping up her course work. She is particularly eager to finish her class on exercise and mental health, which meets at 3 P.M. on Fridays. Her professor is great—this is her second class with him—but keeping focused on Friday afternoon can be a challenge.
>
> On this particular Friday in April, Jessica's professor is lecturing on the relationship between body temperature and anxiety. "This calming effect," he explains, "often stems from a person's increased temperature. . . ."
>
> "Temperature," thinks Jessica, her eyes drifting out the window next to her. "I bet it's almost 75 degrees. Beach weather. I can't wait for Newport in July. . . ."
>
> Sternly, Jessica pulls her attention back to the lecture. Her professor is now reviewing research on regular exercise and the immune system, which Jessica heard about last semester. As a result, her attention wanders once more.
>
> "I haven't been to the gym in five days," she thinks. "But the student gym is always so busy. Maybe I should get a membership at the health club. I wonder how much that would cost."
>
> ". . . a topic that Jessica encountered during her internship last summer," the professor is saying. Uh oh! What topic does the professor mean? Everyone looks at Jessica, as she frantically tries to recall the connection between exercise, the immune system, and her internship.

It's not that Jessica *meant* to lose track of the discussion. But there comes a point at which it's so easy to let your thoughts wander rather than to concentrate on what is being said. After all, concentrating is hard work. Louis Nizer, the famous trial lawyer, once said: "So complete is this concentration that at the end of a court day in which I have only listened, I find myself wringing wet despite a calm and casual manner."[9]

Later in this chapter, we'll look at some things you can do to concentrate better on what you hear.

LISTENING TOO HARD

Until now we have been talking about not paying close attention to what we hear. But sometimes we listen *too* hard. We turn into human sponges, soaking up a speaker's every word as if every word were equally important. We try to remember all the names, all the dates, all the places. In the process we often miss the speaker's main point. What is worse, we may end up confusing the facts as well.

People spend more time listening than in any other communicative activity. One benefit of your speech class is that it can improve your listening skills in a variety of situations.

Shortly after graduating from college, Carlos Molina landed an excellent job as an app developer. Knowing he had never been good at budgeting his money, he signed up for a financial planning workshop.

The first session was about retirement planning. Simone Fisher, who was conducting the workshop, explained that 7 in 10 Americans between the ages of 22 and 35 do not have a monthly budget or a savings plan. Carlos wrote down every number Simone mentioned.

"To have a retirement income equal to 75 percent of your current salary," Simone continued, "you will need to invest at least 6 percent of your present earnings. You also need to account for inflation over time. This afternoon, we will meet with each of you personally to calculate your individual savings needs. In the meantime, I want to stress that the most important thing is to start saving now."

Carlos zealously typed each statistic into his laptop. When Simone opened the floor for questions, Carlos raised his hand and said, "I have two questions. When should I start saving for retirement? And how do I figure out how to account for future inflation?"

This is a typical example of losing the speaker's point by concentrating on details. Carlos had fixed his mind on remembering all the statistics in Simone's presentation, but he blocked out the main message—that it is best to start saving now and that he would get help developing an individual plan.

Rather than trying to remember everything a speaker says, efficient listeners usually concentrate on main points and evidence. We'll discuss these things more thoroughly later in the chapter.

JUMPING TO CONCLUSIONS

Alyssa Shields, a recent college graduate, took a job as an editorial assistant in the research department of a regional magazine. Shortly after Alyssa arrived, the editor in charge of the research department left the magazine for another job. For the next two months, Alyssa struggled to handle the work of the research department by herself. She often felt in over her head, but she knew this was a good opportunity to learn, and she hated to give up her new responsibilities.

One day Michael Perkins, the editor in chief of the magazine, comes into Alyssa's office to talk. The following conversation takes place:

Michael: You've done a great job these last two months, Alyssa. But you know we really need a new editor. So we've decided to make some changes.

Alyssa: I'm not surprised; I know this is an important department.

Michael: Yes, it is. And it's not an easy job. We really need an editor and an assistant to handle all the work. That's why I wanted to tell you . . .

Alyssa: I understand. I knew all along that I was just filling in.

Michael: Alyssa, you're not listening.

Alyssa: Yes, I am. You're trying to be nice, but you're here to tell me that you've hired a new editor and I'll be going back to my old job.

Michael: No, that's not it at all. I think you've done a fine job under difficult circumstances. You've proved yourself, and I intend to make *you* the editor. But I think you'll need an assistant to help you.

Why is there so much confusion here? Clearly, Alyssa is unsure about her future at the magazine. So when Michael starts to talk about making some changes, Alyssa jumps to a conclusion and assumes the worst. The misunderstanding could have been avoided if, when Michael had said, "We've decided to make some changes," Alyssa had asked, "What changes?"—and then *listened.*

This is one form of jumping to conclusions—putting words into a speaker's mouth. It is one reason why we sometimes communicate so poorly with people we are closest to. Because we're so sure we know what they mean, we don't listen to what they actually say.

Another way of jumping to conclusions is prematurely rejecting a speaker's ideas as boring or misguided. That would be a mistake. Let's say the announced topic is "Architecture and History." It sounds dull. So you tune out—and miss a fascinating discussion filled with human-interest stories about buildings and other structures from the ancient pyramids to the latest skyscrapers.

Nearly every speech has something to offer you—whether it be information, point of view, or technique. You are cheating yourself if you prejudge and choose not to listen.

FOCUSING ON DELIVERY AND PERSONAL APPEARANCE

Avid readers of World War II history, Trevor and Megan were thrilled when they saw a poster advertising a lecture by the author of a new book on D-Day. The book had received good reviews, and Trevor and Megan made plans to attend the lecture.

Arriving at the lecture, they took their seats and listened while the speaker discussed his research and major findings. "That was great," Megan exclaimed when they got back to the car. But Trevor was scowling. "What's wrong?" Megan asked.

"I know you're going to think this is stupid," Trevor began. "The guy was a decent speaker, and he seemed to know his stuff. But did you see the sport coat he was wearing? It's so retro—and his tie was atrocious. No matter how I tried, I kept thinking that he hadn't gone shopping since the 1980s."

This story illustrates a common problem. Sometimes we judge people by the way they look or speak and don't listen to what they say. It's easy to become distracted by a speaker's accent, personal appearance, or vocal mannerisms and lose sight of the message. Focusing on a speaker's delivery or personal appearance is one of the major sources of interference in the speech communication process, and it is something we always need to guard against.

How to Become a Better Listener

TAKE LISTENING SERIOUSLY

The first step toward becoming a better listener is to accord listening the seriousness it deserves. Good listeners are not born that way. They have *worked* at learning how to listen effectively. Good listening does not go hand in hand with intelligence, education, or social standing. Like any other skill, it comes from practice and self-discipline. Check your current skills as a listener by completing the Listening Self-Evaluation Worksheet on page 54.[10] Once you have identified your shortcomings as a listener, make a serious effort to overcome them.

BE AN ACTIVE LISTENER

So many aspects of modern life encourage us to listen passively. We listen to Spotify while studying. Parents listen to their children while fixing dinner. Television reporters listen to a politician's speech while walking around the auditorium looking for their next interview.

This type of passive listening is a habit—but so is active listening. Active listeners give their undivided attention to the speaker in a genuine effort to understand his or her point of view. In conversation, they do not interrupt the speaker or finish his or her sentences. When listening to a speech, they do not allow themselves to be distracted by internal or external interference, and they do not prejudge the speaker. They take listening seriously and do the best they can to stay focused on the speaker and his or her message.[11]

active listening

Giving undivided attention to a speaker in a genuine effort to understand the speaker's point of view.

There are a number of steps you can take to improve your skills of active listening. They include resisting distractions, not allowing yourself to be diverted by a speaker's appearance or delivery, suspending judgment until you have heard the speaker out, focusing your listening, and developing note-taking skills. We'll discuss each of these in turn.

LISTENING SELF-EVALUATION

How often do you indulge in the following bad listening habits? Check yourself carefully in each one.

HABIT	FREQUENCY					SCORE
	Almost Always	Usually	Sometimes	Seldom	Almost Never	
1. Giving in to mental distractions	_____	_____	_____	_____	_____	_____
2. Giving in to physical distractions	_____	_____	_____	_____	_____	_____
3. Trying to recall everything a speaker says	_____	_____	_____	_____	_____	_____
4. Rejecting a topic as uninteresting before hearing the speaker	_____	_____	_____	_____	_____	_____
5. Faking paying attention	_____	_____	_____	_____	_____	_____
6. Jumping to conclusions about a speaker's meaning	_____	_____	_____	_____	_____	_____
7. Deciding a speaker is wrong before hearing everything she or he has to say	_____	_____	_____	_____	_____	_____
8. Judging a speaker on personal appearance	_____	_____	_____	_____	_____	_____
9. Not paying attention to a speaker's evidence	_____	_____	_____	_____	_____	_____
10. Focusing on delivery rather than on what the speaker says	_____	_____	_____	_____	_____	_____
					TOTAL	_____

How to score:

For every "almost always" checked, give yourself a score of	2
For every "usually" checked, give yourself a score of	4
For every "sometimes" checked, give yourself a score of	6
For every "seldom" checked, give yourself a score of	8
For every "almost never" checked, give yourself a score of	10

Total score interpretation:	0 to 70	You need lots of training in listening.
	71 to 89	You listen well.
	90 to 100	You listen exceptionally well.

Effective listeners take their task seriously. If you approach listening as an active process, you will significantly sharpen your powers of concentration and comprehension.

RESIST DISTRACTIONS

In an ideal world, we could eliminate all physical and mental distractions. In the real world, however, we cannot. Because we think so much faster than a speaker can talk, it's easy to let our attention wander. Sometimes it's very easy—when the room is too hot, when construction machinery is operating right outside the window, when the speaker is tedious. But our attention can stray even in the best of circumstances—if for no other reason than a failure to stay alert and make ourselves concentrate.

Whenever you find this happening, make a conscious effort to pull your mind back to what the speaker is saying. Then force it to stay there. One way to do this is to think ahead of the speaker—try to anticipate what will come next. This is not the same as jumping to conclusions. When you jump to conclusions, you put words into the speaker's mouth and don't listen to what is said. In this case you *will* listen—and measure what the speaker says against what you had anticipated.

Another way to keep your mind on a speech is to review mentally what the speaker has already said and make sure you understand it. Yet another is to listen between the lines and assess what a speaker implies verbally or says nonverbally with body language. Suppose a speaker is introducing someone to an audience. The speaker says, "It gives me great pleasure to present to you my very dear friend, Ashley Hauser." But the speaker doesn't shake hands with Ashley. He doesn't even look at her—just turns his back and leaves the podium. Is Ashley really his "very dear friend"? Certainly not.

Attentive listeners can pick up all kinds of clues to a speaker's real message. At first you may find it difficult to listen so intently. If you work at it, however, your concentration is bound to improve.

DON'T BE DIVERTED BY APPEARANCE OR DELIVERY

If you had attended Abraham Lincoln's momentous Cooper Union speech of 1860, this is what you would have seen:

> The long, ungainly figure upon which hung clothes that, while new for this trip, were evidently the work of an unskilled tailor; the large feet and clumsy hands, of which, at the outset, at least, the orator seemed to be unduly conscious; the long, gaunt head, capped by a shock of hair that seemed not to have been thoroughly brushed out, made a picture which did not fit in with New York's conception of a finished statesman.[12]

But although he seemed awkward and uncultivated, Lincoln had a powerful message about the moral evils of slavery. Fortunately, the audience at Cooper Union did not let his appearance stand in the way of his words.

Similarly, you must be willing to set aside preconceived judgments based on a person's looks or manner of speech. Gandhi was an unimpressive-looking man who often spoke dressed in a simple white cotton cloth. Renowned physicist Stephen Hawking is severely disabled and can speak only with the aid of a voice synthesizer. Yet imagine how much poorer the world would be if no one listened to them. Even though it may tax your tolerance, patience, and concentration, don't let negative feelings about a speaker's appearance or delivery keep you from listening to the message.

On the other hand, try not to be misled if the speaker has an unusually attractive appearance. It's all too easy to assume that because someone is good-looking and has a polished delivery, he or she is speaking eloquently. Some of the most unscrupulous speakers in history have been handsome people with hypnotic delivery skills. Again, be sure you respond to the message, not to the package it comes in.

SUSPEND JUDGMENT

Unless we listen only to people who think exactly as we do, we are going to hear things with which we disagree. When this happens, our natural inclination is to argue mentally with the speaker or to dismiss everything she or he says. But neither response is fair, and in both cases we blot out any chance of learning or being persuaded.

Does this mean you must agree with everything you hear? Not at all. It means you should hear people out *before* reaching a final judgment. Try to understand their point of view. Listen to their ideas, examine their evidence, assess their reasoning. *Then* make up your mind. The aim of active listening is to set aside "one's own prejudices, frames of reference, and desires so as to experience as far as possible the speaker's world from the inside."[13] It has been said more than once that a closed mind is an empty mind.

FOCUS YOUR LISTENING

As we have seen, skilled listeners do not try to absorb a speaker's every word. Rather, they focus on specific things in a speech. Here are three suggestions to help you focus your listening.

Listen for Main Points

Most speeches contain from two to four main points. Here, for example, are the main points of a speech by Jack Hayes, director of the U.S. National Weather Service:[14]

1. The past 50 years have witnessed a number of pioneering innovations in meteorology.
2. Today, meteorologists can provide better weather warnings than at any time in history.
3. Future advances in meteorology will require visionary ideas and economic resources.

These three main points are the heart of Hayes's message. As with any speech, they are the most important things to listen for.

Unless a speaker is terribly scatterbrained, you should be able to detect his or her main points with little difficulty. Often a speaker will give some idea at the outset of the main points to be discussed in the speech. For example, at the end of his introduction, Hayes said he was going to reflect on "where we were, where we are, and . . . where we go from here." As the speech progressed, Hayes moved from point to point with signposts such as "Let's take a brief look at how far we've come" and "What's on the horizon for us?" After this, only the most inattentive of listeners could have missed his main points.

Listen for Evidence

Identifying a speaker's main points, however, is not enough. You must also listen for supporting evidence. By themselves, Hayes's main points are only assertions. You may be inclined to believe them just because they come from an important meteorologist. Yet a careful listener will be concerned about evidence no matter who is speaking. Had you been listening to Hayes's speech, you would have heard him support his claims with a mass of verifiable evidence. Here is an excerpt:

> Over the past 20 years, advances in science and technology have enabled us to increase public preparation for flash floods from 10 minutes to an hour and 10 minutes, a seven-fold improvement.
>
> We've improved accuracy in hurricane-track forecasting. In 1970, 48-hour track error was about 250 nautical miles. In 2009, it was less than 100 nautical miles. In fact, our current average error at 96 hours is better than our 48-hour forecast was in 1970, giving coastal residents and businesses two more days to prepare for the likes of a hurricane Katrina.

There are four basic questions to ask about a speaker's evidence:

Is it *accurate*?

Is it taken from *objective* sources?

Is it *relevant* to the speaker's claims?

Is it *sufficient* to support the speaker's point?

In Hayes's case, the answer to each question is yes. His figures about meteorological advances are well established in the public record and can be verified by independent sources. The figures are clearly relevant to Hayes's claim that improvements in meteorology are saving lives and money, and they are sufficient to support that claim. If Hayes's evidence were inaccurate, biased, irrelevant, or insufficient, you should be wary of accepting his claim.

We shall discuss these—and other—tests of evidence in detail in Chapters 8 and 17. For now, it's enough to know that you should be on guard against unfounded assertions and sweeping generalizations. Keep an eye out for the speaker's evidence and for its accuracy, objectivity, relevance, and sufficiency.

Listen for Technique

We said earlier that you should not let a speaker's delivery distract you from the message, and this is true. However, if you want to become an effective speaker, you should study the methods other people use to speak effectively.

Analyze the introduction: What methods does the speaker use to gain attention, to relate to the audience, to establish credibility and goodwill? Assess the organization of the speech: Is it clear and easy to follow? Can you pick out the speaker's main points? Can you follow when the speaker moves from one point to another?

Study the speaker's language: Is it accurate, clear, vivid, appropriate? Does the speaker adapt well to the audience and occasion? Finally, diagnose the speaker's delivery: Is it fluent, dynamic, convincing? Does it strengthen or weaken the impact of the speaker's ideas? How well does the speaker use eye contact, gestures, and visual aids?

As you listen, focus on the speaker's strengths and weaknesses. If the speaker is not effective, try to determine why. If he or she is effective, try to pick out techniques you can use in your own speeches. If you listen in this way, you will be surprised by how much you can learn about successful speaking.

DEVELOP NOTE-TAKING SKILLS

Speech students are often amazed at how easily their instructor can pick out a speaker's main points, evidence, and techniques. Of course, the instructor knows what to listen for and has had plenty of practice. But the next time you get an opportunity, watch your instructor during a speech. Chances are she or he will be listening with a laptop or pen and paper. When note taking is done properly, it is a surefire way to improve your concentration and keep track of a speaker's ideas.

The key words here are *when done properly.* Unfortunately, many people don't take notes effectively. Some try to take down everything a speaker says. They view the enterprise as a race that pits their note-taking speed against the speaker's rate of speech. As the speaker starts to talk, the note taker starts to write or type. But soon the speaker is winning the race. In a desperate effort to keep up, the note taker tries to go faster and faster. But even this is not enough. The speaker pulls so far ahead that the note taker can never catch up.[15]

Some people go to the opposite extreme. They arrive armed with pen, laptop, and the best of intentions. They know they can't write down

Research confirms that listening carefully and taking effective notes are vital skills for success in college. They will also benefit you in countless situations throughout life.

everything, so they wait for the speaker to say something that grabs their attention. Every once in a while the speaker rewards them with a joke, a dramatic story, or a startling fact. Then the note taker records a few words and leans back to await the next fascinating tidbit. By the end of the lecture, the note taker has a set of tidbits—and little or no record of the speaker's important ideas.

As these examples illustrate, most inefficient note takers suffer from one or both of two problems: They don't know *what* to listen for, and they don't know *how* to record what they do listen for.[16] The solution to the first problem is to focus on a speaker's main points and evidence. But once you know what to listen for, you still need a sound method of note taking.

Although there are a number of systems, most students find the *key-word outline* best for listening to classroom lectures and formal speeches. As its name suggests, this method briefly notes a speaker's main points and supporting evidence in rough outline form. Suppose a speaker says:

key-word outline

An outline that briefly notes a speaker's main points and supporting evidence in rough outline form.

> The global shark population is in drastic decline. According to the journal *Marine Policy*, 100 million sharks die from human activity every year—the equivalent of 11,000 sharks per hour. Today, almost 30 percent of all shark species are at risk of going extinct. A recent report on National Public Radio states that sharks "are among the most endangered animals in the world."
>
> There are three main causes for the decline in shark populations. The first cause is illegal fishing; humans are killing sharks in unprecedented numbers. A second cause is the slow growth and reproduction rate of sharks; we're wiping out sharks much faster than they can reproduce. The third cause is pollution and habitat destruction, which are disrupting the entire marine ecosystem.

A key-word note taker would record something like this:

Shark population in decline
  100 million die each year
  30 percent at risk of extinction
  Among most endangered in world

Three major causes
  Illegal fishing
  Slow reproduction rate
  Pollution & habitat destruction

Notice how brief the notes are. Yet they accurately summarize the speaker's ideas. They are also very clear. By separating main points from subpoints and evidence, the outline format shows the relationships among the speaker's ideas.

Perfecting this—or any other—system of note taking requires practice. But with a little effort you should see results soon. As you become a better note taker, you will become a better listener. There is also a good chance you will become a better student. Research confirms that students who take effective notes usually receive higher grades than those who do not.[17]

Summary

Most people are poor listeners. Even when we think we are listening carefully, we usually grasp only half of what we hear, and we retain even less. Improving your listening skills can be helpful in every part of your life, including speechmaking.

The most important cause of poor listening is giving in to distractions and letting our thoughts wander. Sometimes, however, we listen too hard. We try to remember every word a speaker says, and we lose the main message by concentrating on details. In other situations, we may jump to conclusions and prejudge a speaker without hearing out the message. Finally, we often judge people by their appearance or speaking manner instead of listening to what they say.

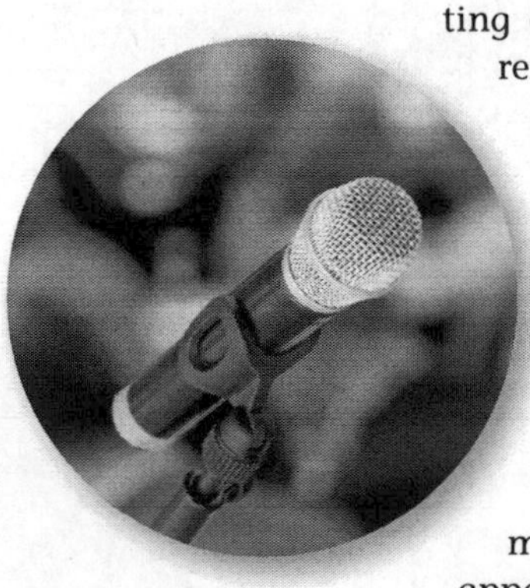

You can overcome these poor listening habits by taking several steps. First, take listening seriously and commit yourself to becoming a better listener. Second, work at being an active listener. Give your undivided attention to the speaker in a genuine effort to understand her or his ideas. Third, resist distractions. Make a conscious effort to keep your mind on what the speaker is saying. Fourth, try not to be diverted by appearance or delivery. Set aside preconceived judgments based on a person's looks or manner of speech. Fifth, suspend judgment until you have heard the speaker's entire message. Sixth, focus your listening by paying attention to main points, to evidence, and to the speaker's techniques. Finally, develop your note-taking skills. When done properly, note taking is an excellent way to improve your concentration and to keep track of a speaker's ideas.

Key Terms

hearing (48)
listening (48)
appreciative listening (49)
empathic listening (49)
comprehensive listening (49)
critical listening (49)
spare "brain time" (50)
active listening (53)
key-word outline (59)

Review Questions

After reading this chapter, you should be able to answer the following questions:

1. What is the difference between hearing and listening?
2. How is listening connected with critical thinking?
3. Why is it important to develop strong listening skills?
4. What are the four main causes of poor listening?
5. What are seven ways to become a better listener?

connect

For further review, go to the LearnSmart study module for this chapter.

Exercises for Critical Thinking

1. Which of the four causes of poor listening discussed in this chapter do you consider the most important? Choose a specific case of poor listening in which you were involved. Explain what went wrong.
2. Using the Listening Self-Evaluation Worksheet on page 54, undertake a candid evaluation of your major strengths and weaknesses as a listener. Explain what steps you need to take to become a better listener.
3. Watch the lead story this week on *60 Minutes, Dateline, 20/20,* or *The Daily Show.* Using the key-word outline method of note taking, record the main ideas of the story.
4. Choose a lecture in one of your other classes. Analyze what the lecturer does most effectively. Identify three things the lecturer could do better to help students keep track of the lecture.

4

Giving Your First Speech

You may be surprised to learn that one of the first assignments in your class is to give a speech. You say to yourself, "What am I going to do? I have barely started this course, yet I'm supposed to stand up in front of everyone and give a speech! I've only read a few pages in the textbook, and I don't know much about public speaking. Where do I begin?"

If these are your thoughts, you aren't alone. Most beginning speech students have a similar reaction. Fortunately, giving your first speech sounds a lot harder than it is. The purpose of this chapter is to help you get started on preparing and delivering your speech. Later chapters will expand on the subjects discussed here and will apply them to different kinds of speeches.

Preparing Your Speech

ice breaker speech

A speech early in the term designed to get students speaking in front of the class as soon as possible.

Usually a brief, simple presentation, the first assignment is often called an ice breaker speech because it is designed to "break the ice" by getting students up in front of the class as soon as possible. This is an important step because much of the anxiety associated with public speaking comes from lack of experience giving speeches. Once you have broken the ice by giving a speech, you will feel less anxious and will have taken the first step on the road to confidence.

DEVELOPING THE SPEECH

There are a number of possible assignments for the first speech. One is a speech of self-introduction that provides insight into the speaker's background, personality, beliefs, or goals. In other cases, students are asked to introduce a classmate, rather than themselves. Some instructors require yet a different kind of speech. Make sure you understand exactly what your instructor requires.

Focusing Your Topic

No matter what kind of introductory speech you are assigned, be sure to focus your presentation sharply so it conforms to the assigned time limit. One of the most common mistakes students make on their first speech is trying to cover too much.

It would be impossible, for example, to tell your audience everything about your life in a two- or three-minute speech. A better approach would be to focus on one or two events that have helped define who you are—competing in the state track meet, tutoring disadvantaged children, getting your first job, and the like. This allows you to make a few well-developed points about a clearly defined subject.

On the other hand, avoid the temptation to narrow the focus of your topic too much. Few listeners would be pleased to hear a two- or three-minute discussion of advanced trumpet-playing techniques. Such a speech would be too specialized for most classroom audiences.

Developing Your Topic

Once you have a topic for your speech, be creative in developing it. Think of ways to structure the speech so it will be interesting and meaningful to your audience. Look, for example, at the sample speeches with commentary at the end of this chapter. The first speaker explains aspects of her personality by referring to her experience as a tap dancer. The second speaker uses the notion of a Third-Culture Kid when introducing one of his classmates. In both cases, the speakers found a creative way to frame their information.

Another possibility is to think of ways you can make your presentation mysterious or suspenseful. Suppose you are telling the audience about meeting a celebrity, visiting a famous place, or participating in a newsworthy event. Rather than identifying the celebrity at the outset, you might save his or her name for the end of your speech. As your story unfolds, tantalize your classmates with clues about your celebrity's gender, physical characteristics, special talents, and the like, but keep the name secret until the last moment.

When developing your first speech, plan what you want to say, organize the material clearly, practice thoroughly, and use the extemporaneous method of delivery. You may be surprised at how much you enjoy the experience.

Audiences are also interested in dangerous situations, adventure, and drama. If your task is to introduce a fellow student, find out if she or he has ever been in danger. Suppose your classmate was caught in a flood or spent a year in Africa with the Peace Corps. The details would make excellent material for a speech.

If you think about it, every person has faced risk, done the unusual, or triumphed over hardship. Try to find ways to include such fascinating experiences in your speech.

You can also make your speech interesting by using colorful, descriptive language. One speaker used this technique when introducing a fellow student, named Alexa, to the class. The speaker began by saying:

> The spotlight shines. The music blares. The crowd cheers. The colors, bright and vibrant, bleed together as Alexa and her partner sail around the dance floor. Her partner touches her hand and her waist, but only briefly. He then spins her away, and she glides across the floor in what seems like a single motion. Alexa has worked many weeks for this moment. Alexa, you see, is a championship ballroom dancer.

connect

View the introduction from "Gotta Dance" in the online Media Library for this chapter (Video 4.1).

The speaker could have said, "Alexa is a terrific ballroom dancer and finds it quite thrilling." Instead, the speaker painted a word picture so listeners could visualize the dance floor, the brilliant colors of the costumes, and the excitement of the competition as Alexa and her partner perform in perfect symmetry. Colorful and concrete illustrations like this are always more interesting than dull language and abstract generalizations.

You might wonder whether you should use humor to make your first speech entertaining. Audiences love witty remarks, jokes, and funny situations, but like anything else, humor is effective only when done well. It should flow naturally out of the speech content rather than being contrived. If you are not normally a funny person, you are better off giving a sincere, enthusiastic speech and leaving out the jokes. In no case should you include humor that involves obscenity, embarrasses individuals, or negatively stereotypes groups of people. The best kind of humor gently pokes fun at ourselves or at universal human foibles.

ORGANIZING THE SPEECH

Regardless of your topic, a speech usually has three main parts—an introduction, a body, and a conclusion. In Chapter 10, we will discuss each of these parts in detail. Here we focus on what you need to know about them as you prepare your introductory speech.

Introduction

introduction

The opening section of a speech.

Your first job in the introduction is to get the attention and interest of the audience. You can do this by posing a question, telling a story, making a startling statement, or opening with a quotation. The purpose of all these methods is to create a dramatic, colorful opening that will make your audience want to hear more.

For an example, look at the speech excerpt on Video 4.2 in the online Media Library for this chapter. The speaker's assignment was to present a narrative about a significant experience in his life. This is how he began:

connect

View the beginning of "The Secret" in the online Media Library for this chapter (Video 4.2).

> I never knew the secret until I took a year off from school, traveled halfway around the world, and lived for a year in Thailand. I was there to teach English, but the trip ended up being much more than a job. It was a voyage of discovery. I didn't know exactly what I would find, but I came home with a truly valuable secret.

After this introduction, the audience was eager to hear more about the speaker's secret.

In addition to gaining attention and interest, the introduction should orient your listeners toward the subject matter of your speech. In the longer speeches you will give later in the term, you will usually need to provide an explicit preview statement that identifies the main points to be discussed in the body of your speech. (For example, "Today I will inform you about the symptoms, causes, and treatment of sleep apnea.")

Because your introductory speech is so short, you may not need a detailed preview statement. But you still need to give your audience a clear sense of your topic and purpose. (Be sure to check with your instructor to see what kind of preview statement he or she prefers for the introductory speech.)

Body

body

The main section of a speech.

After getting the audience's attention and revealing your topic, you are ready to move into the body of your speech. In some speeches, the body seems to organize itself. If you are telling a story about a significant experience in your life, you will relate the events chronologically, in the order they occurred.

chronological order

A method of speech organization in which the main points follow a time pattern.

But not all speeches follow such a format. Suppose you have been asked to give a presentation introducing a classmate. You could organize the most important biographical facts about your subject in chronological order, but this might result in a dull, superficial speech: "Maria was born in Los Angeles in 1996, attended elementary school from 2002 to 2008, and graduated from high school in 2014."

A better way of structuring your remarks might be to discuss three of the most important aspects of Maria's life, such as hobbies, career goals, and family. This is called the topical method of organization, which subdivides the speech topic into its natural, logical, or conventional parts. Although there are many other ways to organize a speech, your first presentation will probably use either chronological or topical order.

topical order

A method of speech organization in which the main points divide the topic into logical and consistent subtopics.

Regardless of the method of organization you use, remember to limit the number of main points in the body of your speech. In a two-minute presentation, you won't have time to develop more than two or three main points.

Once you have selected those points, make sure each one focuses on a single aspect of the topic. For example, if your first point concerns your classmate's hometown, don't introduce irrelevant information about her job or favorite music. Save this material for a separate point, or cut it.

main points

The major points developed in the body of a speech.

Try to make your main points stand out by introducing each with a transition statement. In a speech about a classmate, you might begin the first main point by saying:

> Ashley has been interested in drawing as long as she can remember.

transition

A word or phrase that indicates when a speaker has finished one thought and is moving on to another.

When you reach the second point, you might introduce it like this:

> Ashley's passion for drawing helps explain her desire to major in architecture.

You have now let your audience know that the first main point is over and that you are starting the second one. The third main point might begin as follows:

> As much as Ashley hopes to have a career as an architect, she also wants to keep time for friends and family.

Transitions such as these will help your audience keep track of your main points.

Conclusion

When you finish discussing your final point, you will be ready to move into your conclusion. You need to accomplish two tasks in this part of the speech: let the audience know you are about to finish and reinforce your central idea.

conclusion

The final section of a speech.

If possible, end on a dramatic, clever, or thought-provoking note. For example, when talking about his "secret" in the speech mentioned earlier, the student devoted the body of his presentation to explaining his experiences in Thailand and how they opened his eyes to the universality of human experience. Then, in his conclusion, he wrapped up by saying:

> I needed to be in an entirely different culture to learn the secret—that despite differences in ancestry, language, history, and religion, human beings are pretty much the same wherever they might be. I thought I was going to meet people who were totally alien to me. Instead, I found that family, friendship, kindness, and community are as important on one side of the world as on the other.

connect

View the ending of "The Secret" in the online Media Library for this chapter (Video 4.3).

The final lines end the speech on a strong note and underscore why the speaker's time in Thailand was so important.

Your first speech provides a foundation for speeches you will give later. As you develop your skills of extemporaneous speaking, you will find yourself able to speak confidently and with strong eye contact in class and out.

Delivering Your Speech

Once you have selected a subject and organized the content into a clear structure, it is time to work on the delivery of your speech. Because this is your first speech of the term, no one expects you to give a perfectly polished presentation. Your aim is to do as well as possible while laying a foundation you can build upon in later speeches. With this is mind, we'll look briefly at the extemporaneous method of speech delivery, the importance of rehearsing your speech, and some of the major factors to consider when speech day arrives.

SPEAKING EXTEMPORANEOUSLY

extemporaneous speech

A carefully prepared and rehearsed speech that is presented from a brief set of notes.

You might be inclined, as are many beginning speakers, to write out your speech like an essay and read it word for word to your listeners. The other extreme is to prepare very little for the speech—to wing it by trusting to your wits and the inspiration of the moment. Neither approach is appropriate.

Most experts recommend speaking extemporaneously, which combines the careful preparation and structure of a manuscript presentation with the spontaneity and enthusiasm of an unrehearsed talk. Your aim in an extemporaneous speech is to plan your major points and supporting material without trying to memorize the precise language you will use on the day of the speech.

The extemporaneous method requires you to know the content of your speech quite well. In fact, when you use this method properly, you become so familiar with the substance of your talk that you need only a few brief notes to remind you of the points you intend to cover. The notes should consist of key words or phrases, rather than complete sentences and paragraphs. This way, when you are in front of the audience, you will tell them what you know about the topic in your own words.

Prepare your notes by writing or printing key terms and phrases on index cards or sheets of paper. Some instructors require students to use index cards because they are small and unobtrusive, don't rustle or flop over, and can be held in one hand, which allows the speaker to gesture more easily. Other teachers recommend sheets of paper because you can get more information on them and because it is easier to print out computer files on paper. If you are unsure what your instructor prefers, ask well before your speech is due.

Whether you use index cards or sheets of paper, your notes should be large enough to read clearly at arm's length. Many experienced speakers double- or triple-space their notes because this makes them easier to see at a glance. Write or print on only one side of the index card or paper, and use the fewest notes you can manage and still present the speech fluently and confidently.

connect

View an excerpt from "Life Is a Journey" in the online Media Library for this chapter (Video 4.4).

You can see an example of extemporaneous delivery on Video 4.4 in the online Media Library for this chapter. The speaker is giving a talk of self-introduction. As a returning student, he explains the twists and turns his life has taken during the eight years since he originally enrolled in college. He talks about working in retail, about his wife and daughter, and about what he hopes to do after graduation. As you view this excerpt, notice that even though the speaker's points are well planned, he is not tied to his notes. He speaks personably to his classmates and makes strong eye contact with them.

At first, it may seem very demanding to deliver a speech extemporaneously. In fact, though, you use the extemporaneous method in everyday conversation. Do you read from a manuscript when you tell your friends an amusing story? Of course not. You recall the essential details of your story and tell the tale to different friends, on different occasions, using somewhat different language each time. You feel relaxed and confident with your friends, so you just tell them what is on your mind in a conversational tone. Try to do the same thing in your speech.

REHEARSING THE SPEECH

When you watch a truly effective extemporaneous speaker, the speech comes out so smoothly that it seems almost effortless. In fact, that smooth delivery is the result of a great deal of practice. As your speech course progresses, you will gain more experience and will become more comfortable delivering your speeches extemporaneously.

The first time you rehearse your introductory speech, however, you will probably struggle. Words may not come easily, and you may forget some things you planned to say. Don't become discouraged. Keep going and complete the speech as well as you can. Concentrate on gaining control of the ideas rather than on trying to learn the speech word for word. You will improve every time you practice.

For this approach to work, you must rehearse the speech out loud. Looking silently over your notes is not enough. Speaking the words aloud will help you master the content of your talk. Once you have a fairly good grasp of the speech, ask friends or family members to listen and to give constructive feedback. Don't be shy about asking. Most people love to give their opinion about something, and it's crucial that you rehearse with a live audience before presenting the speech in class.

As you practice, time your speech to make sure it is neither too long nor too short. Because of nerves, most people talk faster during their first speech than when they practice it. When you rehearse at home, make certain your speech runs slightly longer than the minimum time limit. That way, if your speaking rate increases when you get in front of your classmates, your speech won't end up being too short.

PRESENTING THE SPEECH

Delivering your first speech can be a nerve-wracking experience. As your class proceeds and you gain more experience, your confidence (and skill) will grow by leaps and bounds. We will take a detailed look at speech delivery in Chapter 13, but here are a few things to concentrate on in your first presentation.

Starting Your Speech

When it is your turn to speak, move to the front of the room and face the audience. Assume a relaxed but upright posture. Plant your feet a bit less than shoulder-width apart and allow your arms to hang loosely by your side. Arrange your notes before you start to speak. Then take a moment to look over your audience and to smile. This will help you establish rapport with your classmates from the start.

Gestures

gestures

Motions of a speaker's hands or arms during a speech.

Once you are into the speech, feel free to use your hands to gesture, but don't try to plan all your gestures ahead of time. If you don't normally use your hands expressively during informal conversation, you shouldn't feel compelled to gesture a lot during your speech. Whatever gestures you do use should flow naturally from your feelings.

Above all, don't let your gestures or bodily actions distract listeners from your message. Do your best to avoid nervous mannerisms such as twisting your hair, wringing your hands, shifting your weight from one foot to the other, rocking back and forth, or tapping your fingers on the lectern. No matter how nervous you feel, try to appear calm and relaxed.

Eye Contact

eye contact

Direct visual contact with the eyes of another person.

During your talk, look at your classmates as often as you can. One of the major reasons for speaking extemporaneously is to maintain eye contact with your audience. In your own experience, you know how much more impressive a speaker is when she or he looks at the audience while speaking.

If you have practiced the extemporaneous method of delivery and prepared your notes properly, you should be able to maintain eye contact with your audience most of the time. Be sure to look to the left and right of the room, as well as to the center, and avoid the temptation to speak exclusively to one or two sympathetic individuals.

If you are too nervous to look your classmates directly in the eye, try looking just to the side of each person, or just above his or her head. In this way, you will convey a sense of eye contact while easing your nerves.

Voice

Try to use your voice as expressively as you would in normal conversation. Concentrate on projecting to the back of the room and, despite your nerves, fight the temptation to race through your speech. If you make a conscious effort to speak up, slow down, and project clearly, you will be on the right track to an effective presentation.

Look, for example, at Video 4.5 in the online Media Library for this chapter, which presents excerpts from two ice breaker speeches. Neither speaker had taken a public speaking class before, yet both rose to the occasion by focusing on the basic elements of delivery we have just discussed. As you watch the video, notice how both convey a sense of poise and confidence, establish strong eye contact with their classmates, and use the extemporaneous method of delivery. Work on doing the same in your first speech.

connect

View excerpts from "There's an App for That" and "Fork in the Road" in the online Media Library for this chapter (Video 4.5).

Dealing with Nerves

As we saw in Chapter 1, it's normal to be nervous before delivering a speech of any kind. By applying the tips presented in that chapter for managing stage fright, you can stand up for your speech primed for success.

If you have butterflies in your stomach while you wait to go to the lectern, sit quietly in your chair and take several slow, deep breaths. You can also help reduce your tension by tightening and relaxing your leg muscles, or by squeezing your hands together and then releasing them. Keep in mind that while you may be anxious about giving your speech, usually your nervousness will not be visible to your audience.

All the topics discussed in this chapter are developed in much more detail in the rest of this book. For now, keep your introductory assignment in perspective. Remember that neither your audience nor your instructor expects perfection. You are not a professional speaker, and this is the first speech of the class. Do your best on the assignment and have fun with it. Plan what you want to say, organize the material clearly, practice thoroughly, and use the extemporaneous method of delivery. You may be surprised by how much you enjoy giving your first speech.

Sample Speeches with Commentary

The following presentations were prepared by students in beginning speech classes at the University of Wisconsin. The first is a speech of self-introduction; the second is a speech introducing a classmate. As you read the speeches, notice how clearly they are organized and how creatively they are developed. You can watch the delivery of both speeches in the online Media Library for this chapter.

connect

View "Tap, Tap, Tap" and "Third-Culture Kid" in the online Media Library for this chapter (Videos 4.6 and 4.7).

Tap, Tap, Tap

COMMENTARY	SPEECH
As you can see from the online video, the speaker uses a combination of words and brief tap-dance moves to gain attention and interest. She then explains how long she has been tap dancing and previews the main points to be discussed in the body.	When I first started, it sounded like this. But I kept working until it sounded like this. Now it sounds like this. For the past fifteen years, I've been tap dancing. Some may think it's strange to spend ten or fifteen hours a week making shoes click across the floor. But to me, tap dancing represents hard work, patience, and courage—and it has helped shape my life in ways that go far beyond the dance floor.
The speaker's first main point deals with the hard work of learning to tap dance. Her image of hiding under a table at her first dance lesson is memorable and dramatizes how much she has progressed since then.	I started taking tap lessons when I was three years old. Actually, when I started, I just hid under a table, too scared to join the other kids. But my mom kept driving me to class because she knew it was a good outlet for my energy. Slowly, I learned to come out from under that table. It was hard work, but it was definitely worth it in the end.
In her second main point, the speaker performs the pull-back move to help explain how tap dancing has taught her patience. Here, as elsewhere, the performance of tap moves is used to provide insight about the speaker herself, rather than to demonstrate how to tap dance.	Tap dancing has also taught me patience. One of the toughest moves in tap dancing is called the pull back. It involves brushing your toes backwards to create a satisfying click-click-click sound—like this. For months I worked on the pull back, scuffing up the pale wood floors as I tried to move my feet in just the right way. At first I looked at those scuff marks with frustration, but eventually I was at peace with them. Today the pull back is as natural to me as walking down the street.
In her third main point, the speaker relates tap dancing to her speech assignment. She communicates engagingly and with strong eye contact.	Tap dancing has also given me courage, including the courage I needed to give this speech. Earlier this week, I felt the same ice in the pit of my stomach that I do in the days leading up to a dance recital. So I approached this speech just like I approach a dance recital: I worked hard, I practiced a lot, and I concentrated on being positive.
The conclusion summarizes the speaker's main points. It then ties the entire speech together by returning to the brief tap moves of the introduction.	Today, I know I'm not the best tap dancer—or speaker—in the world. But I'm grateful for the hard work, patience, and courage that I've learned over the past fifteen years. It's because of those qualities that I've been able to turn this into this. Thank you.

Third-Culture Kid

COMMENTARY	SPEECH
This paragraph is the speaker's introduction. It gains interest by defining Micah as a Third-Culture Kid and by contrasting his experiences with those of most audience members. The final sentence states the central idea—that Micah's frequent moves have shaped his outlook on life.	People often come up to our classmate Micah and ask where he's from. For many of you, that's probably easy to answer. But it's tough for Micah because he's a Third-Culture Kid. He grew up all over the world, in cultures that were foreign to him and his parents. Because Micah's dad was in the Air Force, he moved almost every year for fifteen years. He tells me that moving so often was never easy, but it has shaped his outlook on life.
The main points in the body are organized chronologically. But rather than simply relating different stages in Micah's life, each point is used to reveal an aspect of Micah's background and personality. The first point deals with Micah's friendliness.	Micah was born in Illinois but moved when he was six months old. The first place he can remember living is Iceland. Then came Belgium, Turkey, and Korea. Moving so often forced him to make new friends every year, but that's why he's a friendly person. He likes to see the best in everyone he meets.
The second main point discusses Micah's fondness for new cultures, which the speaker illustrates with crisp details and vivid imagery.	Later, Micah moved to Kuwait, Japan, and Italy. It was around this time that he started looking forward to the new cultures he and his family would experience. As Micah told me, he can still smell the tea in Kuwait. He can still see the temples in Japan. And, best of all, he can still taste the food in Italy.
In his third main point, the speaker brings Micah's life up to date by placing him at the University of Wisconsin. The speaker has strong eye contact, natural gestures, and an expressive voice.	When Micah was sixteen, he moved back to the United States and settled in Colorado. Now he's here at the University of Wisconsin. Sometimes Wisconsin feels like a foreign country to him, but that's why he loves it. He still has two more years here, and he's looking forward to them. But he's also excited to see where he goes next.
The conclusion ties everything together and imparts a strong sense of unity by echoing ideas and language from the introduction. The final sentence reinforces the positive nature of Micah's experiences as a Third-Culture Kid.	So if you see Micah around campus and ask where he's from, he probably won't have an easy answer. "Home Sweet Home" happens to be wherever he is, wherever his family is, wherever his friends are. That's what it's like being a Third-Culture Kid, and Micah wouldn't have it any other way.

Summary

The purpose of this chapter is to help you get ready for your ice breaker speech. Later chapters will look more closely at all the aspects of speech preparation and delivery discussed here.

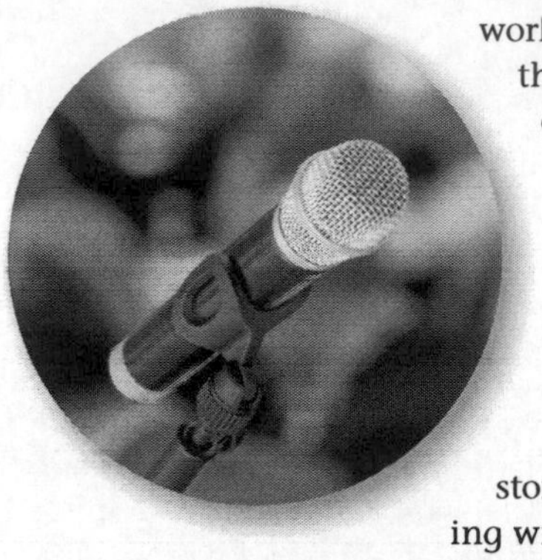

Once you know the exact assignment for your ice breaker speech, you can start working out your ideas. Focus on a limited number of main points and develop them creatively. Your speech will have three parts—introduction, body, and conclusion. Use transition statements to help the audience keep track of your points as the speech progresses.

Your teacher will probably ask you to deliver the speech extemporaneously. This means that the speech is carefully prepared in advance, but the exact language is chosen at the moment of delivery. To be successful, you will need to rehearse the speech multiple times to make sure you have full command of it.

When speech day comes, you will almost surely have butterflies in your stomach. Remember that nervousness is normal. Concentrate on communicating with your audience, rather than on worrying about your nerves. Try to appear calm and relaxed on the outside, no matter how you feel on the inside. Establish eye contact with the audience, use your voice expressively, and make sure your gestures and mannerisms do not distract from your message.

Key Terms

ice breaker speech (64)
introduction (66)
body (66)
chronological order (66)
topical order (67)
main points (67)
transition (67)
conclusion (67)
extemporaneous speech (68)
gestures (70)
eye contact (70)

Review Questions

After reading this chapter, you should be able to answer the following questions:

connect

For further review, go to the LearnSmart study module for this chapter.

1. What two major steps are discussed in this chapter for developing your introductory speech?
2. When organizing your introductory speech, you should divide it into what three sections?
3. What method of delivery does this chapter recommend for your introductory speech?
4. What steps should you take when rehearsing your first speech?
5. What five elements of speech delivery are discussed in this chapter with regard to presenting your first speech?

Exercises for Critical Thinking

1. Examine the two sample speeches with commentary on pages 72–73. Choose one, and answer the following questions about it.
   a. How does the opening paragraph gain the attention of the audience, introduce the subject of the speech, and preview the main points to be discussed in the body?
   b. How clearly is the body of the speech organized? What does the speaker do to help listeners follow the progression of ideas?
   c. How does the speaker conclude? Does the conclusion reinforce the central theme of the speech?
2. Are there occasions outside the classroom on which you might give a speech of self-introduction? Identify such an occasion and explain how you might apply the principles of introductory speeches discussed in this chapter.

Speech Preparation: Getting Started

5

Selecting a Topic and a Purpose

- **Choosing a Topic**
- **Determining the General Purpose**
- **Determining the Specific Purpose**
- **Phrasing the Central Idea**

As you read through this book, you will find examples of hundreds of speeches that were delivered in classrooms, in the political arena, in community and business situations. Here is a very small sample of the topics they cover:

asthma	Native American art
Cesar Chavez	optical illusion
driverless cars	Paralympics
Everglades	Québec
fantasy football	Ramadan
Great Wall	Statue of Liberty
Habitat for Humanity	tropical fish
identity theft	water shortage
Jerusalem	X Games
knitting	Yellowstone
Martin Luther King	zoos

Undoubtedly you noticed that the list runs from A to Z. This array of topics wasn't planned. It happened naturally in the course of presenting many different kinds of speeches. The list is given here to show you that there are literally endless possibilities for speech topics—from A to Z.

Choosing a Topic

topic

The subject of a speech.

The first step in speechmaking is choosing a topic. For speeches outside the classroom this is seldom a problem. Usually the speech topic is determined by the occasion, the audience, and the speaker's qualifications. When Bill Clinton lectures at a college campus, he often speaks about global citizenship. Rachel Maddow will discuss current events. Spike Lee might share his views on new developments in film. The same is true of ordinary citizens. The doctor is asked to inform high-school athletes and their parents about sports injuries, the head of a neighborhood coalition speaks about zoning regulations, the florist discusses how to grow thriving houseplants.

In a public speaking class, the situation is different. Students generally have great leeway in selecting topics. This would appear to be an advantage, since it allows you to talk about matters of personal interest. Yet there may be no facet of speech preparation that causes more gnashing of teeth than selecting a topic.

It is a constant source of amazement to teachers that students who regularly chat with their friends about almost any subject under the sun become mentally paralyzed when faced with the task of deciding what to talk about in their speech class. Fortunately, once you get over this initial paralysis, you should have little trouble choosing a good topic.

There are two broad categories of potential topics for your classroom speeches: (1) subjects you know a lot about and (2) subjects you want to know more about. Let's start with the first.

TOPICS YOU KNOW A LOT ABOUT

Most people speak best about subjects with which they are most familiar. When thinking about a topic, draw on your own knowledge and experience. Everyone knows things or has done things that can be used in a speech.

Think for a moment about unusual experiences you may have had or special expertise you may have acquired. One student, who grew up in Turkey, presented a fascinating speech about daily life in that country. Another used her knowledge as a jewelry store salesperson to prepare a speech on how to judge the value of cut diamonds. A third student, who had lived through a tornado, gave a gripping speech about that terrifying experience.

Too dramatic? Nothing in your life is as interesting? Yet another student, who described herself as "just a housewife who is returning to school to finish the education she started 20 years ago," delivered a witty speech on the adjustments she had to make in coming back to college—sitting in class with students young enough to be her children, balancing her academic work against her family commitments, and the satisfaction of completing the education she had begun years earlier.

When you look for a speech topic, keep in mind special expertise you have or sports, hobbies, travel, and other personal experiences that would make for an interesting presentation.

Here are a few more examples of speech topics based largely on the students' personal knowledge and experience:

Interning at *The Daily Show*

The Basics of Snowboarding

Two Years in the Peace Corps

How to Have a Successful Job Interview

TOPICS YOU WANT TO KNOW MORE ABOUT

On the other hand, you may decide to make your speech a learning experience for yourself as well as for your audience. You may choose a subject about which you already have some knowledge or expertise but not enough to prepare a speech without doing additional research. You may even select a topic that you want to explore for the first time. Say, for example, you've always been interested in Stonehenge but never knew much about it. This would be a perfect opportunity to research a fascinating subject and turn it into a fascinating speech.

Or suppose you run across a subject in one of your other classes that catches your fancy. Why not investigate it further for your speech class? One student used this approach to develop a speech on the subject of neuromarketing, which uses recent advancements in neuroscience to study the way people respond to products and promotions. After hearing about the subject in her marketing class, the student researched the topic further. In the process, she learned that neuromarketing is currently being used by some of the biggest corporations in the world. Using what she learned in her research, she put together a captivating speech that kept everyone's attention from beginning to end.

connect

View an excerpt from "Neuromarketing: Whispers of the Brain" in the online Media Library for this chapter (Video 5.1).

Still another possibility—especially for persuasive speeches—is to think of subjects about which you hold strong opinions and beliefs. They may include national or international concerns such as school safety or environmental protection. Or perhaps you are closely involved in a local issue such as a school board election or a proposal to build a new student center. Not all such topics must be "political." They can deal with anything from graduation requirements to helping people with physical disabilities, from dormitory regulations to building a church recreation center.

BRAINSTORMING FOR TOPICS

brainstorming

A method of generating ideas for speech topics by free association of words and ideas.

After all this, you may still be thinking, "I *don't* care about neuromarketing. I've *never* been to Turkey. I'm *not* active in politics. WHAT am I going to talk about?" If you are having trouble selecting a topic, there are a number of brainstorming procedures you can follow to get started.

Personal Inventory

First, make a quick inventory of your experiences, interests, hobbies, skills, beliefs, and so forth. Jot down anything that comes to mind, no matter how silly or irrelevant it may seem. From this list may come a general subject area out of which you can fashion a specific topic. This method has worked for many students.

Clustering

If the first method doesn't work, try a technique called clustering. Take a sheet of paper and divide it into nine columns as follows: People, Places, Things, Events, Processes, Concepts, Natural Phenomena, Problems, and Plans and Policies. Then list in each column the first four or five items that come to mind. The result might look like this:

People	**Places**	**Things**
Mark Zuckerberg	Syria	drones
Sofía Vergara	Grand Canyon	smart guns
Barack Obama	Mars	4K TV
Erin Andrews	my hometown	movies

Events	**Processes**
graduation	fracking
Yom Kippur	cooking Indian food
Chinese New Year	creating an urban garden
Cinco de Mayo	writing a job resumé

Concepts	**Natural Phenomena**
time travel	sink holes
conservatism	earthquakes
sustainability	tornadoes
bioethics	lightning

Problems	Plans and Policies
campus crime	education reform
heroin	living wage
cyberbullying	legalizing marijuana
political gridlock	immigration policy

Very likely, several items on your lists will strike you as potential topics. If not, take the items you find most intriguing and compose sublists for each. Try to free-associate. Write down a word or idea. What does that trigger in your mind? Whatever it is, write that down next, and keep going until you have four or five ideas on your list. For example, working from the lists printed above, one student composed sublists for movies, campus crime, and lightning:

connect

For an additional resource on speech topics, check the Topic Helper under the Library tab in Connect.

Movies	Campus Crime	Lightning
Academy Awards	police	thunder
prizes	fingerprints	noise
lotteries	hands	traffic
gambling	gloves	air pollution

Can you follow her trail of association? In the first column, movies made her think of the Academy Awards. The Academy Awards are prizes. Prizes reminded her of lotteries. Lotteries are a form of gambling. Suddenly, this student remembered an article she had read on the problem of gambling addiction in America. The idea clicked in her mind. After considerable research, she developed an excellent speech titled "Gambling Addiction: Why You Can't Beat the Odds."

That's a far cry from movies! If you started out free-associating from movies, you would doubtless end up somewhere completely different. This is what clustering is all about.

Internet Search

By clustering, most people come up with a topic rather quickly. But if you are still stymied, try an Internet search. Browse through a subject-based Web site, an online encyclopedia, or some other reference portal until you come across what might be a good topic. As an experiment, one student scanned the *Merriam-Webster Online Dictionary,* limiting herself to the letter *s.* Within 10 minutes, she had come up with these potential topics:

salaries	sleepwalking	sushi	submarines
strip mining	stars	Sphinx	scuba diving
states' rights	Singapore	Sabbath	self-improvement
spiders	stock market	surfing	science fiction

Whatever the means you use for selecting a topic, *start early.* Pay attention to interesting subjects in conversation, on television and the Internet, in newspapers and magazines. Jot down ideas for topics as they occur to you.

Having an inventory of possible topics to choose from is much better than having to rack your brain for one at the last minute. If you get an early start on choosing a topic, you will have plenty of time to pick just the right one and prepare a first-rate speech.

Determining the General Purpose

Along with choosing a topic, you need to determine the general purpose of your speech. Usually it will fall into one of two overlapping categories—to inform or to persuade.

general purpose

The broad goal of a speech.

When your general purpose is to inform, you act as a teacher or lecturer. Your goal is to convey information clearly, accurately, and interestingly. If you describe how to lift weights, narrate the major events of the latest Middle East crisis, or report on your sorority's financial position, you are speaking to inform. Your aim is to enhance the knowledge and understanding of your listeners—to give them information they did not have before.

When your general purpose is to persuade, you act as an advocate or a partisan. You go beyond giving information to espousing a cause. You want to change or structure the attitudes or actions of your audience. If you try to convince your listeners that they should start a regular program of weight lifting, that the United States should modify its policy in the Middle East, or that your sorority should start a fund-raising drive to balance its budget, then you are speaking to persuade. In doing so, you cannot help but give information, but your primary goal is to win over your listeners to your point of view—to get them to believe something or do something as a result of your speech.

In speech classes, the general purpose is usually specified as part of the speech assignment. For speeches outside the classroom, however, you have to make sure of your general purpose yourself. Usually this is easy to do. Are you going to explain, report, or demonstrate something? Then your general purpose is to inform. Are you going to sell, advocate, or defend something? Then your general purpose is to persuade. But no matter what the situation, you must be certain of exactly what you hope to achieve by speaking.

Determining the Specific Purpose

specific purpose

A single infinitive phrase that states precisely what a speaker hopes to accomplish in his or her speech.

Once you have chosen a topic and a general purpose, you must narrow your choices to determine the specific purpose of your speech. The specific purpose should focus on one aspect of a topic. You should be able to state your specific purpose in a single infinitive phrase (to inform my audience about . . . ; to persuade my audience to . . .) that indicates *precisely* what you hope to accomplish with your speech.

For example, Duane Winfield, a student at a large state university, decided to give his first classroom speech on a topic from his personal experience. For the past two years, he had volunteered his time to perform music for patients in mental hospitals, nursing homes, and residences for disabled adults. He had seen how enthusiastically the patients responded to music, even when they remained unmoved by other kinds of stimuli. Duane's experience had given him a better understanding of the benefits of music therapy, and he wanted to share this understanding with his classmates. This gave him a topic and a general purpose, which he stated like this:

Topic: Music therapy

General Purpose: To inform

So far, so good. But what aspect of his topic would Duane discuss? The kinds of facilities in which he had worked? His specific role as a performer? The evidence that music therapy can improve patients' mental health? The needs of patients with different kinds of illnesses? He had to choose something interesting that he could cover in a six-minute speech. Finally, he settled on describing his most memorable experiences with patients to show how music therapy affected them. He stated his specific purpose this way:

Specific Purpose: To inform my audience about the benefits of music therapy for people with psychological or cognitive disabilities.

This turned out to be an excellent choice, and Duane's speech was among the best in the class.

Notice how clear the specific purpose statement is. Notice also how it relates the topic directly to the audience. That is, it states not only what the *speaker* wants to *say* but also what the speaker wants the *audience* to *know* as a result of the speech. This is very important, for it helps keep the audience at the center of your attention as you prepare your speech.

Using public speaking in your CAREER

Your communication degree has helped you land a job as spokesperson for the mayor of a medium-sized city on the West Coast. A year after starting the job, you are selected to organize an information campaign explaining the benefits of a new youth center proposed by the mayor.

To launch this campaign, you've decided to hold a news briefing at the end of the week. To open the briefing, you will present a short set of comments on the mayor's initiative. You decide to focus on four benefits of the youth center: (1) It will offer a range of activities—from sports to the arts—in a safe environment. (2) It will provide social networks for youths from all walks of life. (3) It will operate most hours of the day and night. (4) It will be free and open to everyone.

Following the format used in this chapter, state the general purpose, specific purpose, central idea, and main points of your comments.

Look what happens when the specific purpose statement does not include the audience.

Specific Purpose: To explain the benefits of music therapy for people with psychological or cognitive disabilities.

Explain to whom? To musicians? To medical students? To social workers? Those would be three different speeches. The musicians would want to know about the kinds of music Duane played. The medical students would want to hear about research on the benefits of music therapy. The social workers would want to learn how to implement a music program. Communicating effectively with each group would require preparing a different speech.

When the audience slips out of the specific purpose, it may slip out of the speaker's consciousness. You may begin to think that your task is the general one of preparing "an informative speech," when in fact your task is the specific one of informing a particular group of people. As we shall see in the next chapter, it is almost impossible to prepare a good speech without keeping constantly in mind the *people* for whom it is intended.

TIPS FOR FORMULATING THE SPECIFIC PURPOSE STATEMENT

Formulating a specific purpose is the most important early step in developing a successful speech. When writing your purpose statement, follow the general principles outlined on the following pages.

Write the Purpose Statement as a Full Infinitive Phrase, Not as a Fragment

Ineffective: avalanches.

More Effective: To inform my audience about the three major kinds of avalanches.

The ineffective statement is adequate as an announcement of the speech topic, but it is not thought out fully enough to indicate the specific purpose.

Express Your Purpose as a Statement, Not as a Question

Ineffective: What is Día de los Muertos?

More Effective: To inform my audience about the history of Mexico's Día de los Muertos celebration.

The question might arouse the curiosity of an audience, but it is not effective as a specific purpose statement. It gives no indication about what direction the speech will take or what the speaker hopes to accomplish.

Avoid Figurative Language in Your Purpose Statement

Ineffective: To persuade my audience that the campus policy on student parking really stinks.

Think of opinions you hold when looking for speech topics. One student spoke on the specific purpose "To persuade my audience that stronger measures should be taken to protect Siberian tigers."

More Effective: To persuade my audience that the campus policy on student parking should be revised to provide more spaces for students before 5 P.M.

Although the ineffective statement indicates something of the speaker's viewpoint, it does not state concisely what he or she hopes to achieve. Figurative language can reinforce ideas within a speech, but it is too ambiguous for a specific purpose statement.

Limit Your Purpose Statement to One Distinct Idea

Ineffective: To persuade my audience to become literacy tutors and to donate time to Meals on Wheels.

This purpose statement expresses two unrelated ideas, either of which could be the subject of a speech. The easiest remedy is to select one or the other as a focus for your presentation.

More Effective: To persuade my audience to become literacy tutors.

Or:

More Effective: To persuade my audience to donate time to Meals on Wheels.

Does this mean that you can never use the word "and" in your specific purpose statement? Not at all. Suppose your specific purpose is "To inform my audience about the causes and effects of epilepsy." In this case, "and" is appropriate because it connects two related parts of a unified topic. What you need to avoid is not simply the word "and," but a specific purpose statement that contains two unrelated ideas, either of which could be developed into a speech in its own right.

Make Sure Your Specific Purpose Is Not Too Vague or General

Ineffective: To persuade my audience that something should be done about unsafe school buses.

More Effective: To persuade my audience that the federal government should impose stronger safety standards for school buses in the United States.

The ineffective purpose statement falls into one of the most common traps—it is too broad and ill-defined. It gives no clues about what the speaker believes should be done about school buses. The more effective purpose statement is sharp and concise. It reveals clearly what the speaker plans to discuss.

The more precise your specific purpose, the easier it will be to prepare your speech. Consider this topic and specific purpose:

Topic: Hot-air balloons.

Specific Purpose: To inform my audience about hot-air balloons.

With such a hazy purpose, you have no systematic way of limiting your research or of deciding what to include in the speech and what to exclude. The origins of hot-air balloons, how they work, their current popularity—all could be equally relevant to a speech designed "to inform my audience about hot-air balloons."

In contrast, look at this topic and specific purpose:

Topic: Hot-air balloons.

Specific Purpose: To inform my audience about the scientific uses of hot-air balloons.

Now it is easy to decide what is germane and what is not. The origins of hot-air balloons, how they work, their popularity for recreation—all are interesting, but none is essential to the specific purpose of explaining "the scientific uses of hot-air balloons." Thus you need not worry about researching these matters or about explaining them in your speech. You can spend your preparation time efficiently.

QUESTIONS TO ASK ABOUT YOUR SPECIFIC PURPOSE

Sometimes you will arrive at your specific purpose almost immediately after choosing your topic. At other times you may do quite a bit of research before deciding on a specific purpose. Much will depend on how familiar you are with the topic, as well as on any special demands imposed by the assignment, the audience, or the occasion. But whenever you settle on your specific purpose, ask yourself the following questions about it.

Does My Purpose Meet the Assignment?

Students occasionally stumble over this question. Be sure you understand your assignment and shape your specific purpose to meet it. If you have questions, check with your instructor.

Can I Accomplish My Purpose in the Time Allotted?

Most classroom speeches are quite short, ranging from four to ten minutes. That may seem like a lot of time, but you will quickly find what generations of students have discovered—time flies when you are giving a speech!

Most people speak at an average rate of 120 to 150 words a minute. This means that a six-minute speech will consist of roughly 720 to 900 words. That is not long enough to develop a highly complex topic. Here are some specific purpose statements that would defy being handled well in the time normally allotted for classroom speeches:

> To inform my audience about the rise and fall of ancient Rome.
>
> To inform my audience about the role of technology in human history.
>
> To persuade my audience to convert to Buddhism.

You are much better off with a limited purpose that you have some reasonable hope of achieving in the short span of four to ten minutes.

IS THE PURPOSE RELEVANT TO MY AUDIENCE?

The price of retirement homes in Palm Springs might be an engrossing topic for older citizens who are in the market for such dwellings. And the quality

checklist

Specific Purpose

YES	NO	
☐	☐	1. Is the specific purpose written as a full infinitive phrase?
☐	☐	2. Does the specific purpose include a reference to the audience?
☐	☐	3. Is the specific purpose phrased as a statement rather than a question?
☐	☐	4. Is the specific purpose free of figurative language?
☐	☐	5. Is the specific purpose limited to one distinct subject?
☐	☐	6. Does the specific purpose indicate precisely what I plan to accomplish in the speech?
☐	☐	7. Does the specific purpose meet the requirements of the assignment?
☐	☐	8. Can the specific purpose be accomplished in the time allotted for the speech?
☐	☐	9. Is the specific purpose relevant to my audience?
☐	☐	10. Does the specific purpose deal with a nontrivial subject?
☐	☐	11. Is the specific purpose suitable for a nontechnical audience?

of hot lunches in the elementary schools is of great concern to the students who eat them and the parents who pay for them. But neither subject has much relevance for an audience of college students. No matter how well you construct your speeches, they are likely to fall flat unless you speak about matters of interest to your listeners.

This is not to say you must select only topics that pertain directly to the college student's daily experience. Most students have wide-ranging backgrounds, interests, ideas, and values. And most of them are intellectually curious. They can get involved in an astonishing variety of subjects. Follow your common sense and make sure *you* are truly interested in the topic. Also, when speaking on a subject that is not obviously relevant to your listeners, find a way to tie it in with their goals, values, interests, and well-being. We'll discuss how to do this in the next chapter.

Is the Purpose Too Trivial for My Audience?

Just as you need to avoid speech topics that are too broad or complicated, so you need to steer clear of topics that are too superficial. How to tie a perfect square knot might absorb a group of Cub Scouts, but your classmates would probably consider it frivolous. Unfortunately, there is no absolute rule for determining what is trivial to an audience and what is not. Here are some examples of specific purposes that most people would find too trivial for classroom speeches:

> To inform my audience about the parts of a backpack.
>
> To inform my audience how to do laundry.
>
> To persuade my audience that espresso is better than cappuccino.

Is the Purpose Too Technical for My Audience?

Nothing puts an audience to sleep faster than a dry and technical speech. Beware of topics that are inherently technical and of treating ordinary subjects in a technical fashion. Although you may be familiar with the principles and vocabulary of international finance or clinical psychology, most of your classmates probably are not. There are aspects of these and similar subjects that can be treated clearly, with a minimum of jargon. But if you find that you can't fulfill your specific purpose without relying on technical words and concepts, you should reconsider your purpose.

Here are some examples of specific purposes that are overly technical for most classroom speeches:

> To inform my audience about the solution to Fermat's Last Theorem.
>
> To inform my audience about the principles of neutrino physics.
>
> To inform my audience about the methods of encryption technology.

We will discuss the details of audience analysis and adaptation in Chapter 6. For the moment, remember to make sure that your specific purpose is appropriate for your listeners. If you have doubts, ask your instructor, or circulate a questionnaire among your classmates (see pages 110–113).

Phrasing the Central Idea

WHAT IS THE CENTRAL IDEA?

The specific purpose of a speech is what you hope to accomplish. The *central idea* is a concise statement of what you *expect to say.* Sometimes it is called the thesis statement, the subject sentence, or the major thought. Whatever the term, the central idea is usually expressed as a simple, declarative sentence that refines and sharpens the specific purpose statement.

central idea

A one-sentence statement that sums up or encapsulates the major ideas of a speech.

Imagine that you run into a friend on your way to speech class. She says, "I have to dash to my history lecture, but I hear you're giving a speech today. Can you tell me the gist of it in one sentence?" "Sure," you reply. "America's prison system suffers from three major problems—overcrowding of inmates, lack of effective rehabilitation programs, and high expense to taxpayers."

Your answer is the central idea of your speech. It is more precise than your topic (America's prison system) or your specific purpose statement ("To inform my audience of the three major problems facing America's prison system"). By stating exactly what the three major problems are, the central idea sums up your speech in a single sentence.

Another way to think of the central idea is as your *residual message*—what you want your audience to remember after they have forgotten everything else in the speech. Most of the time the central idea will encapsulate the main points to be developed in the body of the speech. To show how this works, let's take a few of the examples we saw earlier in this chapter and develop them from the topic, general purpose, and specific purpose to the central idea.

residual message

What a speaker wants the audience to remember after it has forgotten everything else in a speech.

We can start with the speech about music therapy.

Topic:	Music therapy.
General Purpose:	To inform.
Specific Purpose:	To inform my audience about the benefits of music therapy for people with psychological or cognitive disabilities.
Central Idea:	Music therapy developed as a formal mode of treatment during the 20th century, utilizes a number of methods, and is explained by several theories that account for its success.

Look carefully at this example. It shows how the speaker might start with a broad subject (music therapy) that becomes narrower and narrower as the speaker moves from the general purpose to the specific purpose to the central idea. Notice also how much more the central idea suggests about the content of the speech. From it we can expect the speaker to address three main points—the first summarizing the development of music therapy, the second looking at methods of music therapy, and the third exploring theories that account for the success of music therapy.

connect

View the introduction from "The Benefits of Music Therapy" in the online Media Library for this chapter (Video 5.2).

This sharpening of focus as one proceeds to the central idea is crucial. Here is another example:

Topic:	Día de los Muertos.
General Purpose:	To inform.

Specific Purpose: To inform my audience about the history of Mexico's Día de los Muertos celebration.

Central Idea: Día de los Muertos can be traced to the Aztecs, was moved from summer to fall by Spanish priests, and today is celebrated in a number of ways in different regions of Mexico.

This central idea is especially well worded. We can assume from it that the body of the speech will contain three main points: (1) on the Aztec origins of Día de los Muertos, (2) on how it was changed by the Spanish, and (3) on the ways it is celebrated today.

Notice in each of these examples how much more the central idea reveals about the content of the speech than does the specific purpose. This is not accidental. Often you can settle on a specific purpose statement early in preparing your speech. The central idea, however, usually emerges later—after you have done your research and have decided on the main points of the speech. The process may work like this:

As an environmental science major, Marcia Esposito had learned that many experts fear the world may face a severe water shortage by the year 2025. She decided this would make a good topic for her informative speech. Tentatively, she adopted the following specific purpose statement: "To inform my audience about the seriousness of the growing international water crisis." Then Marcia started her research.

An article in *Time* magazine, which she located through LexisNexis, explained how the population in countries such as China, India, and Pakistan is outstripping the available supply of fresh water. According to the article, 400 million Chinese do not have access to suitable drinking water and two-thirds of India's 1.1 billion people lack the water they need.

Next Marcia found a report on the United Nations Web site about the impact of pollution on the water supply. The report stated that in developing countries "more than 90 percent of sewage and 70 percent of industrial wastewater is dumped untreated into surface water."

Then Marcia hit upon the idea of interviewing one of her environmental science professors. In addition to confirming Marcia's research about the impact of population growth and pollution, the professor mentioned the problems caused by mismanagement of water supplies. Around the world, 65 to 70 percent of the water people use is lost to waste, evaporation, and other inefficiencies.

Marcia digested all this information. Now she was ready to formulate her central idea: "Population growth, pollution, and mismanagement are creating a serious shortage of fresh water in many parts of the world."

GUIDELINES FOR THE CENTRAL IDEA

What makes a well-worded central idea? Essentially the same things that make a well-worded specific purpose statement. The central idea (1) should be expressed in a full sentence, (2) should not be in the form of a question, (3) should avoid figurative language, and (4) should not be vague or overly general.

Unlike the specific purpose, which you need to settle on early in the speech preparation process, the central idea usually takes shape later, as a result of your research and analysis of the topic.

Here, for example, are four poorly written central ideas. See if you can identify the problem with each and figure out how each might be phrased more effectively:

Ineffective: Paying college athletes a monthly stipend is a good idea.

Ineffective: Problems of fad diets.

Ineffective: What are nanorobots?

Ineffective: South Africa is an awesome place for a vacation.

The first is too general. To say that paying college athletes a monthly stipend is a "good idea" does not convey the speaker's viewpoint sharply and clearly. What does the speaker mean by a "good idea"? A revised central idea for this speech might be:

More Effective: Because college athletes in revenue-producing sports such as football and basketball generate millions of dollars in revenue for their schools, the NCAA should allow such athletes to receive a $300 monthly stipend as part of their scholarships.

The second ineffective central idea is also too general, but it suffers further from not being written as a complete sentence. "Problems of fad diets" does not reveal enough about the content of the speech to serve as the central idea. It should be rewritten as a full sentence that identifies the problems of fad diets to be discussed in the speech:

More Effective: Although fad diets produce quick weight loss, they can lead to serious health problems by creating deficiencies in vitamins and minerals and by breaking down muscle tissue as well as fat.

checklist

Central Idea

YES	NO	
☐	☐	1. Is the central idea written as a complete sentence?
☐	☐	2. Is the central idea phrased as a statement rather than a question?
☐	☐	3. Is the central idea free of figurative language?
☐	☐	4. Does the central idea clearly encapsulate the main points to be discussed in the body of the speech?
☐	☐	5. Can the central idea be adequately discussed in the time allotted for the speech?
☐	☐	6. Is the central idea relevant to the audience?
☐	☐	7. Is the central idea appropriate for a nontechnical audience?

The third poorly written central idea is phrased as a question rather than as a full declarative sentence. Asking "What are nanorobots?" might be a good way to catch the attention of listeners, but it does not encapsulate the main points to be developed in the speech. A more effective central idea would be:

More Effective: Microscopic in size, nanorobots are being developed for use in medicine, weaponry, and daily life.

The final ineffective central idea is flawed by its use of figurative language. To say that South Africa is an "awesome" place for a vacation does not indicate what characteristics of South Africa the speaker intends to discuss. A better central idea might be:

More Effective: South Africa has many attractions for vacationers, including beautiful scenery, exotic wildlife, and bustling cities.

Notice that in all these examples the more effective central idea sums up the main points of the speech in a single sentence. If you are having trouble phrasing your central idea, the reason may be that you do not yet have a firm grasp on the main points of your speech.

Don't worry too much about your central idea until after you have developed the body of your speech (see Chapter 9). If, at that point, you still can't come up with a clear, concise central idea, your speech itself may not be clear or concise. Keep working on the speech until you can compose a central idea that fits the criteria just discussed. The result will be a sharper central idea and a tighter, more coherent speech.

Summary

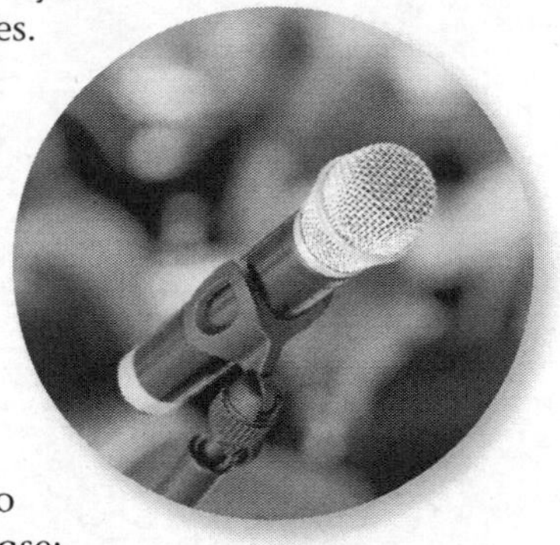

The first step in speechmaking is choosing a topic. For classroom speeches, you can choose a subject you know well or one you research especially for the speech. If you have trouble picking a topic, you can use one of three brainstorming procedures. First, make an inventory of your hobbies, interests, skills, beliefs, and so forth. Second, use clustering to list the first topics that come to mind in several categories. Third, use an Internet subject directory, encyclopedia, or similar reference site to help you scan possible topics.

The general purpose of your speech will usually be to inform or to persuade. When your general purpose is to inform, your goal is to communicate information clearly, accurately, and interestingly. When your general purpose is to persuade, your goal is to win listeners over to your point of view.

Once you know your topic and general purpose, you must focus on a specific purpose statement that indicates precisely what your speech seeks to achieve. The specific purpose statement should (1) be a full infinitive phrase; (2) be worded as a statement, not a question; (3) avoid figurative language; (4) concentrate on one distinct idea; (5) not be vague or general.

Keep several questions in mind as you formulate your specific purpose statement: Does my purpose meet the assignment? Can I accomplish my purpose in the time allotted? Is the purpose relevant to my audience? Is the purpose too trivial or too technical for my audience?

The central idea refines and sharpens your specific purpose. It is a concise statement of what you will say in your speech, and it usually crystallizes in your thinking after you have done your research and have decided on the main points of your speech. The central idea usually encapsulates the main points to be developed in the body of your speech.

Key Terms

topic (78)
brainstorming (80)
general purpose (82)
specific purpose (82)
central idea (89)
residual message (89)

Review Questions

After reading this chapter, you should be able to answer the following questions:

1. What three brainstorming methods can you follow if you are having trouble choosing a topic for your speech?
2. What are the two general purposes of most classroom speeches? How do they differ?
3. Why is determining the specific purpose such an important early step in speech preparation? Why is it important to include the audience in the specific purpose statement?

connect

For further review, go to the LearnSmart study module for this chapter.

4. What are five tips for formulating your specific purpose?
5. What are five questions to ask about your specific purpose?
6. What is the difference between the specific purpose and the central idea of a speech? What are four guidelines for an effective central idea?

Exercises for Critical Thinking

1. Using one of the brainstorming methods described in this chapter, come up with three topics you might like to deal with in your next classroom speech. For each topic, devise a specific purpose statement suitable for the speech assignment. Make sure your specific purpose statements fit the guidelines discussed in the chapter.
2. Here are several specific purpose statements for classroom speeches. Identify the problem (or problems) with each.

   To inform my audience about Portugal.

   To persuade my audience that something has to be done about the problem of corporate tax loopholes.

   Donate blood.

   To inform my audience why square grooves are superior to U-shaped grooves on golf clubs.

   To persuade my audience that the U.S. government should increase funding for the national parks and send an astronaut to Mars by 2025.

   What is the Great Pacific Garbage Patch?

   To inform my audience how to register for classes.
3. Below are three sets of main points for speeches. For each set, supply the general purpose, specific purpose, and central idea.

   General Purpose:

   Specific Purpose:

   Central Idea:

   Main Points:
   I. You should support the school-bond referendum because it will improve classroom facilities.
   II. You should support the school-bond referendum because it will increase the number of teachers.
   III. You should support the school-bond referendum because it will upgrade instructional resources.

   General Purpose:

   Specific Purpose:

   Central Idea:

   Main Points:
   I. The first event in a triathlon is swimming.
   II. The second event in a triathlon is cycling.
   III. The third event in a triathlon is running.

General Purpose:

Specific Purpose:

Central Idea:

Main Points:

I. As a writer, Thomas Jefferson penned the Declaration of Independence and *Notes on the State of Virginia.*

II. As president, Thomas Jefferson negotiated the Louisiana Purchase and approved the Lewis and Clark expedition.

III. As an architect, Thomas Jefferson designed Monticello and the University of Virginia.

6

Analyzing the Audience

- Audience-Centeredness
- Your Classmates as an Audience
- The Psychology of Audiences
- Demographic Audience Analysis
- Situational Audience Analysis
- Getting Information About the Audience
- Adapting to the Audience

Dan Oliver was thrilled. His city was launching its own film festival, and he had been asked to speak on opening night about the importance of modern cinema. A professor of film and an independent filmmaker, Dan was eager to show people that movies could be more than entertainment.

In the weeks leading up to his speech, Dan prepared diligently. He drew upon lecture notes from his upper-level film theory course. He used material from a book he had published the previous year on French new-wave cinema. And he figured this would be a good time to explain some of his recent research on *mise-en-scène* and viewer affect.

Opening night of the film festival was packed. People from all over the community wanted to be part of the festivities. Dan took the stage and began his speech to an audience with wide eyes and shining faces. As the speech went on, however, he noticed a number of blank stares. Then people started fidgeting in their seats and checking their phones. When he finished, he received a ripple of polite applause.

"What happened?" Dan asked the director of the film festival later that night. "I thought I had written such a good speech."

"It would have been a great speech," the director replied, "if all these people had been film scholars. But most of them were just interested in watching some good movies. Once you got into finer points of film theory, you went right over their heads."

Audience-Centeredness

audience-centeredness

Keeping the audience foremost in mind at every step of speech preparation and presentation.

This story points up an important fact: Good public speakers are *audience-centered.* They know the primary purpose of speechmaking is not to browbeat the audience or to blow off steam. Rather, it is to gain a *desired response* from listeners.

Being audience-centered does not involve compromising your beliefs to get a favorable response. Nor does it mean using devious, unethical tactics to achieve your goal. You can remain true to yourself and speak ethically while adapting your message to the goals, values, and attitudes of your audience.

To be audience-centered, you need to keep several questions in mind when you work on your speeches:

To whom am I speaking?

What do I want them to know, believe, or do as a result of my speech?

What is the most effective way of composing and presenting my speech to accomplish that aim?

The answers to these questions will influence every decision you make along the way—selecting a topic, determining a specific purpose, settling on your main points and supporting materials, organizing the message, and, finally, delivering the speech.

In many ways, adapting to an audience during a public speech is not much different from what you do in your daily social contacts. Few people would walk into a party and announce, "You know those people protesting at the administration building are way over the edge!"

People usually prefer to open controversial topics with a fairly noncommittal position. You might say, "What's going on at the administration building?" Then when you have heard and processed your companion's response, you can present your position accordingly. (You don't have to *agree* with a viewpoint different from your own, but neither do you have to hit your listeners over the head with your own opinion.)

When you make a speech, either in class or in some other forum, keep in mind the need to be audience-centered. Think in advance about your listeners' background and interests, about their level of knowledge regarding the speech topic, and about their attitudes regarding your stance on the topic. As you develop the speech, work on explaining your ideas so they will be clear, interesting, and persuasive to the audience.

At this point, you may be nodding your head and saying, "Of course, everyone knows that. It's only common sense." But knowing a precept and putting it into practice are two different matters. The aim of this chapter is to introduce the basic principles of audience analysis and adaption. Chapters 15 and 16 will deal with those features of audience analysis unique to informative and persuasive speaking.

Your Classmates as an Audience

There is a tendency—among students and teachers alike—to view the classroom as an artificial speaking situation. In a way, it is. Your speech class is a testing ground where you can develop your communication skills before applying them outside the classroom. The most serious measure of success or failure is your grade, and that is determined ultimately by your instructor.

Because of this, it is easy to lose sight of your fellow students as an authentic audience. But each of your classmates is a real person with real ideas, attitudes, and feelings. Your speech class offers an enormous opportunity to inform and persuade other people. As one student wrote on her evaluation form at the end of her speech class, "I thought the speeches would all be phony, but they weren't. I've not only learned a lot about speaking—I've learned a lot about other things from listening to the speeches in class."

The best classroom speeches are those that take the classroom audience as seriously as a lawyer, a politician, a minister, or an advertiser takes an audience. You should consider every audience—inside the classroom and out—as worthy of your best efforts to communicate your knowledge or convictions. At the least you show respect for your listeners. At the most you could make a real difference in their lives. The following story demonstrates the latter:

> Crystal Watkins gave an informative speech on the subject of small claims court, where ordinary people can press lawsuits involving up to $10,000 without lawyers. Part of her speech went like this: "It's two weeks after you have moved into a new apartment. A letter arrives from your old landlord. Expecting to get back your $800 security deposit, you joyfully tear open the envelope. Inside is a form letter explaining why your security deposit is not being refunded. What can you do about it? Nothing, right? Wrong! You can file a claim in small claims court."
>
> Lee Callaway, one of Crystal's classmates, paid close attention. At the end of the previous term, he had run into a situation just like the one Crystal described. Not having money to hire a lawyer, he assumed he would have to forfeit his security deposit. But now, as he listened to Crystal's speech, Lee decided he would try to get his money back in small claims court. He filed suit the next week, and within a month he had his money back—thanks in part to his classmate's speech!

Most of your classroom speeches won't have this much immediate impact. Nevertheless, any topic that you handle conscientiously can influence your listeners—can enrich their experience, broaden their knowledge, perhaps change their views about something important.[1]

The Psychology of Audiences

What do you do when you listen to a speech? Sometimes you pay close attention; at other times you let your thoughts wander. People may be compelled to attend a speech, but no one can make them listen. The speaker must make the audience *choose* to pay attention.

Even when people do pay attention, they don't process a speaker's message exactly as the speaker intends. Auditory perception is always selective. Every speech contains two messages—the one sent by the speaker and the one received by the listener.

As we saw in Chapter 1, what a speaker says is filtered through a listener's frame of reference—the sum of her or his needs, interests, expectations, knowledge, and experience. As a result, we listen and respond to speeches not as they are, but as we are. Or, to borrow from Paul Simon's classic song "The Boxer," people hear what they want to hear and disregard the rest.

egocentrism

The tendency of people to be concerned above all with their own values, beliefs, and well-being.

What do people want to hear? Very simply, they usually want to hear about things that are meaningful to them. People are *egocentric.* They pay closest attention to messages that affect their own values, beliefs, and well-being. Listeners approach speeches with one question uppermost in mind: "Why is this important to *me*?" As Harry Emerson Fosdick, the great preacher, once said: "There is nothing that people are so interested in as themselves, their own problems, and the way to solve them. That fact is . . . the primary starting point of all successful public speaking."

What do these psychological principles mean to you as a speaker? First, they mean your listeners will hear and judge what you say on the basis of what they already know and believe. Second, they mean you must relate your message to your listeners—show how it pertains to them, explain why they should care about it as much as you do. Here's an example:

> Luis Rivera is a 20-year veteran of the local police department, specializing in anti-crime initiatives. He frequently gives presentations to groups of schoolchildren and their parents, sometimes to neighborhood-watch organizations and city council meetings. Although his basic message—engaged neighborhoods are safe neighborhoods—never varies, he has learned how important it is to tailor the message to his specific audience.
>
> When Luis speaks to children, his presentations involve humor, colorful stories from his years on the streets, and plenty of visual aids. Sometimes he brings along a police dog, which never fails to get the kids excited. At other times he lets the kids touch real police handcuffs.
>
> When his audience consists of parents of schoolchildren, Luis focuses on how active parenting doesn't have to be overly time-consuming. For neighborhood-watch organizations, he thanks them for their service and gives them pointers on how to spot suspicious activity. When speaking at city council meetings, Luis uses statistics about places where community resources have been effective at lowering crime and where work remains to be done.

As Luis's experience shows, you need some grasp of what your listeners know, believe, and care about. Saul Alinsky, the noted community organizer, advises, "People only understand things in terms of their experience,"

Good speakers are audience-centered. Whether speaking formally or informally, they look for creative ways to communicate their ideas and keep their audience's attention.

which means that to communicate with them, "you must get inside their experience."[2]

Of course, you can't actually get inside another person's experience. But you can learn enough about your audience to know what you should do to make your ideas clear and meaningful. How you can do this is our next topic.

Demographic Audience Analysis

One of the ways speakers analyze audiences is by looking at demographic traits such as age; gender; religion; sexual orientation; group membership; racial, ethnic, or cultural background; and the like. This is called demographic audience analysis. It consists of two steps: (1) identifying the general demographic features of your audience, and (2) gauging the importance of those features to a particular speaking situation.

While demographic audience analysis can be a useful tool in understanding your audience, like all tools, it can be used improperly. When analyzing demographic information about your audience, it is essential that you avoid stereotyping. Stereotyping involves creating an oversimplified image of a particular group of people, usually by assuming that all members of the group are alike. Examples of stereotyping include the erroneous notions that all African Americans are athletic or that all Asians excel in science. Looking at demographic factors can provide important clues about your audience, but you must use those factors prudently and responsibly.

In addition, as we shall see later in this chapter, you should always combine your demographic audience analysis with situational audience analysis.

demographic audience analysis

Audience analysis that focuses on demographic factors such as age, gender, religion, sexual orientation, group membership, and racial, ethnic, or cultural background.

stereotyping

Creating an oversimplified image of a particular group of people, usually by assuming that all members of the group are alike.

The importance of any given demographic factor will vary from audience to audience depending on the occasion and the speech topic. If you keep this in mind, demographic analysis can be a valuable starting point in gauging your audience's background, interests, values, and beliefs. Here are a few of the major demographic factors you should consider.

AGE

As Aristotle noted 2,300 years ago and as researchers have confirmed many times since, few things affect a person's outlook more than his or her age. Of course, no age group is monolithic. There is no generation in which everyone thinks alike, buys the same products, or votes for the same political candidates. Yet each generation has more or less common values and experiences that set it apart from other generations. Whatever your age, you are a product of your world.

You can see what this means for your speeches. Suppose you address an audience of older people. If you refer to Cam'ron, Lorde, or Alter Bridge, your audience may have no idea who you mean. Similarly, if you speak to an audience of young adults and casually mention Watergate, they may not know what you are talking about. Even if younger listeners do recognize the name, it will not produce the same emotional associations as in people who lived through the Watergate break-in and the subsequent resignation of President Richard Nixon.

Depending on the composition of your speech class, you may face an audience that is mostly in their late teens and early twenties. If so, you can assume a common level of age experience. On the other hand, 40 percent of college students today are age 25 or older, and some classrooms include students in their thirties, forties, and beyond. You may then have to tackle two or three generations. This will give you good practice for speeches outside the classroom, where age is usually a major factor in audience analysis.

GENDER

Question: What do you call a female doctor?
Answer: A doctor.

This probably strikes you as a strange question. Few Americans in the second decade of the 21st century identify their doctor by gender. Yet as recently as 1970, only 8 percent of doctors in the United States were women, and the phrase "female doctor" was often heard. Today, 30 percent of American doctors—and 50 percent of medical-school students—are women. The phrase "female doctor" has become extinct.

As in medicine, vocational distinctions between the sexes have been eroding for many years. Women work in construction trades, run corporations, enlist in the armed forces, and serve as college athletic directors. Men work as receptionists, nurses, flight attendants, and day-care attendants.

In addition, the "typical" composition of audiences has changed. At one time, for example, civic groups such as Kiwanis and Rotary clubs were all-male. Today most have sizable contingents of women. Parent associations, which were once composed almost solely of women, now include plenty of interested fathers. Here, as in other areas, the old stereotypes no longer apply.

What does this have to do with public speaking? Speakers who fail to take account of current gender attitudes and practices are almost certain to provoke negative reactions among some listeners, male and female alike. If you're delivering a speech about small businesses, for example, and you refer to business owners generically as "he," or to all shoppers as "she," your word choice will doubtless lead some listeners to raise their eyebrows—or worse.

At the same time, it is important to recognize that men and women are not alike in all their values and beliefs. When it comes to politics, for instance, American women tend to be more concerned about issues such as education, health care, and social justice, whereas men tend to stress economics and national security. But keep in mind that these are generalizations. There are lots of women who believe that national security comes first, just as there are plenty of men who give priority to social issues. An astute speaker will be equally attuned to the differences *and* the similarities between the sexes.[3]

RELIGION

Current events around the world demonstrate that religious views are among the most emotionally charged and passionately defended of all human concerns. Even your small speech class might include a wide range of faiths, as well as atheists and agnostics. You cannot assume that your views on religion—whatever they may be—are shared by your listeners.

As the United States has become more diverse culturally, it has also become more diverse religiously. The traditional mix of Protestantism, Catholicism, and Judaism has been enriched by growing numbers of Buddhists, Muslims, Hindus, Sikhs, Russian Orthodox, and others. One leading scholar on the subject says the United States is "the most religiously diverse nation in the world."[4]

There is also great diversity within different faiths. You cannot assume that all Catholics support the official view of their church on birth control or women in the priesthood, that all Baptists are born-again, or that all Muslims favor a subservient status for women. In matters of religion, the United States is truly a nation of many faiths, many voices, many views.

Whenever you speak on a topic with religious dimensions, be sure to consider the religious orientations of your listeners. Doing so can help you avoid potentially embarrassing pitfalls. In some cases, it may make the difference between an unsuccessful speech and a successful one.

SEXUAL ORIENTATION

Philip Ward, president of a major engineering firm, was hosting his annual awards banquet to recognize outstanding employees. After presenting all the plaques and checks, he said: "Now that we have honored these fine people for their career and community accomplishments, I would like to take a moment to recognize the spouses and partners who have supported their exceptional efforts." The room filled with applause.

After the ceremony, Ward made his way around the room shaking hands and chatting with award winners. "I want to congratulate you again on your superior design for the Houston water project," he said to Joanne Fitzpatrick.

"Thank you for the award," Joanne replied. "And I want to thank you for being sensitive to the fact that many of us are supported by partners as well as by spouses. It really meant a lot to Julie and me to feel recognized and included."

Demographic audience analysis plays a role in every public speaking situation. Here German Vice President Christian Wulff speaks at the German University of Technology in Muscat, Oman.

As an experienced speaker and a successful businessperson, Philip Ward is aware of the need to adapt to his audience on the basis of sexual orientation. By mentioning "partners" as well as "spouses," he took an inclusive stance acknowledging that couples can be same-sex or opposite-sex, married or unmarried.

When you work on your speeches, keep an eye out for language, examples, and other elements that may unintentionally exclude listeners with same-sex partners. The word "homosexual," for example, is considered derogatory by lesbians and gay men. So are references to a gay or lesbian "lifestyle." As there is no single heterosexual lifestyle, there is no single lesbian or gay lifestyle.

Just as audiences often include people of varying occupations, ages, races, and religions, so too do they contain people of different sexual orientations. Effective public speakers take all these demographic factors into account when preparing their remarks.

RACIAL, ETHNIC, AND CULTURAL BACKGROUND

The United States is a multiracial, multiethnic country of unmatched diversity. The majority of Americans support this diversity as a positive development in today's globalized world. Attitudes about race and ethnicity are quite different from what they were even a few decades ago.

These new attitudes are especially evident among Americans born from 1981 to 2000, often referred to as the Millennial Generation. The most racially and ethnically diverse generation in U.S. history, it is also the most tolerant of racial and ethnic differences. As time goes by, this tolerance may continue to grow as the nation becomes even more diverse.

Yet even if you are speaking to an audience composed primarily of Millennials, you must be sensitive to issues of race, ethnicity, and cultural background. Despite their similarities as Americans, people of European descent, blacks, Latinos, Asians, and many others have different customs and beliefs that may bear upon your speech topic.

Because we live in an age of globalization, you may also find yourself addressing listeners from countries other than your own. Not only does the United States contain a substantial percentage of people born in other lands, but more than 5 million Americans (not including those in military service) live abroad. If all those Americans were placed in one state, it would be the 20th largest state in the Union. This is one reason why employers identify the ability to communicate effectively with people of different cultural backgrounds as one of the most desirable skills for current college graduates.

Regardless of where you are speaking, be aware that some of your listeners may have racial, ethnic, or cultural perspectives that will affect their attitudes toward your speech topic. Try to gauge what those perspectives are and how they are likely to affect the audience's response to your message. Adjust your remarks so they will be as clear, suitable, and convincing as possible.

GROUP MEMBERSHIP

"Tell me thy company," says Don Quixote, "and I'll tell thee what thou art." For all our talk about rugged individualism, Americans are very group-oriented. Workers belong to unions, businesspeople to chambers of commerce. Hunters join the National Rifle Association, environmentalists the Sierra Club, feminists the National Organization for Women. Doctors enroll in the American Medical Association, lawyers in the American Bar Association. There are thousands of such voluntary organizations in the United States.

Similar groups abound on campus. Some of your classmates may belong to fraternities or sororities, some to InterVarsity, some to the Young Republicans, some to the film society, some to the ski club, and so forth. For speeches in the classroom, as well as for those outside the classroom, the group affiliations of your audience may provide excellent clues about your listeners' interests and attitudes.

Age; gender; religion; sexual orientation; racial, ethnic, and cultural background; group membership—these are just a few of the variables to consider in demographic audience analysis. Others include occupation, economic position, social standing, education, intelligence, and place of residence. Indeed, *anything* characteristic of a given audience is potentially important to a speaker addressing that audience. For your classroom speeches, you may want to learn about your classmates' academic majors, years in school, extracurricular activities, living arrangements, and job aspirations.

Perhaps the most important thing to keep in mind about demographic audience analysis is that it is not an end in itself. Your aim is not just to list the major traits of your listeners, but to find in those traits clues about how your listeners will respond to your speech. Once you have done that, you are ready to move on to the next stage of audience analysis.

Situational Audience Analysis

situational audience analysis

Audience analysis that focuses on situational factors such as the size of the audience, the physical setting for the speech, and the disposition of the audience toward the topic, the speaker, and the occasion.

Situational audience analysis usually builds on demographic analysis. It identifies traits of the audience unique to the speaking situation at hand. These traits include the size of the audience, the physical setting, and the disposition of the audience toward the subject, the speaker, and the occasion.

SIZE

Outside the classroom, the size of an audience can, with the aid of television and radio, range in the millions. Most speech classes, however, consist of between 20 and 30 people—a small- to medium-sized audience. This is a good size for beginning speakers, most of whom are terrified at the prospect of addressing a huge crowd. As you gain more experience, though, you may welcome the challenge of speaking to larger groups. Some speakers actually prefer a large audience to a small one.

No matter what size group you are addressing, bear in mind one basic principle: The larger the audience, the more formal your presentation must be. Audience size may also affect your language, choice of appeals, and use of visual aids.

PHYSICAL SETTING

Which of the following would you rather address?

> An audience assembled immediately after lunch, crammed into an overheated room with inadequate seating
>
> An audience assembled at 10:00 in the morning, comfortably seated in an airy, well-lighted room

Undoubtedly you chose the second option. Any of the adverse conditions listed in the first could seriously impair your audience's willingness to accept your ideas or even listen to you at all.

When you face any speaking situation, it is important to know in advance if there will be any difficulties with the physical setting. For classroom speeches, of course, you already do know. But speeches outside the classroom can present unpleasant surprises unless you do your homework beforehand.

When you are invited to speak, don't be shy about asking questions of the person who arranged the speech. If possible, look over the room a few days in advance, or else arrive early on the day of your speech to inspect the room. If it is too warm or too cold, see about adjusting the thermostat. Check the seating arrangements and the location of the lectern to be sure your audience can see you. In short, do everything you can to control the influence of physical setting on your audience.

What about circumstances you can't control? Your speech *is* scheduled directly after lunch or dinner. The room *is* too small for the audience expected. The heat *cannot* be regulated. Then you are simply going to have to work harder to adapt to these aspects of your listeners' discomfort.

Above all, don't be influenced *yourself* by the poor physical setting. If your audience sees that you are energetic, alert, and involved with your topic, chances are they will forget their discomfort and come right along with you.

DISPOSITION TOWARD THE TOPIC

As we saw in Chapter 5, you should keep your audience in mind when choosing a topic. Ideally, you will pick a topic that suits them as well as it suits you. Once you have your topic, however, you must consider in more detail their interest in the topic, knowledge about it, and attitudes toward it.

Interest

Outside the classroom, people do not often expend the time and effort to attend a speech unless they are interested in the topic. But the members of your speech class are a captive audience. Sometimes they will be deeply interested in your topic, particularly if it relates directly to them. Most of the time they will range from fairly interested to mildly curious to downright indifferent.

One of your tasks will be to assess their interest in advance and to adjust your speech accordingly. Most important, if your topic is not likely to generate great interest, you must take special steps to get your classmates involved. Here is a brief example of how to do this:

> Kevin wanted to persuade his classmates to support legislation that mandates labels on genetically modified food. He started by saying: "Next time you're at the grocery store, take a look around you. The loaves of bread in the corner, the crackers in aisle seven, the zucchini that was going to be part of your healthy dinner—they all contain genetic modifications. . . . The problem is that we have no way of knowing which foods have been modified and which haven't. That's why I'm here to persuade you to support labels that identify genetically modified foods."

connect

View the beginning of "Know What You Are Eating" in the online Media Library for this chapter (Video 6.1).

In the chapters that follow, we'll look closely at all the ways you can develop interest in your topic—by an arresting introduction, provocative supporting materials, vivid language, dynamic delivery, visual aids, and so forth.

Knowledge

There is often a strong correlation between interest in a topic and knowledge about it. People tend to be interested in what they know about. Likewise, they are inclined to learn about subjects that interest them. But there are exceptions. Few students know much about handwriting analysis, yet most would find it an absorbing topic. On the other hand, almost all know a lot about checking books out of the library, but few would find it a fascinating subject for a speech.

Your listeners' knowledge about your topic will to a large extent determine what you can say in your speech. If your listeners know little about your topic—whether or not they find it interesting—you will have to talk at a more elementary level. If they are reasonably well informed, you can take a more technical and detailed approach.

Attitude

The attitude of your listeners toward your topic can be extremely important in determining how you handle the material. If you know in advance the prevailing attitude among members of your audience, you can adjust your speech to address their concerns or to answer their objections. Consider the experiences of the following two students—one who did not account for listener attitude and one who did:

attitude

A frame of mind in favor of or opposed to a person, policy, belief, institution, etc.

> Jen Salerno spoke about family-leave policies in the workplace. On the basis of her research, she believed there was evidence that such policies unfairly benefited a few parents at the expense of other employees, such as single people and childless couples. Unfortunately, rather than citing her sources and acknowledging that her point of view was controversial, Jen presented her material as though it were general knowledge.
>
> The speech was not well received. As one student commented, "You may be right in what you say, but I have trouble believing it. We've heard so much about the need for businesses to be family-friendly—can it all be wrong? I think you would have been more persuasive if you had looked at both sides of the issue rather than just your own."

Had Jen taken the skepticism of her audience into account and established the credibility of her sources, she might have made her arguments more convincing to her audience.

Compare the approach of Erik Petrovich, who also espoused a controversial viewpoint:

connect

View an excerpt from "The Internet and Our Future" in the online Media Library for this chapter (Video 6.2).

> Concerned about the economic woes of his state, Erik decided to give a persuasive speech calling for a sales tax on goods purchased over the Internet. After distributing an audience-analysis questionnaire among his classmates, Erik found that 80 percent of them opposed his plan. They gave two major reasons. First, they believed they were taxed enough already. Second, they thought an Internet sales tax would be too difficult to implement.
>
> Although Erik disagreed with those beliefs, he realized he could neither ignore them nor insult his classmates for holding them. He knew he would have to discuss these points logically and with hard evidence if he were to have any chance of persuading his audience.

As it turned out, Erik did convince some members of the class to reconsider their beliefs. He could not have done so without first investigating what those beliefs were and then adapting his message to them.[5]

DISPOSITION TOWARD THE SPEAKER

Let's return for a moment to Jen's speech about family leave. Jen was a first-year student with no special background in workplace issues. It's not surprising that her classmates took her statements with a large grain of salt. But suppose Jen had been a recognized expert who had conducted research on the impact of family leave on employee attitudes and business productivity. Then her listeners would have found her much more believable. Why? Because an audience's response to a message is invariably colored by their perception of the speaker.

The more competent listeners believe a speaker to be, the more likely they are to accept what he or she says. Likewise, the more listeners believe that a speaker has their best interests at heart, the more likely they are to respond positively to the speaker's message.

Situational audience analysis provides crucial information that a speaker can use when preparing the speech and when adapting to feedback during the speech.

We will come back to this subject in detail when we deal with strategies for persuasive speaking in Chapter 17. For now, keep in mind that your listeners will always have *some* set of attitudes toward you as a speaker. Estimating what those attitudes are and how they will affect your speech is a crucial part of situational audience analysis.

DISPOSITION TOWARD THE OCCASION

It was graduation day at Valencia High School. The mood was festive as the valedictorian spoke eloquently about the special memories of the graduating class. There was laughter when the principal recounted a well-known prank from the class picnic.

Then, Russell Merritt, the mayor, rose to say a few words. "What a pleasure it is to be here," he said. "I'm so proud of you, the graduates, and you, the parents who raised such a terrific group of kids." He continued in this vein for a couple minutes, interrupted by applause as he heaped praise on the students, their parents, their teachers, and their community.

The listeners' enthusiasm faded as Merritt began talking about building a new library to replace the town's old one. This was a controversial issue, and it was going to be voted on in an upcoming referendum. The more the mayor talked about it, the more irritated his audience became. When he concluded, he was met with grudging applause and quite a few hostile glares.

On other occasions, Merritt's remarks would not have touched off such a negative response. But graduation day was understood by the audience to be a celebratory occasion that focused on the students and their achievements. The last thing anyone expected to hear was a political speech. What angered the audience was not what the mayor said, but that he exploited the occasion for his own purposes.

Using public speaking in your CAREER

As a social media consultant for several local businesses, your work on marketing through social networks has attracted a lot of attention in your community. Now the local chamber of commerce has invited you to speak on the subject at next month's meeting.

Having taken a public speaking class in college, you know how important it is to analyze the audience you will be addressing. To prepare for your speech, you have arranged a phone interview with the chamber's president. List (1) the two most important questions you want to ask the president about the demographics of your audience, and (2) the two most important questions you want to ask about the situational traits of your audience. Be specific in your questions and be prepared, if necessary, to explain your choice of questions.

No matter what the situation, listeners have fairly definite ideas about the speeches they consider appropriate. Speakers who seriously violate those expectations can almost always count on infuriating the audience.

Perhaps most important, the occasion will dictate how long a speech should be. When you are invited to speak, the chairperson will usually say how much time you have for your talk. If not, be sure to ask.

Once you know, pare down your speech so it fits easily within the allotted time. Do not exceed that time under any circumstances, for you are likely to see your audience dwindle as you drone on. (This is one reason why most teachers insist that classroom speeches be kept within the designated time limit. It provides crucial training for speeches you will give outside the classroom.)

There are other audience expectations that apply to your classroom situation. One is that speeches will conform to the assignment. Another is that speakers will observe appropriate standards of taste and decorum. Failure to adhere to these expectations may disturb your classmates and will almost certainly damage your grade.

Getting Information About the Audience

Now that you know *what* to learn about an audience, the next question is, *how* do you learn it? A person running for political office can rely on hired professional pollsters. If, as is more likely, you are invited sometime to address a particular group, the person who invites you can usually provide a good sketch of the audience. Ask your contact where you can find out more about the group's history and mission. If you know someone who has spoken to the same group, be sure to sound out that person.

What about your classmates as an audience? You can learn a lot about them just by observation and conversation, but you may want to know more about their knowledge and attitudes on specific speech topics. Some teachers require students to do a formal audience-analysis questionnaire for at least one of their speeches. In addition to providing information about your classroom audience, such a questionnaire gives you practice in developing the skills of audience analysis you will need for speeches after your class is over.

There are three major types of questions to choose from when developing an audience-analysis questionnaire: fixed-alternative questions, scale questions, and open-ended questions.

Fixed-alternative questions, as their name implies, offer a fixed choice between two or more responses. For example:

fixed-alternative questions

Questions that offer a fixed choice between two or more alternatives.

> Do you know what the insanity plea is in the U.S. legal system?
>
> Yes ______________
>
> No ______________
>
> Not sure ______________

By limiting the possible responses, such questions produce clear, unambiguous answers. They also tend to yield superficial answers. Other techniques are needed to get beneath the surface.

Scale questions resemble fixed-alternative questions, but they allow more leeway in responding. For example:

scale questions

Questions that require responses at fixed intervals along a scale of answers.

> How often do you believe the insanity plea is used in U.S. court cases?
>
> Very seldom ______|______|______|______|______ Very often

Questions like these are especially useful for getting at the strength of a respondent's attitudes.

Open-ended questions give maximum leeway in responding. For example:

open-ended questions

Questions that allow respondents to answer however they want.

> What is your opinion about the insanity plea in U.S. court cases?
>
> Under what circumstances do you think the insanity plea is legitimate in a criminal trial?

Although open-ended questions invite more detailed responses than the other two types of questions, they also increase the likelihood of getting answers that do not give the kind of information you need.

Because each type of question has its advantages and disadvantages, many questionnaires contain all three types. Figure 6.1 (page 112) shows a questionnaire that was distributed before a classroom speech on volunteering. By using all three types of questions, the speaker did two things—elicited specific information about the audience and probed more deeply into their attitudes toward the speech topic. The results broke down as follows:

1. Roughly half of the class had not participated as a volunteer. Therefore, the speaker knew she would have to explain clearly what was involved in this kind of work.
2. Five students knew someone close to them who had benefited from volunteer work by a community, religious, or charitable organization; most said they were not sure. Thus the speaker could not depend on a high degree of personal involvement among the audience.

FIGURE 6.1 Sample Questionnaire

Two fixed-alternative questions establish the listeners' level of knowledge about and degree of involvement with the topic.

1. Have you ever engaged in volunteer work for a community, religious, or charitable organization?

   Yes __________
   No __________

2. Have you or anyone close to you ever benefited from the volunteer work of a community, religious, or charitable organization?

   Yes __________
   No __________
   Not sure __________

This scale question is designed to show the attitudes of listeners who have participated in volunteer work.

3. If you have engaged in volunteer work, how would you rate the experience?

   ☐ Very rewarding
   ☐ Somewhat rewarding
   ☐ Neutral
   ☐ Somewhat unrewarding
   ☐ Very unrewarding

Another scale question gauges the listeners' sense of social obligation.

4. Do you agree or disagree with the following statement? To the extent possible, people have an obligation to help those in less fortunate circumstances.

   ☐ Strongly agree
   ☐ Mildly agree
   ☐ Undecided
   ☐ Mildly disagree
   ☐ Strongly disagree

Two open-ended questions help gauge the listeners' disposition toward volunteer work. The last question is especially important. It probes the specific issues the speaker needs to address for listeners who have not engaged in volunteer work.

5. If you have worked as a volunteer, do you plan to do so again? Why or why not?

6. If you have not worked as a volunteer, what is your major reason for not doing so? Please explain.

3. All but one of the students who had engaged in volunteer work rated it "very rewarding" or "somewhat rewarding." Not only would this portion of the audience be inclined to support the speaker's position, but the speaker could point to their attitude as proof that working as a volunteer is a rewarding experience.
4. Nearly 75 percent of the respondents either "strongly agreed" or "mildly agreed" that people have an obligation to help those in less fortunate circumstances. The speaker could therefore depend on an audience favorably inclined to the basic premise underlying volunteer work.

5. Answers to the fifth question—"If you have worked as a volunteer, do you plan to do so again? Why or why not?"—were interesting. All the respondents indicated that they planned to engage in volunteer work again, but most said they were not likely to do so while in college because they were too busy with other activities.
6. Nearly 90 percent of the students who had not engaged in volunteer work stated that their major reason for not doing so was a lack of time. In combination with the answers to question 5, these responses showed that the speaker would have to deal persuasively with the time issue if she were to be successful in convincing people to volunteer while they were enrolled in school.

connect

View how the speaker in Video 6.2 used an audience-analysis questionnaire in his speech (Video 6.3).

This questionnaire revealed a great deal about the listeners' knowledge, attitudes, and concerns. In putting together your own questionnaire, keep the following principles in mind:

1. Plan the questionnaire carefully to elicit precisely the information you need.
2. Use all three types of questions—fixed-alternative, scale, and open-ended.
3. Make sure the questions are clear and unambiguous.
4. Keep the questionnaire relatively brief.

Adapting to the Audience

Once you have completed the audience analysis, you should have a pretty clear picture of your listeners. But this does not guarantee a successful speech. The key is how well you *use* what you know in preparing and presenting the speech.

This point deserves special attention because it poses one of the hardest tasks facing novice speakers. Most people can identify the major characteristics of their audience, but many have trouble *adapting* their ideas to the audience. There are two major stages in the process of audience adaptation. The first occurs before the speech, as part of your preparation and rehearsal. The second occurs during the presentation of the speech itself.

AUDIENCE ADAPTATION BEFORE THE SPEECH

As we have seen, you must keep your audience in mind at every stage of speech preparation. This involves more than simply remembering who your listeners will be. Above all, it means two things: (1) assessing how your audience is likely to respond to what you say in your speech, and (2) adjusting what you say to make it as clear, appropriate, and convincing as possible.

This is not always easy to do. We are all so wrapped up in our own ideas and concerns that we have trouble seeing things from other people's perspective—especially if their perspective is different from ours. To step outside your own frame of reference and see things from another person's point of view is a real achievement.

Yet this is what a successful speaker eventually learns to do. You must submerge your own views so completely that you can adopt, temporarily, those of your listeners. When you do this, you will begin to hear your speech through the ears of your audience and to adjust it accordingly. Try to imagine what they will like, what they will dislike, where they will have doubts or questions, whether they will need more details here or fewer there, what will interest them and what will not.

At every point you must *anticipate* how your audience will respond. Put yourself in their place and respond to your speech as they would.

Here is how one student worked out his problems of audience adaptation:

> Juan Ruiz, a junior geology major, decided to give an informative speech about how earthquakes occur. From his audience analysis, he learned that only a handful of his classmates knew much about geology. Juan realized that he would have to present his speech at an elementary level and with a minimum of scientific language.
>
> As he prepared the speech, Juan kept asking himself, "How can I make this clear and meaningful to someone who knows nothing about earthquakes or geological principles?" Because he was speaking in the Midwest, he decided to begin by noting that the most severe earthquake in American history took place not in California, but at New Madrid, Missouri, in 1811. If such an earthquake happened today, it would be felt from the Rocky Mountains to the Atlantic Ocean and would flatten most of the cities in the Mississippi Valley. That, he figured, should get his classmates' attention.
>
> Throughout the body of his speech, Juan dealt only with the basic mechanics of earthquakes and carefully avoided technical terms such as "asthenosphere," "lithosphere," and "subduction zones." He also prepared PowerPoint slides to illustrate his points.
>
> To be absolutely safe, Juan asked his roommate—who was not a geology major—to listen to the speech. "Stop me," he said, "anytime I say something you don't understand." Juan's roommate stopped him four times, and at each spot Juan worked out a way to make his point more clearly. Finally, he had a speech that was interesting and perfectly understandable to his audience.

As you work on your speeches, try to keep your listeners constantly in mind. Anticipate how they will respond to your ideas. Be creative in thinking about ways to adapt your message to them. Like Juan, you will give a much better speech.

AUDIENCE ADAPTATION DURING THE SPEECH

No matter how hard you prepare ahead of time, things may not go exactly as planned on the day of your speech. For speeches in the classroom, you may find that the projector for your visual aids is not available or that another student has the same topic as you. For speeches outside the classroom, you might learn that the audience will be much larger (or smaller) than you had anticipated, or that the amount of time available for your speech has been cut in half because a previous speaker has droned on for too long.

If something like this happens to you, don't panic. Find another way to present your visual aids. Modify your introduction to mention the other student's speech on your topic. Adjust your delivery to the changed audience size. If you find that you have less time than you had planned, condense your speech to its most essential points and present them in the time available. Your listeners will sympathize with your predicament and will appreciate

In political campaigns, poll-taking helps the candidates keep track of public opinion. For classroom speeches, you can use an audience-analysis questionnaire to gauge the knowledge and opinions of your listeners.

your regard for their time. This will more than compensate for your lost speaking time.

Finally, be sure to keep an eye out during your speech for audience feedback. If your listeners are sitting forward in their chairs, looking at you with interest, and nodding their heads in approval, you can assume that things are going well. But suppose you find them frowning or responding with quizzical looks. Then you may need to back up and go over your point again, as in this example:

> Saanvi Shah, an economics major, had worked diligently to make sure her speech on digital currency was not too technical for her classmates. She explained everything from the ground up, prepared two excellent visual aids, and practiced giving the speech to her best friend, a music major and self-confessed "economics dummy."
>
> On the day of Saanvi's speech, everything went well until she got to her second main point, when she noticed that several of her classmates seemed puzzled by the process of "mining" in digital currency. Knowing they would be lost for the rest of the speech if they didn't understand mining, Saanvi paused and said, "I can see some of you are confused by my explanation. Let me try it again from a different angle."
>
> As Saanvi went through the material again, she could see her classmates nodding their heads in understanding. She could now go on with the rest of her speech, confident that her audience was ready to go with her.

Adapting to your audience is one of the most important keys to successful public speaking. Like other aspects of speechmaking, it is sometimes easier said than done. But once you master it, you'll see that it pays dividends in more personal facets of your life—when you adapt to an audience of one.

Summary

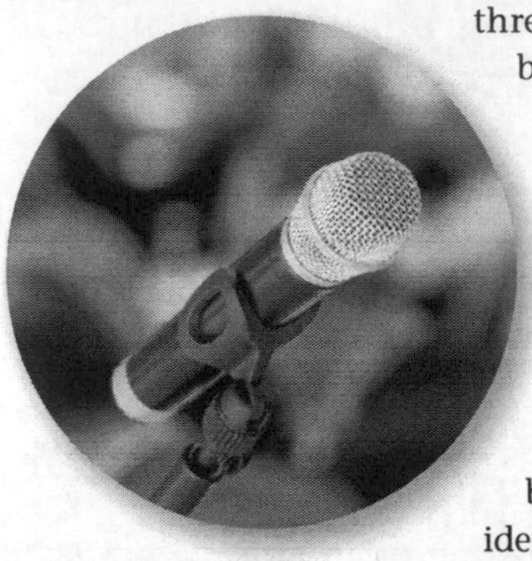

Good speakers are audience-centered. They know that the aim of speechmaking is to gain a desired response from listeners. When working on your speeches, keep three questions in mind: To whom am I speaking? What do I want them to know, believe, or do as a result of my speech? What is the most effective way of composing and presenting my speech to accomplish that aim?

To be an effective speaker, you should know something about the psychology of audiences. People are egocentric. They typically approach speeches with one question uppermost in mind: "Why is this important to *me*?" Therefore, you need to study your audience and adapt your speech to their beliefs and interests.

The first stage in learning about your audience is to identify demographic traits such as age, gender, religion, sexual orientation, group membership, and racial, ethnic, or cultural background. The second stage is identifying traits of the audience unique to the speaking situation. These traits include the size of the audience, attitudes influenced by the physical setting, and your listeners' disposition toward the topic, toward you as a speaker, and toward the occasion.

For speeches outside the classroom, you can best get information about the audience by asking the person who invites you to speak. For classroom speeches, you can learn about your audience by observation and conversation. You also can circulate an audience-analysis questionnaire.

Once you complete the audience analysis, you must adapt your speech so it will be clear and convincing to your listeners. Put yourself in their place. Try to hear the speech as they will. Anticipate questions and objections, and try to answer them in advance. When you deliver your speech, keep an eye out for audience feedback and adjust your remarks in response.

Key Terms

audience-centeredness (98)
egocentrism (100)
demographic audience analysis (101)
stereotyping (101)
situational audience analysis (106)
attitude (108)
fixed-alternative questions (111)
scale questions (111)
open-ended questions (111)

Review Questions

After reading this chapter, you should be able to answer the following questions:

1. Why must a public speaker be audience-centered?
2. What does it mean to say that people are egocentric? What implications does the egocentrism of audiences hold for you as a public speaker?
3. What are the six demographic traits of audiences discussed in this chapter? Why is each important to audience analysis?

4. What is situational audience analysis? What factors do you need to consider in situational audience analysis?
5. How can you get information about an audience?
6. What are the three kinds of questions used in questionnaires? Why is it a good idea to use all three in audience analysis?
7. What methods can you use to adapt your speech to your audience before the speech? During the speech?

connect

For further review, go to the LearnSmart study module for this chapter.

Exercises for Critical Thinking

1. Advertisers are usually very conscious of their audience. Choose an issue of a popular magazine such as *Time, Sports Illustrated, Vanity Fair, Rolling Stone,* or the like. From that issue select three advertisements to analyze. Try to determine the audience being appealed to in each advertisement, and analyze the appeals (verbal and visual) used to persuade buyers. How might the appeals differ if the ads were designed to persuade a different audience?
2. Below are three general speech topics and, for each, two hypothetical audiences to which a speech might be delivered. For each topic, write a brief paragraph explaining how you might adjust your specific purpose and message according to the demographic characteristics of the audience.

   a. *Topic:* "Cryptography"

   Audience #1: 50% computer science majors, 30% physics majors, 20% fine arts majors

   Audience #2: 40% business majors, 40% history majors, 20% computer science majors

   b. *Topic:* "Sexual Assault: The Biggest Campus Crime"

   Audience #1: 80% female, 20% male

   Audience #2: 80% male, 20% female

   c. *Topic:* "The Impeachment of Bill Clinton"

   Audience #1: Day class: 70% age 18 to 22, 30% age 23 and over

   Audience #2: Evening class: 50% age 35 and over, 30% age 23 to 34, 20% age 18 to 22

3. For your next speech, design and circulate among your classmates an audience-analysis questionnaire like that discussed on pages 110–113. Use all three kinds of questions explained in the text: fixed-alternative, scale, and open-ended. After you have tabulated the results of the questionnaire, write an analysis explaining what the questionnaire reveals about your audience and what steps you must take to adapt your speech to the audience.

7

Gathering Materials

- **Using Your Own Knowledge and Experience**
- **Doing Library Research**
- **Searching the Internet**
- **Interviewing**
- **Tips for Doing Research**

Suppose you are planning a trip to Italy. You want to know the major sites so you can work out an itinerary. You also need to know what things will cost, where the hostels are located, and how the train and bus systems work. How do you go about gathering all this information?

You can talk to people who have traveled in Italy and get ideas from them. You can consult guidebooks. You can search the Internet for information. If you have traveled to Europe before, you can draw on that experience. Since you want your trip to be a success, you gather as much information as you can before you leave.

Gathering materials for a speech is like gathering information for any project. There are many resources available if you take advantage of them. You can interview people with specialized knowledge. You can do research on the Internet or in the library. Sometimes you can use yourself as a resource—whenever you have personal experience or above-average knowledge about a subject. Let's turn first to the resource of your own experience.

Using Your Own Knowledge and Experience

Everybody is an expert on something, whether it is video games, child care, or backpacking. As we saw in Chapter 5, we often speak best about subjects with which we are familiar. This is why many teachers encourage students to capitalize on their own knowledge and experience in developing speech topics.

When you choose a topic from your own experience, you may be tempted to depersonalize it by relying solely on facts and figures from books and the Internet. Such outside information is almost always necessary. But supplementing it with the personal touch can really bring your speeches to life.

One student, afflicted with diabetes, chose to explain how a person can live with the disease on a daily basis. He cited statistics on the incidence of diabetes in the United States, identified symptoms of the disease, and explained how it is treated. Along the way, he illustrated his points by talking about his personal experiences. Here is part of what he said:

> Being a diabetic presents a challenge one cannot afford to lose. On a personal note, I have tried not to let my diabetes affect my lifestyle. Last year, I spent nine months traveling in Central and South America. The trip was very memorable, but I had one particularly frightening experience that quickly makes you realize just how vulnerable a diabetic is. On the fifth day of a two-week excursion down the Amazon River, our canoe tipped, dumping everything into the water.
>
> Although I recovered my pack, part of its contents—including my insulin—were swallowed up by the river. Without insulin, I could not eat any food. If I did, my blood sugar level would become too high and I could eventually go into convulsions, slip into a coma, and die. We returned back up the Amazon and traveled three days until we reached the first village and I could radio for more medicine. I was hot and hungry, but alive.

This speech has color and emotion. By drawing on his own experience, the speaker conveyed his point more meaningfully than he could have in any other way.

Even if your life stories are not that dramatic, you can still put them to work for you. By thinking over your past experiences—gathering material from yourself—you can find many supporting materials for your speeches.

Doing Library Research

Even in this age of the Internet, you will get some of the information for your speeches from the library. It contains many resources to help you find what you need, including librarians, the catalogue, reference works, and databases. We'll look at each in turn.

LIBRARIANS

Too often students waste their time wandering aimlessly in the library because they are afraid to ask for assistance. They don't want to appear ignorant or to

FIGURE 7.1 Sample Catalogue Entry for a Book

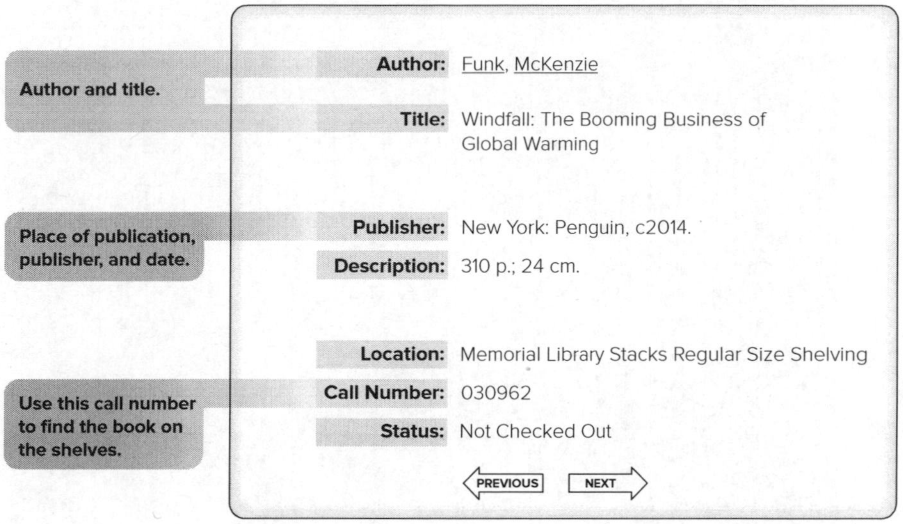

"bother" anyone. But would you be as sensitive about asking a doctor for help with a medical problem? Librarians are experts in their own field, trained in library use and research methods. If you have a question, don't hesitate to ask a librarian. He or she can help you find your way, locate sources, even track down a specific piece of information.

catalogue

A listing of all the books, periodicals, and other resources owned by a library.

THE CATALOGUE

The catalogue lists all the books, periodicals, and other resources owned by the library. Although there are many different computer systems for library catalogues, most allow you to search for books by author, title, subject, or keyword. The catalogue also tells you whether the book you want is available or is already checked out.

Figure 7.1 above shows a sample catalogue entry for a book. The key to finding the book on the shelves is the *call number*. Once you have the call number, all you have to do is find the right section of the shelves (or stacks, as they are called in some libraries) and retrieve your book.

call number

A number used in libraries to classify books and periodicals and to indicate where they can be found on the shelves.

REFERENCE WORKS

Reference works are usually kept in a part of the library called the reference section. The right reference work can save you hours of time by putting at your fingertips a wealth of information that might be difficult to locate through the library catalogue. The major kinds of reference works you are likely to use for your speeches are encyclopedias, yearbooks, quotation books, and biographical aids.

reference work

A work that synthesizes a large amount of related information for easy access by researchers.

Encyclopedias

We are all familiar with general encyclopedias such as the *Encyclopaedia Britannica*. But there are also special encyclopedias that cover their fields in more depth than do general encyclopedias. Some of the most frequently used

Library research is vital for most speeches. Knowing the resources available in your library and how to use them efficiently will make the research process much more productive.

special encyclopedias are the *African American Encyclopedia,* the *Encyclopedia of Religion,* and the *McGraw-Hill Encyclopedia of Science and Technology.*

Yearbooks

As the name implies, yearbooks are published annually. They contain an amazing amount of current information that would otherwise be all but impossible to track down. Two of the most valuable yearbooks are *Facts on File* and *World Almanac and Book of Facts.*

Quotation Books

The best-known collection of quotations is *Bartlett's Familiar Quotations.* With more than 25,000 quotations from historical and contemporary figures, it has long been regarded as an indispensable source for speakers and writers alike. Other excellent quotation books include the *Oxford Dictionary of Quotations, The New Quotable Woman,* and *Ancient Echoes: Native American Words of Wisdom.*

Biographical Aids

When you need information about people in the news, you can turn to one of the many reference works that contain brief life and career facts about contemporary men and women. The most popular biographical aids are published by Who's Who, which produces such titles as *International Who's Who* and *Who's Who in America.* More specialized biographical aids include *Contemporary Black Biography, Dictionary of Hispanic Biography,* and *Who's Who Among Asian Americans.*

NEWSPAPER AND PERIODICAL DATABASES

Newspaper and periodical databases allow you to locate articles in thousands of publications, including *Time, Atlantic,* the *New York Times,* and the *Wall*

Street Journal. Type a subject in your database's search box, and citations for articles on your subject will appear on screen.

In some cases, you may get an *abstract* of the article in addition to—or instead of—the full article. Keep in mind that the abstract is only a summary of the article. You should *never* cite an article in your speech on the basis of the abstract alone. Always consult the full article.

The exact databases you can use will depend on what is available through your library. Here are three major databases; odds are that your library will have at least one of them.

newspaper and periodical database

A research aid that catalogues articles from a large number of magazines, journals, and newspapers.

ProQuest. An excellent database that indexes thousands of periodicals and newspapers. Figure 7.2 below shows a sample screen from ProQuest with a magazine citation and abstract.

LexisNexis Academic. This database provides full-text access to more than 15,000 information sources, including magazines, legal documents, and television broadcast transcripts. LexisNexis also furnishes articles from more than 350 U.S. and international newspapers.

World News Digest. Provides full-text access to news articles from 1940 to the present. Allows searching by topic, country, and decade.

abstract

A summary of a magazine or journal article, written by someone other than the original author.

ACADEMIC DATABASES

At colleges and universities around the world, experts are researching almost every aspect of the natural world and human society. Their work appears in respected, peer-reviewed journals. Academic databases make those journals available to you.

academic database

A database that catalogues articles from scholarly journals.

FIGURE 7.2 Sample Periodical Entry from ProQuest

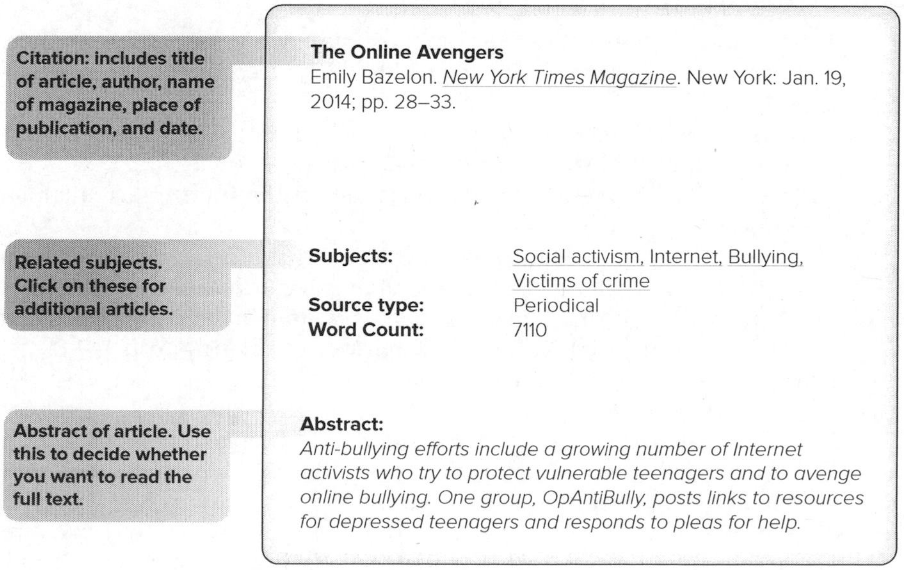

The best place to find scholarly research is in one of the following academic databases. Because each searches across different academic disciplines, you should be able to find what you need in one of the databases.

Academic OneFile. Provides access to millions of scholarly articles in areas from economics and sociology to science and medicine.

JSTOR. In addition to cataloguing more than 1,400 academic journals in various disciplines, JSTOR allows you to search images, letters, and other primary documents.

Google Scholar. A fast and easy way to search a broad range of scholarly literature. Advanced search tools let you narrow your search by author, publication, date, and subject matter.

Searching the Internet

The Internet has been called the world's biggest library. But unlike a library, the Internet has no central information desk, no librarians, no catalogue, and no reference section. Nor does it have a person or department in charge of determining whether materials are of high quality. You can unearth a great deal of information on the Internet, but you cannot always find the same range and depth as in a good library. This is why experts advise that you use the Internet to supplement, not to replace, library research.

In this section, we will look at ways you can go beyond browsing the Web and turn it into a powerful research tool for your speeches. After discussing search engines and other resources for conducting efficient, focused inquiries, we'll explain how to evaluate the reliability and objectivity of the research materials you find on the Web.

SEARCH ENGINES

Search engines are the key to finding materials on the Internet. There are numerous search engines, but the most widely used by far is Google, which provides access to billions of Web pages.

The question is: How can you use Google and other search engines *systematically* to find what you need? The answer is: Develop a search strategy that will allow you to zero in precisely on the information required for your speech.

Suppose you are using Google to look for information on the riskiness of payday loans—those short-term, high-interest loans that target people in already-difficult financial straits. If you simply search for *payday loans*, you will come up with hundreds of businesses offering to give you such a loan.

Instead, you should narrow your search by looking for *dangers of payday loans* or *hidden costs of payday loans*. Another option is to type a question into the search box: *What are the financial risks of taking out a payday loan?* or *What are the legalities of payday loans?*

Google also lets you focus your efforts by identifying the kind of research source that will serve you best. Once your terms are in the Google

Research gives speakers facts and figures to support their ideas. Dr. Nici Vance uses a wide range of supporting materials in her talks about the use of criminal anthropology in solving cold cases.

search box, you can click on *news* to explore recent news stories. You can also click on *images, videos, blogs,* and *books* to search those kinds of resources.

Of course, you will have to adjust your search terms depending on your subject and the kinds of material you are looking for, but once you learn the basic principles for doing precise, pinpointed searches, you will greatly increase your odds of finding exactly what you need for your speeches.

SPECIALIZED RESEARCH RESOURCES

Search engines are extremely helpful, but they are not the only vehicles for finding information. The following specialized resources concentrate on sites that are most likely to be helpful as you work on your speeches.[1]

Virtual Libraries

Search engines help you find what's on the Internet, but they don't evaluate the quality of the sources they retrieve. Librarians and other information specialists are working to make it easier to locate reliable, high-quality Web resources. One result of their efforts is virtual libraries—search engines that combine Internet technology with traditional library methods of assessing data.

virtual library

A search engine that combines Internet technology with traditional library methods of cataloguing and assessing data.

The best virtual library on the Internet is a merger of two previous virtual libraries—Librarians' Internet Index and Internet Public Library. Now called ipl2 (www.ipl.org), this site has more than 20,000 entries organized into 12 main topics, including arts and humanities, education, and health and medical sciences (see Figure 7.3 on page 126). In addition, ipl2 links to a large number of reference sites, as well as to a wide range of constantly evolving special collections.

FIGURE 7.3 Subject screen from ipl2

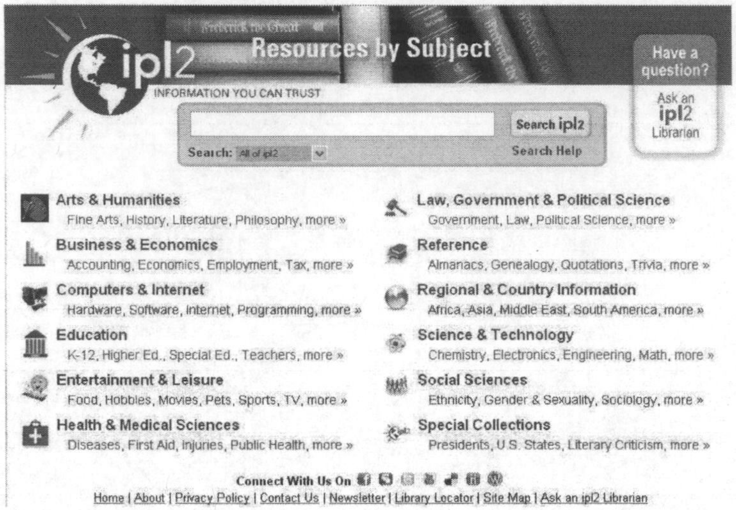

Government Resources

One of the great strengths of the Internet as a research tool is the access it provides to government documents and publications. Whether you are looking for information from the federal government or from a state or local agency, chances are you can find it by starting your search at one of these Web sites:

> *USA.gov* (www.usa.gov). One-stop shopping for all U.S. government information on the Internet. Provides links to Web pages from federal, state, local, and tribal governments.
>
> *United States Census Bureau* (www.census.gov). Contains a wealth of statistical information on social, political, and economic aspects of American life. Much of the information is organized in table form.
>
> *World Factbook* (www.cia.gov/library/publications/the-world-factbook). Published annually by the Central Intelligence Agency, the *World Factbook* is a rich compendium of information on every country in the world. Topics include people, government, economy, communication, transportation, and transnational issues.

Wikipedia

With more than 4.5 million articles in English alone, Wikipedia is the biggest encyclopedia in human history. Each month, some 500 million people access one or more of its articles, making it the fifth most visited Web site in the world.

But is Wikipedia a reliable source of information? Several years ago, it was not. Today, however, its reliability ratings compare favorably with those for print encyclopedias.[2] Major articles have been edited and refined over time to improve currency and accuracy. Articles still in development are flagged so readers know not to take their information at face value.

The most important thing to know about Wikipedia is that it can be a good place to *start* learning about a topic, but it is not a good place to end. Because of its convenience, Wikipedia is used by many people—including teachers and journalists—as a source of basic information. But experienced researchers know not to rely on it as their sole source of information.

One benefit of Wikipedia is that its major articles are followed by an extensive set of additional resources. Those resources include footnotes, a list of references, external links, and, in some cases, video and/or still images. If you take advantage of these resources, they will lead you to a vast amount of information beyond that in Wikipedia.

EVALUATING INTERNET DOCUMENTS

When you do research in a library, everything you find has been evaluated in one way or another before it gets to you. Books, magazines, and journals have editorial procedures to determine whether a given work should or should not be published. Once a work is published, it has to be approved by the acquisitions staff for inclusion in the library.

The Internet, of course, is a very different story. Anyone with a computer and access to the Internet can share his or her opinions with a discussion group, publish an electronic newsletter, or create a personal Web page. Never has the adage been more true than when applied to the Internet: "Don't believe everything you read."

In Chapter 8, we will discuss how to judge the soundness of supporting materials in general. Here we look at three criteria you can use to help distinguish between the jewels and the junk on the Internet.[3]

checklist

Evaluating Internet Documents

YES	NO	
☐	☐	1. Is the author of the document clearly identified?
☐	☐	2. If the author is identified, is he or she an expert on the topic?
☐	☐	3. If the author is not an expert, can his or her opinions be accepted as objective and unbiased?
☐	☐	4. If the author is not identified, can the sponsoring organization be determined?
☐	☐	5. Does the sponsoring organization have a reputation for expertise and objectivity?
☐	☐	6. Does the document include a copyright date, publication date, or date of last revision?
☐	☐	7. If a date is included, is the document recent enough to cite in my speech?

Authorship

Is the author of the Web document you are assessing clearly identified? If so, what are his or her qualifications? Is the author an expert on the topic? Can her or his data and opinions be accepted as objective and unbiased? Just as you should not cite a book or magazine article without identifying the author and his or her credentials, so you should not cite an electronic work in the absence of this information.

In a book or magazine article, information about the author is usually fairly easy to find. Too often, this is not true on the Internet. If you can't find information about the author in the document itself, look for a link to the author's homepage or to another site that explains the author's credentials.

Often you can learn about an author by typing his or her name in the Google search box. If the author is an accepted authority on the subject, there's a good chance Google will turn up information about his or her credentials, publications, and affiliation.

Sponsorship

Many Web documents are published by businesses, government agencies, public-interest groups, and the like rather than by individual authors. In such cases, you must judge whether the sponsoring organization is impartial enough to cite in your speech. Is the organization objective in its research and fair-minded in its statements? Is it economically unbiased with regard to the issue under discussion? Does it have a history of accuracy and nonpartisanship?

sponsoring organization

An organization that, in the absence of a clearly identified author, is responsible for the content of a document on the Internet.

Over the years, some organizations have developed strong reputations for their expertise and objectivity. Many of these are public-interest groups such as Consumers Union, Common Cause, and the American Cancer Society. Others include the National Archives, Centers for Disease Control, and similar government agencies. Private think tanks such as RAND, the Cato Institute, and the Brookings Institution often have definite political leanings but are usually well respected for the quality and substance of their research.

On the other hand, you need to be wary of groups that may sound respectable but in fact are not. Don't let a fancy-sounding name trick you into accepting a sponsoring organization's credibility at face value. One way to gauge the credibility of an organization is to type its name into Google. If commentators have raised serious questions about an organization, those questions will usually surface in the first few pages of search results. You can also check the *About* link on the organization's homepage. Often the resulting screen will identify the site's founders, purpose, and/or philosophy.

What if you can't verify the credentials of an author or identify a credible sponsoring organization for an Internet document? The answer is easy: Don't use the document in your speech!

Recency

One of the advantages of using the Internet for research is that it often has more recent information than you can find in print sources. But just because a document is on the Internet does not mean its facts and figures are up-to-the-minute.

Using public speaking in your CAREER

After receiving your master's degree in education administration, you took a job at the state department of education. At the request of the governor, your section of the department has developed a new early childhood intervention program for children from impoverished households.

Now you have been asked to help publicize the program and to build support for it. You will be speaking to church groups, teachers' associations, family advocacy groups, and others with an interest in children's welfare. You want to prepare a talk that makes good use of statistics and expert testimony to demonstrate the value of early childhood education programs, especially for poor children.

As part of your research, you decide to look on the Web for supporting materials. List three reputable Web sites that provide useful statistics or testimony on the value of early childhood education. Explain why each Web site is reputable and list one statistic or expert quotation you obtain from each source.

The best way to determine the recency of an Internet document is to look for a copyright date, publication date, or date of last revision at the top or bottom of the document. If you are using a source located through a virtual library, you can usually be confident of its currency, as well as its objectivity and reliability. News, government, and academic sites also usually include the date on which a document was last updated.

Once you know the date of the document, you can determine whether it is current enough to use in your speech. This is especially important with regard to statistics, which you should never cite from an undated source, whether in print or on the Internet.

Of course, the date of a Web page is easy to change, so someone who wants to make information appear up-to-date can easily do so. But if you have already verified the credibility of the author and the sponsoring organization, you can usually assume that the date of the information is valid. If you can't find the date on which a Web document was created or last modified, search for another work whose recency you can verify.

Interviewing

Most people think of interviewing in terms of job interviews or conversations with celebrities. But there is another kind of interview—the research (or investigative) interview. Among journalists, it is a time-honored way to collect information. It is also an excellent way to gather materials for speeches.

When done well, interviewing (like many things) looks deceptively easy. In practice, it is a complex and demanding art. The principles of effective interviewing fall into three groups—what to do before the interview, what to do during the interview, and what to do after the interview.

To illustrate, we'll follow the entire interview process for a hypothetical speech about current issues in college athletics.

BEFORE THE INTERVIEW

research interview

An interview conducted to gather information for a speech.

The outcome of most interviews is decided by how well the interviewer prepares. Here are five steps you should take ahead of time to ensure a successful outcome.

Define the Purpose of the Interview

You have done Internet and library research about current issues in college athletics and have a good grasp of the major points of view. But you still have many questions about the situation at your school. You decide that the only way to get answers is to interview someone associated with the athletic program. In that decision you have begun to formulate a purpose for the interview.

Decide Whom to Interview

There are several possibilities, but you elect to start at the top—with the athletic director. That may seem a bit presumptuous, but in dealing with administrative organizations, it is usually best to go to the leaders first. They are likely to have a broad understanding of the issues. And if you need more specific information, they can get it for you or put you in touch with the right person.

Arrange the Interview

Because the athletic director is a busy person, you work out a plan for setting up the interview. Knowing that it's easier to brush off someone over e-mail or the telephone than in person, you go to the athletic office to request the interview. The athletic director agrees, and you set up the interview for three days later.

Decide Whether to Record the Interview

The major advantage of recording an interview is that it gives you an exact record you can check later for direct quotes and important facts. Even if you record the interview, however, you should still take notes by hand in case of technical malfunctions.

If the athletic director does not want the interview recorded, you will need to rely solely on your handwritten notes. Whatever you do, *never* record a conversation without the knowledge or consent of the person being interviewed. Not only is it unethical to do so, but the interviewee is bound to find out and you will only cause yourself trouble.

Prepare Your Questions

You now face the most important of your preinterview tasks—working out the questions you will ask. You should devise questions that are sensible, intelligent, and meaningful. Here are some types of questions to *avoid:*

- Questions you can answer without the interview. (How many sports does your school offer? What is the size of its athletic budget?) Queries like these just waste the subject's time and make you look foolish. Research this information before the interview.

- Leading questions. (Opinion polls show that most Americans believe athletics today have little relation to the academic purposes of a college education. You *do* think it's a problem, too, *don't you*?)
- Hostile, loaded questions. (I think it's disgraceful that many schools spend gobs of money on salaries for football and basketball coaches. Don't you think good teachers for all students are more important than coaches for a few athletes? What do you say to *that,* hmmm?)

You need not shy away from tough questions; just phrase them as neutrally as possible and save them until near the end of the interview. That way, if your interviewee becomes irritated or uncooperative, you'll still get most of the information you want.

Although some experienced journalists conduct interviews with only a few key-word notes on the areas to be covered, you want to be sure not to forget anything during the interview. So you arrange your questions in the order you want to ask them and take the list with you to the interview.

DURING THE INTERVIEW

Every interview is unique. Because the session will seldom go exactly as you plan, you need to be alert and flexible. Here are several steps you can take to make things proceed smoothly.

Dress Appropriately and Be on Time

The athletic director has a busy schedule and is doing you a favor by agreeing to an interview, so you show up on time. Since the interview is a special occasion, you dress appropriately. This is one way of confirming that you regard the interview as serious business.

Interviewing people with expertise on your speech topic can provide valuable information. When conducting an interview, be sure to listen attentively and to take accurate notes.

Repeat the Purpose of the Interview

The athletic director invites you into the office; you exchange a few introductory remarks. Now, before you plunge into your questions, you take a moment to restate the purpose of the interview. You are more likely to get clear, helpful answers if your subject knows why you are following a certain line of questioning.

Set Up the Recorder, if You Are Using One

If your subject has agreed to being recorded, keep one principle in mind: The recorder should be as casual and inconspicuous as possible. Most cell phones now offer applications for audio recording, giving you an easy way to capture the interview.

Keep the Interview on Track

Your goal in the interview is to get answers to the questions you have prepared. Suppose, however, that in answering one of your questions, the athletic director brings up an important point that is not covered on your list of questions. Rather than ignoring the point, you decide to pursue the new issue. You pose a couple of questions about it, get helpful answers, then return to your prepared questions.

Throughout the interview, you pursue new leads when they appear, improvise follow-up questions when called for, then move on again in an orderly fashion. When the interview is over, you have answers to all your prepared questions—and a lot more.

Listen Carefully

During the interview, you listen attentively to the athletic director's answers. When you don't understand something, you ask for clarification. Chances are the athletic director has been misquoted more than once in the press, so he or she will be happy to oblige.

Don't Overstay Your Welcome

Keep within the stipulated time period for the interview, unless your subject clearly wants to prolong the session. When the interview is over, you thank the athletic director for taking the time to talk with you.

AFTER THE INTERVIEW

Although the interview is over, the interviewing process is not. You must now review and transcribe your notes.

Review Your Notes as Soon as Possible

When you leave the athletic director's office, the interview is fresh in your mind. You know what the cryptic comments and scrawls in your notes mean. But as time passes, the details will become hazy. Don't let something like this true story happen to you:

> Years ago, a prominent woman—writer and diplomat—was being interviewed by a young reporter. Among other things, the reporter asked about hobbies and leisure activities. The woman replied that she enjoyed skeet shooting and raised Siamese cats. The reporter scribbled in her notes "shoots" and "cats"—but

didn't bother to put a comma or a dash between the words. The interview was published. And ever since, that prominent woman has been trying to live down the reputation that she "shoots cats."

In reviewing your notes, try to concentrate on two things—discovering the main points that emerged during the interview and pulling out specific information that might be useful in your speech.

Transcribe Your Notes

Once you settle on the most important ideas and information from the interview, you should transcribe that material so it is in the same format as the rest of your research notes (see pages 134–136). By putting all your research notes in a consistent format, you can arrange and rearrange them easily when you start to organize your speech.[4]

Tips for Doing Research

Few people regard doing research as one of life's great joys. But there are ways to make it less tedious and more productive. Here are four ways that are guaranteed to help.

START EARLY

The biggest mistake students make when faced with a research project is waiting too long to begin. The longer you wait, the more problems you will encounter. You may find that a vital book has been checked out of the library or that you no longer have time to arrange a crucial interview. No matter what kind of research you do, you can be sure of one thing: It will *always* take longer than you expect.

Starting early also gives you plenty of time to think about what you find. In researching, you will collect much more material than you will actually use. Preparing a speech is a little like constructing a jigsaw puzzle. Once you gather the pieces, you have to decide how they fit together. The more time you give yourself, the more likely you are to get the pieces to fit just right.

MAKE A PRELIMINARY BIBLIOGRAPHY

In your research, you will run across the titles of books, magazine articles, Internet documents, and so on that look as if they might contain helpful information about your speech topic. Enter *each* item you find in your preliminary bibliography, even though you don't know whether you will use it in your speech. As a result, you may have 15 or 20 works in your preliminary bibliography. But remember that you have not yet examined all those works. Of the 15 or 20 preliminary sources, only 7 or 8 are likely to be of much use. Those final sources will be listed on the bibliography you turn in with your speech outline (see Chapter 11, page 209).

preliminary bibliography

A list compiled early in the research process of works that look as if they might contain helpful information about a speech topic.

There are two major formats for citing documents in a bibliography. One comes from the Modern Language Association (MLA), the other from the

American Psychological Association (APA). Both are widely used by communication scholars; ask your instructor which he or she prefers.

Whichever format you adopt, make sure your bibliography is clear, accurate, and consistent. Figure 7.4 (page 135) lists sample MLA and APA citations for 10 kinds of sources that are cited most frequently in student speeches.

TAKE NOTES EFFICIENTLY

Asia Marshall started her speech preparation with the best of intentions. She was excited about her topic, "Great Women of Jazz," and she started research on the Internet the same day the assignment was announced. She found several interesting sources and took some notes about them. That evening, she checked out a fascinating book about Billie Holiday and read it straight through. She didn't bother taking notes because she was sure she'd remember it all. The next day, she looked through the *Encyclopedia of Jazz* and jotted a few notes on the back of her syllabus.

Then Asia remembered that she had a test in another class. Somewhat panicked, she put aside her speech research to study. When she got back to the speech, the deadline was only four days away. She dug out her notes, but what did they mean? One said, "Medford—*important!!!*" But who or what was Medford? Asia had thought she'd remember all about the Billie Holiday book, but without notes, it was mostly a blur by now. With a sense of doom, she faced up to the fact that she would have to start over—and finish in four days.

Sound familiar? This has happened to almost everyone at least once. But once is enough. There's a better way to take research notes. Here is a method that has worked well for many students:

Take Plenty of Notes

Few things are more aggravating than trying to recall some bit of information you ran across in your research but neglected to record. The moral of Asia Marshall's story is clear: If there is even an outside chance that you may need a piece of information, make a note of it. This will take a little extra time in the short run, but in the long run it can save you much grief.

Record Notes in a Consistent Format

You should use the same format for all your research notes, whether they come from Internet sources, library documents, or personal interviews. In each case, record the note, the source of the note, and a heading indicating the subject of the note (see Figure 7.5 on page 136).

The importance of the subject heading cannot be overemphasized. It is the first step to more efficient note taking. By telling you at a glance what each note is about, it will simplify the task of organizing your notes when you start to compose the speech. Once you start using subject headings, you'll see how helpful they can be.

Make a Separate Entry for Each Note

Many students try to record all the information from one source on a single note. This is not an effective procedure because it makes your notes almost

FIGURE 7.4 Sample Bibliography Formats

Book.	**MLA:**	Fernández-Armesto, Felipe. *Our America: A Hispanic History of the United States*. New York: W. W. Norton, 2014. Print.
	APA:	Fernández-Armesto, F. (2014). *Our America: A hispanic history of the United States.* New York: W. W. Norton.
Magazine article.	**MLA:**	Wallace, Scott. "Blood in the Jungle." *Smithsonian* Feb. 2014: 64–69. Print.
	APA:	Wallace, S. (2014, February). Blood in the jungle. *Smithsonian*, *44(10)*, 64–69.
Newspaper article.	**MLA:**	Timberg, Craig. "Floating Eyes in the Sky Heighten Privacy Worries." *Washington Post* 23 Jan. 2014. Web. 19 April 2014.
	APA:	Timberg, C. (2014, January 23). Floating eyes in the sky heighten privacy worries. *The Washington Post*. Retrieved from www.washingtonpost.com
Article in reference work.	**MLA:**	McConnell, Terrance. "Moral Dilemmas." *Stanford Encyclopedia of Philosophy*. Ed. Edward N. Zalta. Stanford University, Spring 2014. Web. 27 Aug. 2014.
	APA:	McConnell, T. (2014). Moral dilemmas. In E. Zalta (Ed.), *The Stanford encyclopedia of philosophy* (Spring 2014 ed.). Retrieved from http://plato.stanford.edu
Government publication.	**MLA:**	United States Dept. of Labor. Bureau of Labor Statistics. "Foreign-born Workers in the U.S. Labor Force." July 2013. *BLS Spotlight on Statistics*. Web. 27 Sept. 2013.
	APA:	U.S. Department of Labor, Bureau of Labor Statistics. (2013). Foreign-born workers in the U.S. labor force. In *BLS spotlight on statistics*. Retrieved from http://www.bls.gov/spotlight/2013/foreign-born/home.htm
Web site or blog.	**MLA:**	Ferraro, Matthew F., and Daniel Dolgin. "The Snowden Effect: How America's Spy Agencies Can Fix Their Millennials Problem." *Politico*. Politico, 13 Mar. 2014. Web. 20 Sept. 2014.
	APA:	Ferraro, M. F., and Dolgin, D. (2014, March 13). The Snowden effect: How America's spy agencies can fix their Millennials problem. *Politico*. Retrieved from http://www.politico.com/magazine/story/2014/03/the-snowden-effect-104642.html?hp=l17#.UyZKx_ZD29w
Personal interview.	**MLA:**	Chung, Cindy. Personal interview. 8 Oct. 2014.
	APA:	Chung, C. (personal communication, October 8, 2014).
Speech or lecture.	**MLA:**	Abitbol, Eric. "Peace Parks." International Peace and Conflict Resolution 619: Environmental Peacemaking. American University. 31 Mar. 2014. Lecture.
	APA:	Abitbol, E. (2014, March 31). *Peace parks*. Lecture presented in International Peace and Conflict Resolution 619: Environmental Peacemaking. American University.
Television program.	**MLA:**	"League of Denial: The NFL's Concussion Crisis." Narr. Will Lyman. *Frontline*. PBS. WGBH, Boston, 28 Jan. 2014. Television.
	APA:	Lyman W. (Narrator). (2013). League of denial: the NFL's concussion crisis [Television series episode].In M. Kirk, J. Gilmore, & M. Wiser (Producers), *Frontline*. Boston, MA: WGBH Educational Foundation.
Video.	**MLA:**	Milgram, Anne. *Why Smart Statistics Are the Key to Fighting Crime*. TED Talks. *YouTube*. Web. 28 Jan. 2014.
	APA:	Milgram, A. TED Talks (Producer). (2014, January 28). Why smart statistics are the key to fighting crime [Video file]. *YouTube*. Retrieved from http://www.youtube.com

FIGURE 7.5 Sample Research Note

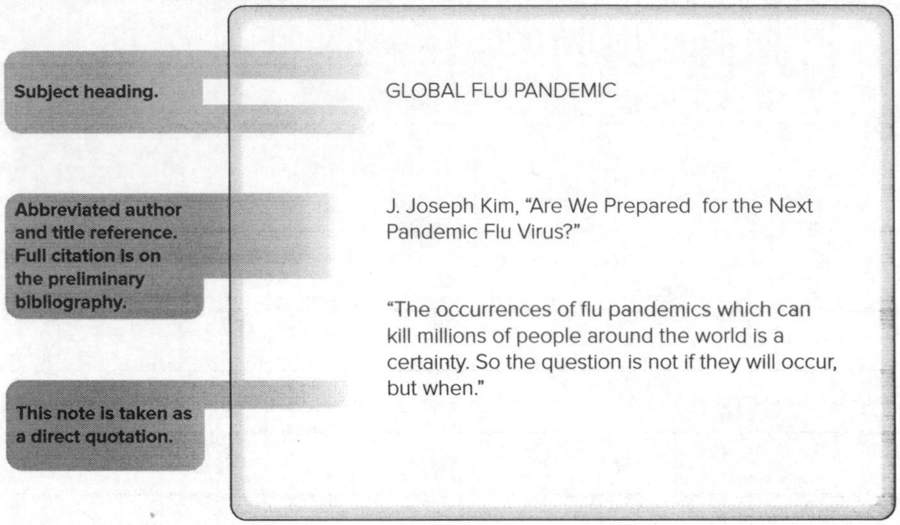

impossible to review and organize. A better approach is to make a separate note for *each* quotation or piece of information you record. Although you may end up with several notes from the same document, you will find that this approach allows you to keep better track of your research.

Distinguish Among Direct Quotations, Paraphrases, and Your Own Ideas

As we saw in Chapter 2, it's easy to plagiarize accidentally by not taking careful research notes. As you do research for your speeches, be sure to use quotation marks whenever you copy the exact words of a source. If you paraphrase, rather than quote verbatim, don't forget to include the source when you record the note.

By keeping track of quotations and paraphrases, you will be able to separate your own words and ideas from those of other people. This will help you avoid the trap of inadvertent plagiarism when you put your speech together.

THINK ABOUT YOUR MATERIALS AS YOU RESEARCH

Students often approach research as a mechanical routine that simply involves gathering the materials to be used in a speech or paper. But when done properly, research can be extremely creative.

If you *think about* what you are finding in your research, you will see your topic just a little bit differently with each note you take. You will find new relationships, develop new questions, explore new angles. You will, in short, begin to write the speech in your head even as you do the research. As you learn more about the topic, you will formulate a central idea, begin to sketch out main points and supporting points, experiment with ways of

To take research notes efficiently, record them in a consistent format; make a separate entry for each note; and distinguish among direct quotations, paraphrases, and your own ideas.

organizing your thoughts. You may even change your point of view, as did this student:

> Francesca Lopez began her speech preparation with this central idea in mind: "Wild animals make more interesting pets than dogs and cats." She went about her research conscientiously, spending many hours online and in the library. In the process, she came upon some disturbing information about the capture of wild animals. She read that young chimpanzees and other apes were literally snatched out of their mothers' arms, and that the mothers were afterward heard to cry almost like humans. Back in her room that night, Francesca couldn't get her mind off the baby chimpanzees.
>
> The next day, Francesca found some more disturbing material. One source told about the extraordinarily high death rate of wild animals during shipment to the United States. Again, that night Francesca brooded about the young animals dying of fear and cold in the cargo holds of airplanes.
>
> By the time she finished her research, Francesca's central idea was completely different. When she spoke, her central idea was "The importation of wild animals for use as pets is inhumane."

This is an example of creative research—and of critical thinking. Francesca kept her mind open, read everything she could find about her topic, and thought seriously about what she found. Because of this thoughtful approach, she changed her mind.[5]

Your own speech preparation may not cause you to reverse your position, but it should give you new insights into your topic. If you approach research in this way, you may find that the time you spend researching is the most productive of all the time you devote to preparing your speech.

Summary

There are many resources you can use when gathering information for a speech. If you have personal experience or above-average knowledge about a topic, you can use yourself as a resource. Most of the time, however, you will need outside information, which you can get in the library, on the Internet, or by interviewing people with specialized information.

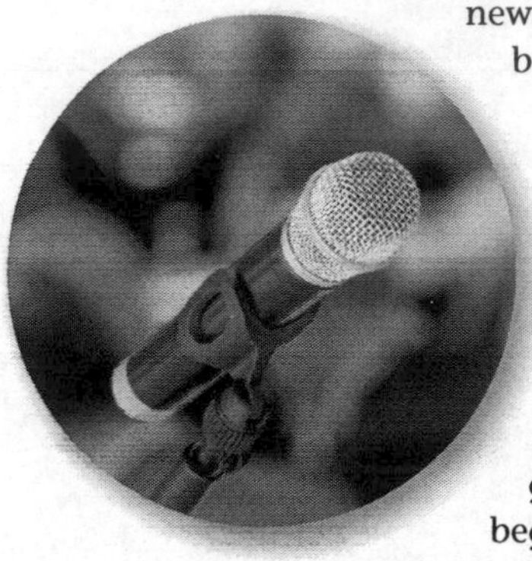

Finding what you need in the library is largely a matter of knowing how to search for information. The catalogue lists all the books, periodicals, and other resources owned by the library. Databases help you find articles in magazines, newspapers, and journals. The reference section includes encyclopedias, yearbooks, biographical aids, and books of quotations. If you have trouble finding something, don't hesitate to ask a librarian.

When looking for information online, you need a search strategy that will help you find exactly what you need. Given the lack of editorial review for most documents on the Web, it is especially important to evaluate the authorship, sponsoring organization, and recency of the research materials you find there.

You can also get information by conducting a personal interview. Before the interview, you should define its purpose, decide whom you are going to interview, and prepare the interview questions. Once the interview begins, be sure to listen attentively and to take accurate notes. Afterward, review and transcribe your notes as soon as possible.

No matter what sources you draw upon in gathering information, your research will be more effective if you start early and make a preliminary bibliography to keep track of all the books, articles, and Internet documents that look as if they might be helpful. By learning to take research notes effectively, you will save yourself time and energy every step of the way. And if you think about your materials as you research, you may find that gathering materials is the most creative part of your speech preparation.

Key Terms

catalogue (121)
call number (121)
reference work (121)
newspaper and periodical database (123)
abstract (123)
academic database (123)
virtual library (125)
sponsoring organization (128)
research interview (130)
preliminary bibliography (133)

Review Questions

After reading this chapter, you should be able to answer the following questions:

1. Why is it important to draw on your own knowledge and experience in gathering materials for your speeches?
2. What are five resources for finding what you need in the library?

3. What are three criteria for evaluating the soundness of research materials that you find on the Internet?
4. What are the three stages of a research interview? What should you do in each stage to help ensure a successful interview?
5. Why is it important to start your speech research early?
6. What is a preliminary bibliography? Why is it helpful to you in researching a speech?
7. What four things should you do to take research notes efficiently?

connect

For further review, go to the LearnSmart study module for this chapter.

Exercises for Critical Thinking

1. Using one of the periodical and newspaper databases discussed on pages 122–123, find three magazine or newspaper articles on the topic of your next speech. Prepare a preliminary bibliography entry for each article. Read the full text of the articles and assess their value for your speech.
2. Using Google or another search engine, find three high-quality documents on the topic of your next speech. Prepare a preliminary bibliography entry for each document. Read the full text of the documents and assess them in light of the criteria for evaluating Internet documents discussed on pages 127–129.
3. Plan to conduct an interview for one of your classroom speeches. Be sure to follow the guidelines presented in this chapter for effective interviewing. Afterward, evaluate the interview. Did you prepare for it adequately? Did you get the information you needed? What would you do differently if you could conduct the interview again?

8

Supporting Your Ideas

Examples

Statistics

Testimony

Citing Sources Orally

A confirmed believer in holistic medicine, Olivia Peck decided to give her first classroom speech on the uses and benefits of aromatherapy. Part of her speech ran like this:

"All of us suffer from things like colds, headaches, nausea, and stress. How would you like to cure these problems without expensive pills or visits to the doctor? Well, you can with aromatherapy. Aromatherapy has been proven to treat many common ailments, and nowadays doctors say it's a great idea. More than any pill you can buy, aromatherapy just works. You should try it!"

After the speech, Olivia's classmates were polite but skeptical. As one remarked, "Olivia made some interesting points, but she's no doctor. I'd be more convinced if she had some medical evidence to back up her opinion."

Good speeches are not composed of hot air and generalizations. They need strong supporting materials to bolster the speaker's point of view. In Olivia's case, there is evidence that aromatherapy is helpful in treating some ailments, but most of the claims about its health benefits have yet to be verified by research. So Olivia's listeners were right to be skeptical about her vague, unsupported generalizations.

The problem with generalizations is that they don't answer the three questions listeners always ask of a speaker: "What do you mean?" "Why should I believe you?" "So what?" Consider the following statements:

General	Less General	Specific
Gender equality has yet to be achieved.	Despite progress on some fronts, women lag behind men in positions of political, economic, and academic leadership.	According to Sheryl Sandberg, CEO of Facebook and author of *Lean In*, of 190 heads of state worldwide, only 9 are women. Women hold 13 percent of legislative seats around the world. In the United States, 15 percent of top corporate jobs are held by women. Only 24 percent of full professors are women.

Which statement do you find most interesting? Most convincing? Chances are you prefer that in the right-hand column. It is sharp and specific, clear and credible—just what a speech needs to come alive.

supporting materials

The materials used to support a speaker's ideas. The three major kinds of supporting materials are examples, statistics, and testimony.

The skillful use of supporting materials often makes the difference between a poor speech and a good one. In Chapters 15 and 17, we will look at special uses of supporting materials in informative and persuasive speeches. In this chapter, we focus on the basic kinds of supporting materials—examples, statistics, and testimony—and on general principles for using them effectively and responsibly.

Examples

> Detective Jim McClelland clicks a button and the grainy close-up of a suspect—bearded, expressionless, and looking away from the camera—disappears from his computer monitor. In place of the two-dimensional image, a disembodied virtual head materializes, rendered clearly in three dimensions. McClelland rotates and tilts the head until the suspect is facing forward and his eyes stare straight out from the screen.

These lines are from the opening of an article in *Popular Science Monthly* about advances in facial recognition software. It illustrates a device well known to magazine writers—and public speakers: Get the audience involved.

example

A specific case used to illustrate or represent a group of people, ideas, conditions, experiences, or the like.

See how skillfully this example accomplishes the goal. It focuses attention on a specific person (Detective Jim McClelland), and it provides vivid details of what happens on his computer screen. We can almost see the grainy image of a suspect looking away from the camera morph into a sharply-rendered virtual head, staring straight at us. We would not be nearly as involved if the article had merely said, "In recent years, there have been many advances in facial-recognition software."

Research has shown that vivid, concrete examples have a strong impact on listeners' beliefs and actions.[1] Without examples, ideas often seem vague, impersonal, and lifeless. With examples, ideas become specific, personal, and lively. This is nowhere better illustrated than in the Bible and the Koran, both of which use all manner of stories, parables, and anecdotes to make abstract principles clear and compelling. There are several kinds of examples you may want to try in your speeches.

BRIEF EXAMPLES

Brief examples—also called specific instances—may be referred to in passing to illustrate a point. The following excerpt uses a brief example to illustrate the miraculous nature of recent advances in creating artificial limbs for accident victims:

> Changes in technology have made it possible for doctors to work wonders that once seemed impossible. Roger Charter, for example, lost both his feet when they were crushed in a truck accident. Now he has new feet—made of a springy plastic alloy that duplicates a normal arch. Not only can Roger walk normally, but he can run and play sports again.

brief example

A specific case referred to in passing to illustrate a point.

Another way to use brief examples is to pile them one upon the other until you create the desired impression. Here is how one speaker used this technique to reinforce the point that Mexican Americans have made many valuable contributions to U.S. life:

> Many of us are familiar with prominent Chicanos and Chicanas such as actress Jessica Alba, boxer Oscar De La Hoya, and guitarist Carlos Santana. But you may be less familiar with other Americans of Mexican origin who have made important contributions to U.S. society. Nancy Lopez played a crucial role in popularizing women's professional golf and won 48 tour championships. Dr. Ellen Ochoa is a former astronaut who logged more than 480 hours in space and invented several optical methods that greatly aid space exploration. Dr. Mario Molina won the 1995 Nobel Prize in Chemistry for his research on the formation and decomposition of the ozone layer.

connect

View this excerpt from "Living in America" in the online Media Library for this chapter (Video 8.1).

EXTENDED EXAMPLES

Extended examples are often called narratives, illustrations, or anecdotes. By telling a story vividly and dramatically, they pull listeners into the speech. Here is such an example, from a speech by Sun Yan, a student at Fudan University in Shanghai, China. Participating in China's national English-language speech competition, Sun Yan used an extended example to illustrate the spirit of the Olympic Games:

extended example

A story, narrative, or anecdote developed at some length to illustrate a point.

> In the history of the Olympic Games, there have been many shining stars. Among them was a European girl. With the lapse of time, her name has faded from memory, yet her unbending spirit shall never perish. It was she who highlighted the Olympic Creed.
>
> In the lead though she had been, she stumbled near the terminus and her leg was injured. Competitors passed her from behind in succession until finally only her weak and lonely figure remained on the track. Doctors came and offered to take her away. Yet she refused. With the only strength left in her, she managed to get up and shuffled feebly to the endpoint with drops of blood along her trail.
>
> But cheers broke out. Though she failed in the race, the girl won applause from people all over the world. It was she who elucidated the Olympic creed of participation. It was she who instilled perseverance in our minds.[2]

connect

View this excerpt from "The Olympic Spirit" in the online Media Library for this chapter (Video 8.2).

This long example captures vividly the courage of the Olympic runner and her personification of the Olympic spirit. The speaker could merely have said, "Olympic athletes often display great fortitude," but the story makes the point far more poignantly.

HYPOTHETICAL EXAMPLES

hypothetical example

An example that describes an imaginary or fictitious situation.

All the examples presented up to now have been factual; the incidents they refer to really happened. Sometimes, however, speakers will use a hypothetical example—one that describes an imaginary situation. Usually such examples are brief stories that relate a general principle.

Here is how one student used a hypothetical example to illustrate the use of honor codes to reduce cheating:

> Imagine this: You're taking your psychology exam when you notice the student sitting next to you is staring at your answers. You also see his open notebook under his desk. You feel your cheeks redden as you become angry that he may get a high score by cheating while you've worked hard to earn your grade. And you feel helpless because you think telling the professor will do nothing.
>
> But now imagine that you attend a school with an honors system. At the beginning of each exam, you sign a statement that says you will not cheat and that you accept the responsibility to report cheating. After the professor hands out the exam, she leaves the room. In this case, you have the power and the duty to report cheaters rather than feel robbed by them.
>
> Such a system has worked elsewhere and it can work at our school. Professor Donald McCabe, president of the Center for Academic Integrity, has surveyed more than 20,000 students at 70 colleges throughout the country, and his research shows that the level of cheating is significantly lower at schools with honor codes than at schools without them.

connect

View this excerpt from "College Cheating: A National Epidemic" in the online Media Library for this chapter (Video 8.3).

This hypothetical example is especially effective. The speaker creates a realistic scenario, relates it directly to her listeners, and gets them involved in the speech. In addition, she uses figures from the president of the Center for Academic Integrity to show that honor codes help reduce the incidence of cheating on college campuses. Whenever you use a hypothetical example, it is a good idea to follow it with statistics or testimony to show that the example is not far-fetched.

TIPS FOR USING EXAMPLES

Use Examples to Clarify Your Ideas

You probably use clarifying examples all the time in everyday conversation. If you were explaining to a friend about different body types, you might say, "Look at Professor Shankar. He's a typical ectomorph—tall, thin, and bony." Examples are an excellent way to clarify unfamiliar or complex ideas. They put abstract ideas into concrete terms that listeners can easily understand.

This principle works exceptionally well in speeches. Suppose you are talking about suspension bridges. You could give a technical description:

> The suspension bridge has a roadway suspended by vertical cables attached to two or more main cables. The main cables are hung on two towers and have their ends anchored in concrete or bedrock.

No matter what the occasion, personal examples are an excellent way to clarify ideas and to build audience interest. To be most effective, they should be delivered sincerely and with strong eye contact.

If your audience were made up of people familiar with structural systems, they might be able to visualize what a suspension bridge looks like. But for listeners lacking this background, you might want to add a simple example:

> Two well-known suspension bridges are the Golden Gate Bridge in San Francisco and the Brooklyn Bridge in New York.

Because almost everyone has at least seen a picture of the Golden Gate Bridge or the Brooklyn Bridge, using them as examples clarifies your meaning quickly and effectively.

Use Examples to Reinforce Your Ideas

In a speech titled "Changing Lives Through the Literacy Network," one student dealt with the problem of low adult literacy and how to alleviate it. She cited figures from the U.S. Department of Education and the National Research Council showing that more than 30 million adults in the United States lack basic literacy skills. After exploring the social consequences of low adult literacy, she then encouraged her classmates to join her as a volunteer tutor at the Literacy Network.

To reinforce her ideas, the speaker cited the example of Dwayne MacNamara, a father of two daughters, who had struggled with reading and writing for years before turning to the Literacy Network for help. She talked about the problems Dwayne faced because of low literacy and of how the Literacy Network helped him acquire the skills he needed to succeed in life.

connect

View this portion of "Changing Lives Through the Literacy Network" in the online Media Library for this chapter (Video 8.4).

This example was very effective because it put the facts and figures about low adult literacy in vivid, human terms that everyone could understand. When you use such an example, make sure it is representative—that it does not deal with rare or exceptional cases. Your listeners are likely to feel betrayed if they suspect that you have chosen an atypical example to prove a general point.

Use Examples to Personalize Your Ideas

People are interested in people. As social psychologist Elliot Aronson explains, "Most people are more deeply influenced by one clear, vivid, personal example than by an abundance of statistical data."[3] Whenever you talk to a general audience (such as your speech class), you can include examples that will add human interest to your speech. So far in this section, we have seen a number of such examples—the heroic Olympic runner, accident victim Roger Charter, and so on. The abstract becomes more meaningful when applied to a person. Which of the following would you be more likely to respond to?

> There are many hungry families in our community who could benefit from food donations.

Or:

> Let me tell you about Arturo. Arturo is four years old. He has big brown eyes and a mop of black hair and an empty belly. In all his four years on this earth, Arturo has never once enjoyed three square meals in a single day.

Try using examples with human interest in your speeches. You will soon discover why accomplished speakers consider them "the very life of the speech."[4]

Make Your Examples Vivid and Richly Textured

The richly textured example supplies everyday details that bring the example to life. Recall the example on page 143 of the Olympic runner. The speaker provided us with many details about the runner's bravery in the face of adverse conditions. The runner stumbles and injures her leg near the end of the race. She is passed by other competitors until she alone is left on the track. Doctors offer to help, but she refuses their assistance and shuffles to the finish line with drops of blood along her trail.

How much less compelling the example would have been if the speaker had merely said:

> One Olympic runner courageously completed her race despite being injured and exhausted.

Instead, the details let us *see* the runner as she battles through her pain and misfortune. She is much more likely to stay in our minds than a "brave runner who completed her race." The more vivid your examples, the more impact they are likely to have on your audience.

Practice Delivery to Enhance Your Extended Examples

An extended example is just like a story or narrative. Its impact depends as much on delivery as on content. Many students have discovered this the hard way. After spending much time and energy developing a splendid example, they have seen it fall flat because they did not make it vivid and gripping for listeners.

Look again at the speaker in Video 8.2. Notice how she uses her voice to increase the impact of her story about the Olympic runner. Like that speaker, you should think of yourself as a storyteller. Don't rush through your examples as though you were reading the newspaper. Use your voice to get listeners involved. Speak faster here to create a sense of action, slower there to

checklist

Using Examples

YES	NO	
☐	☐	1. Do I use examples to clarify my ideas?
☐	☐	2. Do I use examples to reinforce my ideas?
☐	☐	3. Do I use examples to personalize my ideas?
☐	☐	4. Are my examples representative of what they are supposed to illustrate or prove?
☐	☐	5. Do I reinforce my examples with statistics or testimony?
☐	☐	6. Are my extended examples vivid and richly textured?
☐	☐	7. Have I practiced the delivery of my extended examples to give them dramatic effect?

build suspense. Raise your voice in some places; lower it in others. Pause occasionally for dramatic effect.

Most important, maintain eye contact with your audience. The easiest way to ruin a fine example is to read it from your notes. As you practice the speech, "talk through" your extended examples without relying on your notes. By the day of your speech, you should be able to deliver your extended examples as naturally as if you were telling a story to a group of friends.

Statistics

We live in an age of statistics. Day in and day out we are bombarded with a staggering array of numbers: Taylor Swift has sold more than 26 million albums. Thirteen percent of U.S. children under the age of 18 suffer from some type of mental disorder. Americans eat 350 million pounds of peanut butter a year. Hurricane Sandy caused an estimated $60 billion in damages.

What do all these numbers mean? Most of us would be hard-pressed to say. Yet we feel more secure in our knowledge when we can express it numerically. According to Lord Kelvin, the 19th-century physicist, "When you can measure what you are speaking about, and express it in numbers, you know something about it. But when you cannot measure it, when you cannot express it in numbers, your knowledge is . . . meager and unsatisfactory." It is this widely shared belief that makes statistics, when used properly, such an effective way to clarify and support ideas.[5]

statistics

Numerical data.

Like brief examples, statistics are often cited in passing to clarify or strengthen a speaker's points. The following examples show how two students used statistics in their speeches:

> To document the importance of community colleges: "According to the Department of Education, there are more than 1,100 community colleges in the United States, and they enroll 45 percent of all undergraduates."

To illustrate the dramatic increase in pay for professional athletes: "ESPN reports that just 20 years ago, the highest paid baseball player made $5 million. Today, the highest paid player makes $30 million a year."

Statistics can also be used in combination to show the magnitude or seriousness of an issue. We find a good instance of this technique in a student presentation about America's crowded roadways. To demonstrate his point that traffic congestion wastes massive amounts of time and money, the speaker cited the following figures:

connect

View this excerpt from "Stuck in Traffic" in the online Media Library for this chapter (Video 8.5).

According to the Urban Mobility Report from Texas A&M University, Americans collectively spend 4.2 billion hours stuck in traffic each year. All told, traffic congestion results in more than $87 billion in wasted fuel and lost productivity. That number breaks down to about $750 per traveler each year. Clearly, we are wasting far too much time and money on traffic gridlock.

This is a well-supported argument. But what if the speaker had merely said:

Traffic jams are very costly for the United States.

This statement is neither as clear nor as convincing as the one containing statistics. Of course, the audience didn't remember all the numbers, but the purpose of presenting a series of figures is to create an *overall* impact on listeners. What the audience did recall is that an impressive array of statistics supported the speaker's position.[6]

UNDERSTANDING STATISTICS

In his classic book *How to Lie with Statistics,* Darrell Huff exploded the notion that numbers don't lie. Strictly speaking, they don't. But they can be easily manipulated and distorted. For example, which of the following statements is true?

a. Enriched white bread is more nutritious than whole-wheat bread because it contains as much or more protein, calcium, niacin, thiamine, and riboflavin.

b. Whole-wheat bread is more nutritious than white bread because it contains seven times the amount of fiber, plus more iron, phosphorus, and potassium.

As you might expect, *both* statements are true. And you might hear either one of them, depending on who is trying to sell you the bread.

One can play with statistics in all kinds of areas. Which of these statements is true?

a. The cheetah, clocked at 70 miles per hour, is the fastest animal in the world.

b. The pronghorn antelope, clocked at 61 miles per hour, is the fastest animal in the world.

The cheetah, right? Not necessarily. The cheetah can go faster, but only for short sprints. The antelope can maintain its high speed over a much greater distance. So which is faster? It depends on what you're measuring. Put in terms of human races, the cheetah would win the hundred-yard dash, but the antelope would win the marathon.

When used properly, statistics make us feel more secure in our knowledge. A speech that is supported by statistics is usually more persuasive than an undocumented presentation.

When you are dealing with money, statistics become even trickier. Consider the following facts:

a. In 1940, President Franklin D. Roosevelt earned a salary of $75,000.
b. In 1972, President Richard Nixon earned a salary of $200,000.
c. In 2014, President Barack Obama earned a salary of $400,000.

Which president was paid the most money? In purely mathematical terms, Obama is the highest earner. But a dollar does not buy nearly as much today as it did in 1940, when Franklin Roosevelt was president. One measure of the inflation rate is the Consumer Price Index, which lets us gauge the value of the dollar in any given year against its purchasing power in 1972. If we apply the Consumer Price Index to the three presidents' salaries, we can see how much each earned in 1972 dollars:

a. In 1940, President Franklin D. Roosevelt earned a salary of $192,000.
b. In 1972, President Richard Nixon earned a salary of $200,000.
c. In 2014, President Barack Obama earned a salary of $78,000.

In other words, although Obama has the highest salary, the value of his $400,000 is less than half the value of Roosevelt's $75,000.

The point is that there is usually more to statistics than meets the eye.[7] When you track down statistics for your speeches, be sure to evaluate them in light of the following questions.

Are the Statistics Representative?

Say that on your way to class you choose ten students at random and ask them whether they favor or oppose banning recreational vehicles on public lands. Say also that six approve of such a ban and four do not. Would you then be accurate in claiming that 60 percent of the students on your campus favor banning recreational vehicles from public lands?

Of course not. Ten students is not a big enough sample. But even if it were, other problems would arise. Do the ten students interviewed accurately reflect your school's proportion of freshmen, sophomores, juniors, and seniors? Do they mirror the proportion of male and female students? Are the various majors accurately represented? What about part-time and full-time students? Students of different cultural and religious backgrounds?

In short, make sure your statistics are representative of what they claim to measure.

Are Statistical Measures Used Correctly?

Here are two groups of numbers:

Group A	Group B
7,500	5,400
6,300	5,400
5,000	5,000
4,400	2,300
4,400	1,700

mean

The average value of a group of numbers.

median

The middle number in a group of numbers arranged from highest to lowest.

mode

The number that occurs most frequently in a group of numbers.

Let us apply to each group three basic statistical measures—the mean, the median, and the mode.

The *mean*—popularly called the average—is determined by summing all the items in a group and dividing by the number of items. The mean for group A is 5,520. For group B it is 3,960.

The *median* is the middle figure in a group once the figures are put in order from highest to lowest. The median for both group A and group B is exactly the same—5,000.

The *mode* is the number that occurs most frequently in a group of numbers. The mode for group A is 4,400. For group B it is 5,400.

Notice the results:

	Group A	Group B
Mean	5,520	3,960
Median	5,000	5,000
Mode	4,400	5,400

All these measures have the same goal—to indicate what is typical or characteristic of a certain group of numbers. Yet see how different the results are, depending on which measure you use.

The differences among the various measures can be striking. For instance, the *mean* salary of local TV news anchorpersons is $87,000 a year. But the mean is inflated by the huge salaries (up to $1 million a year) paid to a few star anchors in media centers such as New York, Los Angeles, and Chicago. In contrast, the *median* salary of local news anchors is $64,000—not a sum to scoff at, but still $23,000 less than the mean.[8]

How might a speaker use these different measures? The owner of a television station would probably cite the *mean* ($87,000) to show that local news anchors are handsomely compensated for their work. An organization of news anchors might emphasize the *median* ($64,000) to demonstrate that salaries are not nearly as high as the station owner makes them out to be. Both speakers would be telling the truth, but neither would be completely honest unless she or he made clear the meaning of the statistics.

Are the Statistics from a Reliable Source?

Which is the more reliable estimate of the environmental dangers of toxic waste in a landfill—one from the U.S. Environmental Protection Agency or one compiled by the company that owns the landfill? Easy—the estimate by the EPA, which does not have a vested interest in what the figures look like. What about nutritional ratings for fast foods offered by Consumers Union (a highly respected nonprofit organization) or by Burger King? That's easy too—Consumers Union.

But now things get tougher. What about the competing statistics offered by groups for and against charter schools? Or the conflicting numbers tossed out by Republican and Democratic presidential candidates? In these cases, the answer is not so clear, since both sides would present the facts according to their own partisan motives.

As a speaker, you must be aware of possible bias in the use of numbers. Because statistics can be interpreted so many ways and put to so many uses, you should seek figures gathered by objective, nonpartisan sources.

TIPS FOR USING STATISTICS

Use Statistics to Quantify Your Ideas

The main value of statistics is to give your ideas numerical precision. This can be especially important when you are trying to document the existence of a problem. Examples can bring the problem alive and dramatize it in personal terms, but your listeners may still wonder how many people the problem actually affects. In such a situation, you should turn to statistics. Research has shown that the impact of examples is enhanced when they are combined with statistics that show the examples to be typical.[9]

Suppose you are talking about the need for college students to avoid credit-card debt. Part of your speech deals with the large amount of debt the typical college student faces by the time he or she graduates. You give an example, you personalize the subject, you provide many details, as follows:

> Travis Blake left college a changed person. Not only had he earned his degree, but he had racked up almost $4,000 in credit-card debt. Travis was sure he would be able to pay off his debt once he got a full-time job. But when he received his first paycheck, he found that after paying his taxes and living expenses, he could make only the minimum monthly payment on his credit cards. Rather than getting rid of his debt, he would be paying it off for years.

Confronted with this example, a listener might think, "Poor Travis. But I'm not going to end up in his spot because I don't plan to leave college with a lot of credit-card debt." Anticipating just such a response, a sharp speaker would include figures to quantify the extent of credit-card debt among college students in general:

> According to an article in *USA Today,* the average credit-card debt of a graduating college student is $3,100. If someone makes only the minimum monthly payment on his or her credit cards—which is what most people do—they will rack up more than $4,073 in interest charges alone before paying off their original $3,100 debt. This is one reason why the number of people under 25 filing for bankruptcy has increased by more than 50 percent.

Now the audience is much more likely to agree that they need to keep a closer eye on their credit-card balance.

Use Statistics Sparingly

As helpful as statistics can be, nothing puts an audience to sleep faster than a speech cluttered with numbers from beginning to end. Insert statistics only when they are needed, and then make sure they are easy to grasp. Even the most attentive listener would have trouble sorting out this barrage of figures:

> According to the *World Factbook,* life expectancy in the United States ranks 51st in the world. The United States ranks 50th in the world in infant mortality. Sweden ranks 5th. Americans spend more each year on health care than any other nation—$2.8 trillion dollars, or 17.9 percent of gross domestic product—yet Bloomberg ranks the U.S. health care system 46th in the world in overall efficiency.

Instead of drowning your audience in a sea of statistics, use only those that are most important. For example:

> According to the *World Factbook,* the United States has one of the lowest life expectancies among industrialized nations—plus one of the highest rates of infant mortality. Even though we spend more on health care than any other nation, Bloomberg ranks 45 nations ahead of us on the overall performance of our health care system.

This second statement makes the same point as the first statement, but now the ideas are not lost in a torrent of numbers.

Identify the Sources of Your Statistics

As we have seen, figures are easy to manipulate. This is why careful listeners keep an ear out for the sources of a speaker's statistics. One student learned this by experience. In a speech titled "The Dangers of Modern Medicine," she claimed that medical mistakes contribute to the deaths of between 210,000 and 440,000 Americans every year. To clarify the scope of the problem, she stated that this statistic made medical mistakes the third-leading cause of death in the United States, behind only heart disease and cancer. These are startling statistics. But because the student did not say where she got them, her classmates were sure she must be wrong.

As it turned out, the figures were reliable. They had come from a 2013 study published in the peer-reviewed *Journal of Patient Safety* and reported by NPR. If the speaker had mentioned the source in her speech, she would have been more successful.[10]

Explain Your Statistics

Statistics don't speak for themselves. They need to be interpreted and related to your listeners. Notice how effectively one student did this in a speech about Chinese culture in the United States:

> Food is another aspect of Chinese culture that has become part of American life. According to Jennifer Lee's book *The Fortune Cookie Chronicles,* there are some 43,000 Chinese restaurants in the United States. That's more than all the McDonalds, Burger Kings, and KFCs combined.

checklist

Using Statistics

YES	NO	
☐	☐	1. Do I use statistics to quantify my ideas?
☐	☐	2. Are my statistics representative of what they purport to measure?
☐	☐	3. Are my statistics from reliable sources?
☐	☐	4. Do I cite the sources of my statistics?
☐	☐	5. Do I use statistical measures (mean, median, mode) correctly?
☐	☐	6. Do I round off complicated statistics?
☐	☐	7. Do I use visual aids to clarify statistical trends?
☐	☐	8. Do I explain my statistics and relate them to the audience?

Explaining what statistics mean is particularly important when you deal with large numbers, since they are hard to visualize. How, for example, can we comprehend the size of the U.S. national debt, which is approaching $20 trillion? We could explain that a trillion is a thousand billion and a billion is a thousand million. But millions and billions are almost as hard to visualize as trillions. Suppose, instead, we translate the huge numbers into terms a listener can relate to. Here is one speaker's solution:

> How much money is a trillion dollars? Think of it this way. If you had $1 million and spent it at the rate of $1,000 a day, you would run out of money in less than three years. If you had $1 billion and spent it at the rate of $1,000 a day, you would not run out of money for almost 3,000 years. And if you had $1 trillion and spent it at the rate of $1,000 a day, you wouldn't run out of money for nearly 3 million years!

Whenever you use statistics in your speeches, think of how you can make them meaningful to your audience. Rather than simply reciting figures about, say, the continuing destruction of the world's rainforests, find a way to bring those figures home to your audience. You might say, as did one speaker:

> According to the Rainforest Action Network, rainforest is disappearing at an alarming rate. Within the next second, we will lose an area of rainforest equal to two football fields. Within the next fifteen minutes, an area the size of this campus will be erased. By this time tomorrow, 214,000 acres, an area equivalent to the size of New York City, will be gone forever.

connect

View this excerpt from "The Rainforests: Nature's Pharmacy" in the online Media Library for this chapter (Video 8.6).

Be creative in thinking of ways to relate your statistics to your audience. This is probably the single most important step you can take to make statistics work in your speeches.

Round Off Complicated Statistics

Mount Kilimanjaro is 19,341 feet high; the official world land speed record is 763.065 miles per hour; the population of Switzerland is 8,061,516 people; the moon is 238,855 miles from earth.

These are intriguing figures, but they are too complicated to be readily understood by listeners. Unless there is an important reason to give exact numbers, you should round off most statistics. You might say that Mount Kilimanjaro is 19,300 feet high; the world land speed record is 763 miles per hour; the population of Switzerland is more than 8 million; and the moon is 239,000 miles from earth.

Use Visual Aids to Clarify Statistical Trends

Visual aids can save you a lot of time, as well as make your statistics easier to comprehend. Suppose you are discussing the declining purchasing power of the U.S. dollar over the past century. You could start by explaining that in 1913, before the United States entered World War I, the dollar was at an all-time high. It fell off during the war, but it regained value during the 1920s, and in 1933 it stood at 80 cents of its 1913 value. Beginning in the 1940s, however, the dollar started a long decline that has yet to end. A century later, in 2013, it was worth a mere five cents of its original value.

These are interesting statistics, and you could build a good speech around them. But strung together in a few sentences they are hard to digest. Figure 8.1 shows how much more clearly the points can be made with a simple graph. We shall discuss visual aids in detail in Chapter 14. For the moment, keep in mind that they can be helpful in presenting statistical information.

FIGURE 8.1

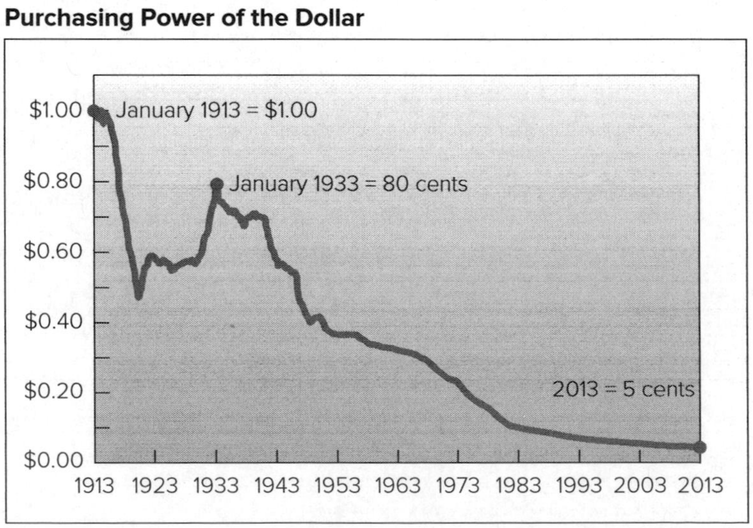

Testimony

Imagine that you are talking with a friend about the classes you plan to take next term. You are not sure whether to sign up for Psychology 230 or Accounting 181. Both are requirements; both meet at the same time of day. Your friend says, "I took those classes last year. They're both good, but Professor Hassam was excellent in Psych 230. If she's teaching it next term, I'd take it for sure." You check the timetable and find that Professor Hassam is indeed slated for Psychology 230. You sign up for her course.

As this story illustrates, we are often influenced by the *testimony* of other people. Just as you are likely to be swayed by your friend's recommendation about which class to take, so audiences tend to respect the opinions of people who have special knowledge or experience on the topic at hand. By quoting or paraphrasing such people, you can give your ideas greater strength and impact. The two major kinds of testimony are expert testimony and peer testimony.

testimony

Quotations or paraphrases used to support a point.

EXPERT TESTIMONY

In most speeches, you will probably rely on expert testimony—testimony from people who are acknowledged authorities in their fields. Citing the views of people who are experts is a good way to lend credibility to your speeches. It shows that you are not just mouthing your own opinions, but that your position is supported by people who are knowledgeable about the topic.[11]

expert testimony

Testimony from people who are recognized experts in their fields.

Expert testimony is even more important when a topic is controversial or when the audience is skeptical about a speaker's point of view. The following story explains how one student enlisted expert testimony for a speech on phony pharmaceuticals:

> The more Leah Giovanni researched her speech topic, the more she became convinced that the growth of fraudulent pharmaceuticals is a serious problem that requires action by the U.S. government. Yet Leah was not an expert on the subject. How could she convince her classmates to accept her ideas?
>
> Statistics helped, and so did examples. But that was not enough. To reinforce her credibility, Leah cited a wide range of experts who agreed with her—including investigative reporter Katherine Eban, author of a book on counterfeit medicines; Graham Jackson, editor of the *International Journal of Clinical Practice;* Tom Kubic, head of the Pharmaceutical Security Institute; and U.S. Representative Steve Israel of New York, who has sponsored legislation in Congress to deal with phony pharmaceuticals. By citing the views of these experts, Leah made her speech much more persuasive.

connect

View an excerpt from "Phony Pharmaceuticals" in the online Media Library for this chapter (Video 8.7).

PEER TESTIMONY

Another type of testimony often used in speeches is peer testimony—opinions of people like ourselves; not prominent figures, but ordinary citizens who have firsthand experience on the topic. This kind of testimony is especially valuable because it gives a more personal viewpoint on issues than can be gained from expert testimony.

peer testimony

Testimony from ordinary people with firsthand experience or insight on a topic.

For example, if you were speaking about the barriers faced by people with physical disabilities, you would surely include testimony from doctors and other medical authorities. But in this case, the expert testimony would be limited because it cannot communicate what it really means to have a physical disability. To communicate that, you need a statement from someone who can speak with the voice of genuine experience—as in the following case:

> Itzhak Perlman, the world-renowned violinist whose legs are paralyzed, once said: "When you are in a wheelchair, people don't talk to you. Perhaps they think it is contagious, or perhaps they think crippled legs mean a crippled mind. But whatever the reason, they treat you like a thing."

There is no way expert testimony could express these ideas with the same authenticity and emotional impact.

QUOTING VERSUS PARAPHRASING

direct quotation

Testimony that is presented word for word.

The statement from Itzhak Perlman is presented as a direct quotation. Testimony can also be presented by paraphrasing. Rather than quoting someone verbatim, you present the gist of that person's ideas in your own words—as did one student in her speech about America's potential water crisis:

> Writing in *Audubon* magazine, Dr. Peter Bourne, president of Global Water, a nonpartisan educational group in Washington, D.C., said most Americans do not yet realize the extent and urgency of the water problem. At the present rate, he says, we are headed for a crisis that will change the way we live in every part of the nation.

paraphrase

To restate or summarize a source's ideas in one's own words.

When should you use a direct quotation as opposed to paraphrasing? The standard rule is that quotations are most effective when they are brief, when they convey your meaning better than you can, and when they are particularly eloquent, witty, or compelling. If you find a quotation that fits these criteria, then recite the quotation word for word.

Paraphrasing is better than direct quotation in two situations: (1) when the wording of a quotation is obscure or cumbersome; (2) when a quotation is longer than two or three sentences. Audiences often tune out partway through lengthy quotations, which tend to interrupt the flow of a speaker's ideas. Since the rest of the speech is in your own words, you should put longer quotations in your own words as well.

TIPS FOR USING TESTIMONY

Quote or Paraphrase Accurately

quoting out of context

Quoting a statement in such a way as to distort its meaning by removing the statement from the words and phrases surrounding it.

Accurate quotation involves three things: making sure you do not misquote someone; making sure you do not violate the meaning of statements you paraphrase; making sure you do not quote out of context.

Of these, the last is the most subtle—and the most dangerous. By quoting out of context, you can twist someone's remarks so as to prove almost anything. Take movie advertisements. A critic pans a movie with these words:

> This movie is a colossal bore. From beginning to end it is a disaster. What is meant to be brilliant dialogue is about as fascinating as the stuff you clean out of your kitchen drain.

But when the movie is advertised in the newspapers, what appears in huge letters over the critic's name? "COLOSSAL! FROM BEGINNING TO END—BRILLIANT! FASCINATING!"

Citing expert testimony is an excellent way for students to lend credibility to their speeches. It shows that the speaker's views are shared by people who have special knowledge on the topic.

This is so flagrant as to be humorous. But quoting out of context can have serious consequences. Consider the following statement by a political candidate:

> Creating a national sales tax would provide needed revenue for programs such as education, health care, and national defense. Several European countries have such a tax, and it could work here. However, I do not support such a tax here—in fact, I don't support new taxes of any kind.

Now look what happens when the first part of that statement is quoted out of context by a competing candidate:

> Americans already pay too much in taxes. Yet my opponent in this election has stated—and I quote: "Creating a national sales tax would provide needed revenue for programs such as education, health care, and national defense. Several European countries have such a tax, and it could work here." Well, my opponent may think new taxes are good for Europe, but they're the last thing we need in the United States.

By quoting the original statement out of context, the competing candidate has created a false impression. Such behavior is highly unethical. Be sure, when you quote or paraphrase someone, that you represent their words and ideas with complete accuracy.

Use Testimony from Qualified Sources

We have all become accustomed to the celebrity testimonial in television and magazine advertising. The professional basketball player endorses a brand of athletic shoes. The movie star praises a hair spray or shampoo. So far, so good. These are the tools of the trade for the people who endorse them.

checklist

Using Testimony

YES	NO	
☐	☐	1. Do I use testimony to support my ideas?
☐	☐	2. Do I use testimony from qualified sources?
☐	☐	3. Do I use testimony from unbiased sources?
☐	☐	4. Do I distinguish between expert testimony and peer testimony?
☐	☐	5. Do I identify the sources of all testimony?
☐	☐	6. Do I quote and paraphrase all sources of testimony with complete accuracy?

But what happens when an Academy Award winner endorses a cell phone company? A tennis player represents a line of watches? Do they know more about these products than you or I? Probably not.

Being a celebrity or an authority in one area does not make someone competent in other areas. Listeners will find your speeches much more credible if you use testimony from sources qualified *on the subject at hand.* As we have seen, this may include either recognized experts or ordinary citizens with special experience on the speech topic.

Use Testimony from Unbiased Sources

In a speech about the use of stun guns by police officers to subdue unruly students in public schools, a student said:

> Steve Tuttle, a spokesman for Taser International, said in a statement that "the Taser device has been shown to be medically safe when used on children" and that there is no reason to prohibit its use when necessary to maintain security in the public schools.

As you might expect, the students' classmates were not persuaded. After all, what would you expect someone at Taser International, the leading manufacturer of stun guns, to say—that its product is unsafe and should be banned?

Careful listeners are suspicious of testimony from biased or self-interested sources. Be sure to use testimony from credible, objective authorities.

Identify the People You Quote or Paraphrase

The usual way to identify your source is to name the person and sketch his or her qualifications before presenting the testimony. The following excerpt is from a speech arguing that excessive time spent at work is harming the quality of education for many American high-school students:

> In their book, *When Children Work,* psychology professors Ellen Greenberger of the University of California and Lawrence Steinberg of Temple University note

> that intensive levels of work among youth tend to produce higher truancy and lower grades. According to Greenberger and Steinberg, one study after another has found that working more than a few hours a week has a negative impact on teenagers' academic performance.

Had the speaker not identified Greenberger and Steinberg, listeners would not have had the foggiest idea who they are or why their opinion should be heeded.

As we saw in Chapter 2, identifying the source of testimony is also an important ethical responsibility. If you use another person's words or ideas without giving credit to that person, you will be guilty of plagiarism. This is true whether you paraphrase the original source or quote it verbatim.

Citing Sources Orally

We have mentioned more than once in this chapter the importance of citing the sources of your supporting materials. Careful listeners are skeptical. They keep an ear out both for a speaker's information and for the sources of that information.

The bibliography in your speech outline should state the sources you used in constructing the speech (see Chapter 11). But listeners do not have access to your outline. You have to identify your sources orally, as you are speaking.

Unlike a written bibliography, oral source citations do not follow a standard format. What you include depends on your topic, your audience, the kind of supporting material you are using, and the claim you are making. The key is to tell your audience enough that they will know where you got your information and why they should accept it as qualified and credible. In most cases, you will need to identify some combination of the following:

- The book, magazine, newspaper, or Web document you are citing.
- The author or sponsoring organization of the document.
- The author's qualifications with regard to the topic.
- The date on which the document was published, posted, or updated.

Here is an example of a speech citation that includes all the above:

> The endangered monarch butterfly population can be seen most clearly in its shrinking migration. Michael Wines, science reporter for the *New York Times*, reported in the paper's January 29, 2014, issue that in only one year, the population of monarchs that migrates to Mexico for the winter shrank by 44 percent.

Because this speaker was citing statistics, she needed to show that they were up-to-date and came from a credible source. In the following example, the speaker is using testimony, but notice how he also establishes the credibility of his source and the recency of his information:

> Human smuggling is big business, and the U.S. government has made little headway in stopping it. Just ask Scott Hatfield, chief of the Human Smuggling division at Immigration and Customs Enforcement, who was quoted last month in the *Houston Chronicle:* "Any time we shut down a smuggling organization, there's always somebody to take their place."

checklist

Citing Sources Orally

YES	NO	
☐	☐	1. Do I identify all the print documents cited in my speech?
☐	☐	2. Do I identify all the Web documents cited in my speech?
☐	☐	3. Do I identify the authors or sponsoring organizations of the documents I cite?
☐	☐	4. Do I establish the authors' credentials with regard to the topic?
☐	☐	5. Do I use documents from sponsoring organizations with established expertise and objectivity?
☐	☐	6. Do I include the dates on which the documents were published, posted, or updated?
☐	☐	7. Do I use a variety of methods in citing my sources?

On the other hand, if you were quoting Abraham Lincoln's Gettysburg Address of November 19, 1863, about "government of the people, by the people, for the people," you would not need to explain Lincoln's qualifications (because he is so well known) or the date of his statement (because it does not affect the relevance of his words).

The same principles apply if you are citing online sources. It is not enough to say, "As I found on the Web," or "As the Internet states." On the other hand, it is not necessary to recite the entire address of the Web page. If you are citing a specific person, you should identify him or her and the name of the Web site on which you found the information—as in this example:

> In an article posted on CNN.com in February 2014, ex-NFL player Ronney Jenkins explained the state of his brain after years of concussions from playing football: "Everything was getting worse. My sleep was getting worse, my moods were getting worse. Your mind just goes crazy."

If you are citing an organization, rather than an individual, you need to provide the name of the organization:

> The U.S. Department of Labor reports on its Web site that over 18 percent of the current labor force is made up of people with disabilities.

Finally, notice how skillfully the speakers quoted above blend their citations into their speeches. They do not always say "According to . . ." or "As stated by. . . ." Nor do they use words like "quote . . . unquote." Usually you can modify your tone of voice or use brief pauses to let your listeners know when you are making a direct quotation.

In Figure 8.2 on the next page, you will find more examples of how you can cite different kinds of sources in your speeches. Keep in mind, however,

FIGURE 8.2 Sample Oral Citations

Book	Elizabeth Kolbert's 2014 book, *The Sixth Extinction*, explains that humans have become the new natural disaster, changing the world "faster than species can adapt."
Newspaper	According to the *Wall Street Journal*, February 4, 2014, lax security around power plants means that a coordinated terrorist attack "could take down the U.S. electric grid and black out much of the country."
Magazine	In last month's issue of *Atlantic Monthly*, senior editor Derek Thompson investigated employment patterns in the United States. He found that despite fears about part-time jobs becoming the new norm, we're actually creating 225 full-time jobs for every new part-time job.
Academic journal	A recent study published in the *Journal of Neuroscience* by researchers at Duke University demonstrates just how problematic sleep deprivation can be for compulsive gamblers. The less sleep a person has, the more he or she is willing to take big risks in the hope of a big score. And the result can be huge losses.
Organization or institution	A December 2013 report from the U.S. Department of Agriculture found that due to improved logistics, technology, and transportation, we now import the same amount of fresh fruit as we produce domestically. That's why you're able to eat avocados, kiwis, strawberries, and blueberries year-round.
Interview	In an interview I conducted for this speech, Professor Elinor Sanchez of the Political Science Department said that the impact of lobbyists has so corrupted the American political system that many people have lost their faith in government to serve the public good.
Television program	The January 31, 2014, episode of *20/20* reported that only fourteen states hold parents criminally liable for failing to store guns safely. Only one state, Massachusetts, requires gun owners to lock up their firearms.
Web site	Former astronaut Ed Lu thinks the biggest threat to human existence is up in the air. An April 10, 2014, article in *Wired.com* explains that Lu's nonprofit B612 Foundation wants to set up a defense perimeter around Earth to protect it from asteroids like the one that killed off the dinosaurs during the Cretaceous period.

that the examples are just that—examples. They are presented to give you a fuller sense of the various methods of oral citation. You can use *any* of the methods with any of the sources. As with other aspects of public speaking, citing sources orally in your speeches is not a matter of following a rigid formula, but of adapting general principles to specific circumstances.

Summary

Good speeches need strong supporting materials to bolster the speaker's point of view. The three basic types of supporting materials are examples, statistics, and testimony.

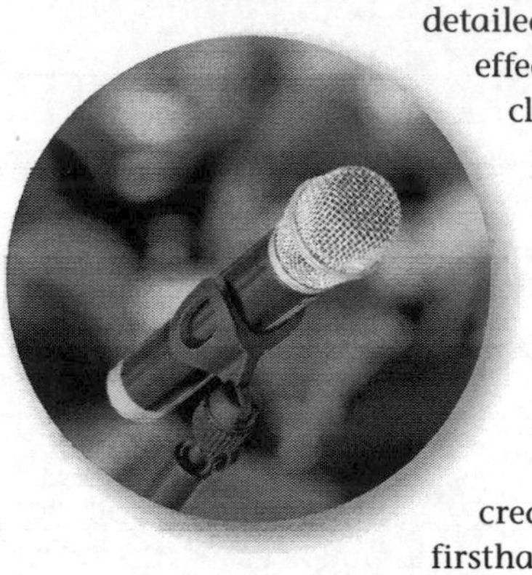

In the course of a speech you may use brief examples—specific instances referred to in passing—and sometimes you may want to give several brief examples in a row to create a stronger impression. Extended examples are longer and more detailed. Hypothetical examples describe imaginary situations and can be quite effective for relating ideas to the audience. All three kinds of examples help clarify ideas, reinforce ideas, or personalize ideas. To be most effective, they should be vivid and richly textured.

Statistics can be extremely helpful in conveying your message as long as you use them sparingly and make them meaningful to your audience. Above all, you should understand your statistics and use them fairly. Make sure your figures are representative of what they claim to measure, that you use statistical measures correctly, and that you take statistics only from reliable sources.

Citing the testimony of experts is a good way to make your ideas more credible. You can also use peer testimony, from ordinary people who have firsthand experience on the topic. Regardless of the kind of testimony, you can either quote someone verbatim or paraphrase his or her words. Be sure to quote or paraphrase accurately and to use qualified, unbiased sources.

When citing sources in a speech, you need to let your audience know where you got your information and why they should accept it as qualified and credible. In most cases, this means identifying the document you are citing, its date of publication or posting, the author or sponsoring organization, and the author's credentials.

Key Terms

supporting materials (142)
example (142)
brief example (143)
extended example (143)
hypothetical example (144)
statistics (147)
mean (150)
median (150)
mode (150)
testimony (155)
expert testimony (155)
peer testimony (155)
direct quotation (156)
paraphrase (156)
quoting out of context (156)

Review Questions

After reading this chapter, you should be able to answer the following questions:

1. Why do you need supporting materials in your speeches?
2. What are the three kinds of examples discussed in this chapter? How might you use each kind to support your ideas?
3. What are five tips for using examples in your speeches?
4. Why is it so easy to lie with statistics? What three questions should you ask to judge the reliability of statistics?
5. What are six tips for using statistics in your speeches?
6. What is testimony? Explain the difference between expert testimony and peer testimony.
7. What are four tips for using testimony in your speeches?
8. What four pieces of information do you usually need to provide when making oral source citations in a speech?

connect™

For further review, go to the LearnSmart study module for this chapter.

Exercises for Critical Thinking

1. Each of the following statements violates at least one of the criteria for effective supporting materials discussed in this chapter. Identify the flaw (or flaws) in each statement.
   a. In the words of one expert, "the prevalence of online multi-tasking is reducing the ability of people to concentrate on a single task, no matter how important the task might be."
   b. Figures compiled by the Bureau of Labor Statistics show that the median salary for petroleum engineers in the United States is $130,280. This shows that petroleum engineers average more than $130,000 a year in salary.
   c. According to a poll conducted for AT&T, most people prefer AT&T's cellular service to that of Sprint or Verizon.
   d. It's just not true that media violence has a strong influence on violent crimes by young people. All my friends watch television, go to the movies, and play video games, and none of us has ever committed a violent crime.
   e. As Leonardo DiCaprio stated in a recent interview, the United States needs to reassess its Middle East policy if it hopes to achieve peace and stability in the region.
   f. According to the U.S. Census Bureau, California has the largest Native American population of any state in the Union—723,225. Oklahoma is second with 482,760 and Arizona is third with 353,386.
   g. In a survey conducted last month among members of People for the Ethical Treatment of Animals, 99 percent of respondents opposed using animals for medical experiments. Clearly, then, the American people oppose such experiments.
2. Analyze "The Dangers of Cell Phones" in the appendix of sample speeches following Chapter 19. Identify the main points of the speech and the supporting materials used for each. Evaluate the speaker's use of supporting materials in light of the criteria discussed in this chapter.

Speech Preparation: Organizing and Outlining

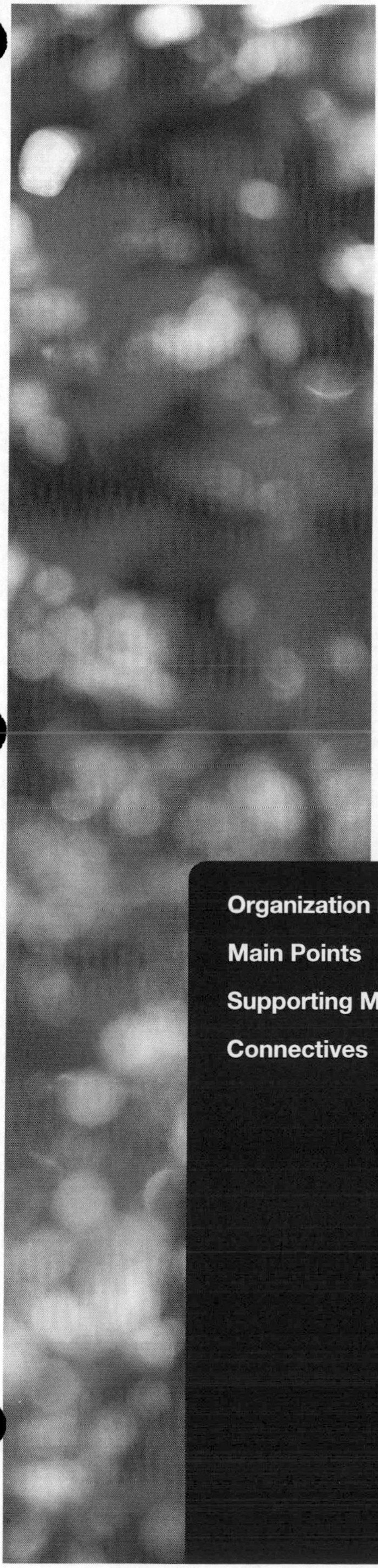

9

Organizing the Body of the Speech

- **Organization Is Important**
- **Main Points**
- **Supporting Materials**
- **Connectives**

Think about shopping in a store such as Ikea, Target, or Best Buy. Many of the items for sale are *organizers*—drawer organizers, desk organizers, closet organizers, kitchen organizers, bathroom organizers, office organizers, audio and video organizers. There is even a nationwide retail chain—The Container Store—devoted entirely to keeping things organized.

Why all this quest for organization? Obviously, when the objects you possess are well organized, they serve you better. Organization allows you to see what you have and to put your hands immediately on the garment, the tool, the piece of paper, the video you want without a frenzied search.

Much the same is true of your speeches. If they are well organized, they will serve you better. Organization allows you—and your listeners—to see what ideas you have and to put mental "hands" on the most important ones.

Organization Is Important

In a classic study, a college professor took a well-organized speech and scrambled it by randomly changing the order of its sentences. He then had a speaker deliver the original version to one group of listeners and the scrambled version to another group. After the speeches, he gave a test to see how well each group understood what they had heard. Not surprisingly, the group that heard the original, unscrambled speech scored much higher than the other group.[1]

A few years later, two professors repeated the same experiment at another school. But instead of testing how well the listeners comprehended each speech, they tested to see what effects the speeches had on the listeners' attitudes toward the speakers. They found that people who heard the well-organized speech believed the speaker to be much more competent and trustworthy than did those who heard the scrambled speech.[2]

strategic organization

Putting a speech together in a particular way to achieve a particular result with a particular audience.

These are just two of many studies that show the importance of organization in effective speechmaking.[3] Listeners demand coherence. Unlike readers, they cannot flip back to a previous page if they have trouble grasping a speaker's ideas. In this respect a speech is much like a movie. Just as a director must be sure viewers can follow the plot of a film from beginning to end, so must a speaker be sure listeners can follow the progression of ideas in a speech from beginning to end. This requires that speeches be organized *strategically.* They should be put together in particular ways to achieve particular results with particular audiences.

Speech organization is important for other reasons as well. As we saw in Chapter 1, it is closely connected to critical thinking. When you work to organize your speeches, you gain practice in the general skill of establishing clear relationships among your ideas. This skill will serve you well throughout your college days and in almost any career you may choose. In addition, using a clear, specific method of speech organization can boost your confidence as a speaker and improve your ability to deliver a message fluently.

The first step in developing a strong sense of speech organization is to gain command of the three basic parts of a speech—introduction, body, and conclusion—and the strategic role of each. In this chapter we deal with the body of the speech. The next chapter will take up the introduction and the conclusion.

There are good reasons for talking first about the body of the speech. The body is the longest and most important part. Also, you will usually prepare the body first. It is easier to create an effective introduction after you know exactly what you will say in the body.

The process of organizing the body of a speech begins when you determine the main points.

Main Points

The main points are the central features of your speech. You should select them carefully, phrase them precisely, and arrange them strategically. Here are the main points of a student speech about the uses of hypnosis:

Specific Purpose: To inform my audience about some of the major uses of hypnosis.

Central Idea: Three major uses of hypnosis today are to control pain in surgery, to help people stop smoking, and to help students improve their academic performance.

Main Points:
I. Hypnosis is used in surgery as an adjunct to chemical anesthesia.
II. Hypnosis is used to help people stop smoking.
III. Hypnosis is used to help students improve their academic performance.

main points

The major points developed in the body of a speech. Most speeches contain from two to five main points.

These three main points form the skeleton of the body of the speech. If there are three major *uses* of hypnosis, then logically there can be three *main points* in the speech.

How do you choose your main points? Sometimes they will be evident from your specific purpose statement. Suppose your specific purpose is "To inform my audience about the history, technology, and benefits of driverless cars." Obviously, your speech will have three main points. The first will deal with the history of driverless cars, the second with the technology behind driverless cars, and the third with the benefits of driverless cars. Written in outline form, the main points might be:

Specific Purpose: To inform my audience about the history, technology, and benefits of driverless cars.

Central Idea: Once a dream of futurists, driverless cars are now a reality, developed through recent technological advancements and capable of saving lives and reducing road congestion.

Main Points:
I. Driverless cars have long been the subject of science-fiction writers and popular imagination.
II. Driverless cars today operate through a combination of network connectivity, intelligent computer processing, and sensors that constantly scan the car's surroundings.
III. Driverless cars have the potential to save lives and to reduce congestion on roadways.

Even if your main points are not stated expressly in your specific purpose, they may be easy to project from it. Let's say your specific purpose is "To inform my audience of the basic steps in making stained-glass windows." You know each of your main points will correspond to a step in the window-making process. They might look like this in outline form:

Specific Purpose: To inform my audience of the basic steps in making stained-glass windows.

Central Idea: There are four steps in making stained-glass windows.

Main Points:
I. The first step is designing the window.
II. The second step is cutting the glass to fit the design.
III. The third step is painting the glass.
IV. The fourth step is assembling the window.

You will not always settle on your main points so easily. Often they will emerge as you research the speech and evaluate your findings. Suppose your specific purpose is "To persuade my audience that our state should not approve proposals for online voting." You know that each main point in the speech will present a *reason* why online voting should not be instituted in your state. But you aren't sure how many main points there will be or what they will be. As you research and study the topic, you decide there are two reasons to support your view. Each of these reasons will become a main point in your speech. Written in outline form, they might be:

Specific Purpose: To persuade my audience that our state should not approve proposals for online voting.

Central Idea: Our state should not approve online voting because it will increase voter fraud and disfranchise people without Internet access.

Main Points:

I. Our state should not approve online voting because it will increase voter fraud.

II. Our state should not approve online voting because it will disfranchise people without access to the Internet.

NUMBER OF MAIN POINTS

You will not have time in your classroom speeches to develop more than four or five main points, and most speeches will contain only two or three. Regardless of how long a speech might run, if you have too many main points, the audience will have trouble sorting them out.

If, when you list your main points, you find that you have too many, you may be able to condense them into categories. Here is a set of main points for a speech about yoga:

Specific Purpose: To inform my audience about the practice of yoga.

Central Idea: Yoga is an ancient practice that involves the whole body.

Main Points:

I. Yoga breathing starts with deep inhalation.

II. Yoga breathing requires slow exhalation.

III. Yoga breathing includes prolonged pauses.

IV. Yoga breathing provides many benefits.

V. Yoga postures involve all parts of the body.

VI. Yoga postures increase flexibility.

VII. Yoga postures strengthen muscle tone.

VIII. Yoga postures demand precise movements.

connect

View an excerpt from "Yoga: Uniting Mind, Body, and Spirit" in the online Media Library for this chapter (Video 9.1).

You have eight main points—which is too many. But if you look at the list, you see that the eight points fall into two broad categories: yoga breathing and yoga postures. You might, therefore, restate your main points this way:

I. One part of practicing yoga involves proper breathing.

II. Another part of yoga involves body postures.

Research studies confirm that clear organization is vital to effective public speaking. As in this address by tribal court judge Theresa Pouley, listeners must be able to follow the progression of ideas in a speech from beginning to end.

STRATEGIC ORDER OF MAIN POINTS

Once you establish your main points, you need to decide the order in which you will present them. The most effective order depends on three things—your topic, your purpose, and your audience. Chapters 15 and 16 will cover special aspects of organizing informative speeches and persuasive speeches. Here we look briefly at the five basic patterns of organization used most often by public speakers.

Chronological Order

Speeches arranged chronologically follow a time pattern. They may narrate a series of events in the sequence in which they happened. For example:

chronological order

A method of speech organization in which the main points follow a time pattern.

Specific Purpose: To inform my audience how the Great Wall of China was built.

Central Idea: The Great Wall of China was built in three major stages.

Main Points:

I. Building of the Great Wall began during the Qin dynasty of 221–206 B.C.

II. New sections of the Great Wall were added during the Han dynasty of 206 B.C.–220 A.D.

III. The Great Wall was completed during the Ming dynasty of 1368–1644.

Chronological order is also used in speeches explaining a process or demonstrating how to do something. For example:

Specific Purpose: To inform my audience of the steps in laser-assisted corrective eye surgery.

Central Idea: There are three main steps in laser-assisted corrective eye surgery.

Main Points:

I. First, a thin layer is sliced off the surface of the eye to expose the cornea.

II. Second, an ultraviolet laser is used to reshape the cornea.

III. Third, the thin layer sliced off at the beginning of the surgery is reaffixed to the eye.

As this outline shows, chronological order is especially useful for informative speeches.

Spatial Order

spatial order

A method of speech organization in which the main points follow a directional pattern.

Speeches arranged in spatial order follow a directional pattern. That is, the main points proceed from top to bottom, left to right, front to back, inside to outside, east to west, or some other route. For example:

Specific Purpose: To inform my audience about the structure of a hurricane.

Central Idea: A hurricane is made up of three parts going from inside to outside.

Main Points:

I. At the center of a hurricane is the calm, cloud-free eye.

II. Surrounding the eye is the eyewall, a dense ring of clouds that produces the most intense wind and rainfall.

III. Rotating around the eyewall are large bands of clouds and precipitation called spiral rain bands.

connect

View an excerpt from "The Wrath of Hurricanes" in the online Media Library for this chapter (Video 9.2).

Or:

Specific Purpose: To inform my audience about the three major regions in Italy.

Central Idea: Northern, central, and southern Italy have their own identities and attractions.

Main Points:

I. Northern Italy is home to Venice and its world-famous canals.

II. Central Italy is home to Rome and its historical treasures.

III. Southern Italy is home to Sicily and its culinary traditions.

Spatial order, like chronological order, is used most often in informative speeches.

Causal Order

causal order

A method of speech organization in which the main points show a cause-effect relationship.

Speeches arranged in causal order organize main points so as to show a cause-effect relationship. When you put your speech in causal order, you have two main points—one dealing with the causes of an event, the other dealing with its effects. Depending on your topic, you can devote your first main point

The main points of a speech should be organized to communicate the speaker's message. Chronological order would work very well for a speech on the history of hot-air balloons.

to the causes and the second to the effects, or you can deal first with the effects and then with the causes.

Suppose your specific purpose is "To persuade my audience that a growing shortage of air-traffic controllers is a serious problem for U.S. aviation." Then you would begin with the causes of the shortage and work toward its effects:

Specific Purpose: To persuade my audience that a growing shortage of qualified air-traffic controllers is a serious problem for U.S. aviation.

Central Idea: The growing shortage of certified air-traffic controllers threatens the safety of air travel.

Main Points:

I. The U.S. aviation system faces a growing shortage of qualified air-traffic controllers.

II. If this shortage continues, it will create serious problems for airline safety.

When the effects you are discussing have already occurred, you may want to reverse the order and talk first about the effects and then about their causes—as in this speech about the Ancient Pueblo peoples that lived in what is now the southwest United States:

Specific Purpose: To inform my audience about possible causes for the collapse of the Ancient Pueblo civilization.

Central Idea: The causes for the collapse of the Ancient Pueblo civilization have not yet been fully explained.

Main Points:

I. Ancient Pueblo civilization flourished for over a thousand years until 1200 A.D., when it mysteriously began to disintegrate.

II. Scholars have advanced three major explanations for the causes of this disintegration.

Because of its versatility, causal order can be used for both persuasive speeches and informative speeches.

Problem-Solution Order

Speeches arranged in problem-solution order are divided into two main parts. The first shows the existence and seriousness of a problem. The second presents a workable solution to the problem. For example:

connect

View an excerpt from "The Horrors of Puppy Mills" in the online Media Library for this chapter (Video 9.3).

Specific Purpose: To persuade my audience that action is needed to combat the abuses of puppy mills.

Central Idea: Puppy mills are a serious problem that can be solved by a combination of legislation and individual initiative.

Main Points:
I. Puppy mills are a serious problem across the United States.
II. Solving the problem requires legislation and individual initiative.

Or:

problem-solution order

A method of speech organization in which the first main point deals with the existence of a problem and the second main point presents a solution to the problem.

Specific Purpose: To persuade my audience that the electoral college should be abolished.

Central Idea: Because the electoral college does not give equal weight to the vote of each citizen, it should be replaced with direct popular election of the President.

Main Points:
I. The electoral college is a serious problem in the U.S. political system because it does not give equal weight to each citizen's vote in electing the President.
II. The problem can be solved by abolishing the electoral college and electing the President by popular vote.

As these examples indicate, problem-solution order is most appropriate for persuasive speeches.

Topical Order

topical order

A method of speech organization in which the main points divide the topic into logical and consistent subtopics.

Topical order results when you divide the speech topic into *subtopics,* each of which becomes a main point in the speech.

Let's say your topic is Josephine Baker, an African-American entertainer and social activist in the middle of the 20th century. You could organize your speech chronologically—by discussing Baker's exploits during each decade of her career. On the other hand, you could arrange the speech topically—by dividing Baker's accomplishments into categories. Then your central idea and main points might be:

Specific Purpose: To inform my audience about the achievements of Josephine Baker.

Central Idea: Josephine Baker was a multitalented figure in the fight for racial justice.

When organizing your speeches, pay special attention to the wording and order of your main points. Choose a method of organization that is most likely to help you achieve your specific purpose.

Main Points:

I. As an entertainer, Baker captivated audiences in Europe and America.

II. As a spy, Baker gathered information on Nazi activities in France during World War II.

III. As a civil rights activist, Baker worked for racial equality on a variety of fronts.

Notice how the main points subdivide the speech topic logically and consistently. Each main point isolates one aspect of Baker's achievements. But suppose your main points look like this:

I. As an entertainer, Baker captivated audiences in Europe and America.

II. As a spy, Baker gathered information on Nazi activities in France during World War II.

III. During the 1950s, Baker expanded her activities and the scope of her influence.

This would *not* be a good topical order because main point III is inconsistent with the rest of the main points. It deals with a *time period* in Baker's life, whereas main points I and II deal with fields of achievement.

The Josephine Baker example refers to an informative speech. But topical order also works for persuasive speeches. Usually the topical subdivisions are the *reasons* why a speaker believes in a certain point of view. Here, for example, are the main points for a speech on why the United States should continue its program of space exploration:

Specific Purpose: To persuade my audience that the United States should continue its program of space exploration.

Using public speaking in your CAREER

You are the purchasing manager for a large jewelry manufacturer. The company's president sent you abroad to find new suppliers of base metals, including brass, copper, nickel, and aluminum. You were asked to evaluate each supplier based on the quality, availability, and cost of its products.

You have just returned from a 12-day trip to suppliers in Cambodia, China, South Korea, and the United Arab Emirates. You will present your findings and recommendations to the company's senior executives, but you're not sure how best to organize your speech.

Your major choices are chronological order, problem-solution order, and topical order. What might be the main points of your speech with each of these methods of organization? Explain which method you think would be most effective for your presentation.

Central Idea: The United States should continue its program of space exploration because it produces scientific knowledge, generates technological breakthroughs, and opens access to natural resources.

Main Points:

I. The space program produces scientific knowledge about the nature of the solar system.

II. The space program generates technological breakthroughs that benefit many aspects of human life.

III. The space program opens access to natural resources that are in short supply on earth.

Because it is applicable to almost any subject and to any kind of speech, topical order is used more often than any other method of speech organization.

TIPS FOR PREPARING MAIN POINTS

Keep Main Points Separate

Each main point in a speech should be clearly independent of the others. Compare these two sets of main points for a speech about the process of producing a Broadway play:

Ineffective

I. The first step is choosing the play.

II. The second step is selecting the cast.

III. The third step is conducting rehearsals and then performing the play.

More Effective

I. The first step is choosing the play.

II. The second step is selecting the cast.

III. The third step is conducting the rehearsals.

IV. The fourth step is performing the play.

The problem with the left-hand list is that point III contains two main points. It should be divided, as shown in the right-hand list.

Try to Use the Same Pattern of Wording for Main Points

Consider the following main points for an informative speech about the benefits of karate:

Ineffective	More Effective
I. Karate gives you better mental discipline.	I. Karate improves your mental discipline.
II. You will become physically stronger through karate.	II. Karate increases your physical strength.
III. Taking karate lessons will teach you self-defense.	III. Karate teaches you self-defense.

The set of main points on the right follows a consistent pattern of wording throughout. Therefore, it is easier to understand and easier to remember than the set on the left.

You will find that it is not always possible to use this kind of parallel wording. Some speeches just don't lend themselves to such a tidy arrangement. But try to keep the wording parallel when you can; it's a good way to make your main points stand out from the details surrounding them.

Balance the Amount of Time Devoted to Main Points

Because your main points are so important, you want to be sure they all receive enough emphasis to be clear and convincing. This means allowing sufficient time to develop each main point. Suppose you discover that the proportion of time devoted to your main points is something like this:

I. 85 percent
II. 10 percent
III. 5 percent

A breakdown of this sort indicates one of two things. Either points II and III aren't really *main* points and you have only one main point, or points II and III haven't been given the attention they need. If the latter, you should revise the body of the speech to bring the main points into better balance.

This is not to say that all main points must receive exactly equal emphasis, but only that they should be roughly balanced. For example, either of the following would be fine:

I. 30 percent	I. 20 percent
II. 40 percent	II. 30 percent
III. 30 percent	III. 50 percent

The amount of time spent on each main point depends on the amount and complexity of supporting materials for each point.

Supporting Materials

By themselves, main points are only assertions. As we saw in Chapter 8, listeners need supporting materials to accept what a speaker says. The outline below demonstrates how supporting materials can be integrated into the body of a speech. (In Chapter 11, we'll look at requirements for a complete speech outline. For now, concentrate on how the supporting materials relate to the main points.)

supporting materials

The materials used to support a speaker's ideas. The three major kinds of supporting materials are examples, statistics, and testimony.

I. Hypnosis is used in surgery as an adjunct to chemical anesthesia.
  A. Hypnosis reduces both the physical and psychological aspects of pain.
    1. Hypnosis can double a person's pain threshold.
    2. It also reduces the fear that intensifies physical pain.
  B. Hypnosis is most useful in cases when the patient is known to have problems with general anesthesia.
    1. Quotation from Dr. Harold Wain of the Mayo Clinic.
    2. Story of Linda Kuay.
    3. Statistics from *Psychology Today.*

II. Hypnosis is used to help people stop smoking.
  A. Many therapists utilize hypnosis to help people break their addiction to cigarettes.
    1. The U.S. Department of Health and Human Services considers hypnosis a safe and effective means of stopping smoking.
    2. Success rates are as high as 70 percent.
      a. Story of Alex Hamilton.
      b. Quotation from New York psychiatrist Dr. Herbert Spiegel.
  B. Hypnosis does not work for all smokers.
    1. A person must want to stop smoking for hypnosis to work.
    2. A person must also be responsive to hypnotic suggestion.

III. Hypnosis is used to help students improve their academic performance.
  A. Hypnosis enables people to use their minds more effectively.
    1. The conscious mind utilizes about 10 percent of a person's mental ability.
    2. Hypnosis allows people to tap more of their mental power.
  B. Studies show that hypnosis can help people overcome many obstacles to academic success.
    1. It improves ability to concentrate.
    2. It increases reading speed.
    3. It reduces test anxiety.

In Chapter 8, we discussed the major kinds of supporting materials and how to use them. Here, we need stress only the importance of *organizing* your supporting materials so they are directly relevant to the main points they are supposed to support. Misplaced supporting materials are confusing. Here's an example:

I. There are several reasons why people immigrate to the United States.
  A. Over the years, millions of people have immigrated to the United States.
  B. Many people immigrate in search of economic opportunity.
  C. Others immigrate to attain political freedom.
  D. Still others immigrate to escape religious persecution.

The main point deals with the reasons immigrants come to the United States, as do supporting points B, C, and D. Supporting point A ("Over the years, millions of people have immigrated to the United States") does not. It is out of place and should not be included with this main point.

If you find such a situation in your own speeches, try to reorganize your supporting points under appropriate main points, like this:

I. Over the years, millions of people have immigrated to the United States.
  A. Since the American Revolution, more than 95 million people have immigrated to the United States.
  B. Today there are 40 million Americans who were born in other countries.

II. There are several reasons why people immigrate to the United States.
  A. Many people immigrate in search of economic opportunity.
  B. Others immigrate to attain political freedom.
  C. Still others immigrate to escape religious persecution.

Now you have two supporting points to back up your "millions of people" point and three supporting points to back up your "reasons" point.

Once you have organized your main points and supporting points, you must give attention to the third element in the body of a speech—connectives.

checklist

Main Points

YES	NO	
☐	☐	1. Does the body of my speech contain two to five main points?
☐	☐	2. Are my main points organized according to one of the following methods of organization? Chronological order Spatial order Causal order Topical order Problem-solution order
☐	☐	3. Are my main points clearly separate from one another?
☐	☐	4. As much as possible, have I used the same pattern of wording for all my main points?
☐	☐	5. Have I roughly balanced the amount of time devoted to each main point?
☐	☐	6. Is each main point backed up with strong, credible supporting materials?
☐	☐	7. Do I use connectives to make sure my audience knows when I am moving from one main point to another?

Connectives

Emily Berenson was speaking to her class about voter I.D. laws. She had rehearsed the speech several times, had a well-defined central idea, three sharp main points, and strong evidence to support her position. But when Emily delivered the speech, she said "All right" every time she moved from one thought to the next. After a while, her classmates started counting. By the end of the speech, most were too busy waiting for the next "All right" to pay attention to Emily's message. Afterward, Emily said, "I never even thought about saying 'All right.' I guess it just popped out when I didn't know what else to say."

connective

A word or phrase that connects the ideas of a speech and indicates the relationships among them.

We all have stock phrases that we use to fill the space between thoughts. In casual conversation they are seldom troublesome. But in speechmaking they distract listeners by calling attention to themselves.

What Emily's speech lacked were strong *connectives*—words or phrases that join one thought to another and indicate the relationship between them. Without connectives, a speech is disjointed and uncoordinated—much as a person would be without ligaments and tendons to join the bones and hold the organs in place. Four types of speech connectives are transitions, internal previews, internal summaries, and signposts.

TRANSITIONS

transition

A word or phrase that indicates when a speaker has finished one thought and is moving on to another.

Transitions are words or phrases that indicate when a speaker has just completed one thought and is moving on to another. Technically, the transitions state both the idea the speaker is leaving and the idea she or he is coming up to. In the following examples, the transitional phrases are underlined:

> Now that we have a clear understanding of the problem, let me share the solution with you.
>
> I have spoken so far of Cesar Chavez the community organizer, but it was his work as a labor leader that truly etched his name into American history.
>
> Keeping these points in mind about sign language, let's return to the sentence I started with and see if we can learn the signs for "You are my friend."

Notice how these phrases remind the listener of the thought just completed, as well as reveal the thought about to be developed.

INTERNAL PREVIEWS

internal preview

A statement in the body of the speech that lets the audience know what the speaker is going to discuss next.

Internal previews let the audience know what the speaker will take up next, but they are more detailed than transitions. In effect, an internal preview works just like the preview statement in a speech introduction, except that it comes in the body of the speech—usually as the speaker is starting to discuss a main point. For example:

> In discussing how Asian Americans have been stereotyped in the mass media, we'll look first at the origins of the problem and second at its continuing impact today.

After hearing this, the audience knows exactly what to listen for as the speaker develops the "problem" main point.

Internal previews are often combined with transitions. For example:

> [*Transition*]: Now that we have seen how serious the problem of faulty credit reports is, let's look at some solutions. [*Internal Preview*]: I will focus on three solutions—instituting tighter government regulation of credit bureaus, holding credit bureaus financially responsible for their errors, and giving individuals easier access to their credit reports.

You will seldom need an internal preview for each main point in your speech, but be sure to use one whenever you think it will help listeners keep track of your ideas.

INTERNAL SUMMARIES

Internal summaries are the reverse of internal previews. Rather than letting listeners know what is coming up next, internal summaries remind listeners of what they have just heard. Such summaries are usually used when a speaker finishes a complicated or particularly important main point or set of main points. For example:

internal summary

A statement in the body of the speech that summarizes the speaker's preceding point or points.

> In short, palm reading is an ancient art. Developed in China more than five thousand years ago, it was practiced in classical Greece and Rome, flourished during the Middle Ages, survived the Industrial Revolution, and remains popular today in many parts of the world.

Internal summaries are an excellent way to clarify and reinforce ideas. By combining them with transitions, you can also lead your audience smoothly into your next main point:

> [*Internal Summary*]: Let's pause for a moment to summarize what we have found so far. First, we have seen that keeping killer whales in captivity stunts their mental and physical development. Second, we have seen that keeping killer whales in captivity endangers other animals and human trainers. [*Transition*]: We are now in a position to see what can be done to keep killer whales out of captivity.

SIGNPOSTS

Signposts are very brief statements that indicate exactly where you are in the speech. Frequently they are just numbers. Here is how one student used simple numerical signposts to help her audience keep track of the major causes for the continuing problem of famine in Africa:

signpost

A very brief statement that indicates where a speaker is in the speech or that focuses attention on key ideas.

> <u>The first cause</u> of this problem is inefficient agricultural production.
>
> <u>The second cause</u> is recurrent drought in the affected countries.
>
> <u>The final cause</u> is mismanagement of available food resources by local leaders.

Another way to accomplish the same thing is to introduce your main points with a question, as did one student in his speech on mail-order fraud.

Experienced speakers include transitions and other connectives to help listeners keep track of their ideas. Here Joseph Jimenez, CEO of Novartis, addresses the 2014 World Economic Forum in Davos, Switzerland.

His first main point showed that mail-order fraud continues to be a serious problem despite the growth of the Internet. He introduced it this way:

> So just how serious is the problem of mail-order fraud? Is it just a few isolated cases, or is it widespread enough to require serious measures to protect consumers?

His second main point dealt with ways to curb mail-order fraud. He introduced it by saying:

> So how can we solve this problem? Is there a way to protect the rights of legitimate mail-order companies while attacking the fraudulent ones?

Questions are particularly effective as signposts because they invite subliminal answers and thereby get the audience more involved with the speech.

Besides using signposts to indicate where you are in the speech, you can use them to focus attention on key ideas. You can do this with a simple phrase, as in the following example:

> The most important thing to remember about abstract art is that it is always based on forms in the natural world.

The underlined words alert the audience to the fact that an especially significant point is coming up. So do phrases such as these:

> Be sure to keep this in mind . . .
>
> This is crucial to understanding the rest of the speech . . .
>
> Above all, you need to know . . .

Depending on the needs of your speech, you may want to use two, three, or even all four kinds of connectives in combination. You needn't worry too much about what they are called—whether this one is a signpost and that a transition. The important thing is to be aware of their functions. Properly applied, connectives can make your speeches more unified and coherent.

Summary

Clear organization is vital to speechmaking. Listeners demand coherence. They get only one chance to grasp a speaker's ideas, and they have little patience for speakers who ramble aimlessly from one idea to another. A well-organized speech will enhance your credibility and make it easier for the audience to understand your message.

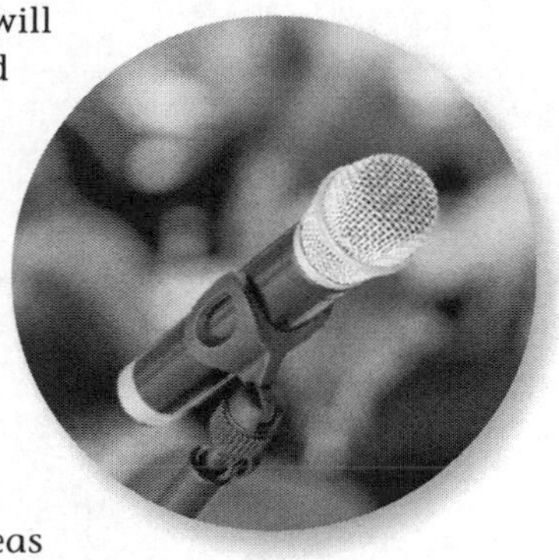

The process of planning the body of a speech begins when you determine the main points. You should choose them carefully, phrase them precisely, and organize them strategically. Because listeners cannot keep track of a multitude of main points, most speeches should contain no more than two to five. Each should focus on a single idea, should be worded clearly, and should receive enough emphasis to be clear and convincing.

You can organize main points in various ways, depending on your topic, purpose, and audience. Chronological order follows a time pattern, whereas spatial order follows a directional pattern. In causal order, main points are organized according to their cause-effect relationship. Topical order results when you divide your main topic into subtopics. Problem-solution order breaks the body of the speech into two main parts—the first showing a problem, the second giving a solution.

Supporting materials are the backup ideas for your main points. When organizing supporting materials, make sure they are directly relevant to the main points they are supposed to support.

Connectives help tie a speech together. They are words or phrases that join one thought to another and indicate the relationship between them. The four major types of speech connectives are transitions, internal previews, internal summaries, and signposts. Using them effectively will make your speeches more unified and coherent.

Key Terms

strategic organization (166)
main points (167)
chronological order (169)
spatial order (170)
causal order (170)
problem-solution order (172)
topical order (172)
supporting materials (176)
connective (178)
transition (178)
internal preview (178)
internal summary (179)
signpost (179)

Review Questions

After reading this chapter, you should be able to answer the following questions:

1. Why is it important that speeches be organized clearly and coherently?
2. How many main points will your speeches usually contain? Why is it important to limit the number of main points in your speeches?
3. What are the five basic patterns of organizing main points in a speech? Which are appropriate for informative speeches? Which is most appropriate for persuasive speeches? Which is used most often?
4. What are three tips for preparing your main points?
5. What is the most important thing to remember when organizing supporting materials in the body of your speech?
6. What are the four kinds of speech connectives? What role does each play in a speech?

connect

For further review, go to the LearnSmart study module for this chapter.

Exercises for Critical Thinking

1. What organizational method (or methods) might you use to arrange main points for speeches with the following specific purpose statements?

   To inform my audience of the geographical regions of South Africa.

   To inform my audience about the major stages in the development of the American film industry.

   To persuade my audience that the state legislature should enact tougher laws to curb the problem of predatory lending to college students.

   To inform my audience about the causes and effects of Lyme disease.

   To inform my audience about the educational philosophy of Maria Montessori.

   To inform my audience about the major kinds of symbols used in Native American art.

2. Turn to the outline of main points and supporting materials for the speech about hypnosis on pages 175–177. Create appropriate transitions, internal previews, internal summaries, and signposts for the speech.
3. Identify the organizational method used in each of the following sets of main points.

   I. The philosophy of hacktivism revolves around free speech, human rights, and online civil disobedience.
   II. The objectives of hacktivism are to expose the corruption and inner workings of governments and corporations.

   I. In ancient Rome, the Colosseum hosted gladiatorial games and other kinds of popular entertainment.
   II. In the Middle Ages, the Colosseum was occupied by religious groups and used as a cemetery.
   III. In modern times, the Colosseum has been restored and turned into a tourist attraction.

I. Caused by a rare genetic mutation, progeria is an inherited disease that has no known treatment.
II. The effects of progeria include the appearance of rapid aging, limited growth, and a shortened lifespan.

I. At the top of the rainforest is the emergent layer, where trees can be 200 feet tall.
II. Below the emergent layer is the canopy, where vegetation is so dense that it filters out 80 percent of the sunlight.
III. Beneath the canopy is the understory, where trees are less than 12 feet tall and grow large leaves to collect the small amount of sunlight.
IV. At the bottom is the forest floor, where there are almost no plants because of the lack of sunlight.

I. Cyberbullying is a widespread national problem.
II. The problem can be solved by a combination of individual awareness and social action.

10

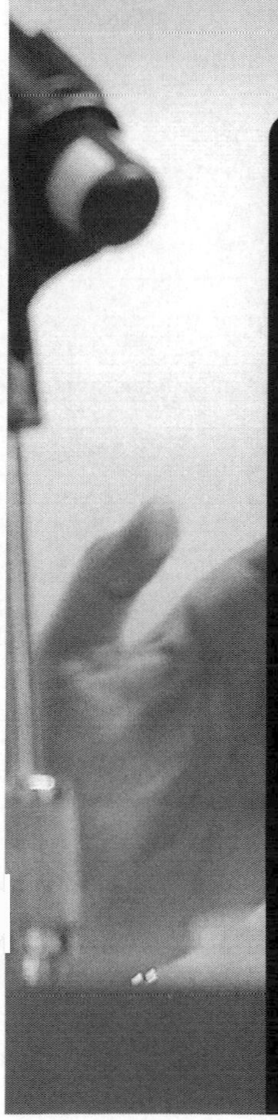

Beginning and Ending the Speech

The Introduction

The Conclusion

On the night of January 26, 1988, a conductor stepped to the podium at the Majestic Theatre in New York City, tapped his baton, raised his arms, and signaled the orchestra to play. Moments later, American theatergoers first heard the dramatic opening chords of *The Phantom of the Opera*. Today, this scene has been repeated more than 11,500 times and *Phantom* has become the longest-running musical in Broadway history.

Like most classic musicals, *Phantom of the Opera* begins with an overture—an orchestral introduction that captures the audience's attention and gives them a preview of the music they are going to hear. Without such an introduction—if the characters simply walked onstage and began singing or speaking—the beginning of the play would seem too abrupt, and the audience would not be suitably "primed" for the entertainment.

Similarly, most musicals end with a finale, when the whole cast is onstage, elements of the dramatic plot are resolved, portions of the principal songs are recalled, and the music is brought to a dramatic climax. If there were no such conclusion, if the actors merely stopped and walked offstage, the audience would be left unsatisfied.

Just as musical plays need appropriate beginnings and endings, so do speeches. The beginning, or introduction, prepares listeners for what is to come. The conclusion ties up the speech and alerts listeners that the speech is going to end. Ideally, it is a satisfying conclusion.

In this chapter, we explore the roles played by an introduction and a conclusion in speechmaking. We also discuss techniques aimed at fulfilling those roles. If you apply these techniques imaginatively, you will take a big step toward elevating your speeches from the ordinary to the splendid.

The Introduction

First impressions are important. A poor beginning may so distract or alienate listeners that the speaker can never fully recover. Moreover, getting off on the right foot is vital to a speaker's self-confidence. What could be more encouraging than watching your listeners' faces begin to register interest, attention, and pleasure? A good introduction, you will find, is an excellent confidence booster.

In most speech situations, the introduction has four objectives:

- Get the attention and interest of your audience.
- Reveal the topic of your speech.
- Establish your credibility and goodwill.
- Preview the body of the speech.

We'll look at each of these objectives in turn.

GET ATTENTION AND INTEREST

"Unless a speaker can interest his audience at once, his effort will be a failure." So said the great lawyer Clarence Darrow. If your topic is not one of extraordinary interest, your listeners are likely to say to themselves, "So what? Who cares?" A speaker can quickly lose an audience if she or he doesn't use the introduction to get their attention and quicken their interest.

Getting the initial attention of your audience is usually easy—even before you utter a single word. After you are introduced and step to the lectern, your audience will normally give you their attention. If they don't, wait patiently. Look directly at the audience without saying a word. In a few moments all talking and physical commotion will stop. Your listeners will be attentive. You will be ready to start speaking.

Keeping the attention of your audience once you start talking is more difficult. Here are the methods used most often. Employed individually or in combination, they will help get the audience caught up in your speech.

Relate the Topic to the Audience

People pay attention to things that affect them directly. If you can relate the topic to your listeners, they are much more likely to be interested in it.

Suppose, for example, one of your classmates begins her speech like this:

> Today I am going to talk about collecting postcards—a hobby that is both fascinating and financially rewarding. I would like to explain the basic kinds of collectible postcards, why they are so valuable, and how collectors buy and sell their cards.

To be most effective, a speech introduction should relate the topic to the audience and be delivered with strong eye contact—as in this presentation by Craig Kielburger, co-founder of Free the Children.

This is certainly a clear introduction, but it is not one to get you hooked on the speech. Now what if your classmate were to begin her speech this way—as one student actually did.

> It's Saturday morning, and you are helping clean out your grandmother's attic. After working a while, you stumble upon a trunk, open it, and discover hundreds of old postcards. Thinking about getting to the football game on time, you start tossing the cards into the trash can. Congratulations! You have just thrown away a year's tuition.

This time the speaker has used just the right bait. Chances are you will be hooked.

Even when you use other interest-arousing lures, you should *always* relate your topic to the audience. At times this will test your ingenuity, but it pays dividends. Here is an excellent example from a student speech about dreams. The speaker began by saying:

> You're being chased by an object of unspeakable horror, yet your legs can only move in slow motion. Each step takes unbearably long, and your frantic struggle to run faster is hopeless. Your pursuer gets closer, and your desperation turns to terror. You're completely helpless—eye to eye with death.
>
> Then you wake up, gasping for air, your heart pounding, your face clammy with sweat. It takes a few minutes for your heart and breathing to slow down. You reassure yourself that it was "just a dream." Soon you drift back to sleep.

connect

View the beginning of "In Your Dreams" in the online Media Library for this chapter (Video 10.1).

By using vivid language to describe something all his classmates had experienced, the speaker made sure of an attentive audience.

State the Importance of Your Topic

Presumably, you think your speech is important. Tell your audience why they should think so too. Here is how Shaun Donovan, U.S. Secretary of Housing and Urban Development, used this method in a speech about the limited lifetime possibilities facing children who grow up in poor neighborhoods:

> There are 3.9 million kids growing up in this country in neighborhoods of concentrated poverty. That's two and a half times the entire population of Manhattan. . . . No matter how hard they work in school, no matter what their parents do to try to get ahead, the single biggest predictor of their life chances, even their lifespan, is the zip code they grow up in.[1]

This is striking information. By citing it in his introduction, Donovan emphasized the importance of his topic and captured the attention of his audience.

Clearly this technique is easy to use when discussing social and political issues such as poverty, endangered species, and domestic surveillance, but it is appropriate for other topics as well. Here is how one student handled it in a speech about beach volleyball:

> Beach volleyball has grown from summer fun to an intensely competitive international sport, with 3 million participants in the United States alone. It's the fastest growing sport in NCAA history, with more than 40 sanctioned programs in three years. High schools around the country are now adding it to their extracurricular offerings. And at the last summer Olympics, tickets to watch beach volleyball sold faster than tickets to any other event.
>
> Today, we'll look at the history of beach volleyball and some of the reasons for its spectacular growth.

Whenever you discuss a topic whose importance may not be clear to the audience, you should think about ways to demonstrate its significance in the introduction.

Startle the Audience

One surefire way to arouse interest quickly is to startle your listeners with an arresting or intriguing statement. Everyone in the audience paid close attention after this speaker's introduction:

> Take a moment and think of the three women closest to you. Who comes to mind? Your mother? Your sister? Your girlfriend? Your wife? Your best friend? Now guess which one will be sexually assaulted during her lifetime. It's not a pleasant thought, but according to the U.S. Department of Justice, one of every three American women will be sexually assaulted sometime during her life.

Notice the buildup to the speaker's arresting statement, "Now guess which one will be sexually assaulted during her lifetime." This statement startles the audience—especially the men—and drives home at a personal level the problem of sexual assault against women.

This technique is highly effective and easy to use. Just be sure the startling introduction relates directly to the subject of your speech. If you choose a strong opening simply for its shock value and then go on to talk about something else, your audience will be confused and possibly annoyed.

Arouse the Curiosity of the Audience

People are curious. One way to draw them into your speech is with a series of statements that progressively whet their curiosity about the subject of the speech. For example:

> This past month, more than 1 billion people around the world skipped lunch every day. They ate no food of any kind and drank no liquid of any kind from sunup to sunset. They did this every day during the month, and they do the same thing every year. I myself did it.
>
> Why? Last month was a time for tending to the mind, the body, and the spirit. Last month was the Muslim holy month of Ramadan.

connect

View the beginning of "Ramadan" in the online Media Library for this chapter (Video 10.2).

By building suspense about her subject, the speaker pulls her audience into the speech. Notice how much less effective the introduction would have been if she had simply said, "Today I am going to talk about Ramadan."

Question the Audience

Asking a *rhetorical question* is another way to get your listeners thinking about your speech. Sometimes a single question will do:

> How would you respond if a loved one was the victim of terrorism?
>
> What would you think if you went to the doctor because you were ill and she told you to watch *The Big Bang Theory* as part of your treatment?

In other circumstances, you may want to pose a series of questions, each of which draws the audience deeper and deeper into the speech. Here is how one speaker used this method:

rhetorical question

A question that the audience answers mentally rather than out loud.

> Have you ever spent a sleepless night studying for an exam? Can you remember rushing to finish a term paper because you waited too long to start writing it? Do you often feel overwhelmed by all the things you have to get done at school? At work? At home?
>
> If so, you may be the victim of poor time management. Fortunately, there are proven strategies you can follow to use your time more effectively and to keep control of your life.

When using this technique, be sure to pause for just a moment after each question. This adds dramatic impact and gives the question time to sink in. The audience, of course, will answer mentally—not out loud.

Begin with a Quotation

Another way to arouse the interest of your audience is to start with an attention-getting quotation. You might choose your quotation from Shakespeare or Confucius, from the Bible or Talmud, from a poem, song, or film. Here is how one student used a humorous quotation to begin a speech about the need for political reform in the U.S. Congress:

> Mark Twain once said, "It could probably be shown by facts and figures that there is no distinctly American criminal class except Congress."

You need not use a famous quotation. The following made an effective introduction for a speech about bird watching:

> "It is a moment I will never forget. I glimpsed a flash of color in the thicket, and then I saw it—a Bachman's Warbler, one of the rarest birds in all of America. I was so excited I could barely keep my binoculars from shaking."
>
> This statement was made by my father. He is just one of the millions of people who have discovered the joys of bird-watching.

Notice that both of the quotations used here as examples are relatively short. Opening your speech with a lengthy quotation is a sure way to set your audience yawning.

Tell a Story

We all enjoy stories—especially if they are provocative, dramatic, or suspenseful. Consider the story one student told to open his speech about the growing epidemic of heroin abuse in the United States:

> He had become an addict in his early 20s. But through willpower, dedication, and the help of family and friends, he got clean. That lasted for 23 years—23 years in which his career reached incredible heights.

checklist

Speech Introduction

YES	NO	
☐	☐	1. Do I gain the attention and interest of my audience by using one or more of the methods discussed in this chapter?
☐	☐	2. Do I relate the speech topic to my audience?
☐	☐	3. Do I clearly reveal the topic of my speech?
☐	☐	4. Do I establish my credibility to speak on this topic?
☐	☐	5. If my topic is controversial, do I take steps to establish my goodwill toward the audience?
☐	☐	6. Do I define any key terms that will be necessary for the audience to understand the rest of my speech?
☐	☐	7. Do I provide a preview statement of the main points to be covered in the body of the speech?
☐	☐	8. Is the introduction limited to 10–20 percent of my entire speech?
☐	☐	9. Have I worked out the language of my introduction in detail?
☐	☐	10. Have I practiced the delivery of my introduction so I can present it fluently, confidently, and with strong eye contact?

As you work on your speeches, keep an eye out for quotations, stories, and other materials you can use to craft an introduction that will capture the attention of your listeners.

> Then the addiction came back. One cold Sunday morning in January, a friend found him dead, a needle in his arm, a bag of heroin nearby. There were more than 50 other bags of heroin in his apartment, along with several bottles of prescription drugs.
>
> This 46-year-old victim of a heroin overdose was not only a loving father of three but also one of the greatest actors of his generation. You may have seen him in *Boogie Nights*, *The Master*, *Hunger Games*, or *Capote*—the role that won him an Oscar. He was Philip Seymour Hoffman, and his overdose in 2014 not only shocked the nation but once again revealed the horrors of heroin.

Like many good introductions, this one does a double job—it arouses the interest of the audience and gets listeners emotionally involved in the speech.

You can also use stories based on your personal experience. Here is how one pre-med student used such a story. She began by recounting the first time she observed doctors performing surgery in the operating room:

> There I stood, wearing a surgical mask, in the middle of a large, brightly lit room. In the center of the room were five figures huddled over a table. I found it difficult to see since everything was draped in blue sheets, yet I didn't dare take a step toward the table.
>
> Then one of the figures called to me, "Angela, get over here and take a closer look." My knees buckled as I walked through the sterile environment. But eventually I was there, standing over an unconscious body in the operating room.

connect

View the beginning of "Hoping to Heal" in the online Media Library for this chapter (Video 10.3).

The effectiveness of any story—especially a personal one—hinges on the speaker's delivery as well as on the content. As you can see from the excerpt of this speech on Video 10.3 in the online Media Library for this chapter, the speaker uses pauses, eye contact, and changes in her tone of voice to help draw her audience into the speech. See if you can do the same in your introduction.

The seven methods discussed above are the ones used most often by student speakers to gain attention and interest. Other methods include referring to the occasion, inviting audience participation, using audio equipment or visual aids, relating to a previous speaker, and beginning with humor. For any given speech, try to choose the method that is most suitable for the topic, the audience, and the occasion.

REVEAL THE TOPIC

In the process of gaining attention, be sure to state clearly the topic of your speech. If you do not, your listeners will be confused. And once they are confused, your chances of getting them absorbed in the speech are almost nil.

This is a basic point—so basic that it may hardly seem worth mentioning. Yet you would be surprised how many students need to be reminded of it. You may hear speeches in your own class in which the topic is not clear by the end of the introduction. So you will know what to avoid, here is such an introduction, presented in a public speaking class:

> Imagine taking a leisurely boat ride along a peaceful waterway. The sun is high in the sky, reflecting brightly off the ripples around you. The banks are lush with mangrove and cypress trees. You see a stately pelican resting on a low-lying branch. You grab your camera, snap a shot, and check the result. The picture is perfect. But will it be perfect in the future?

What is the topic of this speech? Nature photography? No. Birding? No. Tourism in the tropics? No. The student was talking about efforts to restore the natural beauty of the Florida Everglades. But she did not make that clear to her audience. Suppose, instead, she had begun her speech differently:

> Alligators, panthers, otters, brown pelicans—these and other creatures have lost 50 percent of their habitat in south Florida over the past few decades. Now, however, there is an $8 billion program to preserve their home in the Florida Everglades. The largest restoration effort in the history of the world, it will rejuvenate one of America's most diverse ecosystems and protect it for future generations.

This opening would have provided a way to get the audience's attention, but it also would have related directly to the speech topic. If you beat around the bush in your introduction, you may lose your listeners. Even if they already know your topic, you should restate it clearly and concisely at some point in the introduction.

ESTABLISH CREDIBILITY AND GOODWILL

Besides getting attention and revealing the topic, there is a third objective you may need to accomplish in your introduction—establishing your credibility and goodwill.

credibility

The audience's perception of whether a speaker is qualified to speak on a given topic.

Credibility is mostly a matter of being qualified to speak on a given topic—and of being *perceived* as qualified by your listeners. Here is how one student established her credibility on the subject of knitting without sounding like a braggart:

> Once considered something that grandmas did while rocking on the front porch, knitting is becoming more and more popular among our generation—and with good reason. Regardless of your age or gender, knitting can lower stress, produce a sense of accomplishment, and even promote mental health.
>
> I started knitting when I was 10 years old, and I've been doing it ever since. I now sell knit patterns on my own Web site and on Etsy and Pinterest. On weekends, I participate in trunk shows and expos dedicated to the knitting arts.

Telling a story is an excellent way to gain attention in a speech introduction. The story should be clearly relevant to the topic and should be delivered expressively and with strong eye contact.

> Using some of my experience, today I will explain a bit about the process of knitting and why it is so beneficial.

Whether or not you have done any knitting yourself, you will probably be more interested in the speech when you realize that the speaker knows what she is talking about.

Your credibility need not be based on firsthand knowledge and experience. It can come from reading, from classes, from interviews, from friends—as in these cases:

> I have been interested in the myth of Atlantis for several years, and I have read a number of books and articles about it.

> The information I am going to share with you today comes mostly from my biology class and an interview with Reyna Vasquez of the local Audubon Society.

Whatever the source of your expertise, be sure to let the audience know.

Establishing your *goodwill* is a slightly different challenge. It is often crucial outside the classroom, where speakers have well-established reputations and may be identified with causes that arouse hostility among listeners. In such a situation, the speaker must try to defuse that hostility right at the start of the speech.

goodwill

The audience's perception of whether the speaker has the best interests of the audience in mind.

Occasionally you may have to do the same thing in your classroom speeches. Suppose you advocate a potentially unpopular position. You will need to make a special effort to ensure that your classmates will consider your point of view. This is how one student tried to minimize her classmates' opposition in the introduction of a speech urging them to change the way they use their cell phones:

> Now, don't worry, I'm not going to try to persuade you to abandon your constant companion. I still use mine on a regular basis, and I probably always

connect

View this portion of "The Dangers of Cell Phones" in the online Media Library for this chapter (Video 10.4).

> will. But I do hope to persuade you to make one simple change in the way you use your cell phone—a change that will help protect your health.

The speaker was clear about her intentions and reasonable in her expectations. By the end of the introduction, the audience knew she had their best interests at heart.

PREVIEW THE BODY OF THE SPEECH

As we saw in Chapter 3, most people are poor listeners. Even good listeners need all the help they can get in sorting out a speaker's ideas. One way to help your listeners is to tell them in the introduction what they should listen for in the rest of the speech. Here is an excellent example from a speech by Secretary of Defense Robert Gates at the U.S. Military Academy, West Point:

preview statement

A statement in the introduction of a speech that identifies the main points to be discussed in the body.

> Today, I'd like to focus on three interrelated issues—the future of conflict and the implications for the Army; how best to institutionalize the diverse capabilities that will be required; and the kinds of officers the Army will need for the 21st century.[2]

After this introduction, there was no doubt about Gates's topic or the main points he would cover in his speech.

In some types of persuasive speeches, you may not want to reveal your central idea until later in the speech. But even in such a situation you must be sure your audience is not left guessing about the main points they should listen for as the speech unfolds. Nearly always, you should include a *preview statement* like the following:

> I've been fascinated by the Statue of Liberty ever since I was a kid, but I never knew just how amazing it is until I researched it for this speech. This morning, I'd like to tell you a bit about its symbolism, its history, and its architecture.

> I am convinced that we need to take action to combat the problem of phony pharmaceuticals. Later in my speech, I'll share a plan with you for curbing the spread of these dangerous drugs. But let's start by taking a closer look at the problem.

Preview statements such as these serve another purpose as well. Because they usually come at the very end of the introduction, they provide a smooth lead-in to the body of the speech. They signal that the body of the speech is about to begin.

There is one other aspect you may want to cover in previewing your speech. You can use your introduction to give specialized information—definitions or background—that your listeners will need if they are to understand the rest of the speech. Often you can do this very quickly, as in the following example:

> A triathlon is a race made up of three different events completed in succession. The events are usually swimming, biking, and running, though canoeing is sometimes substituted for one of these.

In other circumstances, you may have to explain an important term in more detail. Here is how one student handled the problem in a speech calling for the creation of a living wage policy to replace the current minimum wage:

> What is the living wage, you ask? Well, it's not the same as the minimum wage. The minimum wage is set by Congress and is the same in every part of the country. The living wage goes beyond the minimum wage.
>
> As the *Wall Street Journal* reports, the living wage is tied to the local cost of living and can vary from location to location. Its purpose is to help workers and their families meet a basic standard of living, even when that standard of living is higher than the minimum wage.

connect™

View this excerpt from "The Living Wage Solution" in the online Media Library for this chapter (Video 10.5).

SAMPLE INTRODUCTION WITH COMMENTARY

So far we have seen many excerpts showing how to fulfill the various objectives of an introduction. Now here is a complete introduction from a student speech. The side comments indicate the principles used in developing the introduction.

connect™

View this introduction in the online Media Library for this chapter (Video 10.6).

Surrounded by Stuff

COMMENTARY	SPEECH
The speaker uses a story to gain attention. This story works particularly well because it is richly detailed and is high in human interest. The frequent use of "you" helps relate the story to the audience.	For my Aunt Josefina, life can be empty, even though she's surrounded by tons of stuff. Walking into her living room, you'll see stacks of magazines and newspapers, piles of clean and dirty laundry, and boxes of collectible figurines. But you won't find a place to sit down. In her kitchen, you'll see towers of dishes, scores of empty two-liter bottles, and over a dozen trash bags. But you won't see a kitchen table.
Now the speaker reveals her topic and defines the meaning of hoarding. The way she gradually reveals Aunt Josefina's malady helps build the audience's interest. Her personal involvement with the topic increases her credibility and goodwill.	Some people say Aunt Josefina is lazy. Others say she's just dirty. But my family and I know the truth: Aunt Josefina suffers from a mental disorder known as Collyer's Syndrome, or disposophobia. But you probably know it by its most common name: compulsive hoarding. Those who suffer from compulsive hoarding can't bring themselves to get rid of anything. It doesn't matter if the things are valuable; it only matters that they hold on to them.
The speaker uses statistics to show the importance of her topic. Mentioning her research for the speech further bolsters her credibility.	Over the years, my family and I have become painfully aware of what life is like for a compulsive hoarder. But until researching the topic for this speech, I had no idea how widespread the disorder was. Gail Steketee and Randy Frost, authors of *Stuff: Compulsive Hoarding and the Meaning of Things,* report that anywhere from 6 million to 15 million Americans are compulsive hoarders.
The introduction ends with a clear preview of the main points to be discussed in the body.	Today I would like to introduce you to the world of compulsive hoarding. I will show you the seriousness of the problem, the impact it can have on individuals and families, and the ways it can be treated.

TIPS FOR THE INTRODUCTION

1. Keep the introduction relatively brief. Under normal circumstances it should not constitute more than 10 to 20 percent of your speech.
2. Be on the lookout for possible introductory materials as you do your research. File them with your notes so they will be handy when you are ready for them.
3. Be creative in devising your introduction. Experiment with two or three different openings and choose the one that seems most likely to get the audience interested in your speech.
4. Don't worry about the exact wording of your introduction until you have finished preparing the body of the speech. After you have determined your main points, it will be much easier to make final decisions about how to begin the speech.
5. Work out your introduction in detail. Some teachers recommend that you write it out word for word; others prefer that you outline it. Whichever method you use, practice the introduction over and over until you can deliver it smoothly from a minimum of notes and with strong eye contact.
6. When you present the speech, don't start talking too soon. Make sure the audience has quieted down and is focused on you before you begin. Establish eye contact with the audience, smile, and then launch into your opening words. Give yourself every chance to make sure your introduction has the desired impact.

The Conclusion

"Great is the art of beginning," said Longfellow, "but greater the art is of ending." Longfellow was thinking of poetry, but his insight is equally applicable to public speaking. Many a speaker has marred an otherwise fine speech by a long-winded, silly, or antagonistic conclusion. Your closing remarks are your last chance to drive home your ideas. Moreover, your final impression will probably linger in your listeners' minds. Thus you need to craft your conclusion with as much care as your introduction.

No matter what kind of speech you are giving, the conclusion has two major functions:

- To let the audience know you are ending the speech.
- To reinforce the audience's understanding of, or commitment to, the central idea.

Let us look at each.

SIGNAL THE END OF THE SPEECH

It may seem obvious that you should let your audience know you are going to stop soon. However, you will almost certainly hear speeches in your class in which the speaker concludes so abruptly that you are taken by surprise. Too sudden an ending leaves the audience puzzled and unfulfilled.

The conclusion is your last chance to drive home your ideas. Successful speakers such as San Antonio mayor Julian Castro craft their endings with great care to leave a strong impression.

How do you let an audience know your speech is ending? One way is through what you say. "In conclusion," "My purpose has been," "Let me end by saying"—these are all brief cues that you are getting ready to stop.

You can also let your audience know the end is in sight by your manner of delivery. The conclusion is the climax of a speech. A speaker who has carefully built to a peak of interest and involvement will not need to say anything like "in conclusion." By use of the voice—its tone, pacing, intonation, and rhythm—a speaker can build the momentum of a speech so there is no doubt when it is over.

One method of doing this has been likened to a musical crescendo. As in a symphony in which one instrument after another joins in until the entire orchestra is playing, the speech builds in force until it reaches a zenith of power and intensity.[3] (This does *not* mean simply getting louder and louder. It is a combination of many things, including vocal pitch, choice of words, dramatic content, gestures, pauses—and possibly loudness.)

crescendo ending

A conclusion in which the speech builds to a zenith of power and intensity.

A superb example of this method is the memorable conclusion to Martin Luther King's "I've Been to the Mountaintop," the speech he delivered the night before he was assassinated in April 1968. Speaking to an audience of 2,000 people in Memphis, Tennessee, he ended his speech with a stirring declaration that the civil rights movement would succeed despite the many threats on his life:

> Like anybody, I would like to live a long life. Longevity has its place, but I'm not concerned about that now. I just want to do God's will, and he's allowed me to go up to the mountain, and I've looked over and I've seen the Promised Land. I may not get there with you, but I want you to know tonight that we as a people will get to the Promised Land. So I'm happy tonight. I'm not worried about anything; I'm not fearing any man. Mine eyes have seen the glory of the coming of the Lord.

Another effective method might be compared to the dissolve ending of a concert song that evokes deep emotions: "The song seems to fade away while the light on the singer shrinks gradually to a smaller and smaller circle until it lights only the face, then the eyes. Finally, it is a pinpoint, and disappears with the last note of the song."[4] Here is a speech ending that does much the same thing. It is from General Douglas MacArthur's moving farewell to the cadets at the U.S. Military Academy:

dissolve ending

A conclusion that generates emotional appeal by fading step by step to a dramatic final statement.

> In my dreams I hear again the crash of guns, the rattle of musketry, the strange, mournful mutter of the battlefield. But in the evening of my memory always I come back to West Point. Always there echoes and re-echoes: duty, honor, country.
>
> Today marks my final roll call with you. But I want you to know that when I cross the river, my last conscious thoughts will be of the Corps, and the Corps, and the Corps.
>
> I bid you farewell.

Using public speaking in your CAREER

Your degree in civil engineering has served you well and you are now the chief city planner for a major metropolis. After studying the issue for more than a year, you and the planning commission have decided that the best way to relieve the city's growing traffic congestion is to build a new downtown freeway. Unfortunately, there is no way to build the freeway without knocking down a number of houses and businesses.

Not surprisingly, the neighborhood association that represents the area through which the new freeway will run has expressed a number of concerns about the proposal. Because of your excellent public speaking skills, you have been chosen to represent the city at a meeting of the neighborhood association. You know that if your speech is to be persuasive, you must use the introduction to establish your credibility and goodwill so your listeners will be willing to listen receptively to what you say in the body.

Write a draft of your introduction. Be sure to address all four functions of a speech introduction discussed in this chapter.

The final words fade like the spotlight, bringing the speech to an emotional close.

You may think that you couldn't possibly end a speech with that much pathos—and you'd be right. MacArthur was an eloquent speaker discussing a grave issue with extraordinary poignance. This combination rarely occurs. But that doesn't mean you can't use the dissolve ending effectively. One student used it with great effect in a speech about the immigrant experience in the United States. During the body of the speech, the student spoke about the numbers of immigrants and the challenges they faced. Then, in her conclusion, she created a moving dissolve ending by evoking the emotional images of her grandfather's arrival in the United States:

> On a recent trip to Ellis Island, where my grandfather first stepped on American soil, I saw his name etched into the wall along with the names of tens of thousands of other immigrants. I saw the entry hall where he lined up to process his forms. I saw the room where he underwent a physical examination. I sensed the fear and insecurity he must have felt. But I could also sense his excitement as he looked forward to life in a land of opportunity—a land he came to think of as home.

Both the crescendo and the dissolve endings must be worked out with great care. Practice until you get the words and the timing just right. The benefits will be well worth your time.

REINFORCE THE CENTRAL IDEA

The second major function of a conclusion is to reinforce the audience's understanding of, or commitment to, the central idea. There are many ways to do this. Here are the ones you are most likely to use.

Summarize Your Speech

Restating the main points is the easiest way to end a speech. One student used this technique effectively in his persuasive speech about the resurgence of tuberculosis as a worldwide killer:

> In conclusion, we have seen how tuberculosis has recently returned as a global health crisis. It is infecting and killing on an unprecedented scale. Especially in third-world countries, TB is decimating those who need the most help.
>
> But there is hope. The World Health Organization and privileged countries like the United States can expand their efforts to treat and prevent TB. We have the money and we have the know-how. Now we just need to come together and put an end to this epidemic.

connect

View the conclusion of "TB: An Ancient Plague Returns" in the online Media Library for this chapter (Video 10.7).

The value of a summary is that it explicitly restates the central idea and main points one last time. But as we shall see, there are more imaginative and compelling ways to end a speech. They can be used in combination with a summary or, at times, in place of it.

End with a Quotation

A quotation is one of the most common and effective devices to conclude a speech. Here is a fine example, from a speech on volunteering for Big Brothers or Big Sisters:

> None of us have the extra time that we'd like. But whatever time you can spare, you'll be making a world of difference in the life of an underprivileged child. In the words of the poet Henry Wadsworth Longfellow, "Give what you have. To someone, it may be better than you dare to think."

The closing quotation is particularly good because its urgency is exactly suited to the speech. When you run across a *brief* quotation that so perfectly captures your central idea, keep it in mind as a possible conclusion.

Make a Dramatic Statement

Rather than using a quotation to give your conclusion force and vitality, you may want to devise your own dramatic statement. Some speeches have become famous because of their powerful closing lines. One is Patrick Henry's legendary "Liberty or Death" oration. It takes its name from the final sentences Henry uttered on March 23, 1775, as he exhorted his audience to resist British tyranny:

> Is life so dear, or peace so sweet, as to be purchased at the price of chains and slavery? Forbid it, Almighty God! I know not what course others may take; but as for me, give me liberty, or give me death.

Although your classroom speeches are not likely to become famous, you can still rivet your listeners—as Henry did—with a dramatic concluding statement. What follows is a particularly striking example, from a speech on suicide prevention. Throughout the speech, the student referred to a friend

checklist

Speech Conclusion

YES	NO	
☐	☐	1. Do I signal that my speech is coming to an end?
☐	☐	2. Do I reinforce my central idea by: Summarizing the main points of my speech Ending with a quotation Making a dramatic statement Referring to the introduction
☐	☐	3. Is the conclusion limited to 5–10 percent of my entire speech?
☐	☐	4. Have I worked out the language of my conclusion in detail?
☐	☐	5. Have I practiced the delivery of my conclusion so I can present it fluently, confidently, and with strong eye contact?

who had tried to commit suicide the previous year. Then, in the conclusion, she said:

> My friend is back in school, participating in activities she never did before—and enjoying it. I'm happy and proud to say that she's still fighting for her life and even happier that she failed to kill herself. Otherwise, I wouldn't be here today trying to help you. You see, I am my "friend," and I'm more than glad to say I've made it.

As you can imagine, the audience was stunned. The closing lines brought the speech to a dramatic conclusion. The speaker made it even more effective by pausing just a moment before the last words and by using her voice to give them just the right inflection.

Refer to the Introduction

An excellent way to give your speech psychological unity is to conclude by referring to ideas in the introduction. Here is how one student used the method in her speech about carbon monoxide poisoning:

Introduction It was supposed to be a time of celebration. Five friends had gathered in a south Florida hotel room to celebrate a birthday. Juchen Martial, one of the five, was turning nineteen. But the day after the birthday party, a maid passing by the hotel room glanced through a window and saw five dead bodies. All five friends had been killed.

Their killer was silent, invisible, odorless, and tasteless. Their killer was carbon monoxide. The friends had left their car running in a carport directly beneath their hotel room. Carbon monoxide seeped into the room and took their lives—as it does the lives of 400 people a year in the United States.

In the body of her speech, the student looked in detail at the problem of carbon monoxide poisoning and explained ways to head off the problem. Then, in her closing words, she tied the whole speech together by returning to the story described in her introduction:

Conclusion Remember those five friends I mentioned in the introduction of my speech? Their deaths were tragic and unnecessary. I hope the information I have provided today will help you avoid their fate. By understanding where carbon monoxide comes from, by recognizing the warning signs of carbon monoxide poisoning, and by following the simple preventive steps I've discussed, you can make sure that you don't fall victim to the silent killer.

connect

View the beginning and ending of "The Silent Killer" in the online Media Library for this chapter (Video 10.8).

Summarizing the speech, ending with a quotation, making a dramatic statement, referring to the introduction—all these techniques can be used separately. But you have probably noticed that speakers often combine two or more in their conclusions. Actually, all four techniques can be fused into one—for example, a dramatic quotation that summarizes the central idea while referring to the introduction.

One other concluding technique is making a direct appeal to your audience for action. This technique applies only to a particular type of persuasive speech, however, and will be discussed in Chapter 16. The four methods covered in this chapter are appropriate for all kinds of speeches and occasions.

SAMPLE CONCLUSION WITH COMMENTARY

How do you fit these methods together to make a conclusion? Here is an example, from the speech about compulsive hoarding whose introduction we looked at earlier (page 195).

connect

View this conclusion in the online Media Library for this chapter (Video 10.9).

COMMENTARY	CONCLUSION
The speaker gives an excellent summary of her speech. This is particularly important when speaking to inform because it gives you one last chance to make sure the audience remembers your main points.	Today we have seen that compulsive hoarding is a serious mental disorder whose effects can be devastating for individuals and families. It's also difficult to treat, which means that millions of Americans are left living a life of clutter and chaos.
By referring to her Aunt Josefina, whom she had mentioned in her introduction, the speaker unifies the entire speech. The quotation from Aunt Josefina and the speaker's final sentence end the speech on a strong note.	My Aunt Josefina is one of those people. She says: "People look at my apartment and know I have a problem. I look at my apartment and know I have a problem. I'm trying to get it under control, but it's a really long road." For my Aunt Josefina and millions of others, the good news is that understanding the problem is the first step toward conquering all the stuff.

TIPS FOR THE CONCLUSION

1. As with the introduction, keep an eye out for possible concluding materials as you research and develop the speech.
2. Conclude with a bang, not a whimper. Be creative in devising a conclusion that hits the hearts and minds of your audience. Work on several possible endings, and select the one that seems likely to have the greatest impact.
3. Don't be long-winded. The conclusion will normally make up no more than 5 to 10 percent of your speech.
4. Don't leave anything in your conclusion to chance. Work it out in detail, and give yourself plenty of time to practice delivering it. Many students like to write out the conclusion word for word to guarantee it is just right. If you do this, make sure you can present it smoothly, confidently, and with feeling—without relying on your notes or sounding wooden. Make your last impression as forceful and as favorable as you can.

Summary

First impressions are important. So are final impressions. This is why speeches need strong introductions and conclusions.

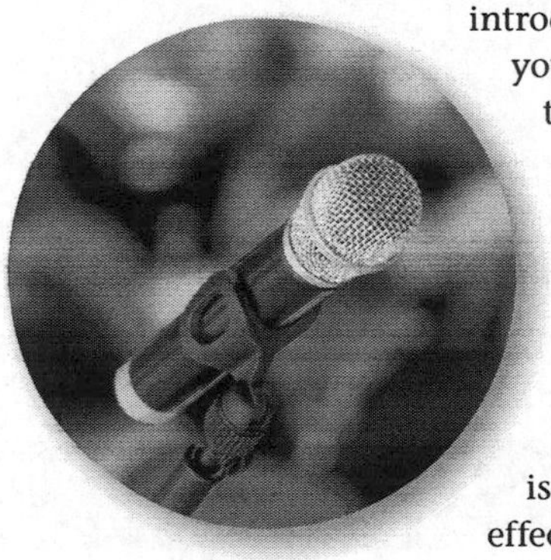

In most speech situations you need to accomplish four objectives with your introduction—get the attention and interest of the audience, reveal the topic of your speech, establish your credibility and goodwill, and preview the body of the speech. Gaining attention and interest can be done in several ways. You can show the importance of your topic, especially as it relates to your audience. You can startle or question your audience or arouse their curiosity. You can begin with a quotation or a story.

Be sure to state the topic of your speech clearly in your introduction so the audience knows where the speech is going. Establishing credibility means that you tell the audience why you are qualified to speak on the topic at hand. Establishing goodwill may be necessary if your point of view is unpopular. Previewing the body of the speech helps the audience listen effectively and provides a smooth lead-in to the body of the speech.

The first objective of a speech conclusion is to let the audience know you are ending, which you can do by your words or by your manner of delivery. The second objective of a conclusion is to reinforce your central idea. You can accomplish this by summarizing the speech, ending with a quotation, making a dramatic statement, or referring to the introduction. Sometimes you may want to combine two or more of these techniques. Be creative in devising a vivid, forceful conclusion.

Key Terms

rhetorical question (189)
credibility (192)
goodwill (193)
preview statement (194)
crescendo ending (197)
dissolve ending (197)

Review Questions

After reading this chapter, you should be able to answer the following questions:

1. What are the four objectives of a speech introduction?
2. What are seven methods you can use in the introduction to get the attention and interest of your audience?
3. Why is it important to establish your credibility at the beginning of your speech?
4. What is a preview statement? Why should you nearly always include a preview statement in the introduction of your speech?
5. What are six tips for your introduction?
6. What are the major functions of a speech conclusion?
7. What are two ways you can signal the end of your speech?
8. What are four ways to reinforce the central idea when concluding your speech?
9. What are four tips for your conclusion?

connect

For further review, go to the LearnSmart study module for this chapter.

Exercises for Critical Thinking

1. Here are six speech topics. Explain how you might relate each to your classmates in the introduction of a speech.

roller coasters	high blood pressure
performance enhancing drugs	coffee
laughter	Social Security

2. Think of a speech topic (preferably one for your next speech in class). Create an introduction for a speech dealing with any aspect of the topic you wish. In your introduction, be sure to gain the attention of the audience, to reveal the topic and relate it to the audience, to establish your credibility, and to preview the body of the speech.
3. Using the same topic as in Exercise 2, create a speech conclusion. Be sure to let your audience know the speech is ending, to reinforce the central idea, and to make the conclusion vivid and memorable.

11

Outlining the Speech

The Preparation Outline

The Speaking Outline

Think what might happen if you tried to build a house without a floor plan or an architect's blueprint. You install a cathedral ceiling so you can have big windows and a huge ceiling fan, but the roof is so high it blocks your bedroom window upstairs. You put in sliding doors to the yard, but they can't be opened because they're too close to the fireplace to slide back without hitting it. You think it's a wonderful idea to have almost no interior walls. But when the first snowfall comes, your (unsupported) roof collapses.

Plans and blueprints are essential to architecture. So, too, are outlines essential to effective speeches. An outline is like a blueprint for your speech. It allows you to see the full scope and content of your speech at a glance. By outlining, you can judge whether each part of the speech is fully developed, whether you have adequate supporting materials for your main points, and whether the main points are properly balanced. An outline helps you make sure that related items are together, that ideas flow from one to another, that the structure of your speech will "stand up"—and not collapse.

Probably you will use two kinds of outlines for your speeches—one very detailed, for the planning stage, and one very brief, for the delivery of the speech.

The Preparation Outline

The preparation outline is just what its name implies—an outline that helps you prepare the speech. Writing a preparation outline means putting your speech together—deciding what you will say in the introduction, how you will organize the main points and supporting materials in the body, and what you will say in the conclusion.

GUIDELINES FOR THE PREPARATION OUTLINE

preparation outline

A detailed outline developed during the process of speech preparation that includes the title, specific purpose, central idea, introduction, main points, subpoints, connectives, conclusion, and bibliography of a speech.

Over the years, a relatively uniform system for preparation outlines has developed. It is explained below and is exemplified in the sample outline on pages 211–213. You should check with your teacher to see what format you are to follow.

State the Specific Purpose of Your Speech

The specific purpose statement should be a separate unit that comes before the outline itself. Including the specific purpose makes it easier to assess how well you have constructed the speech to accomplish your purpose.

Identify the Central Idea

Some instructors prefer that the central idea be given immediately after the purpose statement. Others prefer that it be given and identified in the text of the outline. Check to see which your instructor wants.

Label the Introduction, Body, and Conclusion

If you label the parts of your speech, you will be sure that you indeed *have* an introduction and conclusion and have accomplished the essential objectives of each. Usually the names of the speech parts are placed in the middle of the page or in the far left margin. They are technical labels only and are not included in the system of symbolization used to identify main points and supporting materials.

Use a Consistent Pattern of Symbolization and Indentation

In the most common system of outlining, main points are identified by Roman numerals and are indented equally so as to be aligned down the page. Subpoints (components of the main points) are identified by capital letters and are also indented equally so as to be aligned with each other.

Beyond this, there may be sub-subpoints and even sub-sub-subpoints. For example:

I. Main point
  A. Subpoint
  B. Subpoint
    1. Sub-subpoint
    2. Sub-subpoint
      a. Sub-sub-subpoint
      b. Sub-sub-subpoint

As blueprints are essential to architecture, so outlines are essential to speechmaking. Developing an outline helps ensure that the structure of your speech is clear and coherent.

II. Main point
  A. Subpoint
    1. Sub-subpoint
    2. Sub-subpoint
  B. Subpoint
    1. Sub-subpoint
    2. Sub-subpoint

The clear *visual framework* of this outline immediately shows the relationships among the ideas of the speech. The most important ideas (main points) are farthest to the left. Less important ideas (subpoints, sub-subpoints, and so on) are progressively farther to the right. This pattern reveals the structure of your entire speech.

visual framework

The pattern of symbolization and indentation in a speech outline that shows the relationships among the speaker's ideas.

Once you have organized the body of your speech (see Chapter 9), you should have identified the main points. You need only flesh out your outline with subpoints and sub-subpoints, as necessary, to support the main points. But suppose, as sometimes happens, you find yourself with a list of statements and are not sure which are main points, which are subpoints, and so forth. Such a list might look like this:

There were 13 people at the Last Supper—Jesus and his 12 disciples.

Many superstitions revolve around numbers.

In the United States, 13 is often omitted in the floor numbering of hotels and skyscrapers.

The number 13 has meant bad luck as long as anyone can remember.

Which statement is the main point? The second statement ("Many superstitions revolve around numbers"), which is broader in scope than any of the other statements. This would be one of the main ideas of your speech. The fourth statement is the subpoint; it immediately supports the main point. The other two statements are sub-subpoints; they illustrate the subpoint. Rearranged properly, they look like this:

I. Many superstitions revolve around numbers.
  A. The number 13 has meant bad luck as long as anyone can remember.
    1. There were 13 people at the Last Supper—Jesus and his 12 disciples.
    2. In the United States, 13 is often omitted in the floor numbering of hotels and skyscrapers.

Above all, remember that all points at the same level should immediately support the point that is just above and one notch to the left in your outline. If this sounds confusing, think of it as a business organization chart:

connect

For help formatting your outlines, use the automated Outline Tool in the online Speech Tools for this chapter.

I. President
  A. Vice president—Operations
    1. Manager—Domestic Operations
      a. Assistant manager—East
      b. Assistant manager—West
    2. Manager—International Operations
      a. Assistant manager—Europe
      b. Assistant manager—Asia
      c. Assistant manager—Americas
  B. Vice president—Administration
    1. Manager—Finance
    2. Manager—Personnel

As you can see, every person on this chart reports to the person who is above and one notch to the left—except, of course, the president, who is the "main point."

State Main Points and Subpoints in Full Sentences

Below are two sets of main points and subpoints for the same speech on the life of Martin Luther King.

Ineffective	**More Effective**
I. Montgomery	I. King began his civil rights career in the Montgomery bus boycott of 1955–1956.
II. 1960s	II. King's greatest triumphs came during the early 1960s.
A. Birmingham	A. In 1963, he campaigned against segregation in Birmingham, Alabama.
B. March	B. Later that year, he participated in the famous march on Washington, D.C.
1. 200,000	1. More than 200,000 people took part.
2. "Dream"	2. King gave his "I Have a Dream" speech.
C. Prize	C. In 1964, he received the Nobel Peace Prize.
III. Final years	III. King faced great turmoil during his final years.
A. Criticized	A. He was criticized by more militant blacks for being nonviolent.
B. Vietnam	B. He protested against the war in Vietnam.
C. Assassination	C. He was assassinated in Memphis, Tennessee, on April 4, 1968.

The sample at the left might serve as a speaking outline, but it is virtually useless as a preparation outline. It gives only vague labels rather than distinct ideas. It does not indicate clearly the content of the main points and subpoints. Nor does it reveal whether the speaker has thought out his or her ideas. But there is no concern about any of these matters with the outline on the right.

In sum, a skimpy preparation outline is of little value. Stating your main points and subpoints in full sentences will ensure that you develop your ideas fully.

Label Transitions, Internal Summaries, and Internal Previews

One way to make sure you have strong transitions, internal summaries, and internal previews is to include them in the preparation outline. Usually they are not incorporated into the system of symbolization and indentation but are labeled separately and inserted in the outline where they will appear in the speech.

Attach a Bibliography

You should include with the outline a bibliography that shows all the books, magazines, newspapers, and Internet sources you consulted, as well as any interviews or field research you conducted.

bibliography

A list of all the sources used in preparing a speech.

The two major bibliographic formats are those developed by the Modern Language Association (MLA) and the American Psychological Association (APA). Both are widely used by communication scholars; ask your instructor which he or she prefers. No matter which format you adopt, make sure your statement of sources is clear, accurate, and consistent. For help, turn to page 135 in Chapter 7, where you will find sample citations for the kinds of sources used most frequently in classroom speeches.

Give Your Speech a Title, If One Is Desired

In the classroom you probably do not need a title for your speech unless your teacher requires one. In some other situations, however, a speech title is necessary—as when the speech is publicized in advance or is going to be published. Whatever the reason, if you do decide to use a title, it should (1) be brief, (2) attract the attention of your audience, and (3) encapsulate the main thrust of your speech.

A good title need not have what Madison Avenue would call "sex appeal"—lots of glitter and pizzazz. By the same token, there is certainly nothing wrong with a catchy title—as long as it is germane to the speech. Here are two groups of titles. Those on the left are straightforward and descriptive. Those on the right are figurative alternatives to the ones on the left.

Group I	Group II
Gambling Addiction	Against All Odds
The Rage to Diet	The Art of Wishful Shrinking
Living with Deafness	The Sounds of Silence
Unsafe Drinking Water	Toxins on Tap

Which group do you prefer? There are advantages and disadvantages to both. Those in the first group clearly reveal the topic, but they are not as provocative as those in the second group. Those in the second group are sure to arouse interest, but they do not give as clear an idea of what the speeches are about.

checklist

Preparation Outline

YES	NO	
☐	☐	1. Does my speech have a title, if one is required?
☐	☐	2. Do I state the specific purpose before the text of the outline itself?
☐	☐	3. Do I state the central idea before the text of the outline itself?
☐	☐	4. Are the introduction, body, and conclusion clearly labeled?
☐	☐	5. Are main points and subpoints written in full sentences?
☐	☐	6. Are transitions, internal summaries, and internal previews clearly labeled?
☐	☐	7. Does the outline follow a consistent pattern of symbolization and indentation?
☐	☐	8. Does the outline provide a clear visual framework that shows the relationships among the ideas of my speech?
☐	☐	9. Does the bibliography identify all the sources I consulted in preparing the outline?
☐	☐	10. Does the bibliography follow the format required by my instructor?

There is one other kind of title you should consider—the question. Phrasing your title as a question can be both descriptive and provocative. Using this method, we can construct a third set of titles combining the virtues of groups I and II:

Group III

Do You Really Think You Can Beat the Odds?

Diets: How Effective Are They?

Can You See What I'm Saying?

Is Your Water Safe to Drink?

Sometimes you will choose a title for your speech very early. At other times you may not find one you like until the last minute. Either way, try to be resourceful about creating titles for your speeches. Experiment with several and choose the one that seems most appropriate.

SAMPLE PREPARATION OUTLINE WITH COMMENTARY

The following outline for a six-minute informative speech illustrates the principles just discussed. The commentary explains the procedures used in organizing the speech and writing the outline. (Check with your teacher to see if she or he wants you to include a title with your outline.)

Beneficial Bacteria

COMMENTARY

Stating your specific purpose and central idea as separate units before the text of the outline makes it easier to judge how well you have constructed the outline to achieve your purpose and to communicate your central idea.

Labeling the introduction marks it as a distinct section that plays a special role in the speech.

The opening gets attention and, as it progresses, reveals the topic of the speech.

Here the speaker establishes his credibility and previews the main points to be discussed in the body.

Including transitions ensures that the speaker has worked out how to connect one idea to the next. Notice that the transition is not included in the system of symbolization and indentation used for the rest of the speech.

Labeling the body marks it as a distinct part of the speech.

Main point I is phrased as a full sentence. The three subpoints of main point I are shown by the capital letters A, B, and C and are also written in full sentences to ensure that the speaker has thought them out fully.

OUTLINE

Specific Purpose: To inform my audience about the role of beneficial bacteria in our bodies and in the environment.

Central Idea: Beneficial bacteria are crucial to human health and to the health of our environment.

Introduction

I. Hold up your hand and look closely.
   A. You can't see them, but millions of creatures—bacteria—are living there.
   B. You've been taught to scrub off those bacteria in the sink.
   C. That's fine advice—but only up to a point.

II. The truth is that most bacteria are not something to be washed away.

III. Dr. Martin Blaser states in his book *Missing Microbes* that bacteria are vital to human life and to the world in general.

IV. I learned about the importance of bacteria in my biology class, and I did additional research for this speech.

V. Today, I'd like to inform you about some of the ways beneficial bacteria help our bodies and our environment.

(*Transition:* Let's start by looking at the beneficial bacteria inside us.)

Body

I. Beneficial bacteria play a crucial role in our bodies.
   A. All of us have had bacteria on—and in—our bodies since we were born.
      1. As stated in *Scientific American*, the human body is "a complex ecosystem . . . containing trillions of bacteria."
      2. Each square centimeter of your skin is home to as many as 100,000 bacteria.

The progressive indentation shows visually the relationships among main points, subpoints, and sub-subpoints.

3. There are more than 100 different kinds of bacteria in your mouth.
4. Overall, there are 10 times more bacteria in your body than there are human cells.

B. One positive function of bacteria is to help us digest food and maintain our body weight.
   1. Yogurt is famous for its positive bacteria.
   2. Other foods high in positive bacteria include sauerkraut, kefir, kimchi, and some soft cheeses.

Points below the level of subpoint are indicated by Arabic numerals and lowercase letters. Sometimes they are not written as full sentences. Check to see what your instructor prefers.

C. According to the *British Journal of Nutrition*, bacteria help our bodies in other ways as well.
   1. They strengthen our immune systems by helping cells divide and reproduce.
   2. They promote healthy organs by synthesizing the enzymes needed for vitamins.
   3. Perhaps most important, they help create the energy we need to live.

The transition shows how the speaker will get from main point I to main point II.

Like main point I, main point II is phrased as a full sentence.

(*Transition:* Just as important as the bacteria in our bodies are the bacteria in the world around us.)

II. Beneficial bacteria play a crucial role in our environment.
   A. The Web site for the master gardener program at Colorado State University notes that healthy soil is "a dynamic living ecosystem."
      1. In every cup of soil, you'll find some 200 million bacteria.
      2. These bacteria help produce nutrients in the soil that allow plants to grow.
      3. In other words, a good garden requires good bacteria.

Notice the pattern of subordination in this section. Subpoint B states that beneficial bacteria can combat pollution. Sub-subpoint 2 notes that bacteria can help clean up oil spills. Because items a and b expand upon the point about oil spills, they are subordinated to it.

   B. In addition to enriching the soil, bacteria play an important role in combatting pollution.
      1. As a natural part of the environment, bacteria reduce contaminants in lakes, rivers, and oceans.
      2. Scientists are now using bacteria to help clean up oil spills.
         a. Remember the Deepwater Horizon oil spill in the Gulf of Mexico a few years ago?
         b. A recent article in *U.S. News and World Report* states that bacteria released by scientists ate through a significant portion of the oil.
      3. Some bacteria can even eat through discarded plastic and radioactive waste.

Conclusion

Labeling the conclusion marks it as a distinct part of the speech.

Summarizing the main points is standard procedure in an informative speech.

The speaker's closing quotation reinforces his central idea.

I. While bacteria can be dangerous, many are so beneficial that life as we know it could not survive without them.
II. The health of our bodies and the health of our environment both depend on beneficial bacteria.
III. In the words of award-winning science writer Richard Conniff, we should see bacteria "not as enemies, but as intimate partners" in our journey through life.

This is the final bibliography. It lists the sources actually used in writing the speech and is shorter than the preliminary bibliography compiled in the early stages of research. (See Chapter 7 for a discussion of the preliminary bibliography.)

This bibliography follows the Modern Language Association (MLA) format. Check with your instructor to see what format you should use for your bibliography.

Bibliography

Ackerman, Jennifer. "The Ultimate Social Network." *Scientific American* June 2012: 36–43. Print.

Alonso, Virginia Robles, and Francisco Guarner. "Linking the Gut Microbiota to Human Health." *British Journal of Nutrition* Jan. 2013: S21–S26. Print.

Blaser, Martin J. *Missing Microbes: How the Overuse of Antibiotics Is Fueling Our Modern Plagues*. New York: Henry Holt, 2014. Print.

Colorado Master Gardener Program. "The Living Soil." *Colorado State University Extension*. Colorado State University, Dec. 2011. Web. 5 Apr. 2014.

Conniff, Richard. "The Body Eclectic: You're Not Just Human." *Smithsonian Magazine* May 2013: 40. Print.

Koebler, Jason. "Study: Oil-Eating Bacteria Mitigated Deepwater Horizon Oil Spill." *U.S. News & World Report* 8 Apr. 2013. Web. 7 Apr. 2014.

Still have questions about outlining? If you log on to Connect, you will find additional resources to help you create effective preparation outlines. The Outline Tool will help you construct your own outlines from scratch following the guidelines in this chapter. There is also a program called EasyBib that can automatically format your speech bibliography in either APA or MLA format. Like many students before you, you can take advantage of these resources to improve your command of outlining principles and practices.

connect

The Outline Tool and EasyBib can be accessed through the Library tab on the Connect home page.

The Speaking Outline

"I was never so excited by public speaking before in my life," wrote one listener in 1820 after listening to Daniel Webster. "Three or four times I thought my temples would burst with the gush of blood. . . . I was beside myself, and am so still."[1]

Such reactions were not unusual among Webster's audiences. He thrilled two generations of Americans with his masterful orations. Incredible as it seems today, he did so while speaking for several hours at a time, often without using any notes! A reporter once asked how he managed this. "It is my memory," Webster said. "I can prepare a speech, revise and correct it in my memory, then deliver the corrected speech exactly as finished."[2]

Few people have Webster's remarkable powers of memory. Fortunately, it is no longer customary to speak from memory. Today most people speak extemporaneously—which means the speech is carefully prepared and practiced in advance, but much of the exact wording is selected while the speech is being delivered (see Chapter 13). Your speeches will probably be of this type. You should know, then, about the *speaking outline*—the most widely recommended form of notes for extemporaneous speeches.

speaking outline

A brief outline used to jog a speaker's memory during the presentation of a speech.

The aim of a speaking outline is to help you remember what you want to say. In some ways, it is a condensed version of your preparation outline. It should contain key words or phrases to jog your memory, as well as essential statistics and quotations that you don't want to risk forgetting. But it should also include material *not* in your preparation outline—especially cues to direct and sharpen your delivery.

Most speakers develop their own variations on the speaking outline. As you acquire more experience, you, too, should feel free to experiment. But for now, your best bet is to follow the basic guidelines below and to use the sample speaking outline on pages 216–217 as your model.

GUIDELINES FOR THE SPEAKING OUTLINE

Follow the Visual Framework Used in the Preparation Outline

Your speaking outline should use the same visual framework—the same symbols and the same pattern of indentation—as your preparation outline. This will make it much easier to prepare the speaking outline. More important, it will allow you to see instantly where you are in the speech at any given moment while you are speaking. You will find this a great advantage. As you speak, you will look down at your outline periodically to make sure you are covering the right ideas in the right order.

Compare the following two versions of a partial speaking outline. They are from an informative speech about the history of the U.S. women's rights movement.

Ineffective

I. 1840–1860
A. World Anti-Slavery Convention
B. Seneca Falls convention
1. Lucretia Mott
2. Elizabeth Cady Stanton
3. Declaration of Sentiments
II. 1900–1920
A. National American Woman Suffrage Association
1. Founding
2. Objectives
B. Nineteenth Amendment
1. Campaign
2. Ratification

More Effective

I. 1840–1860
    A. World Anti-Slavery Convention
    B. Seneca Falls convention
        1. Lucretia Mott
        2. Elizabeth Cady Stanton
        3. Declaration of Sentiments
II. 1900–1920
    A. National American Woman Suffrage Association
        1. Founding
        2. Objectives
    B. Nineteenth Amendment
        1. Campaign
        2. Ratification

The wording of both outlines is exactly the same. But the visual framework of the one on the right makes it easier to take in at a glance and reduces the odds of the speaker losing her or his place.

Make Sure the Outline Is Legible

Your speaking outline is all but worthless unless it is instantly readable at a distance. When you make your outline, use large lettering, leave extra space between lines, provide ample margins, and write or type on only one side of the paper.

Some speakers put their notes on index cards. Most find the 3 × 5 size too cramped and prefer the 4 × 6 or 5 × 8 size instead. Other people write their speaking outlines on regular paper. Either practice is fine, as long as your notes are immediately legible to you while you are speaking.

Keep the Outline as Brief as Possible

If your notes are too detailed, you will have difficulty maintaining eye contact with your audience. A detailed outline will tempt you to look at it far too often, as one student discovered:

Angela Rossi was speaking about the benefits of Pilates. She had prepared the speech thoroughly and practiced it until it was nearly perfect. But when she delivered the speech in class, she referred constantly to her detailed notes. As a result, her delivery was choppy and strained. After the speech, Angela's classmates remarked on how often she had looked at her notes, and she was amazed. "I didn't even know I was doing it," she said. "Most of the time I wasn't even paying attention to the outline. I knew the speech cold."

Many experienced speakers are more comfortable with a brief set of notes, or no notes at all, which allows them to communicate directly with the audience.

Using public speaking in your CAREER

As the defense attorney in a car theft case, you need to prepare your closing argument to the jury before it begins its deliberations. After reviewing evidence from the trial, you decide to stress the following points to demonstrate the innocence of your client:

a. The stolen car was found abandoned three hours after the theft with the engine still warm; at the time the car was found, your client was at the airport to meet the flight of a friend who was flying into town.
b. Lab analysis of muddy shoe prints on the floor mat of the car indicates that the prints came from a size 13 shoe; your client wears a size 10.
c. Lab analysis shows the presence of cigarette smoke in the car, but your client does not smoke.
d. The only eyewitness to the crime, who was 50 feet from the car, said the thief "looked like" your client; yet the eyewitness admitted that at the time of the theft she was not wearing her glasses, which had been prescribed for improving distance vision.
e. The car was stolen at about 1 P.M.; your client testified that he was in a small town 250 miles away at 11 A.M.
f. In a statement to police, the eyewitness described the thief as blond; your client has red hair.

As you work on the outline of your speech, you see that these points can be organized into three main points, each with two supporting points. Compose an outline that organizes the points in this manner.

Many students have had the same experience. "As long as I have plenty of notes," they feel, "disaster will not strike." In fact, most beginning speakers use too many notes. Like Angela, they don't need all of them to remember the speech, and they find that too many notes can actually interfere with good communication.

To guard against this, keep your speaking outline as brief as possible. It should contain key words or phrases to help you remember major points, subpoints, and connectives. If you are citing statistics, you will probably want to include them in your notes. Unless you are good at memorizing quotations, write them out fully as well. Finally, there may be two, three, or four key ideas whose wording is so important that you want to state them in simple complete sentences. The best rule is that your notes should be the *minimum* you need to jog your memory and keep you on track.

Give Yourself Cues for Delivering the Speech

A good speaking outline reminds you not only of *what* you want to say but also of *how* you want to say it. As you practice the speech, you will decide that certain ideas and phrases need special emphasis—that they should be spoken more loudly, softly, slowly, or rapidly than other parts of the speech. You will also determine how you want to pace the speech—how you will control its timing, rhythm, and momentum. But no matter how you work these things out ahead of time, no matter how often you practice, it is easy to forget them once you get in front of an audience.

delivery cues

Directions in a speaking outline to help a speaker remember how she or he wants to deliver key parts of the speech.

The solution is to include in your speaking outline *delivery cues*—directions for delivering the speech. One way to do this is by underlining or otherwise highlighting key ideas that you want to be sure to emphasize. Then, when you reach them in the outline, you will be reminded to stress them. Another way is to jot down on the outline explicit cues such as "pause," "repeat," "slow down," "louder," and so forth. Both techniques are good aids for beginning speakers, but they are also used by experienced speakers.

SAMPLE SPEAKING OUTLINE WITH COMMENTARY

Below is a sample speaking outline for a six-minute informative talk about beneficial bacteria. By comparing it with the preparation outline for the same speech on pages 211–213, you can see how a detailed preparation outline is transformed into a concise speaking outline.

COMMENTARY

These comments remind the speaker to establish eye contact and not to race through the speech.

Including the main points of the introduction helps keep the speaker on track at the start of the speech.

OUTLINE

Eye Contact!!

Slow Down

I. Hold up hand—look closely.
   A. Can't see millions of creatures there—bacteria.
   B. Taught to scrub off in sink.
   C. Fine—up to a point.
II. Most bacteria should <u>not</u> be washed away.
III. Dr. Martin Blaser, *Missing Microbes*: co-exist with bacteria vital to human life and the world.

IV. Learned in biology; did additional research.
V. Today: bacteria help bodies, environment.

(Start with bacteria <u>in</u> us.)

It's usually a good idea to pause briefly before launching into the first main point. This is another way of signaling that you are moving from the introduction to the body.

—*Pause*—

Most speakers label the body of the speech in the speaking outline as well as in the preparation outline.

Notice how the body of the speech follows the same visual format as the preparation outline. This makes the outline easy to read at a glance.

Body

I. Beneficial bacteria in <u>bodies</u>.
  A. We have all lived with bacteria since birth.
    1. *Scientific American*: Human body is "a complex ecosystem . . . containing trillions of bacteria."
    2. Each square centimeter—100,000.
    3. 100 kinds in mouth.
    4. 10 times more in body than human cells.
  B. One <u>positive</u> function: digest food, maintain weight.
    1. Yogurt.
    2. Others: sauerkraut, kefir, kimchi, soft cheeses.
  C. *British Journal of Nutrition*: help other ways.
    1. Strengthen immune systems.
    2. Promote healthy organs.
    3. Create energy needed to live.

Throughout the outline, key words are used to jog the speaker's memory. Because the final wording of an extemporaneous speech is chosen at the moment of delivery, it will not be exactly the same as that in the preparation outline.

(Just as important as bacteria in the body are bacteria in the <u>world</u>.)

Inserting transitions makes sure the speaker doesn't forget them.

Quotations are usually written out in full in the speaking outline.

Underlining reminds the speaker to stress key words or ideas.

II. Beneficial bacteria in environment.
  A. Web site for master gardener program at Colorado State: healthy soil "a dynamic living ecosystem."
    1. Cup of soil—200 million.
    2. Provide nutrients that allow plants to grow.
    3. <u>Good garden</u>—<u>good bacteria</u>.
  B. In addition to enriching soil, bacteria can combat pollution.
    1. Reduce contaminants in lakes, rivers, oceans.
    2. Scientists use to clean up oil spills.
      a. Remember Deepwater Horizon?
      b. *U.S. News and World Report*: bacteria ate oil.
    3. Can also eat plastic and radioactive waste.

Sources of statistics or testimony should be included in the speaking outline to make sure the speaker identifies them in the speech.

It's usually a good idea to pause before entering the conclusion.

—*Pause*—

Conclusion

Including key ideas and phrases from the conclusion jogs the speaker's memory and ensures that the speech will end as planned.

I. Some bacteria dangerous, many beneficial.
II. Health of bodies, health of environment depend on them.
III. Science writer Richard Conniff: see bacteria "not as enemies, but as intimate partners" in journey through life.

Summary

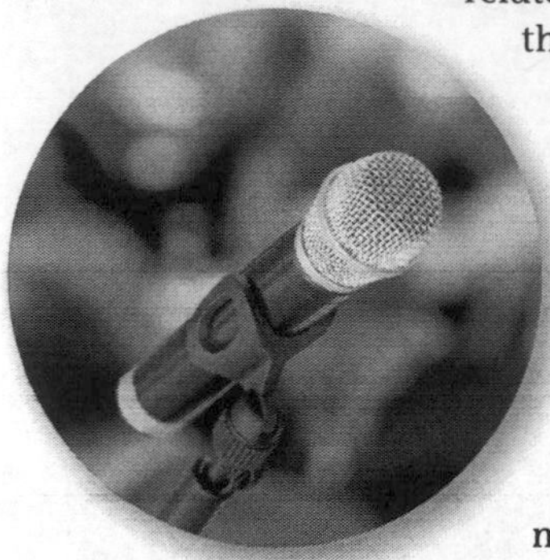

Outlines are essential to effective speeches. By outlining, you make sure that related ideas are together, that your thoughts flow from one to another, and that the structure of your speech is coherent. You will probably use two kinds of outlines for your speeches—the detailed preparation outline and the brief speaking outline.

In the preparation outline, you state your specific purpose and central idea; label the introduction, body, and conclusion; and designate transitions, internal summaries, and internal previews. You should identify main points, subpoints, and sub-subpoints by a consistent pattern of symbolization and indentation. Your instructor may require a bibliography with your preparation outline.

The speaking outline should contain key words or phrases to jog your memory, as well as essential statistics and quotations. Make sure your speaking outline is legible, follows the same visual framework as your preparation outline, and includes cues for delivering the speech.

Key Terms

preparation outline (206)
visual framework (207)
bibliography (209)
speaking outline (213)
delivery cues (216)

Review Questions

connect

For further review, go to the LearnSmart study module for this chapter.

After reading this chapter, you should be able to answer the following questions:

1. Why is it important to outline your speeches?
2. What is a preparation outline? What are the eight guidelines discussed in this chapter for writing a preparation outline?
3. What is a speaking outline? What are four guidelines for your speaking outline?

Exercises for Critical Thinking

1. In the left-hand column on page 219 is a partially blank outline from a speech about the Golden Gate Bridge. In the right-hand column, arranged in random order, are the subpoints to fill in the outline. Choose the appropriate subpoint for each blank in the outline.

Outline	Subpoints
I. More than 20 years passed from the time the Golden Gate Bridge was proposed to the time it opened.	Today, those towers make it the world's fourth tallest suspension bridge.
A.	Construction finally began in 1933 and ended in 1937.
B.	The span between its towers is 4,200 feet.
C.	At the time it was built, the Golden Gate was also the longest suspension bridge in the world.
D.	In 1923, the State of California passed legislation authorizing construction of the bridge.
II. Now nearly 80 years old, the Golden Gate Bridge remains a marvel of engineering.	Its two towers rise almost 750 feet above the waters of the Pacific Ocean.
A.	Once construction of the bridge was authorized, it took ten years to approve the design and financing.
1.	That span makes it the twelfth longest suspension bridge in the world today.
2.	At the time it was built, the Golden Gate was the tallest suspension bridge in the world.
B.	The bridge was originally proposed in 1916 but faced years of legal hurdles.
1.	
2.	

connect

For additional practice with scrambled outlines, go to the LearnSmart module for this chapter.

2. From the preparation outline on the Golden Gate Bridge you constructed in Exercise 1, create a speaking outline that you might use in delivering the speech. Follow the guidelines for a speaking outline discussed in this chapter.

Presenting the Speech

12

Using Language

Contrary to popular belief, language does not mirror reality. It does not simply describe the world as it is. Instead, language helps create our sense of reality by giving meaning to events. The words we use to label an event determine to a great extent how we respond to it.

For example, if you see the medical use of stem cells as "immoral," as "scientifically irresponsible," and as a "violation of human life," you will likely oppose it. But if you see the medical use of stem cells as "moral," as "scientifically responsible," and as a way to "alleviate pain and suffering," you will likely support it.

What separates these two viewpoints? Not the conditions of people with genetic disorders; not the medical procedures of using stem cells. Both are the same regardless of one's viewpoint. The difference is in the *meaning* given to them by the words that label them.[1]

Words are the tools of a speaker's craft. They have special uses, just like the tools of any other profession. Have you ever watched a carpenter at work? The job that would take you or me a couple of hours is done by the carpenter in 10 minutes—with the right tools. You can't drive a nail with a screwdriver or turn a screw with a hammer. It is the same with public speaking. You must choose the right words for the job you want to do.

Good speakers are aware of the meaning of words—both their obvious and their subtle meanings. They also know how to use language accurately, clearly, vividly, appropriately, and inclusively. This chapter will explore each of these areas.

Meanings of Words

denotative meaning

The literal or dictionary meaning of a word or phrase.

Words have two kinds of meanings—denotative and connotative. *Denotative* meaning is precise, literal, and objective. It describes the object, person, place, idea, or event to which the word refers. One way to think of a word's denotative meaning is as its dictionary definition. For example, denotatively, the noun "school" means "a place, institution, or building where instruction is given."

Connotative meaning is more variable, figurative, and subjective. The connotative meaning of a word is what the word suggests or implies. For instance, the connotative meaning of the word "school" includes all the feelings, associations, and emotions that the word touches off in different people. For some people, "school" might connote personal growth, childhood friends, and a special teacher. For others, it might connote frustration, discipline, and boring homework assignments.

connotative meaning

The meaning suggested by the associations or emotions triggered by a word or phrase.

Connotative meaning gives words their intensity and emotional power. It arouses in listeners feelings of anger, pity, love, fear, friendship, nostalgia, greed, guilt, and the like. Speakers, like poets, often use connotation to enrich their meaning. For example:

> Terrorists neither listen to reason nor engage in reasoning with others. Their aim is to generate fear—to frighten people into submission. They measure success by the magnitude of the fear they generate through brutal, savage acts of violence. Terrorists are prepared to kill to further whatever cause they claim to be pursuing. And the heinousness of these murders is accentuated by the fact that terrorists murder without passion. They murder with cool deliberation and deliberate planning. They are utterly amoral.

The underlined words in this passage have powerful connotations that are almost certain to produce a strong emotional revulsion to terrorism.

Here, in contrast, is another version of the same statement—this time using words with a different set of connotations:

> Terrorists do not seek to negotiate with their opponents. They seek victory by using political and psychological pressure, including acts of violence that may endanger the lives of some people. To the terrorist, ultimate objectives are more important than the means used to achieve them.

With the exception of "terrorist," the words in this statement are less likely to evoke an intensely negative response than those in the first statement.

Which statement is preferable? That depends on the audience, the occasion, and the speaker's purpose. Do you want to stir up your listeners' emotions, rally them to some cause? Then select words with more intense connotative meanings. Or are you addressing a controversial issue and trying to seem completely impartial? Then stick with words that touch off less intense reactions. Choosing words skillfully for their denotative and connotative meanings is a crucial part of the speaker's craft.

Words are the tools of the speaker's craft. Good speakers use them accurately and correctly. They also use language that will be clear, vivid, and appropriate for their listeners.

Using Language Accurately

Using language accurately is as vital to a speaker as using numbers accurately is to an accountant. One student found this out the hard way. In a speech about America's criminal justice system, he referred several times to "criminal *persecution*." What he meant, of course, was "criminal *prosecution*." This one error virtually ruined his speech. As one of his classmates said, "How can I believe what you say about our courts when you don't even know the difference between prosecution and persecution?"

Fortunately, such outright blunders are relatively rare among college students. However, we all commit more subtle errors—especially using one word when another will capture our ideas more precisely. Every word has shades of meaning that distinguish it from every other word. As Mark Twain said, "The difference between the right word and the almost right word is the difference between lightning and the lightning bug."

If you look in a thesaurus, you'll find the following words given as synonyms:

thesaurus

A book of synonyms.

education knowledge expertise

All mean roughly the same thing—special grasp of a subject matter or skill. But all these words have different shades of meaning. See if you can fill in the best word to complete each of the sentences below:

1. Because he won a scholarship to a top university, Enrique received an excellent ____________.
2. Sophia acquired her ____________ of Chinese history by reading a number of books on the subject.
3. Jasmine's ____________ as a business consultant comes from having worked with many clients over the years.

The best answers for the three statements are:

1. education 2. knowledge 3. expertise

Each of the words means something a little different from the others, and each says something special to listeners.

As you prepare your speeches, ask yourself constantly, "What do I *really* want to say? What do I *really* mean?" When in doubt, consult a dictionary or thesaurus to make sure you have the best words to express your ideas.

Using Language Clearly

People are different. What makes perfect sense to some may be gobbledygook to others. You cannot assume that what is clear to you is clear to your audience. Listeners, unlike readers, cannot turn to a dictionary or reread an author's words to discover their meaning. A speaker's meaning must be *immediately* comprehensible; it must be so clear that there is no chance of misunderstanding. You can ensure this by using familiar words, by choosing concrete words over abstract words, and by eliminating verbal clutter.

USE FAMILIAR WORDS

One of the biggest barriers to clear speech is using big, bloated words where short, sharp ones will do the job better.[2] This is especially true when it comes to technical language that may be familiar to the speaker but not to the audience. Yet, if you work at it, you will almost always be able to translate even the most specialized topic into clear, familiar language.

Here, for instance, are two passages explaining the devastating effects of a pregnant woman's drinking on her unborn child. The first passage is technically accurate, but it contains too many obscure words.

> The deleterious effects of alcohol on the unborn child are very serious. When a pregnant mother consumes alcohol, the ethanol in the bloodstream easily crosses the placenta from mother to child and invades the amniotic fluid. This can produce a number of abnormal birth syndromes, including central-nervous-system dysfunctions, growth deficiencies, a cluster of facial aberrations, and variable major and minor malformations.

Well-informed listeners can probably figure out "deleterious effects," "central-nervous-system dysfunctions," and "facial aberrations." But these terms don't create sharp mental images of what the speaker is trying to say.

Here, in contrast, is the second passage. It is utterly clear and shows what can be done with work, imagination, and a healthy respect for everyday words:

> When the expectant mother drinks, alcohol is absorbed into her bloodstream and distributed throughout her entire body. After a few beers or a couple of martinis, she begins to feel tipsy and decides to sober up. She grabs a cup of coffee, two aspirin, and takes a little nap. After a while she'll be fine.
>
> But while she sleeps, the fetus is surrounded by the same alcoholic content as its mother had. After being drowned in alcohol, the fetus begins to feel the

> effect. But it can't sober up. It can't grab a cup of coffee. It can't grab a couple of aspirin. For the fetus's liver, the key organ in removing alcohol from the blood, is just not developed. The fetus is literally pickled in alcohol.[3]

This kind of plain talk is what listeners want. You cannot go wrong by following the advice of Winston Churchill to speak in "short, homely words of common usage." If you think big words (or a lot of words) are needed to impress listeners, bear in mind that the Gettysburg Address—considered the finest speech in the English language—contains 271 words, of which 251 have only one or two syllables.

CHOOSE CONCRETE WORDS

Concrete words refer to tangible objects—people, places, and things. They differ from abstract words, which refer to general concepts, qualities, or attributes. "Carrot," "pencil," "nose," and "door" are concrete words. "Humility," "science," "progress," and "philosophy" are abstract words.

concrete words

Words that refer to tangible objects.

Of course, few words are completely abstract or concrete. "Apple pie" is concrete, but in the United States, the phrase also has abstract values of patriotism and conventional morals. Usually, the more specific a word, the more concrete it is. Let us say you are talking about basketball. Here are several words and phrases you might use:

abstract words

Words that refer to ideas or concepts.

physical activity	abstract/general
sports	
basketball	
professional basketball	
LeBron James	concrete/specific

As you move down the list, the words become less abstract and more concrete. You begin with a general concept (physical activity), descend to one type of activity (sports), to a particular sport (basketball), to a division of that sport (professional basketball), to one specific professional basketball player (LeBron James).

Although abstract words are necessary to express certain kinds of ideas, they are much easier to misinterpret than are concrete words. Also, concrete words are much more likely to claim your listeners' attention. Suppose you make a speech about bed bugs, which are plaguing people from coast to coast. Here are two ways you could approach the subject—one featuring abstract words, the other concrete words:

Abstract Words

> Bed bugs are highly newsworthy in the United States. They affect people regardless of social strata, demographic group, or region of the country. They are found in a wide range of social locations, some of which one might not expect. No matter where one lives, bed bugs are a growing problem.

Concrete Words

> In recent months, bed bugs have made headlines across the country, affecting the rich and the poor, the clean and the dirty, the East Coast, the West Coast, and every place in between.

In New York City, bed bugs have been found in fancy hotels, crowded subways, even the Victoria's Secret store on Lexington Avenue. In Los Angeles, they have infiltrated public housing and posh Beverly Hills neighborhoods alike. In college towns, they are almost everywhere—dorm rooms, apartments, restaurants, movie theaters, bars, even sports arenas.

Bed bugs are becoming a pest of epidemic proportions.

connect

View this excerpt from "The Plague of Bed Bugs" in the online Media Library for this chapter (Video 12.1).

Notice how much more persuasive the second version is. A speech dominated by concrete words will almost always be clearer, more interesting, and easier to recall than one dominated by abstract words.

ELIMINATE CLUTTER

Cluttered speech has become a national epidemic. Whatever happened to such simple words as "before," "if," and "now"? When last seen they were being routed by their cluttered counterparts: "prior to," "in the eventuality of," and "at this point in time." By the same token, why can't politicians say, "We have a crisis," instead of saying, "We are facing a difficult crisis situation that will be troublesome to successfully resolve"?

clutter

Discourse that takes many more words than are necessary to express an idea.

This type of clutter forces listeners to hack through a tangle of words to discover the meaning. When you make a speech, keep your language lean and lively. Beware of using several words where one or two will do. Avoid flabby phrases. Let your ideas emerge sharply and firmly. Above all, watch out for redundant adjectives and adverbs. Inexperienced speakers (and writers) tend to string together two or three synonymous adjectives, such as "a learned and educated person" or "a hot, steamy, torrid day."

Here is part of a student speech that has been revised to eliminate clutter:

Sitting Bull was one of the most important ~~and significant of all~~ Native American leaders. He was born in ~~the year of~~ 1831 near Grand River, in ~~an area that is now part of the state of~~ present-day South Dakota. A fearless ~~and courageous~~ warrior, he ~~ended up being~~ was elected chief of the Hunkpapa Sioux in 1867. In the following years, he also attracted a large ~~and numerous~~ following among the ~~tribes of the~~ Cheyenne and Arapaho. He is best known ~~to people in this day and age~~ today for his ~~instrumental~~ role in ~~helping to lead the defeat of~~ defeating General Custer at the Battle of Little Big Horn in 1876. Although eventually ~~required against his will~~ forced to live ~~his life~~ on the Standing Rock Reservation in South Dakota, he never surrendered ~~to anyone~~ his dignity or his ~~personal~~ devotion to the Sioux way of life.

Notice how much cleaner and easier to follow the revised version is. No longer are the speaker's ideas hidden in a thicket of wasted words.

This kind of pruning is easy once you get the knack of it. The hardest part—and it is often very hard—is recognizing clutter and forcing yourself to throw away the unnecessary words. Watch for clutter when you write your speech outlines. Be prepared to revise the outline until your ideas emerge clearly and crisply.

Even when discussing technical subjects, effective speakers such as renowned scholar Henry Louis Gates look for ways to communicate their ideas in clear, familiar language.

You can also help eliminate clutter by practicing your speeches with a digital recorder. As you play the speech back, keep an ear out not just for flabby phrases but for verbal fillers such as "you know," "like," and "really." Practice delivering the speech again, this time making a special effort to trim it of wasted or distracting words. This will not only make you a better public speaker, it will also help you present ideas more effectively in meetings, conversations, and group discussions.[4]

Using Language Vividly

Just as you can be accurate without being clear, so you can be both accurate and clear without being interesting. Here, for example, is how Martin Luther King *might have* phrased part of his "I Have a Dream" speech:

> Turning back is something we cannot do. We must continue to work against police brutality, segregated housing, disfranchisement, and alienation. Only when these problems are solved will we be satisfied.

Here is what King *actually* said:

> We cannot turn back. There are those who ask the devotees of civil rights, "When will you be satisfied?" We can never be satisfied as long as the Negro is the victim of the unspeakable horrors of police brutality. We can never be satisfied as long as our bodies, heavy with the fatigue of travel, cannot gain lodging in the motels of the highways and the hotels of the cities. . . . We cannot be satisfied as long as a Negro in Mississippi cannot vote and a Negro in New York believes he has nothing for which to vote.
>
> No, no, we are not satisfied, and we will not be satisfied until justice rolls down like waters and righteousness like a mighty stream.

Much more stirring, isn't it? If you want to move people with your speeches, use vivid, animated language. Although there are several ways to do this, two of the most important are imagery and rhythm.

IMAGERY

imagery

The use of vivid language to create mental images of objects, actions, or ideas.

One sign of a good novelist is the ability to create word pictures that let you "see" the haunted house, or "hear" the birds chirping on a warm spring morning, or "taste" the hot enchiladas at a Mexican restaurant.

Speakers can use imagery in much the same way to make their ideas come alive. Three ways to generate imagery are by using concrete words, simile, and metaphor.

Concrete Words

As we saw earlier in this chapter, choosing concrete words over abstract words is one way to enhance the clarity of your speeches. Concrete words are also the key to effective imagery. Consider the following excerpt from Ronald Reagan's famous address commemorating the 40th anniversary of D-Day. Speaking at the scene of the battle, Reagan dramatically recounted the heroism of the U.S. Rangers who scaled the cliffs at Pointe du Hoc to help free Europe from Hitler's stranglehold:

> We stand on a lonely, windswept point on the northern shore of France. The air is soft, but 40 years ago at this moment, the air was dense with smoke and the cries of men, and the air was filled with the crack of rifle fire and the roar of cannon.
>
> At dawn, on the morning of the 6th of June, 1944, 225 Rangers jumped off the British landing craft and ran to the bottom of these cliffs. . . . The Rangers looked up and saw the enemy soldiers—at the edge of the cliffs shooting down at them with machine guns and throwing grenades. And the American Rangers began to climb. They shot rope ladders over the face of these cliffs and began to pull themselves up.
>
> When one Ranger fell, another would take his place. When one rope was cut, a Ranger would grab another and begin his climb again. They climbed, shot back, and held their footing. Soon, one by one, the Rangers pulled themselves over the top, and in seizing the firm land at the top of these cliffs, they began to seize back the continent of Europe.

Concrete words call up mental impressions of sights, sounds, touch, smell, and taste. In Reagan's speech, we do not merely learn that the U.S. Rangers helped win the battle of D-Day. We visualize the Rangers landing at the foot of the cliffs. We see them fighting their way up the cliffs in the face of enemy grenades and machine guns. We hear the crack of rifle fire and the cries of the soldiers. The concrete words create images that pull us irresistibly into the speech.

Simile

simile

An explicit comparison, introduced with the word "like" or "as," between things that are essentially different yet have something in common.

Another way to create imagery is through the use of simile. Simile is an explicit comparison between things that are essentially different yet have something in common. It always contains the words "like" or "as." Here are some examples from student speeches:

> Walking into my grandparents' home when I was a child was like being wrapped in a giant security blanket.
>
> Personal data is flowing like a torrent into NSA servers.

Audience-oriented speakers put a premium on clear, vivid, uncluttered language. They give a great deal of thought to finding just the right words to express their ideas.

These are bright, fresh similes that clarify and vitalize ideas. Some similes, however, have become stale through overuse. Here are a few:

fresh as a daisy	hungry as a bear
fit as a fiddle	busy as a bee
strong as an ox	happy as a lark

Such *clichés* are fine in everyday conversation, but you should avoid them in speechmaking. Otherwise, you are likely to be "dull as dishwater" and to find your audience "sleeping like a log"!

cliché

A trite or overused expression.

Metaphor

You can also use metaphor to create imagery in your speeches. Metaphor is an implicit comparison between things that are essentially different yet have something in common. Unlike simile, metaphor does not contain the words "like" or "as." For example:

> America's cities are the windows through which the world looks at American society. (Henry Cisneros)

> With globalization, the same sea washes all of humankind. We are all in the same boat. There are no safe islands. (Kofi Annan)

metaphor

An implicit comparison, not introduced with the word "like" or "as," between two things that are essentially different yet have something in common.

These are both brief metaphors. Sometimes, however, a speaker will develop a longer metaphor. Here is an excellent example, from Al Gore's speech accepting the Nobel Peace Prize for his efforts to help the world deal with climate change:

> The earth has a fever. And the fever is rising. The experts have told us it is not a passing affliction that will heal by itself. We asked for a second opinion.

And a third. And a fourth. And the consistent conclusion, restated with increasing alarm, is that something basic is wrong.

When used effectively, metaphor—like simile—is an excellent way to bring color to a speech, to make abstract ideas concrete, to clarify the unknown, and to express feelings and emotions.[5]

RHYTHM

rhythm

The pattern of sound in a speech created by the choice and arrangement of words.

Language has a rhythm created by the choice and arrangement of words. Speakers, like poets, sometimes seek to exploit the rhythm of language to enhance the impact of their words. Winston Churchill was a master at this. Here is a passage from one of his famous speeches during World War II. To emphasize its cadence, the passage has been printed as if it were poetry rather than prose:

> We cannot tell what the course
>   of this fell war will be. . . .
> We cannot yet see
>   how deliverance will come,
> or when it will come.
>   But nothing is more certain
> than that every trace of Hitler's footsteps,
>   every stain of his infected and corroding fingers,
> will be sponged and purged
>   and, if need be,
> blasted from the surface of the earth.

The impact of the passage was heightened by Churchill's superb delivery; but even by themselves the words take on an emphatic rhythm that reinforces the message. You can see why one observer said that Churchill "mobilized the English language and sent it into battle."[6]

A speech, however, is not a poem. You should never emphasize sound and rhythm at the expense of meaning. The aim is to think about ways you can use the rhythm and flow of language to enhance your meaning. Although you may never have paid much conscious attention to this subject, you can develop an ear for vocal rhythms by study and practice. What's more, you can easily begin now to use four basic stylistic devices employed by Churchill and other fine speakers to improve the rhythm of their prose.

Parallelism

parallelism

The similar arrangement of a pair or series of related words, phrases, or sentences.

The first device is parallelism—the similar arrangement of a pair or series of related words, phrases, or sentences. For example:

> *Rich and poor, intelligent and ignorant, wise and foolish, virtuous and vicious, man and woman*—it is ever the same, each soul must depend wholly on itself. (Elizabeth Cady Stanton)

The effects of parallelism are perhaps best illustrated by seeing what happens when it is absent. For instance, compare this statement:

> I speak as a Republican. I speak as a woman. I speak as a United States Senator. I speak as an American. (Margaret Chase Smith)

Using public speaking in your CAREER

Since graduating from college, you have developed a successful business that is located near the campus. As part of its plan to involve more alumni and community members in college affairs, the school has asked you to speak with new students during registration week for the fall term.

In the opening section of your speech, you want the audience to feel what you felt the first few days you were on campus as a new student. The best strategy, you decide, is to present two or three similes that complete the sentence "Beginning college is like. . . ." Write your similes.

with this one:

> I speak as a Republican. I speak as a woman. I speak as a United States Senator. And I am also addressing you as an American.

The first statement is clear, consistent, and compelling. The second is not. By violating the principle of parallel structure, its final sentence ("And I am also addressing you as an American") destroys the progression begun by the preceding three sentences. It turns a strong, lucid, harmonious statement into one that is fuzzy and jarring.

Repetition

Repetition means reiterating the same word or set of words at the beginning or end of successive clauses or sentences. For example:

repetition

Reiteration of the same word or set of words at the beginning or end of successive clauses or sentences.

> *If not* now, when? *If not* us, who? *If not* together, how? (Gordon Brown)
>
> *We do not* give up. *We do not* quit. *We do not* allow fear or division to break our spirit. (Barack Obama)

As you can see, repetition usually results in parallelism. In addition to building a strong cadence, it unifies a sequence of ideas, emphasizes an idea by stating it more than once, and helps create a strong emotional effect.

Alliteration

The third device you can use to enhance the rhythm of your speeches is alliteration. The most common method of alliteration is repeating the initial consonant sound of close or adjoining words. For example:

alliteration

Repetition of the initial consonant sound of close or adjoining words.

> *P*eace is essential for *p*rogress, but *p*rogress is no less essential for *p*eace. (Liaquat Ali Khan)
>
> Nothing great is accomplished without *c*ooperation, *c*ompromise, and *c*ommon *c*ause. (Ban Ki-moon)

By highlighting the sounds of words, alliteration catches the attention of listeners and can make ideas easier to remember. Used sparingly, it is a marvelous way to spruce up your speeches. Used to excess, however, it can draw attention to itself, so that listeners get more involved in listening for the next alliteration than in absorbing the content of the speech.

Antithesis

antithesis

The juxtaposition of contrasting ideas, usually in parallel structure.

Finally, you might try using antithesis—the juxtaposition of contrasting ideas, usually in parallel structure. For example:

> Ask not what your country can do for you; ask what you can do for your country. (John F. Kennedy)
>
> Let us never negotiate out of fear. But let us never fear to negotiate. (John F. Kennedy)

It is no accident that both of these examples are from speeches by President Kennedy. Antithesis was one of his favorite language devices, and the one he used in his most memorable phrases. Because it nearly always produces a neatly turned phrase, it is a fine way to give your speeches a special touch of class.

You may be thinking that imagery and rhythm are too fancy for ordinary speeches like yours. This is not true. Take a look at the following excerpt from one student's speech about the Massachusetts 54th, the regiment of African-American soldiers during the Civil War featured in the movie *Glory:*

connect

View this excerpt from "The Massachusetts 54th" in the online Media Library for this chapter (Video 12.2).

> To join an army that didn't believe in you. To fight with an army who didn't like you. To die for an army that didn't respect you. This was the Massachusetts 54th. Today they lay where they died, on the beaches of South Carolina. Colonel Shaw and his men were piled together in a mass grave, which has since been covered by the shifting tides of the Atlantic. A small statue stands in Boston—a reminder of their sacrifice.
>
> Bravery, patriotism, and sacrifice. These are qualities of the Massachusetts 54th. With the help of their efforts, along with all the other black regiments that followed them, slavery did eventually come to an end.

This is vivid, moving language. The imagery is sharp and poignant, the rhythm strong and insistent. Think of how you can do similar things in your own speeches.

Using Language Appropriately

Here is part of a famous oration given by John Hancock in 1774, during the American Revolution. Speaking of the British soldiers who killed five Americans in the Boston Massacre, Hancock exclaimed:

> Ye dark designing knaves, ye murderers, parricides! How dare you tread upon the earth, which has drank in the blood of slaughtered innocents shed by your wicked hands? . . . Tell me, ye bloody butchers, ye villains high and low, ye wretches, do you not feel the goads and stings of conscious guilt pierce through your savage bosoms?

This is certainly vivid language—and Hancock's audience loved it. But can you imagine speaking the same way today? In addition to being accurate,

Language needs to be appropriate to a speaker's topic, as well as to the audience. A speech on zip-lining would use more action-oriented words than would a speech about theories of psychology.

clear, and vivid, language should be appropriate—to the occasion, to the audience, to the topic, and to the speaker.

APPROPRIATENESS TO THE OCCASION

Language that is appropriate for some occasions may not be appropriate for others. As a simple example, a coach might address the football team as "you guys" (or worse!), whereas the speaker in a more formal situation would begin with "distinguished guests." Try reversing these two situations, and see how ridiculous it becomes. It's only common sense to adjust your language to different occasions.

APPROPRIATENESS TO THE AUDIENCE

Appropriateness also depends on the audience. If you keep this in mind, it will help you greatly when dealing with technical topics. When addressing an audience of physicians, you might use the word "parotitis" to refer to a viral disease marked by the swelling of the parotid glands. Your audience would know just what you meant. But when talking to a nonmedical audience, such as your classmates, the appropriate word would be "mumps."

You should be especially careful to avoid language that might offend your audience. Off-color humor or profanity might be appropriate in a comedy routine, but most listeners would find it offensive in a formal public speech. Remember, speakers are expected to elevate and polish their language when addressing an audience.

Of course, you cannot always be sure of how listeners will respond to what you say. When it comes to appropriateness, you will seldom go wrong by erring on the side of caution. (Put simply, "erring on the side of caution" means "when in doubt—don't.")

APPROPRIATENESS TO THE TOPIC

Language should also be appropriate to the topic. You would not use metaphor, antithesis, and alliteration when explaining how to change a bicycle tire.

But you might use all three in a speech honoring U.S. soldiers who have died in defense of their country. The first topic calls for straightforward description and explanation. The second calls for special language skills to evoke emotion, admiration, and appreciation.

APPROPRIATENESS TO THE SPEAKER

No matter what the occasion, audience, or topic, language should also be appropriate to the speaker. Every public speaker develops his or her own language style.

"Terrific," you may be thinking. "I have my own style too. I feel more comfortable using abstract words, slang, and technical jargon. That's *my* way of speaking." But to say that language should be appropriate to the speaker does not justify ignoring the other needs for appropriateness. There is a difference between one's everyday style and one's *developed* style as a public speaker. Accomplished speakers have developed their speaking styles over many years of trial, error, and practice. They have *worked* at using language effectively.

You can do the same if you become language-conscious. One way to develop this consciousness is to read and listen to effective speakers. Study their techniques for achieving accuracy, clarity, and vividness, and try to adapt those techniques to your own speeches. But do not try to "become" someone else when you speak. Learn from other speakers, blend what you learn into your own language style, and seek to become the best possible you.

A Note on Inclusive Language

inclusive language

Language that does not stereotype, demean, or patronize people on the basis of gender, race, religion, disability, sexual orientation, or other factors.

As the United States has become more diverse, our language has evolved to reflect that diversity. Regardless of the situation, audiences expect public speakers to use inclusive language that is respectful of the different groups that make up American society. They also expect speakers to avoid stereotypes based on age, race, gender, disability, and other factors.

Today a number of principles for inclusive language have become so widespread that no aspiring speaker (or writer) can afford to ignore them. Here are a few of the most important.

Avoid the Generic "He"

generic "he"

The use of "he" to refer to both women and men.

Ineffective: Each time a surgeon walks into the operating room, *he* risks being sued for malpractice.

More Effective: Each time a surgeon walks into the operating room, *he or she* risks being sued for malpractice.

Often, a more graceful alternative is to pluralize. For example:

More Effective: Whenever surgeons walk into the operating room, *they* risk being sued for malpractice.

Avoid the Use of "Man" When Referring to Both Men and Women

Ineffective: If a large comet struck the Earth, it could destroy all of mankind.

More Effective: If a large comet struck the Earth, it could destroy all human life.

Avoid Stereotyping Jobs and Social Roles by Gender

Ineffective: Being a small businessman in the current economic climate is not easy.

More Effective: Being a small businessperson in the current economic climate is not easy.

Sometimes you can solve this problem with a simple twist in sentence construction. For example:

More Effective: Owning a small business is not easy in the current economic climate.

Use Names That Groups Use to Identify Themselves

One of the most fundamental ways of showing respect for others is to refer to them by the names they use to identify themselves and to avoid names they consider offensive.

Ineffective: Despite progress in recent years, homosexuals still face many forms of discrimination.

More Effective: Despite progress in recent years, lesbians and gay men still face many forms of discrimination.

Ineffective: The Paralympics show what handicapped people can accomplish in the athletic arena.

More Effective: The Paralympics show what people with disabilities can accomplish in the athletic arena.

Like many other aspects of American life, issues of inclusive language can sometimes be confusing. Language is alive and constantly evolving, so what is considered inclusive today may shift down the road. If you have questions in any particular case, check the Internet for the most up-to-date information. Using inclusive and respectful language is not a matter of political correctness, but it is a matter of P.C.—personal courtesy.[7]

Summary

Good speakers have respect for language and how it works. As a speaker, you should be aware of the meanings of words and know how to use language accurately, clearly, vividly, and appropriately.

Words have two kinds of meanings—denotative and connotative. Denotative meaning is precise, literal, and objective. Connotative meaning is more variable, figurative, and subjective. It includes all the feelings, associations, and emotions that a word touches off in different people.

Using language accurately is vital to a speaker. Never use a word unless you are sure of its meaning. If you are not sure, look up the word in a dictionary. As you prepare your speeches, ask yourself constantly, "What do I *really* want to say? What do I *really* mean?" Choose words that are precise and accurate.

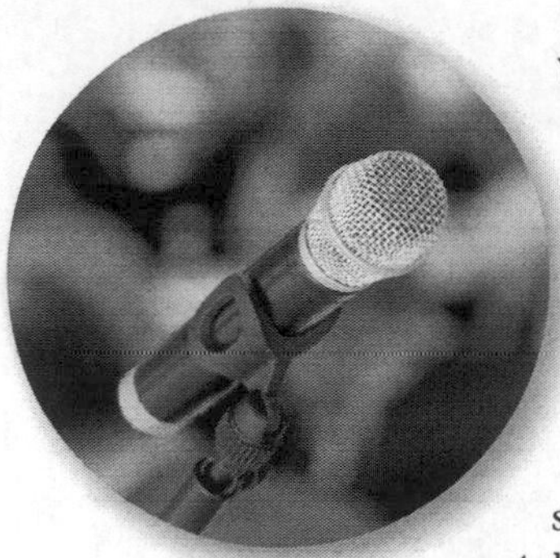

Using language clearly allows listeners to grasp your meaning immediately. You can ensure this by using words that are known to the average person and require no specialized background, by choosing concrete words in preference to more abstract ones, and by eliminating verbal clutter.

Using language vividly helps bring your speech to life. One way to make your language more vivid is through imagery, which you can develop by using concrete language, simile, and metaphor. Another way to make your speeches vivid is by exploiting the rhythm of language with parallelism, repetition, alliteration, and antithesis.

Using language appropriately means adapting to the particular occasion, audience, and topic at hand. It also means developing your own language style instead of trying to copy someone else's.

The subject of inclusive language can be complex, but a number of inclusive usages have become so widely accepted that no aspiring speaker can afford to ignore them. They include avoiding the generic "he," dropping the use of "man" when referring to both men and women, refraining from stereotyping jobs and social roles by gender, and using names that groups use to identify themselves.

Key Terms

denotative meaning (222)
connotative meaning (222)
thesaurus (223)
concrete words (225)
abstract words (225)
clutter (226)
imagery (228)
simile (228)
cliché (229)
metaphor (229)
rhythm (230)
parallelism (230)
repetition (231)
alliteration (231)
antithesis (232)
inclusive language (234)
generic "he" (234)

Review Questions

After reading this chapter, you should be able to answer the following questions:

1. How does language help create our sense of reality?
2. What is the difference between denotative and connotative meaning? How might you use each to convey your message most effectively?
3. What are four criteria for using language effectively in your speeches?
4. What are three things you should do to use language clearly in your speeches?
5. What are two ways to bring your speeches to life with vivid, animated language?
6. What does it mean to say you should use language appropriately in your speeches?
7. Why is it important for a public speaker to use inclusive language? What four usages of inclusive language have become so widely accepted that no speaker can afford to ignore them?

connect

For further review, go to the LearnSmart study module for this chapter.

Exercises for Critical Thinking

1. Arrange each of the sequences below in order, from the most abstract word to the most concrete word.
   a. housing complex, building, dining room, structure, apartment
   b. *Mona Lisa,* art, painting, creative activity, portrait
   c. automobile, vehicle, Ferrari, transportation, sports car
2. Rewrite each of the following sentences using clear, familiar words.
   a. My employment objective is to attain a position of maximum financial reward.
   b. All professors at this school are expected to achieve high standards of excellence in their instructional duties.
   c. In the eventuality of a fire, it is imperative that all persons evacuate the building without undue delay.
3. Each of the statements below uses one or more of the following stylistic devices: metaphor, simile, parallelism, repetition, alliteration, antithesis. Identify the device (or devices) used in each statement.
   a. "We are a people in a quandary about the present. We are a people in search of our future. We are a people in search of a national community." (Barbara Jordan)
   b. "The vice presidency is the sand trap of American politics. It's near the prize, and designed to be limiting." (Howard Fineman)
   c. "People the world over have always been more impressed by the power of our example than by the example of our power." (Bill Clinton)
   d. "I speak so those without a voice can be heard. Those who have fought for their rights: Their right to live in peace. Their right to be treated with dignity. Their right to equality of opportunity." (Malala Yousafzai)

13

Delivery

If you were to record one of Ellen DeGeneres's comedy routines, memorize it word for word, and stand up before your friends to recite it, would you get the same response DeGeneres does? Not very likely. And why not? Because you would not *deliver* the jokes as DeGeneres does. Of course, the jokes are basically funny. But Ellen DeGeneres brings something extra to the jokes—her manner of presentation, her vocal inflections, her perfectly timed pauses, her facial expressions, her gestures. All these are part of an expert delivery. It would take you years of practice—as it took DeGeneres—to duplicate her results.

No one expects your speech class to transform you into a multimillion-dollar talk show host. Still, this example demonstrates how important delivery can be to any public speaking situation. Even a mediocre speech will be more effective if it is presented well, whereas a wonderfully written speech can be ruined by poor delivery.

This does not mean dazzling delivery will turn a mindless string of nonsense into a triumphant oration. You cannot make a good speech without having something to say. But having something to say is not enough. You must also know *how* to say it.

nonverbal communication

Communication based on a person's use of voice and body, rather than on the use of words.

Speech delivery is a matter of *nonverbal communication.* It is based on how you use your voice and body to convey the message expressed by your words. There is a great deal of research showing that the impact of a speaker's words is powerfully influenced by his or her nonverbal communication. In this chapter, we will explain how you can use nonverbal communication to deliver your speeches effectively and to increase the impact of your verbal message.

What Is Good Delivery?

Wendell Phillips was a leader in the movement to abolish slavery in the United States during the 1800s. Some people considered him the greatest speaker of his time. The following story suggests one reason why:

> Shortly before the Civil War an Andover student, learning that Phillips was to lecture in Boston, made a 22-mile pilgrimage on foot to hear him. At first the trip seemed hardly worthwhile, for the student discovered that Phillips was not an orator in the grand manner, but spoke in an almost conversational style. He stood on the platform, one hand lightly resting on a table, talked for what seemed to be about 20 minutes, concluded, and sat down. When the student looked at his watch, he found to his astonishment that he had been listening for an hour and a half![1]

Good delivery does not call attention to itself. It conveys the speaker's ideas clearly, interestingly, and without distracting the audience. Most audiences prefer delivery that combines a certain degree of formality with the best attributes of good conversation—directness, spontaneity, animation, vocal and facial expressiveness, and a lively sense of communication.

Speech delivery is an art, not a science. What works for one speaker may fail for another. And what succeeds with today's audience may not with tomorrow's. You cannot become a skilled speaker just by following a set of rules in a textbook. In the long run, there is no substitute for experience. But take heart! A textbook *can* give you basic pointers to get you started in the right direction.

When you plan your first speech (or your second or third), you should concentrate on such basics as speaking intelligibly, avoiding distracting mannerisms, and establishing eye contact with your listeners. Once you get these elements under control and begin to feel fairly comfortable in front of an audience, you can work on polishing your delivery to enhance the impact of your ideas. Eventually, you may find yourself able to control the timing, rhythm, and momentum of a speech as skillfully as a conductor controls an orchestra.

Methods of Delivery

There are four basic methods of delivering a speech: (1) reading verbatim from a manuscript, (2) reciting a memorized text, (3) speaking impromptu, and (4) speaking extemporaneously. Let us look at each.

READING FROM A MANUSCRIPT

Certain speeches *must* be delivered word for word, according to a meticulously prepared manuscript. Examples include a Pope's religious proclamation, an engineer's report to a professional meeting, or a President's message to Congress. In such situations, absolute accuracy is essential. Every word of the speech will be analyzed by the press, by colleagues, perhaps by enemies. In the case of the President, a misstated phrase could cause an international incident.

manuscript speech

A speech that is written out word for word and read to the audience.

Although it looks easy, delivering a speech from manuscript requires great skill. Some people do it well. Their words "come alive as if coined on the spot."[2] Others ruin it every time. Instead of sounding vibrant and conversational, they come across as wooden and artificial. They falter over words, pause in the wrong places, read too quickly or too slowly, speak in a monotone, and march through the speech without even glancing at their audience. In short, they come across as *reading to* their listeners, rather than *talking with* them.

If you are in a situation where you must speak from a manuscript, practice aloud to make sure the speech sounds natural. Work on establishing eye contact with your listeners. Be certain the final manuscript is legible at a glance. Above all, reach out to your audience with the same directness and sincerity that you would if you were speaking extemporaneously.

RECITING FROM MEMORY

Among the feats of the legendary orators, none leaves us more in awe than their practice of presenting even the longest and most complex speeches entirely from memory. Nowadays it is no longer customary to memorize any but the shortest of speeches—toasts, congratulatory remarks, acceptance speeches, introductions, and the like.

If you are giving a speech of this kind and want to memorize it, by all means do so. However, be sure to memorize it so thoroughly that you will be able to concentrate on communicating with the audience, not on trying to remember the words. Speakers who gaze at the ceiling or stare out the window trying to recall what they have memorized are no better off than those who read dully from a manuscript.

SPEAKING IMPROMPTU

An impromptu speech is delivered with little or no immediate preparation. Few people choose to speak impromptu, but sometimes it cannot be avoided. In fact, many of the speeches you give in life will be impromptu. You might be called on suddenly to "say a few words" or, in the course of a class discussion, business meeting, or committee report, want to respond to a previous speaker.

impromptu speech

A speech delivered with little or no immediate preparation.

When such situations arise, don't panic. No one expects you to deliver a perfect speech on the spur of the moment. If you are in a meeting or discussion, pay close attention to what the other speakers say. Take notes of major points with which you agree or disagree. In the process, you will automatically begin to formulate what you will say when it is your turn to speak.

Whenever you are responding to a previous speaker, try to present your speech in four simple steps: First, state the point you are answering. Second, state the point you wish to make. Third, support your point with appropriate statistics, examples, or testimony. Fourth, summarize your point. This four-step method will help you organize your thoughts quickly and clearly.

If time allows, sketch a quick outline of your remarks on a piece of paper before you rise to speak. This will help you remember what you want to say and will keep you from rambling.

If the situation calls for you to speak from a lectern, walk to it calmly, take a deep breath or two (not a visible gasp), establish eye contact with your audience, and begin speaking. No matter how nervous you are inside, do your best to look calm and assured on the outside.

Once you begin speaking, maintain eye contact with the audience. Help the audience keep track of your ideas with signposts such as "My first point is . . . ; second, we can see that . . . ; in conclusion, I would like to say. . . ." By stating your points clearly and concisely, you will come across as organized and confident.

As with other kinds of public speaking, the best way to become a better impromptu speaker is to practice. You can do this on your own. Simply choose a topic on which you are already well informed, and give a one- or two-minute impromptu talk on some aspect of that topic. Any topic will do, no matter how serious or frivolous it may be. You don't even need an audience—you can speak to an empty room. Better yet, record the speech and play it back to hear how you sound. The purpose is to gain experience in pulling your ideas together quickly and stating them succinctly.

SPEAKING EXTEMPORANEOUSLY

In popular usage, "extemporaneous" means the same as "impromptu." But technically the two are different. Unlike an impromptu speech, which is delivered off-the-cuff, an extemporaneous speech is carefully prepared and practiced in advance. In presenting the speech, the extemporaneous speaker uses only a brief set of notes or a speaking outline to jog the memory (see Chapter 11). The exact wording is chosen at the moment of delivery.

extemporaneous speech

A carefully prepared and rehearsed speech that is presented from a brief set of notes.

This is not as hard as it sounds. Once you have your outline (or notes) and know what topics you are going to cover and in what order, you can begin to practice the speech. Every time you run through it, the wording will be slightly different. As you practice the speech over and over, the best way to present each part will emerge and stick in your mind.

The extemporaneous method has several advantages. It gives more precise control over thought and language than does impromptu speaking; it offers greater spontaneity and directness than does speaking from memory or from a full manuscript; and it is adaptable to a wide range of situations. It also encourages the conversational quality audiences look for in speech delivery.

conversational quality

Presenting a speech so it sounds spontaneous no matter how many times it has been rehearsed.

"Conversational quality" means that no matter how many times a speech has been rehearsed, it still *sounds* spontaneous. When you speak extemporaneously—and have prepared properly—you have full control over your ideas, yet you are not tied to a manuscript. You are free to establish strong eye contact, to gesture naturally, and to concentrate on talking *with* the audience rather than declaiming *to* them.

For an example of extemporaneous delivery, look at Video 13.1 in the online Media Library for this chapter. The student is demonstrating how to breathe when doing yoga. She clearly has rehearsed a great deal, and she

Whether talking extemporaneously or from a manuscript, a speaker needs to gesture naturally, establish eye contact with the audience, and establish a strong communicative bond with listeners.

knows what she wants to say, but she has not memorized the speech. She has a brief set of speaking notes in case she needs them, but she is not tied to the notes. Rather, she selects her words as she goes along, maintains strong eye contact with the audience, and has excellent conversational quality.

Like thousands of previous students, you can become adept at speaking extemporaneously by the end of the term. As one student commented in looking back at his class: "At the start, I never thought I'd be able to give my speeches without a ton of notes, but I'm amazed at how much progress I've made. It's one of the most valuable things I learned in the entire class."

connect

View an excerpt from "Yoga: Uniting Mind, Body, and Spirit" in the online Media Library for this chapter (Video 13.1).

Most experienced speakers prefer the extemporaneous method, and most teachers emphasize it. Later in this chapter (pages 251–252), we'll look at a step-by-step program for practicing your extemporaneous delivery.

The Speaker's Voice

What kind of voice do you have? Is it rich and resonant like Morgan Freeman's? Soft and alluring like Scarlett Johansson's? Loud and irritating like Dick Vitale's? Whatever the characteristics of your voice, you can be sure it is unique. Because no two people are exactly the same physically, no two people have identical voices.

A golden voice is certainly an asset for a public speaker, but some of the most famous speakers in history have had undistinguished voices. Abraham Lincoln had a harsh and penetrating voice; Winston Churchill suffered from a slight lisp and an awkward stammer. Like them, you can overcome natural disadvantages and use your voice to the best effect. Lincoln and Churchill learned to *control* their voices. You can do the same thing.

The aspects of voice you should work to control are volume, pitch, rate, pauses, vocal variety, pronunciation, articulation, and dialect.

VOLUME

volume

The loudness or softness of the speaker's voice.

At one time, a powerful voice was essential for an orator. Today, electronic amplification allows even a soft-spoken person to be heard in any setting. But in the classroom you will speak without a microphone. When you do, be sure to adjust your voice to the acoustics of the room, the size of the audience, and the level of background noise. If you speak too loudly, your listeners will think you boorish. If you speak too softly, they will not understand you.

Remember that your own voice always sounds louder to you than to a listener. Soon after beginning your speech, glance at the people farthest away from you. If they look puzzled, are leaning forward in their seats, or are otherwise straining to hear, you need to talk louder.

PITCH

pitch

The highness or lowness of the speaker's voice.

inflections

Changes in the pitch or tone of a speaker's voice.

monotone

A constant pitch or tone of voice.

Pitch is the highness or lowness of a speaker's voice. The faster sound waves vibrate, the higher their pitch; the slower they vibrate, the lower their pitch.

Changes in pitch are known as *inflections.* Inflection is what makes the difference between the "Aha!" triumphantly exclaimed by Sherlock Holmes upon discovering a seemingly decisive clue and the "Aha" he mutters when he learns the clue is not decisive after all. If you were to read the preceding sentence aloud, your voice would probably go up in pitch on the first "Aha" and down on the second.

In ordinary conversation, we instinctively use inflections to convey meaning and emotion. People who do not are said to speak in a *monotone,* a trait whose only known benefit is to cure insomnia in one's listeners.

Although few people speak in an absolute monotone, with no variation whatever in pitch, many fall into repetitious pitch patterns that are just as hypnotic. You can guard against this by recording your speeches as you practice them. If all your sentences end on the same inflection—either upward or downward—work on varying your pitch patterns to fit the meaning of your words.

RATE

rate

The speed at which a person speaks.

Rate refers to the speed at which a person talks. People in the United States usually speak at a rate between 120 and 150 words per minute, but there is no uniform rate for effective speechmaking. Franklin Roosevelt spoke at 110 words per minute, John Kennedy at 180. Martin Luther King opened his "I Have a Dream" speech at 92 words per minute and finished it at 145. The best rate of speech depends on several things—the vocal attributes of the speaker, the mood she or he is trying to create, the composition of the audience, and the nature of the occasion.

Two obvious faults to avoid are speaking so slowly that your listeners become bored or so quickly that they lose track of your ideas. Novice speakers are particularly prone to racing through their speeches at a frantic rate. Fortunately, this is usually an easy habit to break, as is the less common one of crawling through one's speech at a snail's pace.

The key in both cases is becoming aware of the problem and concentrating on solving it. Use a recording device to check how fast you speak. Pay special attention to rate when practicing your speech. Finally, be sure to include reminders about delivery on your speaking outline so you won't forget to make the adjustments when you give your speech in class.

PAUSES

Learning how and when to pause is a major challenge for most beginning speakers. Even a moment of silence can seem like an eternity. As you gain more poise and confidence, however, you will discover how useful the pause can be. It can signal the end of a thought unit, give an idea time to sink in, and lend dramatic impact to a statement. "The right word may be effective," said Mark Twain, "but no word was ever as effective as a rightly timed pause."

pause

A momentary break in the vocal delivery of a speech.

Developing a keen sense of timing is partly a matter of common sense, partly a matter of experience. You will not always get your pauses just right at first, but keep trying. Listen to accomplished speakers to see how they use pauses to modulate the rate and rhythm of their messages. Work on pauses when you practice your speeches.

Make sure you pause at the end of thought units and not in the middle. Otherwise, you may distract listeners from your ideas. Most important, do not fill the silence with "uh," "er," or "um." These *vocalized pauses* can create negative perceptions about a speaker's intelligence and often make a speaker appear deceptive.[3]

vocalized pause

A pause that occurs when a speaker fills the silence between words with vocalizations such as "uh," "er," and "um."

VOCAL VARIETY

Just as variety is the spice of life, so is it the spice of public speaking. A flat, listless, unchanging voice is as deadly to speechmaking as a flat, listless, unchanging routine is to daily life. When giving a speech, you should strive for vocal variety—changes in rate, pitch, and volume that will give your voice interest and expressiveness.

vocal variety

Changes in a speaker's rate, pitch, and volume that give the voice variety and expressiveness.

For an excellent example of vocal variety, look at Video 13.2 in the online Media Library for this chapter. The speaker, Sajjid Zahir Chinoy, was born and raised in Bombay, India, before coming to the United States to attend college at the University of Richmond. At the end of his senior year, Chinoy was selected as the student commencement speaker in a campus-wide competition. He spoke of the warm reception he received at Richmond and of how cultural differences can be overcome by attempting to understand other people.

The best rate of speech depends partly on the mood a speaker wants to create. To communicate the splendor of a rainbow over Victoria Falls, you would probably speak at a slower-than-normal rate.

connect

View an excerpt from "Questions of Culture" in the online Media Library for this chapter (Video 13.2).

At the end of his speech, Chinoy received thunderous applause—partly because of what he said, but also because of how he said it. Addressing the audience of 3,000 people without notes, he spoke extemporaneously with strong eye contact and excellent vocal variety. The speech was so inspiring that the main speaker, Harvard psychiatrist Robert Coles, began his presentation by paying tribute to Chinoy. "I've been to a number of commencements," said Coles, "but I've never heard a speech quite like that!"

How can you develop a lively, expressive voice? Above all, by approaching every speech as Chinoy approached his—as an opportunity to share with your listeners ideas that are important to you. Your sense of conviction and your desire to communicate will give your voice the same spark it has in spontaneous conversation.

PRONUNCIATION

We all mispronounce words now and again. Here, for example, are four words with which you are probably familiar. Say each one aloud.

pronunciation

The accepted standard of sound and rhythm for words in a given language.

genuine	arctic
err	nuclear

Very likely you made a mistake on at least one, for they are among the most frequently mispronounced words in the English language. Let's see:

Word	**Common Error**	**Correct Pronunciation**
genuine	gen-u-wine	gen-u-win
arctic	ar-tic	arc-tic
nuclear	nu-cu-lar	nu-cle-ar
err	air	ur

Every word leads a triple life: it is read, written, and spoken. Most people recognize and understand many more words in reading than they use in ordinary writing, and about three times as many as occur in spontaneous speech.[4] This is why we occasionally stumble when speaking words that are part of our reading or writing vocabularies. In other cases, we may mispronounce the most commonplace words out of habit.

The problem is that we usually don't *know* when we are mispronouncing a word. If we are lucky, we learn the right pronunciation by hearing someone else say the word properly or by having someone gently correct us in private. If we are unlucky, we mispronounce the word in front of a roomful of people, who may raise their eyebrows, groan, or laugh.

All of this argues for practicing your speech in front of as many trusted friends and relatives as you can corner. If you have any doubts about the proper pronunciation of certain words, be sure to check a dictionary.

ARTICULATION

Articulation and pronunciation are not identical. Sloppy articulation is the failure to form particular speech sounds crisply and distinctly. It is one of several causes of mispronunciation, but you can articulate a word sharply and still mispronounce it. For example, if you say the "s" in "Illinois" or the "p" in "pneumonia," you are making a mistake in pronunciation, regardless of how precisely you articulate the sounds.

Among college students, poor articulation is more common than ignorance of correct pronunciation. We know that "let me" is not "lemme," that "going to" is not "gonna," that "did you" is not "didja," yet we persist in articulating these words improperly. Here are some other common errors in articulation you should work to avoid:

articulation

The physical production of particular speech sounds.

Word	**Misarticulation**
ought to	otta
didn't	dint
don't know	dunno
have to	hafta
want to	wanna
will you	wilya

If you have sloppy articulation, work on identifying and eliminating your most common errors. Like other bad habits, careless articulation can be broken only by persistent effort—but the results are well worth it. As Shakespeare advised, "Mend your speech a little, lest you may mar your fortunes."

DIALECT

Most languages have dialects, each with a distinctive accent, grammar, and vocabulary. Dialects are usually based on regional or ethnic speech patterns. The United States has four major regional dialects—Eastern, New England, Southern, and General American. We also have multiple ethnic dialects. As the nation has become more diverse culturally, it has also become more diverse linguistically.[5]

dialect

A variety of a language distinguished by variations of accent, grammar, or vocabulary.

Linguists have concluded that no dialect is inherently better or worse than another. Dialects are not linguistic badges of superiority or inferiority. They are usually shaped by our regional or ethnic background, and every dialect is "right" for the community of people who use it.

When is a given dialect appropriate in public speaking? The answer depends above all on the composition of your audience. Heavy use of any dialect—regional or ethnic—can be troublesome when the audience does not share that dialect. In such a situation, the dialect may cause listeners to make negative judgments about the speaker's personality, intelligence, and competence. This is why professional speakers have been known to invest large amounts of time (and money) to master the General American dialect used by most television news broadcasters.

Does this mean you must talk like a television news broadcaster if you want to be successful in your speeches? Not at all. Regional or ethnic dialects do not pose a problem as long as the audience is familiar with them and finds them appropriate. When speaking in the North, for example, a southern politician may avoid regional dialect. But when addressing audiences in the South, the same politician may intentionally include regional dialect as a way of creating common ground with listeners.

Although not strictly speaking a matter of dialect, the proficiency of non-native speakers of English often arises in the speech classroom. Fortunately, teachers and students alike usually go out of their way to be helpful and encouraging to international students and others for whom English is not the primary language. Over the years, many non-native speakers of English have found speech class a supportive environment in which to improve their proficiency in spoken English.[6]

The Speaker's Body

Imagine yourself at a party. During the evening you form impressions about the people around you. Jonte seems relaxed and even-tempered, Nicole tense and irritable. Kyndra seems open and straightforward, Sun-Hi hostile and evasive. Amin seems happy to see you; Seth definitely is not.

How do you reach these conclusions? To a surprising extent, you reach them not on the basis of what people say with words, but because of what they say with their posture, gestures, eyes, and facial expressions. Suppose you are sitting next to Amin, and he says, "This is a great party. I'm really glad to be here with you." However, his body is turned slightly away from you, and he keeps looking at someone across the room. Despite what he says, you know he is *not* glad to be there with you.

Much the same thing happens in speechmaking. Posture, facial expression, gestures, eye contact—all affect the way listeners respond to a speaker. How we use these and other body motions to communicate is the subject of a fascinating area of study called kinesics. One of its founders, Ray Birdwhistell, estimated that more than 700,000 physical signals can be sent through bodily movement. Studies have shown that these signals have a significant impact on the meaning communicated by speakers.

kinesics

The study of body motions as a systematic mode of communication.

Research has also lent support to what the Greek historian Herodotus observed more than 2,400 years ago: "People trust their ears less than their eyes." When a speaker's body language is inconsistent with his or her words, listeners may well believe the body language rather than the words.[7] Here are the major aspects of physical action that will affect the outcome of your speeches.

PERSONAL APPEARANCE

If you were Lady Gaga, you could show up to make an MTV Music Video Award presentation speech wearing a bizarre creation that left little to the imagination. If you were Albert Einstein, you could show up to address an international science conference wearing wrinkled trousers, a sweater, and tennis shoes. While the members of your audience would certainly comment on your attire, your reputation would not be harmed. In fact, it might be enhanced. You would be one of the few, the very few, who live outside the rules, who are expected to be unusual.

Now imagine what would happen if the president of a corporation showed up to address a stockholders' meeting attired like Lady Gaga, or if the President of the United States spoke on national television wearing wrinkled clothes and tennis shoes. Both presidents would soon be looking for work. Barring the occasional eccentric, every speaker is expected by her

Good speakers use a lively voice to bring their ideas to life. They also use gestures, eye contact, and facial expressions to create a bond with their audience.

or his audience to exhibit a personal appearance in keeping with the occasion of the speech.

Many studies have confirmed that personal appearance plays an important role in speechmaking.[8] Listeners always see you before they hear you. Just as you adapt your language to the audience and the occasion, so should you dress and groom appropriately. Although the force of your speech can sometimes overcome a poor impression created by personal appearance, the odds are against it. Regardless of the speaking situation, you should try to evoke a favorable first impression.

MOVEMENT

Novice speakers are often unsure about what to do with their body while giving a speech. Some pace back and forth across the podium, shift their weight from one foot to the other, fidget with their notes, or jingle coins in their pockets. Still others turn into statues, standing rigid and expressionless from beginning to end.

Such quirks usually stem from nervousness. If you are prone to distracting mannerisms, your teacher will identify them so you can work on controlling them. With a little concentration, these mannerisms should disappear as you become more comfortable speaking in front of an audience.

As important as how you act during the speech is what you do just *before* you begin and *after* you finish. As you rise to speak, try to appear calm, poised, and confident, despite the butterflies in your stomach. When you reach the lectern, don't lean on it, and don't rush into your speech. Give yourself time to get set. Arrange your notes just the way you want them. Stand quietly as you wait to make sure the audience is paying attention. Establish eye contact with your listeners. Then—and only then—should you start to talk.

When you reach the end of your speech, maintain eye contact for a few moments after you stop talking. This will give your closing line time to sink in. Unless you are staying at the lectern to answer questions, collect your notes and return to your seat. As you do so, maintain your cool, collected demeanor. Whatever you do, don't start to gather your notes before you have finished talking, and don't cap off your speech with a huge sigh of relief or some remark like, "Whew! Am I glad that's over!"

When practicing your speeches, spend a little time rehearsing how you will behave at the beginning and at the end. It is one of the easiest—and one of the most effective—things you can do to improve your image with an audience.

GESTURES

gestures

Motions of a speaker's hands or arms during a speech.

Few aspects of delivery cause students more anguish than deciding what to do with their hands. "Should I clasp them behind my back? Let them hang at my sides? Rest them on the lectern? And what about gesturing? When should I do that—and how?" Even people who use their hands expressively in everyday conversation seem to regard them as awkward appendages when speaking before an audience.

Over the years, more nonsense has been written about gesturing than any other aspect of speech delivery. Adroit gestures *can* add to the impact of a speech; but effective speakers do not need a vast repertoire of gestures. Some accomplished speakers gesture frequently, others hardly at all. The primary rule is this: Whatever gestures you make should not distract from your message. They should *appear* natural and spontaneous, help clarify or reinforce your ideas, and be suited to the audience and occasion. For a good example, look at Video 13.3 in the online Media Library for this chapter.

connect

View an excerpt from "Third-Culture Kid" in the online Media Library for this chapter (Video 13.3).

Gesturing tends to work itself out as you acquire experience and confidence. For now, make sure your hands do not upstage your ideas. Avoid flailing them about, wringing them together, or toying with your rings. Once you have eliminated these distractions, forget about your hands. Think about communicating with your listeners, and your gestures will take care of themselves—just as they do in conversation.

EYE CONTACT

The eyes have been called "the windows of the soul." We look to them to help gauge a speaker's truthfulness, intelligence, attitudes, and feelings.

eye contact

Direct visual contact with the eyes of another person.

Although patterns of eye contact in everyday conversation vary from culture to culture, there is wide agreement across cultures on the importance of eye contact in public speaking. In most circumstances, one of the quickest ways to establish a communicative bond with your listeners is to look at them personally and pleasantly. Avoiding their gaze is one of the surest ways to lose them.

Speakers in the United States who fail to establish eye contact are perceived as tentative or ill at ease and may be seen as insincere or dishonest. It is no wonder, then, that teachers urge students to look at the audience 80 to 90 percent of the time they are talking. You may find this disconcerting at first. But after one or two speeches, you should be able to meet the gaze of your audience fairly comfortably.

It isn't enough just to look at your listeners; *how* you look at them also counts. Beware of the tendency to gaze intently at one part of the audience while ignoring the rest. In speech class, some students look only at the section of the room where the teacher is sitting. Others avoid looking anywhere near the teacher and focus on one or two sympathetic friends. You should try to establish eye contact with your whole audience.

When addressing a small audience such as your class, you can usually look briefly from one person to another. For a larger group, you can scan the

Research shows that eye contact is one of the most important elements in speech delivery. No matter what the situation, you want your eyes to convey confidence, sincerity, and conviction.

audience rather than try to engage the eyes of each person individually. No matter what the size of your audience, you want your eyes to convey confidence, sincerity, and conviction.

Look at Video 13.4 in the online Media Library for this chapter to see a fine example of eye contact. The speaker is telling her classmates how they can become volunteers for the Special Olympics. Notice how she uses her eyes to connect with her listeners at a personal level. This is the kind of strong communication you should strive for in your speeches.[9]

connect

View an excerpt from "Making a Difference Through the Special Olympics" in the online Media Library for this chapter (Video 13.4).

Practicing Delivery

Popular wisdom promises that practice makes perfect. This is true, but only if we practice properly. You will do little to improve your speech delivery unless you practice the right things in the right ways. Here is a five-step method that has worked well for many students:

1. Go through your preparation outline *aloud* to check how what you have written translates into spoken discourse. Is it too long? Too short? Are the main points clear when you speak them? Are the supporting materials distinct, convincing, interesting? Do the introduction and conclusion come across well? As you answer these questions, revise the speech as needed.
2. Prepare your speaking outline. In doing so, be sure to follow the guidelines in Chapter 11. Use the same visual framework as in the preparation outline. Make sure the speaking outline is easy to read at a glance. Give yourself cues on the outline for delivering the speech.

3. Practice the speech aloud several times using only the speaking outline. Be sure to "talk through" all examples and to recite in full all quotations and statistics. If your speech includes visual aids, use them as you practice. The first couple of times, you will probably forget something or make a mistake, but don't worry. Keep going and complete the speech as well as you can. Concentrate on gaining control of the *ideas;* don't try to learn the speech word for word. After a few tries you should be able to get through the speech extemporaneously with surprising ease.
4. Now begin to polish and refine your delivery. Practice the speech in front of a mirror to check for eye contact and distracting mannerisms. Record the speech to gauge volume, pitch, rate, pauses, and vocal variety. Most important, try it out on friends, roommates, family members—anyone who will listen and give you an honest appraisal. Because your speech is designed for people rather than for mirrors or recorders, you need to find out ahead of time how it goes over with people.
5. Finally, give your speech a dress rehearsal under conditions as close as possible to those you will face in class. Some students like to try the speech a couple times in an empty classroom the day before the speech is due. No matter where you hold your last practice session, you should leave it feeling confident and looking forward to speaking in your class.

If this or any practice method is to work, you must start early. Don't wait until the night before your speech to begin working on delivery. A single practice session—no matter how long—is rarely enough. Allow yourself *at least* a couple of days, preferably more, to gain command of the speech and its presentation.

Answering Audience Questions

If you have ever watched a press conference or heard a speaker answer questions after a talk, you know the question-and-answer session can make or break a presentation. A speaker who handles questions well can strengthen the impact of his or her speech. On the other hand, a speaker who evades questions or shows annoyance will almost certainly create the opposite effect.

The question-and-answer session is a common part of public speaking, whether the occasion is a press conference, business presentation, public hearing, or classroom assignment. An answer to a question is often the final word an audience hears and is likely to leave a lasting impression.

PREPARING FOR THE QUESTION-AND-ANSWER SESSION

The first step to doing well in a Q&A session is to take it as seriously as the speech itself. The two major steps in preparing are working out answers to possible questions and practicing the delivery of those answers.

Formulate Answers to Possible Questions

Once you know that your presentation will include questions from the audience, you should be thinking about possible questions even as you are writing your speech. If you practice your speech in front of friends, family, or coworkers, ask them to jot down questions. Keep track of all the questions and formulate answers. Write your answers in full to make sure you have thought them through completely.

If you are giving a persuasive speech, be sure to work out answers to objections the audience may have to your proposal. No matter how careful you are to deal with those objections in your speech, you can be sure they will come up in the Q&A session.

If you are speaking on a topic with technical aspects, be ready to answer specialized inquiries about them, as well as questions that seek clarification, in nontechnical terms. You might even prepare a handout that you can distribute afterward for people who want more information.

Practice the Delivery of Your Answers

You would not present a speech to a room full of people without rehearsing. Neither should you go into a Q&A session without practicing the delivery of your answers.

One possibility is to have a friend or colleague listen to your presentation, ask questions, and critique your answers. This method is used by political candidates and business leaders before debates or press conferences. Another possibility is to record your answers to anticipated questions, play them back, and revise them until they are just right.

As you rehearse, work on making your answers brief and to the point. Many simple questions can be answered in 30 seconds, and even complex ones should usually be answered in a minute or two. If you practice answering questions beforehand, you will find it much easier to keep to these time limits.

Of course, there is no way to predict every question you will receive. But if you go into the Q&A period fully prepared, you will be able to adapt to whatever occurs.

MANAGING THE QUESTION-AND-ANSWER SESSION

If you have ever watched a skillful speaker field inquiries from the audience, you know there is an art to managing a question-and-answer session. Entire books have been written on this subject, but the following suggestions will help get you started on the right foot.

Using public speaking in your CAREER

Utilizing your business degree and computer savvy, you have made a success of the online marketing company you started after graduating from college. Now in its third year, the company has prepared a proposal to design the e-commerce site for a major sporting goods retailer. In your 30-minute presentation to the retailer's management team, you will review the homepage designs, site maps, and security protocols.

You notice on the agenda that another 30 minutes has been allotted after your presentation for questions and answers. Knowing from your previous experience with clients how important the Q&A session can be, you want to be sure you are ready for it. What steps will you take to prepare?

Approach Questions with a Positive Attitude

A positive attitude will help you answer questions graciously and respectfully. Try to view questions from the audience as signs of genuine interest and a desire to learn more about your subject. If someone asks about a point that seems clear to you, don't respond by saying, "I discussed that at the beginning of my talk," or "The answer seems obvious." Instead, use moments like these to reiterate or expand upon your ideas.

A speaker who adopts a sharp or defensive tone while answering questions will alienate many people in the audience. Even if you are asked a hostile question, keep your cool. Avoid the temptation to answer defensively, sarcastically, or argumentatively. Most people in the audience will respect you for trying to avoid a quarrel.

Listen Carefully

It's hard to answer a question well if you don't listen carefully to it. Give the questioner your full attention. When faced with an unclear or unwieldy question, try to rephrase it by saying something like, "If I understand your question, it seems to me that you are asking. . . ." Another option is simply to ask the audience member to repeat the question. Most people will restate it more succinctly and clearly.

Direct Answers to the Entire Audience

When you are being asked a question, look at the questioner. Direct your answer, however, to the entire audience. Make occasional eye contact with the questioner as you answer, but speak primarily to the audience as a whole. If you speak just to the questioner, the rest of your audience may drift off.

When speaking to a large audience, repeat or paraphrase each question after it is asked. This involves the entire audience and ensures that they know the question. In addition, repeating or paraphrasing the question gives you a moment to frame an answer before you respond.

Be Honest and Straightforward

If you don't know the answer to a question, say so. Don't apologize, don't evade, and most important, don't try to bluff. Do, however, let the questioner know that you take the question seriously. Offer to check into the answer as soon as possible after the speech. If a more knowledgeable person is at hand, ask if she or he knows the answer.

Stay on Track

It's easy to get diverted or lose control of time in a lively Q&A session. Unless there is a moderator, the speaker is responsible for keeping things on track. Allow one follow-up question from each person, and don't let yourself be dragged into a personal debate with any questioner. If someone attempts to ask more than two questions, respond graciously yet firmly by saying, "This is an interesting line of questioning, but we need to give other people a chance to ask questions."

Sometimes, a listener will launch into an extended monologue instead of posing a question. When this happens, you can retain control of the situation by saying something like, "Those are very interesting ideas, but do you have a specific question I can answer?" If the person persists, offer to talk individually with him or her after the session.

Question-and-answer sessions are an important part of public speaking around the globe. Here Spanish delegates talk with reporters in Dublin, Ireland, about the 2014 European Parliament elections.

On some occasions, the length of the question-and-answer session is predetermined. On other occasions, it's up to the speaker. Make sure you allow enough time to get through issues of major importance, but don't let things drag on after the momentum of the session has started winding down. As the end approaches, offer to respond to another question or two. Then wrap things up by thanking the audience for its time and attention.[10]

Presenting Your Speech Online

The head of a small tech start-up, Matthew Rhee was excited about his presentation later that morning. He was going to speak to librarians around the state about new online catalogue software he was developing. The software promised to simplify the process of searching, finding, and even previewing library books from computers and mobile devices.

Matthew was particularly excited because he could talk without leaving his apartment. His potential clients would log in to a virtual meeting room, and he would speak from his computer to people in a half-dozen cities. Having made a couple of successful speeches to in-person audiences, he was confident about the outcome. He ran through his planned remarks a couple of times, but he didn't make any special adjustments for the online speaking situation.

Unfortunately, things did not go as smoothly as Matthew had expected. Because his computer was facing a window behind him, the audience had a hard time seeing his face. But they could see the clutter on his desk and the plain white t-shirt he was wearing—neither of which did much for his credibility. Nor did he help himself by slouching in his chair and drinking coffee as he spoke. By the end of the presentation, many of Matthew's listeners had either zoned out or had started checking their email.

Like Matthew, many people underestimate the difficulty of presenting a speech online. An online speech is not simply a speech to an in-person audience that has been uploaded on YouTube or a campus server. An online speech, as defined here, is one that has been created specifically for an audience that will view it online and in real time, often using software designed for that purpose. Such a speech requires all the skills of speech preparation and delivery discussed throughout this book, but it also poses special challenges unique to the online environment.

online speech

A speech that has been created specifically for an audience that will view it online and in real time.

Whether or not you give an online presentation in your speech class, there is a good chance that, like Matthew, you will one day find yourself speaking via the Internet to an audience that is spread across multiple locations. You may need to give a brief speech of self-introduction during an online job interview. You may be required, as part of your job, to present an online training session or to speak with potential clients about a service or a product. You may address a meeting of the school board or the city zoning commission from a remote location.

Some 12 million Web meetings take place in the United States every day, plus millions more around the world. As with other aspects of public speaking, there is no substitute for experience when it comes to giving speeches online. The following eight points, however, will help you get started in the right direction.

UNDERSTAND THE SPECIAL NATURE OF THE ONLINE ENVIRONMENT

When you deliver a traditional in-person speech, you're in the same room as your audience. You can see how many people are present. You can look them in the eye to keep them engaged. You have multiple forms of feedback to assess how fully they are paying attention and how well they are grasping your message.

In the online environment, you have a fundamentally different relationship with your audience. Because you are not in the same room with them, gauging their response can be difficult. Even if your software allows you to see the audience, you can't make direct eye contact with them. You might not know if they begin staring out the window, checking Facebook, or reading the news online.

The first step to a successful online speech is realizing that the online environment will transform almost every aspect of your presentation—including technology, the visual environment, nonverbal communication, pacing, Q&A, rehearsal, and adapting to unforeseen contingencies. We'll look at each of these in turn.

KNOW YOUR TECHNOLOGY

There are a number of software programs designed for online presentations—WebEx, GoToMeeting, Adobe Connect, Google Hangouts, and Cisco TelePresence, to name a few of the most popular. Beyond the basic function of allowing you to speak to people in remote locations, these programs have different features that may be more or less applicable to your presentation. Some programs allow you to combine audio and video with visual aids. Some allow you to see, hear, and chat with your audience. Some let you share documents and collaborate in real time. As a speaker,

Whether presenting online or to an in-person audience, you should rehearse under conditions as close as possible as to those you will face during the speech. Thorough preparation will increase your skill and confidence.

it is imperative that you know the capabilities and limitations of the software you'll be using.

Because some software programs are quite complex, you may be able to find someone who can help manage the technological side of your presentation. This is not always possible, but many businesses, universities, and nonprofit organizations have an IT person who is prepared to assist. This person may also have special equipment that will improve the video and audio quality of your speech.

CONTROL THE VISUAL ENVIRONMENT

The Internet is often informal. We Skype with family members, post photos of our social lives to Instagram, and watch cat videos on YouTube. Your online speech, however, should *not* be informal. It should be as polished and professional as an in-person speech. This requires, among other things, controlling the visual environment so it works *for* you rather than against you.

Pay attention to lighting. You don't want the room to seem too dark; neither do you want so much light that it washes you out. You can usually gauge what the audience will see on their screens through the video preview window—sometimes called "participant view"—that is included in most software programs.

When previewing yourself, check your distance from the webcam. If you sit too far away, you'll seem small and removed from your listeners. If you sit too close, you'll look like a selfie. If you aim the camera too low, you'll have a disproportionate amount of blank space above your head. A good rule of thumb is to sit two to three feet from the webcam so you fill most of the frame and the audience can see you from the chest up (look at Figure 13.1 on the next page).[11]

FIGURE 13.1

Another way to control the visual environment is to clean up what's around you. Get rid of clutter—cups, dishes, pens, paper, erasers, staplers—anything that can distract the audience's attention.

Finally, controlling the visual environment means taking your personal appearance seriously. Dress for your online speech as if you were delivering an in-person speech. The more professional you look on screen, the more professional you will feel when presenting—and the more professional you will appear to your audience.

ADAPT YOUR NONVERBAL COMMUNICATION

Your nonverbal communication is magnified dramatically when you speak via a camera of any kind. Gestures, facial expressions, eye movements—all become more noticeable, and potentially distracting.

This is something newscasters have long known. Their on-camera tricks can be useful for your online presentation. Because much of your speech will involve sitting in front of the webcam, your posture will need to be straight, but not rigid. The goal is to appear professional, relaxed, and confident.

Well-planned and deliberate hand gestures are also important. If your hands are too close to the camera, they'll draw attention to themselves. Too many hand movements can make you seem nervous and fidgety. Concentrate on using gestures that are natural but controlled. As one expert in online presentations explains, "The more defined your hands appear, the more defined your message will appear to your audience."[12]

Also be mindful of your eyes. As experienced online presenters know, the camera will heighten every eye movement. Avoid looking up or down, and make sure your eyes do not dart back and forth. Learning to speak to a camera is an acquired skill. Look into the camera as naturally as you can and imagine yourself establishing eye contact with an audience right in front of you. This will help your eye movements seem deliberate, controlled, and confident.

ADJUST YOUR PACING FOR THE ONLINE ENVIRONMENT

As speech consultant Cynthia Clay explains, online audiences have more ways to tune out than do in-person listeners, and the temptation to multitask is often irresistible.[13] Phones, coworkers, what's happening outside the window—all will be competing with you for attention. The pacing of your speech can help keep the audience focused on you instead of on the temptations around them.

One way to adjust the pacing of your speech for the online environment is to alter what appears on the audience's screen. Your listeners aren't likely to pay attention for long if they see only your talking head for 10 minutes. Try to incorporate visual aids into your presentation (see Chapter 14 for a full discussion of visual aids). Altering what's on screen can help keep your speech fresh and engaging.

Effective pacing also requires that you pay close attention to time constraints. Ask the person who invites you to speak how long your presentation should be. Make sure you meet or beat that length.

Regardless of the length of your speech, try to keep it moving at a brisk pace. People are accustomed to a crisp tempo when watching videos of almost any kind. Make sure you explain your ideas fully enough that the audience understands your message, but doesn't get bogged down in digressions or unnecessary details.

MANAGE Q&A FOR THE ONLINE ENVIRONMENT

Earlier in this chapter, we looked at how to handle question-and-answer sessions in traditional speech settings. Everything discussed there remains true in the online environment. But there is one additional factor you will need to consider—whether to invite questions as the speech proceeds or to keep them for the end.

Some experienced speakers like to encourage questions during the presentation because it can help keep the audience involved. The downside of this approach is that it can easily throw the speech off track. One audience member might have a laundry list of questions that will consume your time and encourage other listeners to direct their attention elsewhere.

For first-time online speakers, the best bet is usually to save Q&A for the end of the speech. This will allow you to communicate your message in an orderly fashion *and* to answer whatever questions your listeners may have.

REHEARSE FOR THE ONLINE ENVIRONMENT

Many people assume that an online speech requires less rehearsal than an in-person speech. In fact, it usually requires more.

There are two general stages to rehearsing an online speech. First, as with an in-person speech, you should try to practice in front of family, friends, or coworkers. They can give you feedback on such things as the structure of your speech, the clarity of your ideas, the tone of your voice, the pacing of your remarks, and so forth. Once you have these matters under control, you are ready to move to the second stage of rehearsal.

In this stage, you need to focus specifically on adapting your delivery for the online environment. Practice with the computer and software you will use on the day of your speech. Make sure you know all the computer commands and can execute them flawlessly. Practice with your visual aids so you

checklist

Presenting an Online Speech

YES	NO	
☐	☐	1. Have I considered the special nature of the online speech environment?
☐	☐	2. Do I understand the capabilities and limitations of my presentation software?
☐	☐	3. Do I control the visual environment of my presentation so it will work to my advantage?
☐	☐	4. Have I adapted my nonverbal communication so it will be effective when viewed online?
☐	☐	5. Will the pacing of my speech keep the audience focused on my message?
☐	☐	6. Have I considered how best to handle questions and answers?
☐	☐	7. Have I taken all the steps necessary to rehearse my speech for online presentation?
☐	☐	8. Do I have a backup plan in case I run into technical problems?

can integrate them seamlessly into your speech. Do everything you can to control the technical side of your presentation.

Because your audience will view the speech on either a computer screen or a projection screen, it is imperative that you rehearse with this in mind. Once you have mastered the technology and practiced in front of a live audience, deliver the speech into your webcam, record it, and play it back. Some online presentation software has a recording function built into the program.

Watching the video of your speech will help you frame the shot, hear your voice, gauge your eye contact, check your gestures, and see yourself through your audience's eyes. Make the necessary adjustments and record the speech again until you're happy with the final result.

HAVE A BACKUP PLAN

Have you ever run into problems logging on to a Web site? Encountered server errors? Waited impatiently for a video to buffer? All these things—and others—can play havoc with an online presentation. No matter how much time speakers invest in mastering the technology at their end, they can still be undermined by technological glitches at the audience's end.

This is why experts recommend that you *always* have a backup plan in case the technology fails. That plan might be to distribute an outline of your speech via email. It might be to move the speech to an audio-only conference call. It might even be to reschedule the speech once the technical problems are resolved. Because we have all been sabotaged by technology at one time or another, audiences usually have sympathy for a speaker who encounters such problems. Having a backup plan will make you look conscientious and considerate.

Summary

Speech delivery is a matter of nonverbal communication. It is based on how you use your voice and body to convey the message expressed by your words. Rather than calling attention to itself, effective delivery conveys the speaker's ideas clearly, engagingly, and without distracting the audience.

There are four basic methods of delivering a speech: reading verbatim from a manuscript, reciting a memorized text, speaking impromptu, and speaking extemporaneously. When speaking extemporaneously, you will have a brief set of notes or a speaking outline and will choose the exact wording of your speech at the moment of delivery.

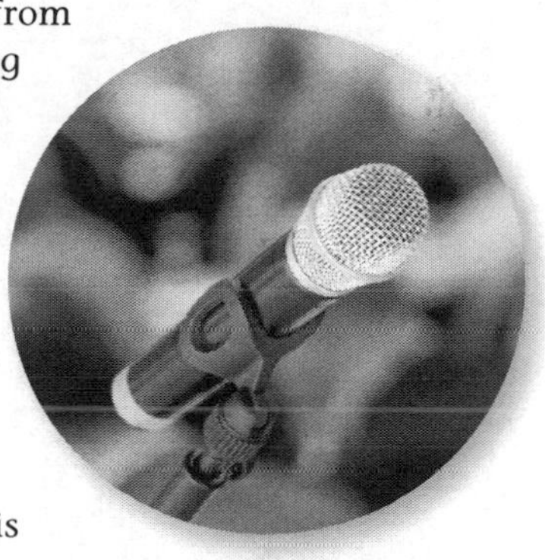

To use your voice effectively you should work on controlling your volume, pitch, rate, pauses, vocal variety, pronunciation, articulation, and dialect. Volume is the relative loudness of your voice, and pitch is the relative highness or lowness. Rate refers to the speed at which you talk. Pauses, when carefully timed, can add punch to your speech, but you should avoid vocalized pauses ("er," "um," and the like).

Vocal variety refers to changes in volume, pitch, rate, and pauses, and is crucial to making your voice lively and animated. You also need correct pronunciation and distinct articulation. Avoid heavy use of dialect in situations where the audience does not share the dialect or will find it inappropriate.

Posture, personal appearance, facial expression, gestures, and eye contact also affect the way listeners respond to speakers. Dress and groom appropriately, use gestures and bodily movement to enhance your message, and make eye contact with your listeners.

You should practice all these aspects of delivery along with the words of your speech. Start your practice sessions early so you will have plenty of time to gain command of the speech and its presentation.

If your speech includes a question-and-answer session, anticipate the most likely questions, prepare answers to them, and practice delivering those answers. During the Q&A period, listen carefully to the questions, approach them positively, and respond to them briefly, graciously, and straightforwardly. Direct your answers to the full audience, rather than to the questioner alone, and make sure to end the session in a timely fashion.

If you are delivering a speech online, you will have to take a number of special steps. They include understanding the nature of the online environment, knowing the capabilities and limitations of your presentation software, controlling the visual environment, and adapting your pacing and nonverbal communication. You will also need to rehearse specifically for online presentation, decide how to handle Q&A, and develop a backup plan in case the technology fails you.

Key Terms

nonverbal communication (240)
manuscript speech (241)
impromptu speech (241)
extemporaneous speech (242)
conversational quality (242)
volume (244)
pitch (244)
inflections (244)
monotone (244)
rate (244)
pause (245)
vocalized pause (245)
vocal variety (245)
pronunciation (246)
articulation (247)
dialect (247)
kinesics (248)
gestures (250)
eye contact (250)
online speech (256)

Review Questions

After reading this chapter, you should be able to answer the following questions:

1. What is nonverbal communication? Why is it important to effective public speaking?
2. What are the elements of good speech delivery?
3. What are the four methods of speech delivery?
4. What are the eight aspects of voice usage you should concentrate on in your speeches?
5. What are four aspects of bodily action you should concentrate on in your speeches?
6. What are the five steps you should follow when practicing your speech delivery?
7. What steps should you take when preparing for a question-and-answer session? What should you concentrate on when responding to questions during the session?
8. What eight steps should you take if you are faced with presenting an online speech?

connect

For further review, go to the LearnSmart study module for this chapter.

Exercises for Critical Thinking

1. An excellent way to improve your vocal variety is to read aloud selections from poetry that require emphasis and feeling. Choose one of your favorite poems that falls into this category, or find one by leafing through a poetry anthology.

   Practice reading the selection aloud. As you read, use your voice to make the poem come alive. Vary your volume, rate, and pitch. Find the appropriate places for pauses. Underline the key words or phrases you think should be stressed. Modulate your tone of voice; use inflections for emphasis and meaning.

For this to work, you must overcome your fear of sounding affected or "dramatic." Most beginning speakers do better if they exaggerate changes in volume, rate, pitch, and expression. This will make you more aware of the ways you can use your voice to express a wide range of moods and meanings. Besides, what sounds overly "dramatic" to you usually does not sound that way to an audience. By adding luster, warmth, and enthusiasm to your voice, you will go a long way toward capturing and keeping the interest of your listeners.

If possible, practice reading the selection into a digital recorder. Listen to the playback. If you are not satisfied with what you hear, practice the selection some more and record it again.

2. Watch a 10-minute segment of a television drama with the sound turned off. What do the characters say with their dress, gestures, facial expressions, and the like? Do the same with a television comedy. How do the nonverbal messages in the two shows differ? Be prepared to report your observations in class.

3. Attend a speech on campus. You may choose either a presentation by a guest speaker from outside your school or a class session by a professor who has a reputation as a good lecturer. Prepare a brief report on the speaker's delivery.

   In your report, first analyze the speaker's volume, pitch, rate, pauses, vocal variety, pronunciation, and articulation. Then evaluate the speaker's personal appearance, bodily action, gestures, and eye contact. Explain how the speaker's delivery added to or detracted from what the speaker said. Finally, note at least two techniques of delivery used by the speaker that you might want to try in your next speech.

14

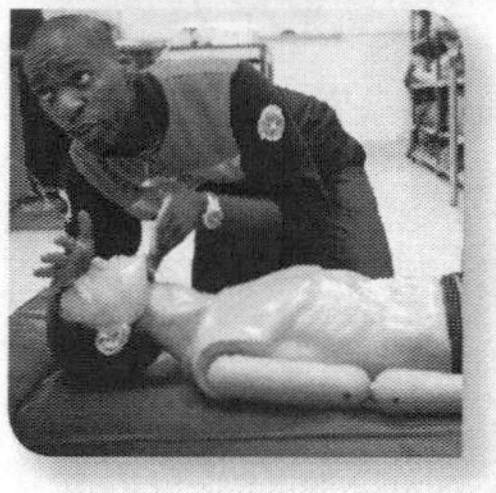

Using Visual Aids

Diagnosed with high blood pressure when he was in high school, Devin Marshall decided to give his persuasive speech on the excessive amount of salt in the American diet. On the day of his speech, he brought to class a large box, which he set on the table next to him. This immediately aroused the curiosity of his audience. Devin took from the box a container of Morton Salt, a measuring cup, and two plates. Then he began his speech.

First, he explained the monthly salt consumption recommended by the American Medical Association. To illustrate, he measured a cup of salt onto one plate and showed it to the audience. Next, he gave statistics about how much salt the average American consumes in a month. Again, as he spoke, he measured. When he was finished measuring, the second plate had three cups, almost two pounds of salt.

Finally, Devin said, "Now let's multiply that amount by 12 and see how much salt we eat over the course of a year." And he began taking out of the box one container of Morton Salt after another, until he had piled up a pyramid of 14 containers, or nearly 24 pounds of salt!

As the old saying tells us, one picture is worth a thousand words. Can you picture two pounds of salt? Or 24 pounds of salt? You could if you had watched Devin measure out the salt and stack up the Morton containers. This dramatic visual evidence brought home Devin's point more forcefully than would have been possible with words alone.

People find a speaker's message more interesting, grasp it more easily, and retain it longer when it is presented visually as well as verbally. In fact, when used properly, visual aids can enhance almost *every* aspect of a speech. An average speaker who uses visual aids will come across as better prepared, more credible, and more professional than a dynamic speaker who does not use visual aids. Visual aids can even help you combat stage fright. They heighten audience interest, shift attention away from the speaker, and give the speaker greater confidence in the presentation as a whole.[1]

For all these reasons, you will find visual aids of great value in your speeches. In this chapter, we will concentrate primarily on visual aids suitable for classroom speeches, but the same principles apply in all circumstances. For speeches outside the classroom—in business or community situations, for instance—you should have no difficulty if you follow the suggestions given here.

Let us look first at the kinds of visual aids you are most likely to use, then at guidelines for preparing visual aids, and finally at guidelines for using visual aids.

Kinds of Visual Aids

OBJECTS AND MODELS

Bringing the object of your speech to class can be an excellent way to clarify your ideas and give them dramatic impact. If your specific purpose is "To inform my audience how to choose the right ski equipment," why not bring the equipment to class to show your listeners? Or suppose you want to inform your classmates about the Peruvian art of doll making. You could bring several dolls to class and explain how they were made.

Some objects, however, cannot be used effectively in classroom speeches. Some are too big. Others are too small to be seen clearly. Still others may not be available to you. If you were speaking about a rare suit of armor in a local museum, you could, theoretically, transport it to class, but it is most unlikely that the museum would let you borrow it.

If the object you want to discuss is too large, too small, or unavailable, you may be able to work with a model. For an example, check Video 14.1 in the online Media Library for this chapter. The speaker is talking about CPR, which he demonstrates on a training dummy he borrowed from the local Red Cross.

connect

View an excerpt from "CPR" in the online Media Library for this chapter (Video 14.1).

PHOTOGRAPHS AND DRAWINGS

In the absence of an object or a model, you may be able to use photographs or drawings. Neither, however, will work effectively unless they are large enough for the audience to see without straining. Normal-size photos are too

Photographs make excellent visual aids if they are large enough to be seen easily. Check Video 14.2 in the online Media Library for this chapter to see how one speaker used this photograph of the famous ruins at Angkor Wat.

small to be seen clearly without being passed around—which only diverts the audience from what you are saying. The same is true of photographs and drawings in books.

The most effective way to show drawings and photographs is with a presentation program such as PowerPoint or Keynote. Notice, for example, how the speaker in Video 14.2 uses PowerPoint to present a photograph of the famous ruins at Angkor Wat in Cambodia. No other method of showing the photograph would work as well.

For another example, take a look at Figure 14.1 (below), which shows a drawing used in a speech about the kinds of problems faced by people who have dyslexia. It allowed the speaker to translate complex ideas into visual terms the audience could grasp immediately.

connect

View an excerpt from "The Splendor of Angkor Wat" in the online Media Library for this chapter (Video 14.2).

GRAPHS

Audiences often have trouble grasping a complex series of numbers. You can ease their difficulty by using graphs to show statistical trends and patterns.

graph

A visual aid used to show statistical trends and patterns.

FIGURE 14.1

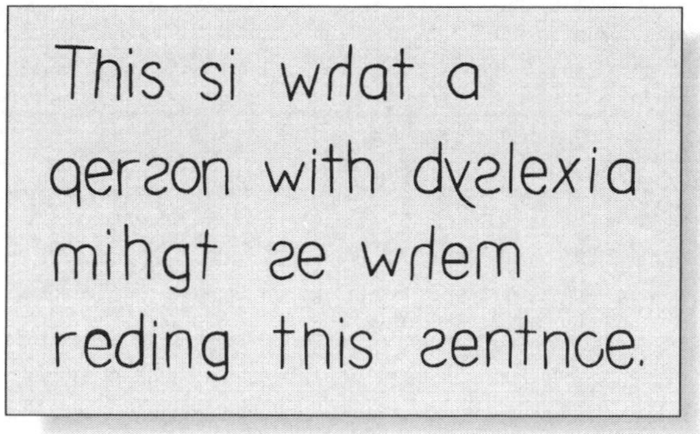

FIGURE 14.2

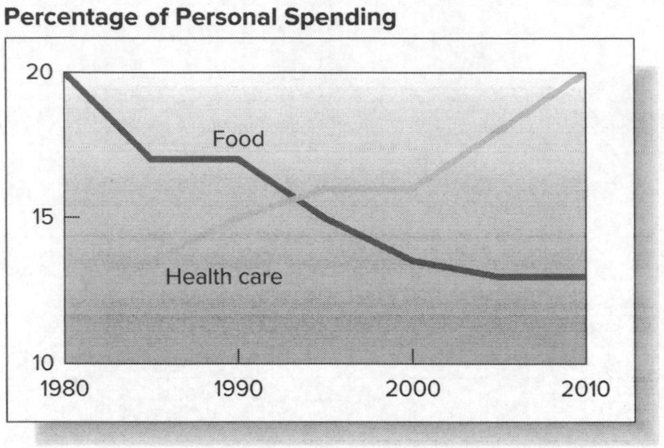

line graph

A graph that uses one or more lines to show changes in statistics over time or space.

The most common type is the *line graph*. Figure 14.2 (above) shows such a graph, used in a speech about the rising cost of health care. If you look at Video 14.3 in the online Media Library for this chapter, you can see how the speaker explained the graph. She said:

connect

View the presentation of this graph in "The Cost of Health Care" in the online Media Library for this chapter (Video 14.3).

> As you can see from this graph, based on figures from the U.S. government, health care continues to eat away at our budgets. Since 1980, it's risen from 13 percent of personal spending to 20 percent. Compare that to what we spend on food. In 1980, 20 percent of personal spending was on food; today it is 13 percent. That's right, over the past three decades health care has completely changed places with food as the largest category of personal expense.

The *pie graph* is best suited for illustrating simple distribution patterns. Figure 14.3 (below) shows how one speaker used a pie graph to help listeners

FIGURE 14.3

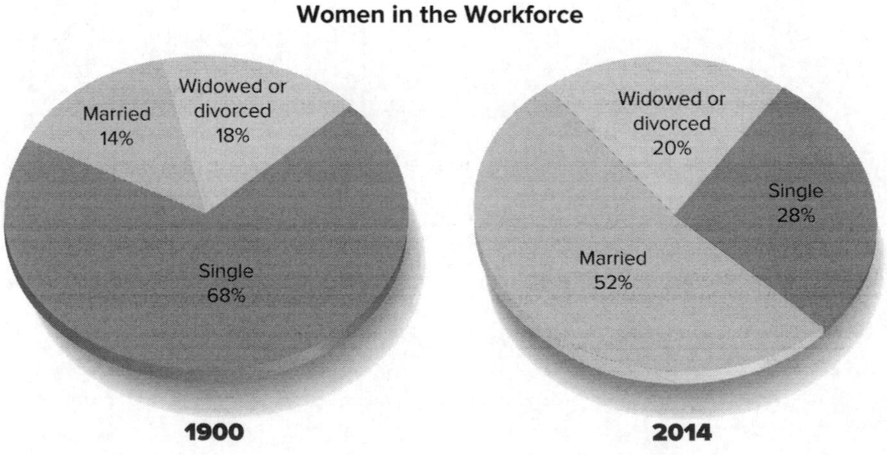

pie graph

A graph that highlights segments of a circle to show simple distribution patterns.

FIGURE 14.4

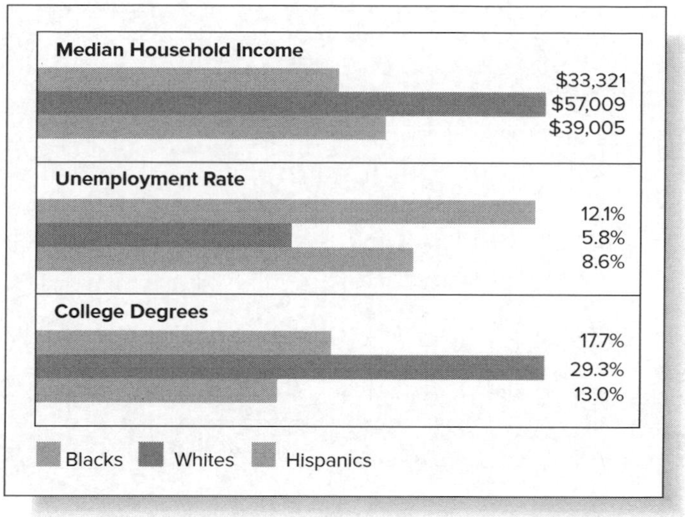

bar graph

A graph that uses vertical or horizontal bars to show comparisons among two or more items.

visualize changes in marital status among working women in the past century. The graph on the left shows the percentages of working women who were single, married, and widowed or divorced in 1900. The graph on the right shows percentages for the same groups in 2014.

Because a pie graph is used to dramatize relationships among the parts of a whole, you should keep the number of different segments in the graph as small as possible. A pie graph should ideally have from two to five segments; under no circumstances should it have more than eight.

The *bar graph* is a particularly good way to show comparisons among two or more items. It also has the advantage of being easy to understand, even by people who have no background in reading graphs.

Figure 14.4 (above) is an example of a bar graph from a speech titled "The Politics of Race in America." It shows visually the relative standing of blacks, whites, and Hispanics with respect to median household income, unemployment, and college education. By using a bar graph, the speaker made her points more vividly than if she had just cited the numbers orally.[2]

CHARTS

Charts are particularly useful for summarizing large blocks of information. One student, in a speech titled "The United States: A Nation of Immigrants," used a chart to show the leading regions of the world for U.S. immigrants (Figure 14.5, page 270). These are too many categories to be conveyed in a pie graph. By listing them on a chart, the speaker made it easier for listeners to keep the information straight. Look at Video 14.4 in the online Media Library for this chapter to see how the student presented the chart during her speech.

connect

View an excerpt from "The United States: A Nation of Immigrants" in the online Media Library for this chapter (Video 14.4).

The biggest mistake made by beginning speakers when using a chart is to include too much information. As we will discuss later, visual aids should be clear, simple, and uncluttered. Lists on a chart should rarely exceed seven or eight items, with generous spacing between items. If you cannot fit everything on a single chart, make a second one.

FIGURE 14.5

Region of Birth	Percent of U.S. Immigrants
Asia	36 percent
Mexico	14 percent
Europe	11 percent
Caribbean	11 percent
South America	10 percent
Africa	9 percent
Central America	5 percent
Other	4 percent

chart

A visual aid that summarizes a large block of information, usually in list form.

VIDEO

If you are talking about the impact caused by a low-speed automobile accident, what could be more effective than showing slow-motion video of crash tests? Or suppose you are explaining the different kinds of roller coasters found in amusement parks. Your best visual aid would be a video showing those coasters in action.

Despite its advantages, however, adding video to a speech can cause more harm than good if it is not done carefully and expertly. First, make sure the clip is not too long. While a 30-second video can illustrate your ideas in a memorable way, anything much longer will distract attention from the speech itself. Second, make sure the video is cued to start exactly where you want it. Third, if necessary, edit the video to the precise length you need so it will blend smoothly into your speech. Fourth, beware of low-resolution video that may look fine on a computer but is blurry and distorted when projected on a screen or monitor.

THE SPEAKER

Sometimes you can use your own body as a visual aid—by illustrating how a conductor directs an orchestra, by revealing the secrets behind magic tricks, by showing how to perform sign language, and so forth. In addition to clarifying a speaker's ideas, doing some kind of demonstration helps keep the audience involved. It also can reduce a speaker's nervousness by providing an outlet for extra adrenaline.

connect

View an excerpt from "Yoga: Uniting Body, Mind, and Spirit" in the online Media Library for this chapter (Video 14.5).

Doing a demonstration well requires special practice to coordinate your actions with your words and to control the timing of your speech. You can see an excellent example on Video 14.5 in the online Media Library for this chapter. After talking about the role of proper breathing in yoga, the speaker demonstrates three yoga poses. Notice how clearly she explains each pose, communicates directly with the audience, and maintains eye contact throughout her demonstration.

Special care is required if you are demonstrating a process that takes longer to complete than the time allotted for your speech. If you plan to show

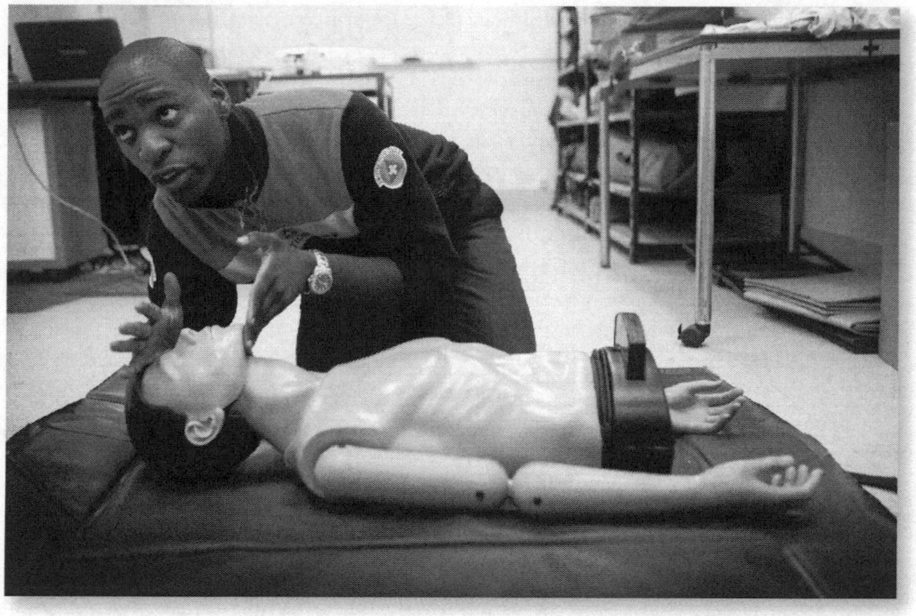

Demonstration speeches usually involve a visual aid of some kind. Such speeches require careful practice to coordinate the speaker's actions and words while maintaining eye contact with the audience.

a long process, you might borrow the techniques of television chefs. They work through most of the steps in making a perfect marinated chicken, but they have a second, finished chicken ready to show you at the last minute.

Presentation Technology

Presentation technology allows you to integrate a variety of visual aids—including charts, graphs, photographs, and video—in the same talk. The most widely used presentation program is PowerPoint, but in recent years it has been joined by a host of competitors, including Keynote, Prezi, Google Docs, and Zoho Show. Depending on the resources at your school, you may be able to use one of these programs in your speech class. If so, it will provide training for speeches outside the classroom—especially in business settings, where presentation technology is used every day.

Later in this chapter, we will look at guidelines for preparing and presenting visual aids effectively. In the process, we'll pay special attention to what you can do to create and deliver high-quality slides. For now, consider the following factors when thinking about employing presentation technology in your speeches.

PLUSES AND MINUSES OF PRESENTATION TECHNOLOGY

When used well, presentation technology is a great boon to communication. Unfortunately, it is not always used well. Too often speakers allow it to dominate their talks, wowing the audience with their technical proficiency while losing the message in a flurry of sounds and images.

This can be especially true with some of the new presentation programs. Prezi, for example, promises that you can "captivate your audience by zooming through your story." The danger is that Prezi's zooming, panning, and transition effects can easily become a barrier to communication. As one leading expert on presentation technology warns, Prezi too often turns speeches into "heavily decorated and animated affairs with excessive motion that distracts from even well-researched content."[3]

At the other extreme are mind-numbing presentations that gave rise to the phrase "Death by PowerPoint." In such cases, the speaker plods through one poorly designed slide after another, virtually reading the speech to the audience as the words appear on screen. This is no more effective than reading dully from a manuscript.

PLANNING TO USE PRESENTATION TECHNOLOGY

If you are going to employ presentation technology effectively, you need a clear idea of exactly why, how, and when to use it. Rather than putting everything you say on screen for the audience to read, you need to choose which aspects of your speech to illustrate. This requires careful planning.

connect

View this excerpt from "Medical Robots: From Science Fiction to Science Fact" in the online Media Library for this chapter (Video 14.6).

The first step is deciding where you can use PowerPoint, Keynote, or some other program to greatest advantage. After you have finished developing the speech, think about where well-chosen slides will clarify or strengthen your ideas. Rather than using slides to illustrate every thought, look for spots where they will genuinely enhance your message.

One student, for example, used PowerPoint splendidly in a speech on medical robots. Part of the speech dealt with orderly robots, which transport medicine, food, and lab supplies around the hospital without a human by their side. The robots navigate by using "light whiskers"—invisible beams of sonar, infrared, and laser that constantly scan the environment to avoid collisions. Because the light whiskers are invisible, the speaker needed to find a way to make them visible for his audience. He did so by creating a PowerPoint slide in which colored lines representing the light whiskers popped on

Using public speaking in your CAREER

As a veterinarian and owner of a small-animal practice, you work closely with your local humane society to help control a growing population of unwanted dogs and cats. You and your staff devote many hours annually in free and reduced-cost medical services to animals adopted from the society. Now you have been asked to speak to the city council in support of legislation proposed by the society for stronger enforcement of animal licensing and leash laws.

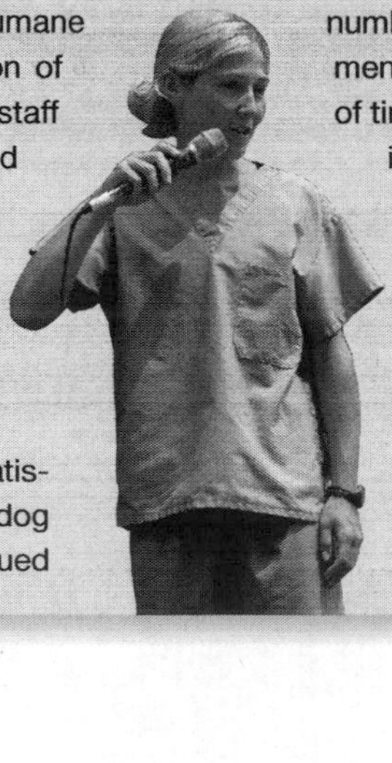

In your speech, you plan to include statistics that (1) compare estimates of the city's dog population with the number of licenses issued during the past five years and (2) show the small number of citations given by local law enforcement for unleashed pets during the same period of time. Knowing from your college public speaking class how valuable visual aids can be in presenting statistics, you decide to illustrate one set of statistics with a chart and the other with a graph.

For which set of statistics will a chart be more appropriate? For which set will a graph be more appropriate? Of the three kinds of graphs discussed in this chapter—bar, line, pie—which will work best for your statistics, and why?

screen in perfect coordination with the speaker's words. As you can see from Video 14.6, it was an ingenious solution.

As you plan your speeches, think about how you can use presentation technology to enhance your ideas. At the same time, remember that too many visuals—or poor visuals—can do more harm than good. Be creative and resourceful without allowing technology to overpower your entire speech.

Guidelines for Preparing Visual Aids

Whether you are creating visual aids by hand or with PowerPoint, the following guidelines will help you design aids that are clear and visually appealing.

PREPARE VISUAL AIDS WELL IN ADVANCE

Preparing visual aids well in advance has two advantages. First, it means you will have the time and resources to devise creative, attractive aids. Second, it means you can use them while practicing your speech. Visual aids are effective only when they are integrated smoothly with the rest of the speech. If you lose your place, drop your aids, or otherwise stumble around when presenting them, you will distract your audience and shatter your concentration.

KEEP VISUAL AIDS SIMPLE

Visual aids should be simple, clear, and to the point. If you look back at the aids presented earlier in this chapter, you will see that all of them are clear and uncluttered. They contain enough information to communicate the speaker's point, but not so much as to confuse or distract the audience.

Limit your slides to a manageable amount of information, and beware of the tendency to go overboard. It is possible to create a graphic that displays two charts, a photograph, and ten lines of text in five different typefaces with 250 colors. But who would be able to read it?

MAKE SURE VISUAL AIDS ARE LARGE ENOUGH

A visual aid is useless if no one can see it. Keep in mind the size of the room in which you will be speaking and make sure your aid is big enough to be seen easily by everyone. As you prepare the aid, check its visibility by moving to a point as far away from it as your most distant listener will be sitting.

If you are using a presentation program such as PowerPoint, make sure your text and images are easy for everyone in your audience to see. By making sure your visual aid is large enough, you will avoid having to introduce it with the comment "I know some of you can't see this, but . . .."

What about using all capital letters? That might seem a great way to ensure that your print is large enough to be read easily. But research has shown that a long string of words in ALL CAPS is actually harder to read than is normal text. Reserve ALL CAPS for titles or for individual words that require special emphasis.

USE A LIMITED AMOUNT OF TEXT

When displaying text on visual aids, follow this general rule: Briefer is better. Succinct phrases containing only essential key words will help listeners grasp your basic point and process the information as you're speaking.

FIGURE 14.6

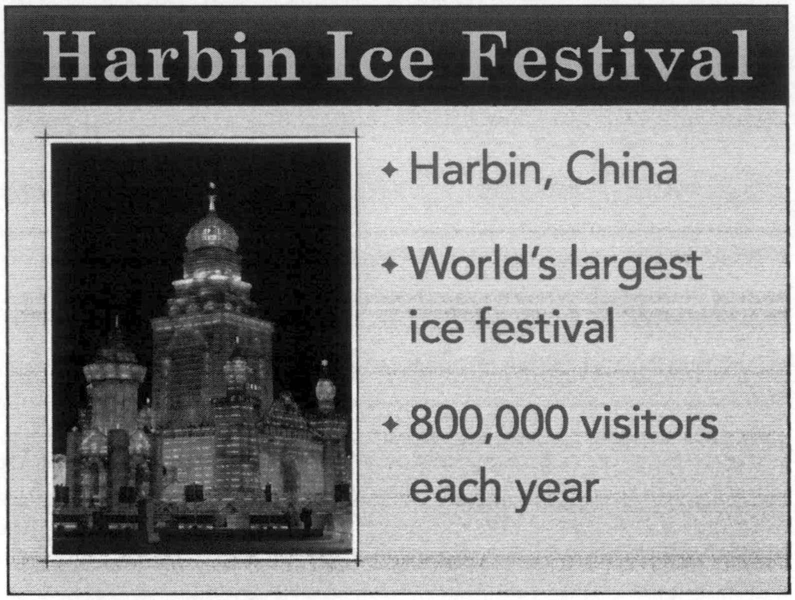

One of the biggest mistakes people make with presentation technology is putting too much text on a single slide. A general rule for slides that contain only text is to include no more than a half-dozen lines of type. If you are combining text with images, you may need to limit yourself to fewer lines to keep the text from getting too small. If you have a number of important points to cover, spread them out over multiple slides.

Figure 14.6 (above) shows a slide from a speech about the Harbin International Ice and Snow Sculpture Festival, held each year in Harbin, China. Notice that the slide is not bogged down with information. It presents only an image of an ice sculpture, plus a title and text noting the location of the festival, the fact that it is the largest such event in the world, and the number of visitors it attracts each year. Because the slide is simple and clear, the speaker was able to present it succinctly and move on to her next point.

USE FONTS EFFECTIVELY

font

A complete set of type of the same design.

Not all fonts are suitable for visual aids. For the most part, you should avoid decorative fonts such as those on the left in Figure 14.7 (page 275). Those on the right of the figure, however, will help make your aids audience-friendly.

Using fonts effectively can make a huge difference in your slides. In general, keep the following guidelines in mind when selecting fonts:

- Choose fonts that are clear and easy to read.
- Avoid using ALL CAPS because they are difficult to read.
- Don't use more than two fonts on a single slide—one for the title or major heading and another for subtitles or other text.
- Use the same fonts on all your slides.
- Put titles and major headings in at least 36- to 44-point type; make subheads and other text at least 24- to 30-point.

FIGURE 14.7

Ineffective	More Effective
Blackmoor	Arial
Bradley Hand	Baskerville
Cracked	Cambria
ECCENTRIC	Courier
Handwriting	Gill Sans
ROSEWOOD	Optima
SchoolHouse	Times New Roman
Snell Roundhand	Verdana

If you use one of the built-in themes in Keynote or PowerPoint, you can be confident that the fonts, which have been preselected according to the design of the theme, are clear, legible, and consistent.

USE COLOR EFFECTIVELY

When used effectively, color can dramatically increase the impact of a visual aid. The key words, of course, are "when used effectively." Some colors do not work well together. Red and green are a tough combination for anyone to read, and they look the same to people who are color-blind. Many shades of blue and green are too close to each other to be easily differentiated—as are orange and red, blue and purple.

You can use either dark print on a light background or light print on a dark background, but in either case make sure there is enough contrast between the background and the text so listeners can see everything clearly. Avoid such colors as yellow on a white background or purple on a red background.

Also, stick to a limited number of colors and use them consistently. Use one color for background, one color for titles, and one color for other text throughout all your slides. This consistency will unify the slides and give your speech a professional appearance.

USE IMAGES STRATEGICALLY

One of the benefits of presentation technology is the ease with which it allows you to include photographs, charts, graphs, and other images, including video. Unfortunately, some speakers are prone to adding images simply because it is easy, rather than because it is essential for communicating their message. You should *never* add images of any sort to a slide unless they are truly needed. There is a great deal of research showing that extraneous images distract listeners and reduce comprehension of the speaker's point.[4]

In addition to keeping your slides free of extraneous images, keep these guidelines in mind:

- Make sure images are large enough to be seen clearly.
- Choose high-resolution images that will project without blurring.
- Keep graphs and charts clear and simple.

- In most cases, include a title above charts and graphs so the audience knows what they are viewing.
- Edit video so it is integrated seamlessly into your slides.[5]

Guidelines for Presenting Visual Aids

No matter how well designed your visual aids may be, they will be of little value unless you display them properly, discuss them clearly, and integrate them effectively with the rest of your presentation. Here are seven guidelines that will help you get the maximum impact out of your visual aids.

DISPLAY VISUAL AIDS WHERE LISTENERS CAN SEE THEM

Check the speech room ahead of time to decide exactly where you will display your visual aids. If you are displaying an object or a model, be sure to place it where it can be seen easily by everyone in the room. If necessary, hold up the object or model while you are discussing it.

Once you have set the aid in the best location, don't undo all your preparation by standing where you block the audience's view of the aid. Stand to one side of the aid, and point with the arm nearest it. Using a pen, a ruler, or some other pointer will allow you to stand farther away from the visual aid, thereby reducing the likelihood that you will obstruct the view.

checklist

Preparing Visual Aids

YES	NO	
☐	☐	1. Have I prepared my visual aids well in advance?
☐	☐	2. Are my visual aids clear and easy to comprehend?
☐	☐	3. Does each visual aid contain only the information needed to make my point?
☐	☐	4. Are my visual aids large enough to be seen clearly by the entire audience?
☐	☐	5. Do the colors on my visual aids work well together?
☐	☐	6. Is there a clear contrast between the lettering and background on my charts, graphs, and drawings?
☐	☐	7. Do I use line graphs, pie graphs, and bar graphs correctly to show statistical trends and patterns?
☐	☐	8. Do I limit charts to no more than eight items?
☐	☐	9. Do I use fonts that are easy to read?
☐	☐	10. Do I use a limited number of fonts?

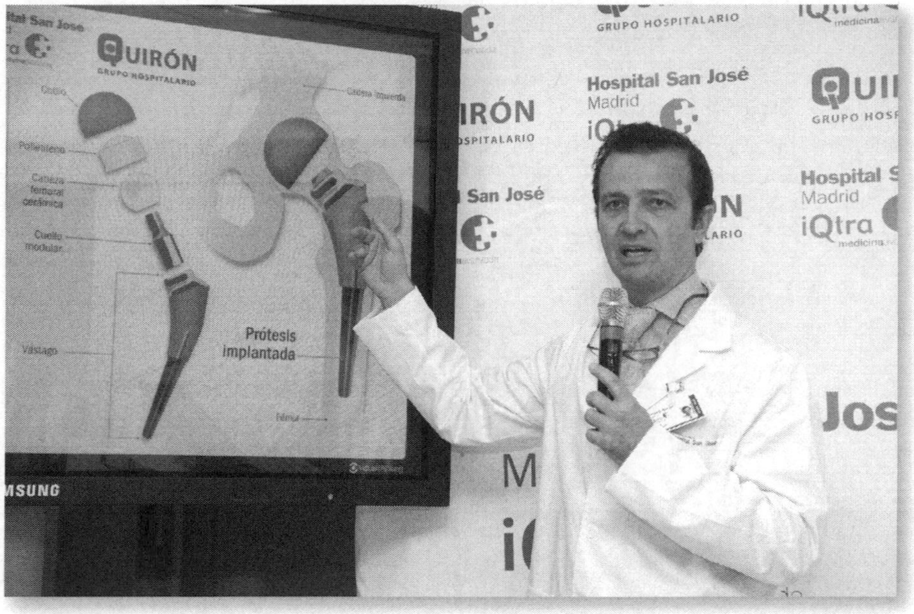

Speakers should select their visual aids carefully and explain them concisely. Adequate rehearsal helps ensure that the speaker is fully prepared and can maintain eye contact with the audience while discussing his or her visual aids.

If you are using a projection screen, check ahead of time to make sure it is not located where you will cast a shadow on it while you are speaking. If necessary, move the lectern to the side of the screen.

AVOID PASSING VISUAL AIDS AMONG THE AUDIENCE

Once visual aids get into the hands of your listeners, you are in trouble. At least three people will be paying more attention to the aid than to you—the person who has just had it, the person who has it now, and the person waiting to get it next. By the time the visual aid moves on, all three may have lost track of what you are saying.[6]

Nor do you solve this problem by preparing a handout for every member of the audience. They are likely to spend a good part of the speech looking over the handout at their own pace, rather than listening to you. Although handouts can be valuable, they usually just create competition for beginning speakers.

Every once in a while, of course, you will want listeners to have copies of some material to take home. When such a situation arises, keep the copies until after you've finished talking and distribute them at the end. Keeping control of your visual aids is essential to keeping control of your speech.

DISPLAY VISUAL AIDS ONLY WHILE DISCUSSING THEM

Just as circulating visual aids distracts attention, so does displaying them throughout a speech. If you are using an object or a model, keep it out of sight until you are ready to discuss it. When you finish your discussion, place the object or model back out of sight.

The same principle applies to PowerPoint slides. They should be visible only while you are discussing them. You can accomplish this by adding blank slides as needed, so the audience's attention will not be diverted by the previous slide. It is also a good idea to add a blank slide at the end of your presentation, so your last content slide will not continue to be exposed after you have finished discussing it.

FIGURE 14.8

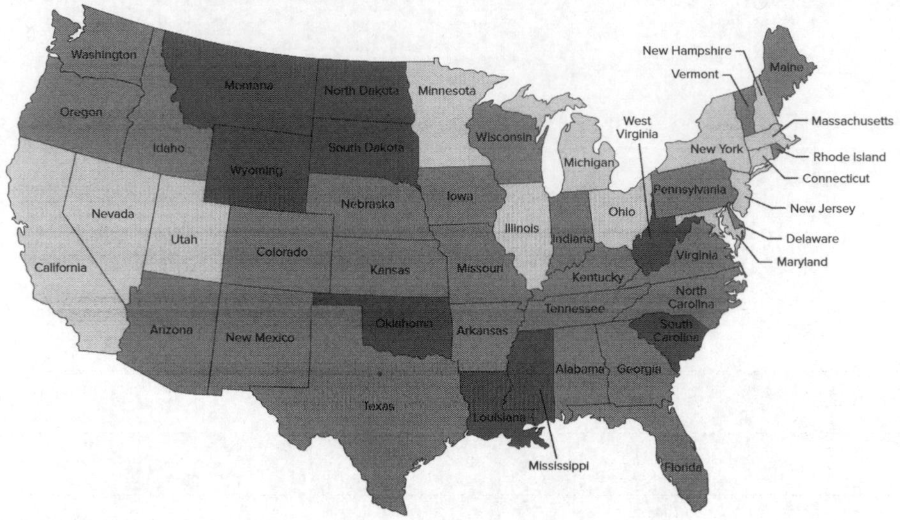

EXPLAIN VISUAL AIDS CLEARLY AND CONCISELY

Visual aids don't explain themselves. Like statistics, they need to be translated and related to the audience. For example, Figure 14.8 (above) is an excellent visual aid, but do you know what it represents? Probably not, unless you've kept up on the latest statistics of U.S. drunk-driving deaths. But even then, the full meaning of the map may not be clear until it is explained to you.

A visual aid can be of enormous benefit—but only if the viewer knows what to look for and why. Unfortunately, speakers often rush over their visual aids without explaining them clearly and concisely. Don't just say "As you can see . . ." and then pass quickly over the aid. Tell listeners what the aid means. Describe its major features. Spell out the meaning of charts and graphs. Interpret statistics and percentages. Remember, a visual aid is only as useful as the explanation that goes with it.

connect

View an excerpt from "The Tragedy of Drunk Driving" in the online Media Library for this chapter (Video 14.7).

As you can see from Video 14.7 in the online Media Library for this chapter, the speaker who used the map of drunk-driving deaths discussed above did an excellent job explaining how each color on the map corresponds to a different per-capita death rate. Having used the map during her practice sessions, she was able to work it into the speech smoothly and skillfully—and to maintain eye contact with the audience throughout her discussion of it. You should strive to do the same when you present visual aids in your speeches.

TALK TO YOUR AUDIENCE, NOT TO YOUR VISUAL AID

When explaining a visual aid, it is easy to break eye contact with your audience and speak to the aid. Of course, your listeners are looking primarily at the aid, and you may need to glance at it periodically as you talk. But if you keep your eyes fixed on the visual aid, you will lose your audience. By keeping eye contact with your listeners, you can also pick up feedback about how the visual aid and your explanation of it are coming across.

PRACTICE WITH YOUR VISUAL AIDS

This chapter has mentioned several times the need to practice with visual aids, but the point bears repeating. No matter what kind of visual aid you choose, be sure to employ it when you practice. Go through the speech multiple times, rehearsing how you will show your aids, the gestures you will make, and the timing of each move. In using visual aids, as in other aspects of speechmaking, there is no substitute for preparation.

If you are using presentation technology, don't just click the mouse casually or rush quickly over your words when you practice. Make sure you know exactly when you want each slide to appear and disappear, and what you will say while each is on screen. Mark your speaking notes with cues that will remind you when to display each slide and when to remove it.

Rehearse with the mouse, keyboard, or iPad until you can use them without looking down for more than an instant when advancing your slides. Also concentrate on presenting the speech without looking back at the screen to see what is being projected. For a good example, check Video 14.8 in the online Media Library for this chapter. Notice how the speaker's visual aids are perfectly coordinated with her words and how she keeps eye contact with her audience while she is presenting the aids.

Given all the things you have to work on when practicing a speech with any kind of presentation technology, you need to allow extra time for rehearsal. So get an early start and give yourself plenty of time to ensure that your delivery is as impressive as your slides.[7]

connect

View an excerpt from "The Living-Wage Solution" in the online Media Library for this chapter (Video 14.8).

checklist

Presenting Visual Aids

YES	NO	
☐	☐	1. Have I checked the speech room to decide where I can display my visual aids most effectively?
☐	☐	2. Have I practiced presenting my visual aids so they will be clearly visible to everyone in the audience?
☐	☐	3. Have I practiced presenting my visual aids so they are perfectly timed with my words and actions?
☐	☐	4. Have I practiced keeping eye contact with my audience while presenting my visual aids?
☐	☐	5. Have I practiced explaining my visual aids clearly and concisely in terms my audience will understand?
☐	☐	6. If I am using handouts, have I planned to distribute them after the speech rather than during it?
☐	☐	7. Have I double-checked all equipment to make sure it works properly?
☐	☐	8. If I am using PowerPoint, do I have a backup of my slides that I can take to the speech with me?

CHECK THE ROOM AND EQUIPMENT

For classroom speeches, you will already be familiar with the room and equipment. If any of the technology fails, a technician can make the necessary adjustments. For speeches outside the classroom, however, the situation is very different. There is wide variation among computers and projectors, as well as among rooms equipped with multimedia connections. Even if you have used PowerPoint or Keynote on previous occasions, you need to check the setup in the room where you will be speaking.

If possible, look at the room and equipment before the day of your speech. Hook up your computer to make sure everything works properly. If you are using a computer that is installed in the room, bring your slides on a flash drive so you can see how they work with that computer. If your presentation includes audio or video, double-check them using the room's audiovisual system. Arrange ahead of time to have a technician present so he or she can take care of any problems.

Sometimes, of course, it is not possible to visit the room before the day of your speech. In that case, plan to arrive an hour early to familiarize yourself with the equipment and to make sure it's working properly. Never assume that everything will be "just fine." Instead, assume that things will not be fine and that they need to be checked ahead of time.

Finally, *always* bring a backup of your slides on a flash drive even if you plan on using your own computer during the speech. This may seem like a lot of fuss and bother, but anyone who has given speeches with PowerPoint—or any other kind of visual aid—will tell you that it is absolutely essential.

Summary

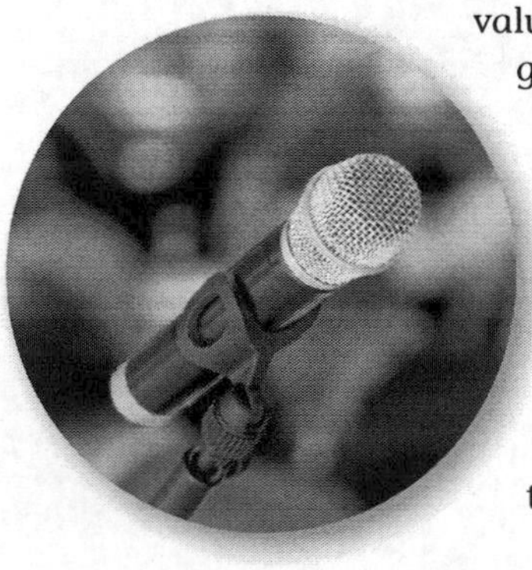

There are many kinds of visual aids. Most obvious is the object about which you are speaking, or a model of it. Diagrams, sketches, and other kinds of drawings are valuable because you can design them to illustrate your points exactly. Photographs should be large enough to be seen clearly by all your listeners. Graphs are an excellent way to illustrate any subject dealing with numbers, while charts are used to summarize large blocks of information. Video can be useful as a visual aid, but it needs to be carefully edited and integrated into the speech. You can act as your own visual aid by performing actions that demonstrate processes or ideas.

If you use presentation technology such as PowerPoint, Keynote, or Prezi, plan carefully why, how, and when you will utilize it. Rather than putting everything you say on screen for your audience to read, use the technology only when it will genuinely enhance your message.

No matter what kind of visual aid you use, you need to prepare it carefully. You will be most successful if you prepare your aids well in advance, keep them simple, make sure they are large enough to be seen clearly, and use a limited amount of text. If you are creating visual aids on a computer, use fonts, color, and images strategically and effectively.

In addition to being designed with care, visual aids need to be presented skillfully. Avoid passing visual aids among the audience. Display each aid only while you are talking about it, and be sure to place it where everyone can see it without straining. When presenting a visual aid, maintain eye contact with your listeners and explain the aid clearly and concisely. If you are using presentation technology, make sure you check the room and equipment prior to the time of delivery. Above all, practice with your visual aids so they fit into your speech smoothly and expertly.

Key Terms

graph (267)
line graph (268)
pie graph (268)
bar graph (269)
chart (270)
font (274)

Review Questions

After reading this chapter, you should be able to answer the following questions:

1. What are the major advantages of using visual aids in your speeches?
2. What kinds of visual aids might you use in a speech?
3. What factors should you consider when planning to use presentation technology in a speech?
4. What guidelines are given in the chapter for preparing visual aids?
5. What guidelines are given in the chapter for presenting visual aids?

connect

For further review, go to the LearnSmart study module for this chapter.

Exercises for Critical Thinking

1. Watch a how-to television program (a cooking show, for example) or the weather portion of a local newscast. Notice how the speaker uses visual aids to help communicate the message. What kinds of visual aids are used? How do they enhance the clarity, interest, and retainability of the speaker's message? What would the speaker have to do to communicate the message effectively without visual aids?
2. Consider how you might use visual aids to explain each of the following:
   a. How to perform the Heimlich maneuver to help a choking victim.
   b. The proportion of the electorate that votes in major national elections in the United States, France, Germany, England, and Japan, respectively.
   c. Where to obtain information about student loans.
   d. The wing patterns of various species of butterflies.
   e. The increase in the amount of money spent by Americans on health care since 1985.
   f. How to change a bicycle tire.
   g. The basic equipment and techniques of rock climbing.
3. Plan to use visual aids in at least one of your classroom speeches. Be creative in devising your aids, and be sure to follow the guidelines discussed in the chapter for using them. After the speech, analyze how effectively you employed your visual aids, what you learned about the use of visual aids from your experience, and what changes you would make in using visual aids if you were to deliver the speech again.

Varieties of Public Speaking

Ins

15

Speaking to Inform

Types of Informative Speeches: Analysis and Organization

Guidelines for Informative Speaking

Sample Speech with Commentary

Hayley Walden is the chief designer at a fast-growing company that creates and sells innovative sportswear. On a bright Tuesday in October, Hayley begins her workday by talking to a colleague from tech support about her computer problems. She shows what goes wrong when she boots up, and she explains the mistakes in her internal backup system.

Later that morning, Hayley has a long meeting with her design team. They discuss their new line of spring products, going over everything from the manufacturing process to the marketing campaign. As the other team members talk, Hayley takes careful notes and asks questions to make sure she doesn't miss anything.

In the afternoon, Hayley rushes to a meeting with the company president, so she can report on what the design team discussed earlier in the day. She reviews the manufacturing process for the new outfits, discusses the distribution chain, and explains different marketing options. Afterward, the president compliments Hayley for giving such a clear presentation. "Anyone who can communicate that well," the president says, "is going to go a long way in this company."

Hayley doesn't consider herself a "public speaker," but much of her job involves absorbing and communicating information clearly and effectively. Although Hayley is just a single person, her experience is not unusual. In one survey, graduates from five U.S. colleges were asked to rank the speech skills most important to their jobs. They rated informative speaking number one. In another survey, 62 percent of the respondents said they used informative speaking "almost constantly."[1]

Public speaking to inform occurs in a wide range of everyday situations. The business manager explains next year's budget. The architect reviews plans for a new building. The union leader informs members about a new contract. The church worker outlines plans for a fund drive. There are endless situations in which people need to inform others. Competence in this form of communication will prove valuable to you throughout your life.

informative speech

A speech designed to convey knowledge and understanding.

One of your first classroom assignments probably will be to deliver an informative speech in which you will act as a lecturer or teacher. You may describe an object, show how something works, report on an event, explain a concept. Your aim will be to convey knowledge and understanding—not to advocate a cause. Your speech will be judged in light of three general criteria:

Is the information communicated accurately?

Is the information communicated clearly?

Is the information made meaningful and interesting to the audience?

In this chapter, we will look at four types of informative speeches and the basic principles of informative speaking. Along the way, we will apply various general principles discussed in previous chapters.

Types of Informative Speeches: Analysis and Organization

There are many ways to classify informative speeches. Here we focus on the kinds you are most likely to give in your speech class: (1) speeches about objects, (2) speeches about processes, (3) speeches about events, and (4) speeches about concepts.

SPEECHES ABOUT OBJECTS

object

Anything that is visible, tangible, and stable in form.

As the word is used here, "objects" include anything that is visible, tangible, and stable in form. Objects may have moving parts or be alive; they may include places, structures, animals, even people. Here are examples of subjects for speeches about objects:

Legos	service dogs
graphene	Susan B. Anthony
Matterhorn	dreamcatchers

You will not have time to tell your classmates everything about any of these subjects. Instead, you will choose a specific purpose that focuses on one aspect of your subject. Working from the topics presented above, the following are examples of good specific purpose statements for informative speeches about objects:

To inform my audience about three major kinds of service dogs.

To inform my audience about the role of Susan B. Anthony in the U.S. women's rights movement.

To inform my audience about the worldwide fascination with Legos.

Notice how precise these statements are. As we saw in Chapter 5, you should select a specific purpose that is not too broad to achieve in the allotted time. "To inform my audience about Pablo Picasso" is far too general for a classroom speech. "To inform my audience about the major contributions of Pablo Picasso to modern art" is more precise and is a purpose you could reasonably hope to achieve in a brief talk.

If your specific purpose is to explain the history or evolution of your subject, you will put your speech in *chronological* order. For example:

Specific Purpose: To inform my audience about the major achievements of Frederick Douglass.

Central Idea: Although born in slavery, Frederick Douglass became one of the greatest figures in American history.

Main Points:

I. Douglass spent the first 20 years of his life as a slave in Maryland.

II. After escaping to the North, Douglass became a leader in the abolitionist movement to end slavery.

III. During the Civil War, Douglass helped establish black regiments in the Union Army.

IV. After the war, Douglass was a tireless champion of equal rights for his race.

If your specific purpose is to describe the main features of your subject, you may organize your speech in *spatial* order:

Specific Purpose: To inform my audience about the geographical regions of the Mississippi River.

Central Idea: The Mississippi River is divided into three sections, each with its own unique features.

Main Points:

I. The upper Mississippi is known for its scenic parks and system of dams and locks.

II. The middle Mississippi is known for its wildlife refuges and fishing opportunities.

III. The lower Mississippi is known for its heavy river traffic and connection to the Gulf of Mexico.

As often as not, you will find that speeches about objects fall into *topical* order. For example:

Specific Purpose: To inform my audience about the three major features of the Taj Mahal.

Central Idea: The three major features of the Taj Mahal are the mausoleum, the garden, and the reflecting pool.

Main Points:

I. The Taj Mahal's mausoleum is famous for its brilliant white marble and massive dome.

II. The Taj Mahal's garden is famous for its symmetry and carefully sculpted greenery.

III. The Taj Mahal's reflecting pool is famous for its mirror-like surface and expansive layout.

No matter which of these organizational methods you use—chronological, spatial, or topical—be sure to follow the guidelines discussed in Chapter 9: (1) limit your speech to between two and five main points; (2) keep main points separate; (3) try to use the same pattern of wording for all main points; (4) balance the amount of time devoted to each main point.

SPEECHES ABOUT PROCESSES

process

A systematic series of actions that leads to a specific result or product.

A process is a systematic series of actions that leads to a specific result or product. Speeches about processes explain how something is made, how something is done, or how something works. Here are examples of good specific purpose statements for speeches about processes:

To inform my audience how flash floods develop.

To inform my audience how to write an effective job resumé.

To inform my audience how U.S. currency is made.

As these examples suggest, there are two kinds of informative speeches about processes. One kind explains a process so that listeners will *understand* it better. Your goal is to have your audience know the steps of the process and how they relate to one another. If your specific purpose is "To inform my audience how a nuclear power plant works," you will explain the basic procedures of a nuclear power plant. You will not instruct your listeners on how they can *operate* a nuclear power plant.

A second kind of speech explains a process so listeners will be better able to *perform* the process themselves. Your goal in this kind of speech is to have the audience learn a skill. Suppose your specific purpose is "To inform my audience how to take pictures like a professional photographer." You will present photographic techniques and show your listeners how they can utilize them. You want the audience to be able to *use* the techniques as a result of your speech.

Both kinds of speeches about processes may require visual aids. At the very least, you should prepare a chart outlining the steps or techniques of your process. In some cases you will need to demonstrate the steps or techniques by performing them in front of your audience. One student did sleight-of-hand magic tricks to show the techniques behind them. Another executed elementary tai chi maneuvers. In each case, the demonstration not only

Informative speeches can be organized in many ways. A speech on the history of the Taj Mahal would likely be in chronological order, while a speech on its major features would fall into topical order.

clarified the speaker's process, but captivated the audience as well. (If you are using visual aids of any kind, be sure to review Chapter 14.)

When informing about a process, you will usually arrange your speech in *chronological* order, explaining the process step by step from beginning to end. For example:

Specific Purpose: To inform my audience about the three major stages of dementia.

Central Idea: Dementia is a loss of cognitive ability that proceeds through early, middle, and late stages.

Main Points:

I. The early stage of dementia includes forgetfulness, losing track of time, and being uncomfortable in familiar places.

II. The middle stage of dementia includes serious memory lapses, anxiety, and social withdrawal.

III. The late stage of dementia includes inability to recognize family members and full dependence on others.

Sometimes, rather than moving through a process step by step, you will focus on the major principles or techniques involved in performing the process. Then you will organize your speech in *topical* order. Each main point will deal with a separate principle or technique. For example:

Specific Purpose: To inform my audience of the common methods used by stage magicians to perform their tricks.

Central Idea: Stage magicians use two common methods to perform their tricks—mechanical devices and sleight of hand.

Main Points:

I. Many magic tricks rely on mechanical devices that may require little skill by the magician.

II. Other magic tricks depend on the magician's skill in fooling people by sleight-of-hand manipulation.

Concise organization is especially important in speeches about processes. You must make sure each step is clear and easy to follow. If your process has more than four or five steps, group the steps into units to limit the number of main points. For example, in a speech explaining how to set up a home aquarium, a student presented the following main points:

I. First you must choose the size of your tank.
II. Then you must determine the shape of your tank.
III. You must also decide how much you can afford to pay for a tank.
IV. Once you have the tank, you need a filter system.
V. A heater is also absolutely necessary.
VI. You must also get an air pump.
VII. Once this is done, you need to choose gravel for the tank.
VIII. You will also need plants.
IX. Other decorations will round out the effects of your aquarium.
X. Now you are ready to add the fish.
XI. Freshwater fish are the most common.
XII. Saltwater fish are more expensive and require special care.

Not surprisingly, this was too much for the audience to follow. The speaker should have organized the points something like this:

I. The first step in establishing a home aquarium is choosing a tank.
   A. The size of the tank is important.
   B. The shape of the tank is important.
   C. The cost of the tank is important.

II. The second step in establishing a home aquarium is equipping the tank.
   A. You will need a filter system.
   B. You will need a heater.
   C. You will need an air pump.
   D. You will need gravel.
   E. You will need plants.
   F. You may also want other decorations.

III. The third step in establishing a home aquarium is adding the fish.
   A. Freshwater fish are the most common for home aquariums.
   B. Saltwater fish are more expensive and require special care.

The subpoints cover the same territory as the original twelve points, but three main points are much easier to understand and remember.

SPEECHES ABOUT EVENTS

event

Anything that happens or is regarded as happening.

The *Random House Dictionary* defines an event as "anything that happens or is regarded as happening." By this definition, the following are examples of suitable topics for informative speeches about events:

Boston Marathon	cyberterrorism
sleep deprivation	Battle of Little Big Horn
Festival of the Sun	therapeutic massage

As usual, you will need to narrow your focus and pick a specific purpose you can accomplish in a short speech. Here are examples of good specific purpose statements for informative speeches about events:

> To inform my audience about the events at Peru's Festival of the Sun ceremony.
>
> To inform my audience about the major types of therapeutic massage.
>
> To inform my audience about what occurred at the Battle of Little Big Horn.

There are many ways to discuss events. If your specific purpose is to recount the history of an event, you will organize your speech in *chronological* order, relating the incidents one after another in the order they occurred. For example:

Specific Purpose: To inform my audience about the history of the Paralympics.

Central Idea: Olympic-style games for athletes with physical disabilities have made great strides since the first competition more than 60 years ago.

Main Points:

I. What would eventually become the Paralympics began in 1948 with a sports competition in Great Britain involving World War II veterans with spinal cord injuries.

II. In 1952, the event expanded when athletes from the Netherlands took part.

III. In 1960, the first Paralympic Games for international athletes took place in Rome.

IV. In 2001, an agreement was signed officially holding the Paralympic Games alongside the summer and winter Olympic Games.

You can approach an event from almost any angle or combination of angles—features, origins, implications, benefits, future developments, and so forth. In such cases, you will put your speech together in *topical* order. And you should make sure your main points subdivide the subject logically and consistently. For instance:

Specific Purpose: To inform my audience about three aspects of the Mardi Gras celebration in New Orleans.

Central Idea: The Mardi Gras celebration in New Orleans is renowned for its parades, costumes, and food.

Main Points:

I. The parades are lavish events that take place over the course of several weeks.

II. The costumes include disguises, medallions, and the official Mardi Gras colors of purple, green, and gold.

III. The food features Cajun and Creole dishes common to southern Louisiana.

SPEECHES ABOUT CONCEPTS

concept

A belief, theory, idea, notion, principle, or the like.

Concepts include beliefs, theories, ideas, principles, and the like. They are more abstract than objects, processes, or events. The following are examples of subjects for speeches about concepts:

numerology	sustainability
philosophies of education	original-intent doctrine
Net neutrality	Confucianism

Taking a few of these general subjects, here are some specific purpose statements for speeches about concepts:

To inform my audience about the philosophy of Net neutrality.

To inform my audience about the doctrine of original intent in constitutional interpretation.

To inform my audience about the basic principles of Confucianism.

Speeches about concepts are usually organized in *topical* order and focus on the main features or aspects of your concept. For example:

Specific Purpose: To inform my audience about the basic principles of nonviolent resistance.

Central Idea: The basic principles of nonviolent resistance stress using moral means to achieve social change, refusing to inflict violence on one's enemies, and using suffering as a social force.

Main Points:

I. The first major principle of nonviolent resistance is that social change must be achieved by moral means.

II. The second major principle of nonviolent resistance is that one should not inflict violence on one's enemies.

III. The third major principle of nonviolent resistance is that suffering can be a powerful social force.

Another approach is to define the concept you are dealing with, identify its major elements, and illustrate it with specific examples. An excellent instance of this came in a student speech about homeschooling:

Specific Purpose: To inform my audience about different philosophies of homeschooling.

Central Idea: Approaches to homeschooling include the classical model, the Charlotte Mason model, the Montessori model, and the unschooling model.

Main Points:

I. The classical model focuses on language, critical thinking, and communication skills.

II. The Charlotte Mason model focuses on hands-on learning and the study of nature.

The need to communicate information is essential for most occupations. Here General George W. Casey addresses members of the international press.

III. The Montessori model focuses on an interactive environment that children navigate on their own.

IV. The unschooling model focuses on escaping formal instruction and letting children learn through experience.

Speeches about concepts are often more complex than other kinds of informative speeches. When dealing with concepts, pay special attention to avoiding technical language, to defining terms clearly, and to using examples and comparisons to illustrate the concepts.

Look, for example, at Video 15.1 in the online Media Library for this chapter, which presents an excerpt from a student speech about the Chinese philosophy of Confucianism. Notice how the student defines Confucianism and then explains its unifying principle of *jen*. If you give an informative speech about a concept, give special thought to how you can make that concept clear and comprehensible to your listeners.

connect

View an excerpt from "Confucianism" in the online Media Library for this chapter (Video 15.1).

The lines dividing speeches about objects, processes, events, and concepts are not absolute. Some subjects could fit into more than one category, depending on how you develop the speech. For example, a speech about the destruction of ancient Pompeii by the eruption of Mount Vesuvius would probably deal with its subject as an event, but a speech on what causes volcanoes to erupt would most likely treat its subject as a process. The important step is to decide whether you will handle your subject as an object, a process, an event, or a concept. Once you do that, you can develop the speech accordingly.

Regardless of how you approach your topic, be sure to give listeners plenty of help in sorting out facts and ideas. One way is by using enough transitions, internal previews, internal summaries, and signposts (see Chapter 9). Another way is to follow the old maxim "Tell 'em what you're going to say; say it; then tell 'em what you've said." In other words, preview the main points of your speech in the introduction and summarize them in the conclusion. This will make your speech easier to understand and easier to remember.

Guidelines for Informative Speaking

All the previous chapters of this book relate to the principles of informative speaking. Selecting a topic and specific purpose, analyzing the audience, gathering materials, choosing supporting details, organizing the speech, using words to communicate meaning, delivering the speech—all must be done effectively if an informative speech is to be a success. Here we emphasize six additional points that will help make yours a success.

DON'T OVERESTIMATE WHAT THE AUDIENCE KNOWS

In a speech about meteorology, a student said, "If modern methods of weather forecasting had existed in 1900, the Galveston hurricane disaster would never have taken place." Then he was off to other matters, leaving his listeners to puzzle over what the Galveston hurricane was, when it happened, and what kind of destruction it wreaked.

The speaker assumed his audience already knew these things. But they were not experts on meteorology or on American history. Even those who had heard of the hurricane had only a fuzzy notion of it. Only the speaker knew that the hurricane, which killed more than 6,000 people when it unexpectedly struck on September 8, 1900, is still the deadliest natural disaster in American history.

As many speakers have discovered, it is easy to overestimate the audience's stock of information. In most informative speeches, your listeners will be only vaguely knowledgeable (at best) about the details of your topic. You cannot *assume* they will know what you mean. Rather, you must be *sure* to explain everything so thoroughly that they cannot help but understand. As you work on your speech, always consider whether it will be clear to someone who is hearing about the topic for the first time.

Suppose you are talking about bulletproof vests. Surely all of your classmates have heard of bulletproof vests, but most probably don't know how the vests work. How will you tell them? Here's one way:

> Ballistic vests, more commonly known as bulletproof vests, are pieces of personal body armor that protect human beings from damage incurred by explosively propelled projectiles. How? Intricately woven synthetic fibers such as Kevlar form a powerful mesh that laterally disperses a projectile's kinetic energy while at the same time deforming the projectile and stopping its momentum.

To someone who knows a lot about physics or textiles, this is probably perfectly clear. But someone who does not may get lost along the way. The tone of the statement is that of a speaker reviewing information already familiar to the audience—not of a speaker introducing new information.

Here, in contrast, is another explanation of bulletproof vests:

> So how do bulletproof vests actually stop bullets? Let me explain with an example.
>
> Imagine a police officer investigating a strange noise down a dark alley. He startles a drug dealer trying to make a sale, and before he knows it, bang! Luckily, the officer was wearing his bulletproof vest.
>
> Instead of entering the officer's body, the bullet enters layer upon layer of strong, tightly woven fibers. Because of their strength and intricate pattern, the fibers begin to twist and deform the bullet. The fibers are so strong that they flatten the bullet out and absorb its energy. While the bullet may go through a couple of layers of fabric, it stops well before going through the entire vest.
>
> Thanks to these strong, tightly woven fibers, our police officer lives to put the drug dealer in cuffs.

This explanation is clear and simple. Its tone is that of a teacher unraveling a new subject.

Is it too simple? Not at all. The test of a good speaker is to communicate even the most complex ideas clearly and simply. Anyone can go to a book and find a learned-sounding definition of a bulletproof vest. But to say in plain English how a bulletproof vest works—that takes hard work and creative thinking.

Also, remember that readers can study a printed passage again and again until they extract its meaning, but listeners don't have that luxury. They must understand what you say in the time it takes you to say it. The more you assume they know about the topic, the greater your chances of being misunderstood.

RELATE THE SUBJECT DIRECTLY TO THE AUDIENCE

> The British dramatist Oscar Wilde arrived at his club after the disastrous opening-night performance of his new play.
>
> "Oscar, how did your play go?" asked a friend.
>
> "Oh," Wilde quipped, "the play was a great success, but the audience was a failure."

Speakers have been known to give much the same answer in saving face after a dismal informative speech. "Oh," they say, "the speech was fine, but

Informative speeches take place in a wide range of situations. Here journalist Rachel Maddow presents a lecture at the John F. Kennedy School of Government.

the audience just wasn't interested." And they are at least partly right—the audience *wasn't* interested. But there is no such thing as a fine speech that puts people to sleep. It is the speaker's job to get listeners interested—and to keep them interested.

Informative speakers have one big hurdle to overcome. They must recognize that what is fascinating to them may not be fascinating to everybody. Once you have chosen a topic that could possibly be interesting to your listeners, you should take special steps to relate it to them. You should tie it in with their interests and concerns.

Start in the introduction. Instead of saying,

> I want to talk with you about the Ironman competition.

you could say:

> Your body can't go any further. Your toenails fell off long ago. Your lungs are on fire. Your heart is one beat away from exploding. Are you dying? Are you dreaming? Neither. You're about to cross the finish line of your first Ironman competition—and nothing could feel better.

connect

View this excerpt from "Not Your Everyday Competition" in the online Media Library for this chapter (Video 15.2).

But don't stop with the introduction. Whenever you can, put your listeners into the body of the speech. After all, nothing interests people more than themselves. Find ways to talk about your topic in terms of your listeners. Bring your material home to them. Get it as close to them as possible.

Here's an example. Let's say you are explaining how bed bugs spread from person to person and location to location. You have plenty of facts and could recite them like this:

> High-traffic areas provide ideal environmental conditions for bed bugs to spread. High-density locations such as dormitories, apartment buildings, and transportation terminals are among the most likely places to find bed bugs. Because bed bugs are attracted to items that allow them to hide, they often attach themselves to clothing, backpacks, purses, and the like. Bed bugs also thrive in cluttered locations that have a lot of items lying about.

This is valuable information, but it is not related to the audience. Let's try again:

> Bed bugs spread most rapidly in places that have lots of people coming and going. If *you* live in the dorms or an apartment, if *you* travel through airports, train stations, and bus stations, or if *you* stay in hotels and motels, *you're* passing through prime breeding grounds for bed bugs.
>
> Bed bugs are like tiny hitchhikers. They'll insert themselves in *your* clothes, *your* luggage, *your* purse, *your* backpack, *your* coat—anything that has fabric and folds.
>
> Bed bugs are also drawn to locations where they can hide easily. So the more clutter *you* have in *your* environment, the more bed bugs will like to be *your* tiny companions.

connect

View this excerpt from "Don't Let the Bed Bugs Bite" in the online Media Library for this chapter (Video 15.3).

Look at the frequent use of "you" and "your." The facts are the same, but now they are pointed directly at the audience. Research shows that using personal terms such as "you" and "your" in an informative speech significantly increases audience understanding of the speaker's ideas.[2]

DON'T BE TOO TECHNICAL

What does it mean to say that an informative speech is too technical? It may mean the subject matter is too specialized for the audience. Any subject can be popularized—but only up to a point. The important thing for a speaker to know is what can be explained to an ordinary audience and what cannot.

Say your subject is power amplifiers. It's no trick to demonstrate how to operate an amplifier (how to turn it on and off, adjust the volume, set the tone and balance controls). It's also relatively easy to explain what an amplifier does (it boosts the sound received from a DVD, mobile device, or live performance). But to give a full scientific account of how an amplifier works cannot be done in any reasonable time unless the audience knows the principles of audio technology. The material is just too technical for a general audience.

Even when the subject matter is not technical, the language used to explain it may be. Every activity has its jargon, whether it be golf (bogey, wedge, match play); chemistry (colloid, glycogen, heavy water); or financial analysis (covered call, reverse bid, toehold acquisition). If you are talking to a group of specialists, you can use technical words and be understood. But you must do all you can to avoid technical words when informing a general audience such as your speech class.

Here, for instance, are two statements explaining graphene, a revolutionary material that is thin and bendable, yet incredibly strong. The first is heavily laden with specialized language that would have little impact on ordinary listeners:

> Graphene is a two-dimensional material composed of a single layer of carbon atoms. The structure of graphene is a hexagonal lattice of 0.33-nanometer thickness. A semi-metal or zero-gap semiconductor, graphene allows electrons to flow through it at one one-hundredth the speed of light, as if they carried no mass.

Using public speaking in your CAREER

As a financial planner at a local investment firm, you have been asked to speak to a group of recent college graduates about long-term financial planning. After considering what recent college graduates need to know about saving for their future, you decide to organize your presentation around four general stages of investing:

1. The early years of investing, which include putting aside small amounts of money that will grow over time.
2. The years of acquisition, which include balancing investments with large expenses such as raising children and paying a mortgage.
3. The years of accumulation, which include putting away as much money as possible in anticipation of retirement.
4. The retirement years, which include living off of savings and adjusting investments as needed.

As you look over these stages of investing, you think back to the public speaking course you took in college. You remember that informative speakers should relate their speech directly to the audience, should not be too technical, should not overestimate what the audience knows about the subject, and should be creative. How might each of these guidelines influence your presentation to recent college graduates? Be specific.

The second statement is perfectly understandable and shows how technical information can be made clear to the average person:

> It's the strongest, thinnest, most conductive material in the world. The *New York Times* calls it the "material of tomorrow." But you can call it by its official name—graphene.
>
> Nick Bilton, technology writer for the *Times,* explains graphene's miraculous properties. A million times thinner than a single hair on your head, it is 200 times stronger than steel and can conduct electricity faster than anything known to exist. It is also bendable and can be stretched by up to 20 percent of its original length.
>
> Cell phones made of graphene will be the width of a piece of paper. Airplanes made of it will be lighter, stronger, and faster. In these ways—and countless others—graphene will transform our lives in the years to come.

Much clearer, isn't it? The only specialized word in the whole passage is "graphene." The rest of the language is straightforward, the ideas easy to grasp. This is what you should strive for in your informative speeches.

AVOID ABSTRACTIONS

"My task," said the novelist Joseph Conrad, "is, before all, to make you see." And make the reader see is just what Conrad did. Witness this passage, in which Conrad describes the aftermath of an explosion aboard a ship:

> The first person I saw was Mahon, with eyes like saucers, his mouth open, and the long white hair standing straight on end round his head like a silver halo. . . . I stared at him in unbelief, and he stared at me with a queer kind of shocked curiosity. I did not know that I had no hair, no eyebrows, no eyelashes, that my young mustache was burnt off, that my face was black, one cheek laid open, my nose cut, and my chin bleeding.[3]

A speech is not a novel. Still, many informative speeches would be vastly improved by the novelist's bent for color, specificity, and detail.

description

A statement that depicts a person, event, idea, or the like with clarity and vividness.

One way to avoid abstractions is through *description.* When we think of description, we usually think of external events such as the explosion described by Conrad. But description is also used to communicate internal feelings. Here is how one student tried to convey to his audience the sensations he experienced when he first began sky diving:

> As we wait for the plane to climb to the jump altitude of 12,000 feet, my mind races with a frenzied jumble of thoughts: "OK, this is the moment you've been waiting for. It's going to be great. Am I really going to jump out of an airplane from 12,000 feet? What if something goes wrong? Can I still back out? Come on now, don't worry. It'll be fine."

Even if we have not been sky diving, we have all had the same kinds of emotions on similar occasions. So what happened next?

> Now it is time to jump. My palms are sweating and my heart is pounding so hard I think it may burst. "Get ready," yells the instructor. As I jump into the blue, I wonder, "What am I doing here?"

Yes—and then what?

> The blast of air resistance blows me backward like a leaf at the mercy of an autumn wind. In about 10 seconds my body levels out and accelerates to a speed of 120 miles an hour. The air supports my body like an invisible flying carpet. There is no sound except for the wind rushing around my face. Any fears or doubts I had are gone in the exhilaration of free flight. Every nerve in my body is alive with sensation; yet I am overcome by a peaceful feeling and the sense that I am at one with the sky.

As we listen to the speaker we share his thoughts, feel his heart pound, and join his exhilaration as he floats effortlessly through the sky. The vivid description lends reality to the speech and draws us further in.

Another way to escape abstractions is with *comparisons* that put your subject in concrete, familiar terms. Do you want to convey what would happen if a comet or large asteroid struck the earth? You could say this:

comparison

A statement of the similarities among two or more people, events, ideas, etc.

> If a comet or large asteroid struck the earth, the impact would be devastating.

True, but the statement is vague and abstract. It does not communicate your meaning clearly and concretely. Now suppose you add this:

> To give you an idea how devastating the impact would be, it would be like all the nuclear bombs in the world going off at one spot.

Now you have made the abstract specific and given us a sharp new slant on things.

Like comparison, *contrast* can put an idea into concrete terms. Suppose you want to illustrate the size of the fantasy football market in the United States. You could say, "Americans spend a whopping $15 billion playing fantasy football every year." The word "whopping" suggests that you consider $15 billion a significant amount, but significant in comparison to what? One speaker offered this contrast:

contrast

A statement of the differences among two or more people, events, ideas, etc.

> Last year, Americans spent $15 billion playing fantasy football. In contrast, the total revenue for the National Football League was only $10 billion. Think about it: Americans spend $5 billion more on NFL fantasy football than they do on the real thing.

This puts an abstract fact into meaningful perspective.

PERSONALIZE YOUR IDEAS

Listeners want to be entertained as they are being enlightened.[4] Nothing takes the edge off an informative speech more than an unbroken string of facts and figures. And nothing enlivens a speech more than personal illustrations. Whenever possible, you should try to *personalize* your ideas and dramatize them in human terms.

personalize

To present one's ideas in human terms that relate in some fashion to the experience of the audience.

Let's say you are talking about family homelessness, which most often involves mothers and their children living on the streets, in cars, or in shelters. You would surely note that 41 percent of the homeless population

Whether in the classroom or out, effective informative speakers work to communicate their ideas in clear, nontechnical language that relates the topic to their listeners' knowledge and interests.

consists of families, leaving 1.6 million children without a home. You would also note that these children are much more likely than their peers to experience violence, physical and mental health problems, and developmental difficulties.

But these are dry facts and figures. If you really want to get your audience involved, you will weave in some examples of families who have experienced homelessness. One speaker began by telling this story:

> Lydia. She was the new girl in school. We were in a couple of the same classes, sometimes we sat together at lunch, and we would see each other during recess. Lydia was kind, funny, and supportive. But for six months, I didn't know the secret she was hiding.
>
> Lydia didn't like to talk about her family. She never wanted me to meet her mom, and she never invited me over to her house. She always insisted that we meet somewhere like the mall. But then one day I found out why: Lydia never invited me to her house because she did not have a house. For more than a year she, her mother, and her little brother had been homeless. They had been living in shelters, staying with relatives, and resting their heads wherever they could.

During the body of the speech, the speaker mentioned Lydia twice more to illustrate different aspects of family homelessness. Then, at the end of the speech, she brought Lydia's story to a hopeful conclusion:

> We have seen how family homelessness affects millions of Americans and can lead to poor physical and mental health, episodes of violence, and a range of developmental difficulties. Homelessness is not just the

> disheveled man sitting by himself on the street—the image we've seen countless times in the media. Homelessness affects families; it affects people like Lydia.
>
> Or, I should say, it *used* to affect Lydia. After two difficult years, her mother found a job that paid her enough to rent an apartment. Lydia herself now works part time and takes classes at a community college. She made it through the stressful time that affects far too many families. And she remains my friend.

connect
View this excerpt from "Family Homelessness" in the online Media Library for this chapter (Video 15.4).

It was a powerful ending. By putting a human face on the topic, the speaker took family homelessness out of the realm of statistics and social services and communicated it in personal terms.

BE CREATIVE

Whether you are seeking alternatives to technical language, avoiding abstractions, personalizing ideas, or adapting to the audience's knowledge about the topic, you need to be creative in thinking about ways to achieve your objectives. A good informative speech is not an oral encyclopedia article. Like any other kind of speech, it requires a healthy dose of creativity.

If you look back at the examples on the previous few pages, you will see that all of them involve creative thinking by the speaker. As in these examples, creativity is often a matter of using language imaginatively and resourcefully. But creativity can involve *any* aspect of an informative speech, including visual aids—as can be seen in the speech on the Statue of Liberty that is reprinted on pages 300–302.

Part of the speech deals with the architecture of the statue. The exterior of the Statue of Liberty is made of thin copper, which is supported by a massive iron skeleton. Because the skeleton can't be seen in photographs, the speaker needed to find a way to make it visible for his audience. He did so by using a PowerPoint slide in which a photograph of the statue faded away and black lines representing the iron skeleton appeared in coordination with the speaker's words. The black lines seemed to "build" the skeleton right before the audience's eyes. As you can see from Video 15.5, it was an effective—and creative—solution.

connect
View this excerpt from "Lady Liberty" in the online Media Library for this chapter (Video 15.5).

If, like this speaker, you think creatively when constructing your informative speech, you are much more likely to be successful.

Sample Speech with Commentary

The following classroom speech provides an excellent example of how to apply the guidelines for informative speaking discussed in this chapter. Notice how the speaker takes what could be a dry and technical topic and makes it interesting. Well-chosen supporting materials and superb visual aids help the speech come alive—as does the speaker's dynamic delivery. You can view the speech in the online Media Library for this chapter.

connect
View "Lady Liberty" in the online Media Library for this chapter (Video 15.6).

Lady Liberty

COMMENTARY	SPEECH
The speaker gains attention and interest by arousing the audience's curiosity. After identifying the topic, he displays a photo of the Statue of Liberty.	If you've ever been to New York, you've probably seen it. I used to see it almost every day growing up on Staten Island, in New York Harbor. And even though its skin has turned green with age, it remains vibrant. I'm talking, of course, about the Statue of Liberty. This 220 tons of copper and iron is a powerful symbol of our country.
The speaker relates his subject directly to the audience and explains why it is important. His repeated use of "we" creates common ground with the audience.	Now, America isn't perfect, and we sometimes fall short of our ideals, but the Statue of Liberty remains a part of our lives. We see it all the time in movies, on television, and in advertisements. The statue has become so familiar that we sometimes don't think about it. But we should. As Neil Kotler, an historian at the Smithsonian Institute, says, the statue is "a monument of breathtaking proportions."
The speaker establishes his credibility, previews the main points to be discussed in the rest of the speech, and provides a transition to the body.	I've been fascinated with the Statue of Liberty ever since I was a kid, but I never knew just how amazing it is until I started researching it for this speech. This morning, I'd like to tell you a bit about its symbolism, its history, and its architecture. By the end, I hope you'll understand why this familiar structure is a modern marvel. Let's start with its symbolism, moving from the top of the statue to the bottom.
Main point one deals with the Statue of Liberty's symbolism, starting with the torch at the top of the statue. As you can see from the video, the speaker uses well-chosen photographs throughout the body to help illustrate his points.	At the top is the statue's most famous symbol—the torch. Ever since the statue was built, the torch has been a beacon to immigrants. It's the torch that prompted the poet Emma Lazarus to pen the famous lines that are inscribed on the pedestal of the statue: "Give me your tired, your poor, your huddled masses yearning to breathe free. . . . I lift my lamp beside the golden door!"
Here the speaker explains the symbolism of the statue's crown.	Down from the torch is the Statue of Liberty's crown. Coming out from the crown are seven rays—one for each continent. As the National Park Service explains on its Statue of Liberty Web site, these rays symbolize the importance of liberty around the world.
The speaker completes his look at the statue's symbolism by discussing the broken chains at the foot of the statue.	Less famous than the crown and the torch are the chains at the foot of the Statue of Liberty. As you can see here, the chains are broken. *National Geographic* explains that the broken chains represent the abolition of slavery and the Union's victory in the U.S. Civil War, which ended not long before the statue was built.

A signpost signals that the speaker is moving to his second main point, on the history of the Statue of Liberty. As in other parts of the speech, he relies on expert testimony to support his ideas. Notice how clearly he identifies the source he is citing.

As we shall see next, the symbolism of the statue takes on added significance when we take a look at its history. Historian Edward Berenson, author of *The Statue of Liberty: A Transatlantic Story*, explains how the statue was created. At a dinner party in France in 1865, two men, Edouard de Laboulaye and Frederic Bartholdi, came up with the idea of building a statue for the United States. Laboulaye was an expert on American politics and wanted to commemorate the end of slavery. Bartholdi was a brilliant young sculptor who envisioned a colossal monument he called "Liberty Enlightening the World."

This paragraph focuses on construction of the Statue of Liberty. The speaker's dramatic photographs complement his words and keep the audience involved.

Construction of the statue began in 1876 and was completed 10 years later. All the building was done in France. You can see in this photo what the statue looked like with the buildings of Paris in the background. After the statue was finished, it was taken down as you can see here, put in boxes, and shipped to New York, where it was reconstructed.

Throughout the speech, vivid descriptions help bring the speaker's ideas to life.

When the statue was unveiled in New York, more than 1 million people flocked to the harbor to see it. Shown in this painting, the celebration was one of the biggest in American history. "Liberty Enlightening the World" had finally found its permanent home.

Now the speaker begins his third main point, which deals with the statue's architecture.

Today we take the Statue of Liberty for granted, but it was considered an architectural marvel when it was built. If you look at the statue from the outside, it looks solid—like it's made completely of stone. But looks can be deceiving.

By comparing the thickness of the statue's exterior to that of a penny, the speaker turns an abstraction into a concrete image.

The statue's exterior is not made of stone, but of copper. And it's only 2.4 millimeters thick—not much thicker than this penny. Yet despite its thin copper skin, the statue stands 151 feet tall and towers 305 feet above the water, if you include the pedestal. Think about the wind and the weather that have beaten against it for 130 years. The thin copper skin wouldn't be able to survive without something really strong underneath.

This paragraph is a fine example of how to communicate technical information clearly and concisely. In addition to his words, the speaker employs a creative visual aid to help listeners visualize the statue's internal structure.

So what is underneath? As represented in this slide, there's an iron skeleton underneath the copper skin. Darcy Grigsby, author of the 2012 book *Colossal*, explains that the skeleton is made of a 92-foot-tall pylon that is stuck deep in the stone pedestal. The skeleton has flat metal bars that connect the copper skin to the pylon. These bars work like springs; they provide the strength and flexibility that allow the Statue of Liberty to survive the harsh weather of New York Harbor.

A comparison with the Eiffel Tower further clarifies the engineering principles employed in the Statue of Liberty.

If the interior design of the Statue of Liberty reminds you at all of this structure, that's because it was created by the same man who would later build the Eiffel Tower. You can definitely see similarities between the open structure of the Eiffel Tower and the engineering principles employed in the interior design of the Statue of Liberty.

As in other places, the speaker's use of high-quality expert testimony lends credibility to his statements.

Architectural historian Yasmin Sabina Khan says in her 2010 book *Enlightening the World* that the statue's design was such a stunning technical achievement that people referred to it at the time as the eighth wonder of the world.

"In conclusion" signals that the speech is coming to an end. After summarizing the main points of the body, the speaker closes by echoing language from the introduction.

In conclusion, I hope I've shown you some of the reasons why the Statue of Liberty remains a wonder of the world. Its symbolism, history, and architecture make this 220 tons of copper and iron a modern marvel. So the next time you're in New York City, the next time you see the statue on television, in movies, in magazines, just remember—there's a lot more to it than meets the eye.

Summary

Speaking to inform occurs in a wide range of everyday situations. Improving your ability to convey knowledge effectively will be valuable to you throughout your life.

Informative speeches may be grouped into four categories—speeches about objects, speeches about processes, speeches about events, and speeches about concepts.

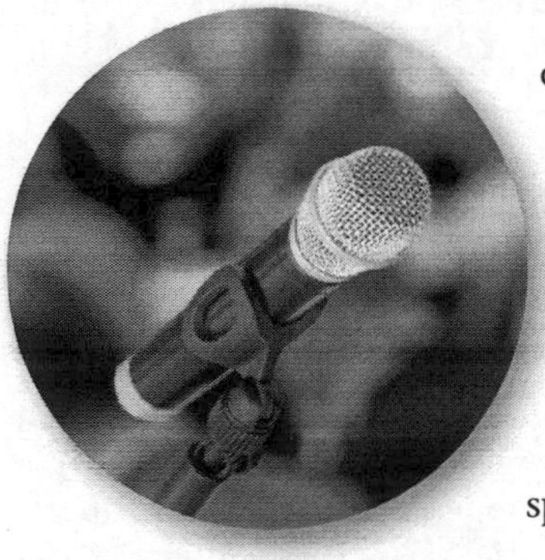

Objects include places, structures, animals, even people. Speeches about objects usually are organized in chronological, spatial, or topical order. A process is a series of actions that work together to produce a final result. Speeches about processes explain how something is made, how something is done, or how something works. The most common types of organization for speeches about processes are chronological and topical.

An event is anything that happens or is regarded as happening. Speeches about events are usually arranged in chronological or topical order. Concepts include beliefs, theories, ideas, and principles. Speeches about concepts are often more complex than other kinds of informative speeches, and they typically follow a topical pattern of organization.

No matter what the subject of your informative speech, be careful not to overestimate what your audience knows about it. Explain everything so thoroughly that they can't help but understand. Avoid being too technical. Make sure your ideas and your language are fully comprehensible to someone who has no specialized knowledge about the topic.

Equally important, recognize that what is fascinating to you may not be fascinating to everybody. It is your job to make your informative speech interesting and meaningful to your audience. Find ways to talk about the topic in terms of your listeners. Avoid too many abstractions. Use description, comparison, and contrast to make your audience *see* what you are talking about. Try to personalize your ideas and dramatize them in human terms. Finally, be creative in thinking of ways to communicate your ideas.

Key Terms

informative speech (284)
object (284)
process (286)
event (288)
concept (290)
description (296)
comparison (297)
contrast (297)
personalize (297)

Review Questions

After reading this chapter, you should be able to answer the following questions:

1. What are the four types of informative speeches discussed in the chapter? Give an example of a good specific purpose statement for each type.
2. Why must informative speakers be careful not to overestimate what the audience knows about the topic? What can you do to make sure your ideas don't pass over the heads of your listeners?
3. What should you do as an informative speaker to relate your topic directly to the audience?
4. What two things should you watch out for in making sure your speech is not overly technical?
5. What are three methods you can use to avoid abstractions in your informative speech?
6. What does it mean to say that informative speakers should personalize their ideas?
7. Why is it important for informative speakers to be creative in thinking about ways to communicate their ideas?

connect

For further review, go to the LearnSmart study module for this chapter.

Exercises for Critical Thinking

1. Below is a list of subjects for informative speeches. Your task is twofold: (a) Select four of the topics and prepare a specific purpose statement for an informative speech about each of the four. Make sure your four specific purpose statements include at least one that deals with its topic as an object, one that deals with its topic as a process, one that deals with its topic as an event, and one that deals with its topic as a concept. (b) Explain what method of organization you would most likely use in structuring a speech about each of your specific purpose statements.

hobbies	sports	education
animals	music	media
science	cultural customs	technology

2. Analyze "Medical Robots: From Science Fiction to Science Fact" in the appendix of sample speeches that follows Chapter 19. Identify the specific purpose, central idea, main points, and method of organization. Evaluate the speech in light of the guidelines for informative speaking discussed in this chapter.

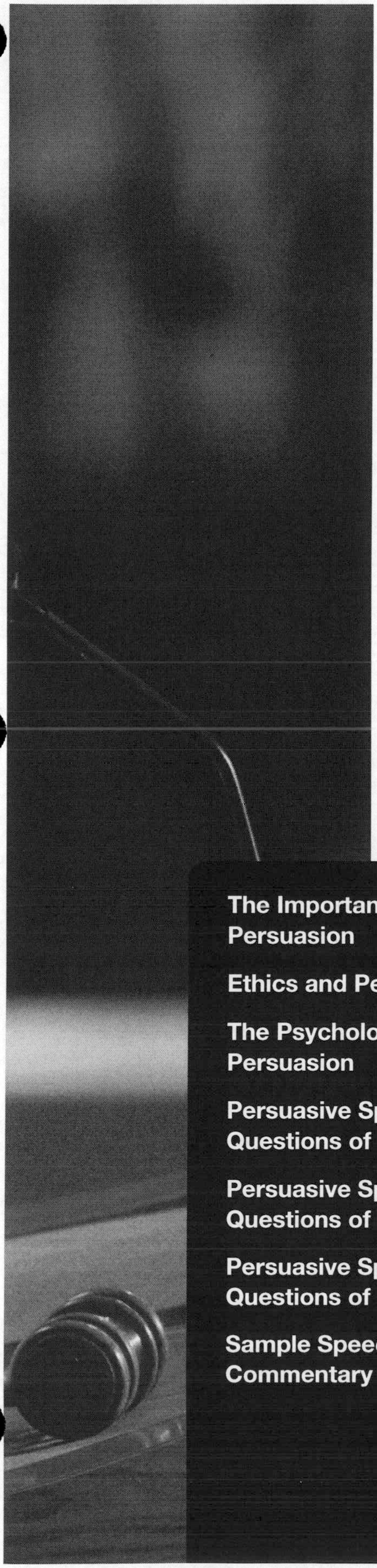

16

Speaking to Persuade

- **The Importance of Persuasion**
- **Ethics and Persuasion**
- **The Psychology of Persuasion**
- **Persuasive Speeches on Questions of Fact**
- **Persuasive Speeches on Questions of Value**
- **Persuasive Speeches on Questions of Policy**
- **Sample Speech with Commentary**

Nicolás Navarro started his day on campus by stopping at his history professor's office hours. "I don't normally do this," he said, "but I'm wondering if I can have a 24-hour extension on my paper. I have two exams on the same day and I've really been overwhelmed lately." The professor hemmed and hawed. Then she said, "Okay. You've turned in all your other work just fine, so you can have an extension this one time."

With a sigh of relief, Nicolás headed off for classes. Walking across the quad, he ran into some friends. "Are we still on for basketball today?" one of them asked. "I wish I could," Nicolás said, "but I'm handing out flyers for the dance marathon for the children's hospital. Next week, though, for sure."

In the afternoon, Nicolás went to his part-time job at the marketing department of a local independent music label. "I've been thinking about how we can keep people interested in our music," he said at a meeting with other members of the marketing team. "People have a great time at our concerts, and we want them to remember that. What if we gave away audio from the concerts—kind of like the Grateful Dead used to? This would increase interest among our fans, and we already record the concerts."

The head of marketing looked skeptical, but then replied: "Okay. Let's try it for a few months and see what happens. But first I want you to figure out the details."

If you asked Nicolás how he spent his day, he might say, "I talked to my history professor. I handed out flyers for the dance marathon. I had a staff meeting at work." In fact, he spent a large part of his day *persuading*—persuading people to do things they were reluctant to do or that had not occurred to them.

The Importance of Persuasion

persuasion

The process of creating, reinforcing, or changing people's beliefs or actions.

Persuasion is the process of creating, reinforcing, or changing people's beliefs or actions.[1] The ability to speak (and write) persuasively will benefit you in every part of your life, from personal relations to community activities to career aspirations. When economists added up the number of people—lawyers, sales representatives, public relations specialists, counselors, administrators, and others—whose jobs depend largely on persuading people to adopt their point of view, they concluded that persuasion accounts for 26 percent of the U.S. gross domestic product![2]

Understanding the principles of persuasion is also vital to being an informed citizen and consumer. Politicians and advertisers, salespeople and interest groups, fund-raisers and community activists—all vie for your attention, votes, money, time, and support. The more you know about persuasion, the more effective you can be in using your powers of critical thinking to assess the barrage of persuasive messages you are exposed to every day.

Although persuasion has been studied for more than 2,000 years, it is still the subject of lively debate among scholars. There are a number of scientific models of the persuasive process and a wide range of respected theories about how persuasion works. In this chapter and the next, we will explore the principles of persuasion as they apply to public speaking.

When you speak to persuade, you act as an advocate. Your job is to get listeners to agree with you and, perhaps, to act on that belief. Your goal may be to defend an idea, to refute an opponent, to sell a program, or to inspire people to action. Because persuasive speakers must communicate information clearly and concisely, you will need all the skills you used in speaking to inform. But you will also need new skills that take you from giving information to affecting your listeners' attitudes, beliefs, or actions.

Ethics and Persuasion

No matter what the speaking situation, you need to make sure your goals are ethically sound and that you use ethical methods to communicate your ideas. Meeting these obligations can be especially challenging when you speak to persuade. Would you be willing to shade the truth "just a bit" if it would guarantee a successful speech? How about juggling statistics, doctoring quotations, passing off opinions as facts, or pandering to prejudice and stereotypes?

Unfortunately, there is no shortage of speakers—and other persuaders—who are willing to take ethical shortcuts to achieve their objectives. Yet, as Martin Luther King stated years ago, it is not possible to bring about a truly beneficial result by using unethical methods. Maintaining the bond of trust with listeners is also vital to a speaker's credibility. As in other kinds of public speaking, the ideal of effective persuasion is the good person speaking well.

When you work on your persuasive speech, keep in mind the guidelines for ethical speaking discussed in Chapter 2. Make sure your goals are ethically sound and that you can defend them if they are questioned or challenged. Study the topic thoroughly so you won't mislead your audience through shoddy research or muddled thinking. Learn about all sides of an issue, seek out competing viewpoints, and get your facts right.

But knowing the facts is not enough. You also need to be honest in what you say. There is no place in ethical speechmaking for deliberately false or deceptive statements. Also be on guard against more subtle forms of dishonesty such as quoting out of context, portraying a few details as the whole story, and misrepresenting the sources of facts and figures. Take care to present statistics, testimony, and other kinds of evidence fairly and accurately.

Keep in mind as well the power of language and use it responsibly. Show respect for the rights of free speech and expression, and stay away from name-calling and other forms of abusive language. Finally, check the section of Chapter 17 that discusses the role of emotional appeal (pages 348–352). Make sure that any emotional appeal you use is appropriate to the topic and that you build your speech on a firm base of facts and logic before appealing to your audience's emotions. Aim at the highest standards and construct your speech so it will be both convincing *and* ethically sound.[3]

The Psychology of Persuasion

Persuasion is a psychological process. It occurs in a situation where two or more points of view exist. The speaker supports right-to-work laws, but many listeners do not. The speaker considers genetic screening unethical, but some in the audience think it is justified in certain circumstances. The different points of view may be completely opposed, or they may simply be different in degree. Whichever the case, there must be a disagreement, or else there would be no need for persuasion.

THE CHALLENGE OF PERSUASIVE SPEAKING

Of all the kinds of public speaking, persuasion is the most complex and the most challenging. Your objective is more ambitious than in speaking to inform, and audience analysis and adaptation become much more demanding. In some persuasive speeches, you will deal with controversial topics that touch on your listeners' basic attitudes, values, and beliefs. This may increase their resistance to persuasion and make your task more difficult.

It is much easier, for example, to explain the history of the war on drugs than to persuade an audience either that marijuana should be legalized in every state or once again be outlawed across the country. In the persuasive speech, you must contend not only with your audience's knowledge about marijuana but also with their attitudes toward recreational drugs and their beliefs about the impact of marijuana use on human health and social mores.

Lines of argument that work with one part of the audience may fail with—or even upset—another part. What seems perfectly logical to some listeners may seem wildly irrational to others. No matter how expert you are on the topic, no matter how skillfully you prepare the speech, no matter how captivating your delivery—some listeners will not agree with you.

This does not mean that persuasion is impossible. It does mean you should have a realistic sense of what you can accomplish. You can't expect a group of die-hard Democrats to become Republicans or a steak lover to turn vegetarian as a result of one speech.

In every persuasive speech, you will face some listeners who are strongly in favor of your position, some who are neutral, and some who are adamantly opposed. If listeners are neutral or only moderately committed one way or another, you can realistically hope your speech will move at least some of them toward your side. If listeners are strongly opposed to your position, you can consider your speech a success if it leads even a few to reexamine their views.

When thinking about the range of persuasive responses, you may find it helpful to visualize listeners on a scale such as that shown in Figure 16.1 (below). Persuasion involves any movement by a listener from left to right on the scale, no matter where the listener begins and no matter how great or small the movement.[4]

How successful you are in any particular persuasive speech will depend above all on how well you tailor your message to the values, attitudes, and beliefs of your audience. In Chapter 6, we considered the general principles of audience analysis and adaptation. Here we emphasize two additional principles that are crucial to the psychology of persuasion. The first deals with how listeners process and respond to persuasive messages. The second pertains to the target audience for persuasive speeches.

HOW LISTENERS PROCESS PERSUASIVE MESSAGES

We often think of persuasion as something a speaker does *to* an audience. In fact, persuasion is something a speaker does *with* an audience. Listeners do not

FIGURE 16.1

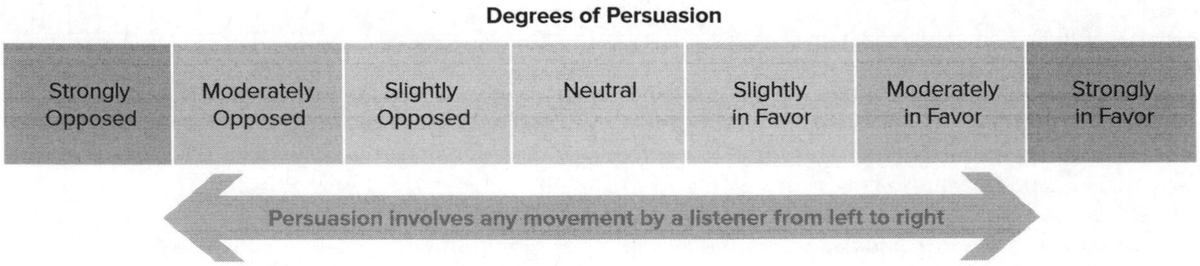

No matter what the situation, a persuasive speaker needs to adapt to the target audience. Here Washington University student Daniel Giuffra speaks in support of the Youth Tobacco Prevention Campaign.

just sit passively and soak in everything the speaker has to say. Instead, they engage in a mental give-and-take with the speaker. While they listen, they assess the speaker's credibility, delivery, supporting materials, language, reasoning, and emotional appeals. They may respond positively at one point, negatively at another. At times they may argue, inside their own minds, with the speaker. This mental give-and-take is especially vigorous when listeners are highly involved with the topic and believe it has a direct bearing on their lives.[5]

In a sense, the psychological interaction between a speaker and audience during a persuasive speech is similar to what happens vocally during a conversation—as in this example:

Karyn: It's better to donate your time to charity than to donate your money. Plenty of charities are well supported financially, but they lack the volunteers they need.

Naomi: It's true that volunteering is important, but most of us just don't have the time. It's easier to send a donation online. I'm sure the charities would rather have me give money than nothing at all.

Karyn: You're right about that. But you'd be surprised how easy it is to find an hour or two a week. Between classes, on the weekends, in the evenings—most people have more flexibility than they realize.

Naomi: Perhaps, but showing up at some strange place to volunteer makes me nervous. Even if I could find the time, I get uncomfortable in new situations like that.

Karyn: I used to feel the same way, but charities are set up to help volunteers feel welcome. I got over my nervousness quickly, and now I'm excited to volunteer.

Much the same kind of interaction might occur during a persuasive speech, except that the listener would respond internally rather than out loud.

mental dialogue with the audience

The mental give-and-take between speaker and listener during a persuasive speech.

What does this mean to you as a speaker? It means you must think of your persuasive speech as a kind of *mental dialogue* with your audience. You must anticipate possible objections the audience will raise to your point of view and answer them in your speech. You cannot convert skeptical listeners unless you deal directly with the reasons for their skepticism.

As you prepare your persuasive speech, put yourself in the place of your audience and imagine how they will respond. Be as tough on your speech as your audience will be. Every place they will raise a question, answer it. Every place they will have a criticism, deal with it. Every place they will see a hole in your argument, fill it. Leave nothing to chance.[6]

THE TARGET AUDIENCE

Unfortunately, no matter how carefully you plot your speech, you will seldom be able to persuade all your listeners. Like most audiences, yours will probably contain some listeners who are hostile to your position, some who favor it, some who are undecided, and some who just don't care. You would like to make your speech equally appealing to everyone, but this is rarely possible. Most often you will have a particular *part* of the whole audience that you want to reach with your speech. That part is called the *target audience.*

target audience

The portion of the whole audience that the speaker most wants to persuade.

Advertising gives us an effective model. Successful commercials are aimed at particular segments of the market. Investment funds now direct many of their advertisements at women. Why? Because more and more women are investing in the stock market. Beer commercials, on the other hand, are directed at men because they drink the most beer.

For your classroom speeches, you don't have the sophisticated research capability of a large advertising agency. But as we saw in Chapter 6, you can use questionnaires to find out where your classmates stand on your speech topic. This is your equivalent of market research. Once you know where your target audience stands, you can tailor your speech to fit their values and concerns—aim at the target, so to speak.

Here, for example, is how one student, Vivian Xu, determined her target audience for a persuasive speech advocating lifetime GPS tracking of high-risk serial sex offenders:

> There are 22 students in my audience. My audience-analysis questionnaires show that 4 are absolutely opposed to my plan. I can't persuade them no matter what I say. My questionnaires also show that 6 already support my position. I don't need to persuade them. The other 12 students could be persuaded if they knew more about how the GPS tracking program would work and about its privacy implications.

Not only did Vivian pinpoint her target audience, she also knew from her audience-analysis questionnaire the issues she would have to discuss to be convincing:

> The members of my target audience break down this way: 5 give "concerns over cost" as their primary concern; 5 are worried about "privacy and government surveillance"; and 2 think sex offenders will just remove the monitoring devices.

With all this information, Vivian was able to put together a speech that focused directly on her classmates' attitudes and beliefs. As a result, she was able to convince several to support her position.

In the next chapter, we'll discuss the methods you can use to hit the target in your persuasive speeches. In the rest of this chapter, we focus on the three major kinds of persuasive speeches and how to organize them most effectively.

Persuasive Speeches on Questions of Fact

WHAT ARE QUESTIONS OF FACT?

What college basketball team has won the most games since 2000? Who was the first African American to sit on the U.S. Supreme Court? How far is it from Los Angeles to Cairo? These questions of fact can be answered absolutely. The answers are either right or wrong.

question of fact

A question about the truth or falsity of an assertion.

But many questions of fact cannot be answered absolutely. There is a true answer, but we don't have enough information to know what it is. Some questions like this involve prediction: Will the economy be better or worse next year? Who will win the Super Bowl this season?

Other questions deal with issues on which the facts are murky or inconclusive. Is there intelligent life in other parts of the solar system? What will happen next in the Middle East? No one knows the final answers to these questions, but that doesn't stop people from speculating about them or from trying to convince other people that they have the best possible answers.

ANALYZING QUESTIONS OF FACT

In some ways, a persuasive speech on a question of fact is similar to an informative speech. But the two kinds of speeches take place in different kinds of situations and for different purposes.

The situation for an informative speech is *nonpartisan.* The speaker acts as a lecturer or a teacher. The aim is to give information as impartially as possible, not to argue for a particular point of view.

On the other hand, the situation for a persuasive speech on a question of fact is *partisan.* The speaker acts as an advocate. The aim is not to be impartial, but to present one view of the facts as persuasively as possible. The speaker may mention competing views of the facts, but only to refute them.

For example, consider the assassination of John F. Kennedy. After 50 years, there is still much debate about what really happened in Dallas on November 22, 1963. Did Lee Harvey Oswald act alone, or was he part of a conspiracy? How many shots were fired at President Kennedy and from what locations? If there was a conspiracy, who was involved in it? The informative speaker would recite the known facts on both sides of these questions without drawing a conclusion about which side is correct. The persuasive speaker, however, would draw a conclusion from the known facts and try to convert listeners to his or her point of view.

If there were no possibility of dispute on questions of fact, there would be no need for courtroom trials. In a criminal trial there is usually at least one known fact—a crime has been committed. But did the defendant commit the crime? The prosecuting attorney tries to persuade the jury that the defendant is guilty. The defense attorney tries to persuade the jury that the defendant is innocent. The jury must decide which view of the facts is more persuasive.[7]

ORGANIZING SPEECHES ON QUESTIONS OF FACT

Persuasive speeches on questions of fact are usually organized *topically.* Suppose, for example, that you want to convince your classmates that an earthquake of 9.0 or above on the Richter scale will hit California within the next ten years. Each main point in your speech will present a *reason* why someone should agree with you:

Specific Purpose: To persuade my audience that an earthquake of 9.0 or above on the Richter scale will hit California in the next ten years.

Central Idea: There are three good reasons to believe that an earthquake of 9.0 or above on the Richter scale will hit California in the next ten years.

Main Points:

I. California is long overdue for a major earthquake.

II. Many geological signs indicate that a major earthquake may happen soon.

III. Experts agree that an earthquake of 9.0 or above could strike California any day.

To take another example, suppose you are trying to persuade your classmates that the plays attributed to William Shakespeare were not actually written by him. Your specific purpose, central idea, and main points might be:

Specific Purpose: To persuade my audience that William Shakespeare did not write the plays attributed to him.

Central Idea: There is considerable evidence that the plays attributed to William Shakespeare were actually written by Francis Bacon or Edward de Vere.

Main Points:

I. Biographical and textual evidence suggest that William Shakespeare did not write the plays attributed to him.

II. Historical evidence indicates that Shakespeare's plays were probably written by either Sir Francis Bacon or Edward de Vere, 17th Earl of Oxford.

Notice in these examples that the speaker's purpose is limited to persuading the audience to accept a particular view of the facts. Sometimes, however, the dispute that gives rise to a persuasive speech will go beyond a question of fact and will turn on a question of value.

Many persuasive speeches revolve around questions of fact. There is much debate, for example, about the impact of climate change on violent weather events around the world.

Persuasive Speeches on Questions of Value

WHAT ARE QUESTIONS OF VALUE?

What is the best movie of all time? Is solitary confinement morally justifiable? What are the ethical responsibilities of journalists? Such questions not only involve matters of fact, but they also demand *value judgments*—judgments based on a person's beliefs about what is right or wrong, good or bad, moral or immoral, proper or improper, fair or unfair.

question of value

A question about the worth, rightness, morality, and so forth of an idea or action.

Take the issue of solitary confinement. It can be discussed at a purely factual level by asking such questions as "What are the laws about solitary confinement?" or "How widespread is solitary confinement as a punishment in American prisons?" These are factual questions. The answers you reach are independent of your belief about the morality of solitary confinement.

But suppose you ask, "Is it morally justifiable to keep prisoners in solitary confinement for extended periods of time?" Now you are dealing with a question of value. How you answer will depend not only on your factual knowledge about solitary confinement, but also on your moral values.

ANALYZING QUESTIONS OF VALUE

Contrary to what many people think, questions of value are not simply matters of personal opinion or whim. If you say, "I enjoy bicycle riding," you do not have to give a reason why you enjoy it. You are making a statement about your personal taste. Even if bicycle riding were the most unpleasant activity ever invented, it could still be one of your favorites.

On the other hand, if you say, "Bicycle riding is the ideal form of land transportation," you are making a statement about a question of value. Whether bicycling is the ideal form of land transportation does not depend on your own likes and dislikes. To defend the statement, you cannot say, "Bicycle riding is the ideal form of land transportation because I like it."

Instead, you must *justify* your claim. The first step is to define what you mean by an "ideal form of land transportation." Do you mean a mode of transportation that gets people where they want to go as fast as possible? That is relatively inexpensive? That is fun? Nonpolluting? Beneficial for the user? In other words, you must establish your *standards* for an "ideal form of land transportation." Then you can show how bicycle riding measures up against those standards.

Whenever you give a speech on a question of value, be sure to give special thought to the standards for your value judgment.

ORGANIZING SPEECHES ON QUESTIONS OF VALUE

Persuasive speeches on questions of value are almost always organized *topically*. The most common approach is to devote your first main point to establishing the standards for your value judgment and your second main point to applying those standards to the subject of your speech.

Think back for a moment to the speech about bicycle riding as the ideal form of land transportation. If you organized this speech in topical order, your first main point would identify the standards for an ideal form of land transportation. Your second main point would show how biking measures up against those standards. Here is how your specific purpose, central idea, and main points might look:

Specific Purpose: To persuade my audience that bicycle riding is the ideal form of land transportation.

Central Idea: Bicycle riding is the ideal form of land transportation because it is faster than walking or running, is nonpolluting, and promotes the health of the rider.

Main Points:

I. An ideal form of land transportation should meet three major standards.
   A. It should be faster than running or walking.
   B. It should be nonpolluting.
   C. It should be beneficial for the person who uses it.

II. Bicycle riding meets all these standards for an ideal form of land transportation.
   A. Bicycle riding is faster than walking or running.
   B. Bicycle riding is not a source of air, land, water, or noise pollution.
   C. Bicycle riding is extremely beneficial for the health of the rider.

When you speak on a question of value, you must make sure to justify your judgment against some identifiable standards. In the following example, notice how the speaker devotes her first main point to judging capital punishment against moral standards and her second main point to judging it against legal standards:

Specific Purpose:	To persuade my audience that capital punishment is morally and legally wrong.
Central Idea:	Capital punishment violates both the Bible and the U.S. Constitution.
Main Points:	I. Capital punishment violates the biblical commandment "Thou shalt not kill."
	II. Capital punishment violates the constitutional ban on "cruel and unusual punishment."

As you can see, speeches on questions of value may have strong implications for our actions. A person who is persuaded that capital punishment is morally and legally wrong is more likely to support legislation abolishing the death penalty. But speeches on questions of value do not argue directly for or against particular courses of action. Once you go beyond arguing right or wrong to arguing that something should or should not be done, you move from a question of value to a question of policy.

Persuasive Speeches on Questions of Policy

WHAT ARE QUESTIONS OF POLICY?

Questions of policy arise daily in almost everything we do. At home we debate what to do during spring vacation, whether to buy a new laptop, which movie to see on the weekend. At work we discuss whether to ask for a raise, what strategy to use in selling a product, how to improve communication between management and employees. As citizens we ponder whether to vote for or against a political candidate, what to do about national defense, how to promote economic growth.

All these are questions of policy because they deal with specific courses of action. Questions of policy inevitably involve questions of fact. (How can we decide whether to vote for a candidate unless we know the facts of her or his stand on the issues?) They may also involve questions of value. (The policy you favor on abortion will be affected by whether you think abortion is moral or immoral.) But questions of policy *always* go beyond questions of fact or value to decide whether something should or should not be done.

question of policy

A question about whether a specific course of action should or should not be taken.

When put formally, questions of policy usually include the word "should," as in these examples:

What measures should be taken to protect people's privacy online?

Should the electoral college be abolished?

What steps should be taken to reduce the erosion of America's coastlines?

TYPES OF SPEECHES ON QUESTIONS OF POLICY

When you speak on a question of policy, your goal may be either to gain passive agreement or to motivate immediate action from your listeners. Deciding which goal you want to achieve will affect almost every aspect of your speech.

Speeches to Gain Passive Agreement

speech to gain passive agreement

A persuasive speech in which the speaker's goal is to convince the audience that a given policy is desirable without encouraging the audience to take action in support of the policy.

If your goal is passive agreement, you will try to get your audience to agree with you that a certain policy is desirable, but you will not necessarily encourage the audience to do anything to enact the policy. For example, suppose you want to persuade people that the United States should abolish the electoral college and elect the President by direct popular vote. If you seek passive agreement, you will try to get your audience to concur, but you will not urge them to take any action right now to help change presidential election procedures.

Here are some specific purpose statements for policy speeches that seek passive agreement:

> To persuade my audience that there should be stricter safety standards on amusement-park rides.
>
> To persuade my audience that the U.S. patent system should be overhauled so as to promote innovation.
>
> To persuade my audience that a balanced-budget amendment should be added to the U.S. Constitution.

In each case, the speaker's aim is to convince listeners that the speaker's policy is necessary and practical. The speaker is not trying to get listeners to take action in support of the policy.

Speeches to Gain Immediate Action

speech to gain immediate action

A persuasive speech in which the speaker's goal is to convince the audience to take action in support of a given policy.

When your goal is immediate action, you want to do more than get your listeners to nod their heads in agreement. You want to motivate them to action—to sign a petition for abolishing the electoral college, to campaign for lower tuition, to contribute to a fund drive, and so forth.

Here are some examples of specific purpose statements for policy speeches that seek immediate action:

> To persuade my audience to participate in alternate spring break.
>
> To persuade my audience to give time to Big Brothers or Big Sisters.
>
> To persuade my audience to establish retirement accounts early in their careers.

Some experts say you should seek action from your audience whenever possible. Although it is much easier to evoke passive agreement than to elicit action, the listener is not making much of a commitment by thinking, "Sure, I agree with you." Within a day or two that same listener may forget entirely about your speech—and about her or his agreement with it.

Action, however, reinforces belief. A great deal of research shows that if you can persuade a listener to take some kind of action—even if it is no more than signing a petition, putting a bumper sticker on a car, or attending a meeting—you have gained a more serious commitment. Once a listener acts on behalf of a speaker's position, she or he is more likely to remain committed to it.[8]

When you call for action in a persuasive speech, you should make your recommendations as specific as possible. Don't just urge listeners to "do something." Tell them exactly what to do and how to do it.

connect

View this excerpt from "Making a Difference Through the Special Olympics" in the online Media Library for this chapter (Video 16.1).

For an excellent example, look at Video 16.1 in the online Media Library for this chapter. The speaker's aim was to convince her classmates to donate time to the Special Olympics. After talking about the mission of Special

Persuasive speeches on questions of policy are given whenever people debate specific courses of action. Here U.S. Senator Elizabeth Warren presents a plan to improve wages for American workers.

Olympics, the need for volunteers, and the rewarding feelings experienced by volunteers, she explained how students can get involved for whatever amount of time they are able to commit at the moment. She also brought along brochures with additional information to pass out after her speech. When you construct your persuasive speech, remember that the more specific your instructions, the more likely it is that your call to action will succeed.[9]

ANALYZING QUESTIONS OF POLICY

Regardless of whether your aim is to elicit passive agreement or to gain immediate action, you will face three basic issues whenever you discuss a question of policy—need, plan, and practicality.

Need

There is no point in arguing for a policy unless you can show a need for it:

> Is there a need for more student parking on campus?
>
> Is there a need for the school district to replace traditional textbooks with e-textbooks?
>
> Is there a need for a national ID card in the United States?

Your first step is to convince listeners that there is a serious problem with things as they are. People are not inclined to adopt a new policy unless they are convinced that the old one is not working. This is why the *burden of proof* always rests with the speaker who advocates change. (Of course, you may be defending present policy, in which case you will argue that there is *no* need to change—that things are already working as well as can be expected.)

need

The first basic issue in analyzing a question of policy: Is there a serious problem or need that requires a change from current policy?

burden of proof

The obligation facing a persuasive speaker to prove that a change from current policy is necessary.

Plan

The second basic issue of policy speeches is plan. Once you have shown that a problem exists, you must explain your plan for solving it:

> What can we do to get more student parking on campus?
>
> How much will e-textbooks cost? Who will pay for them? What devices will students use to read them?
>
> What information should be included on a national ID card? Who will be responsible for collecting the information and creating the cards?

plan

The second basic issue in analyzing a question of policy: If there is a problem with current policy, does the speaker have a plan to solve the problem?

Answering such questions is especially important if you call for a new policy. It's easy to complain about problems; the real challenge is developing solutions.

connect

View this excerpt from "The Horrors of Puppy Mills" in the online Media Library for this chapter (Video 16.2).

In most classroom speeches, you will not have time to describe your plan in detail, but you should at least identify its major features. Look, for example, at the plan section in the speech on puppy mills in the online Media Library for this chapter. First, the speaker proposes legal measures to punish dog breeders that do not take proper care of their animals. Second, he presents four steps that individual listeners can take when buying a dog to make sure they are not supporting puppy mills. The speech would have been much less persuasive if the speaker had not spelled out the major features of his plan.

Practicality

practicality

The third basic issue in analyzing a question of policy: Will the speaker's plan solve the problem? Will it create new and more serious problems?

The third basic issue of policy speeches is practicality. Once you have presented a plan, you must show that it will work. Will it solve the problem? Or will it create new and more serious problems?

> Building a multilevel parking garage on campus would provide more student parking, but the cost would require a sharp increase in tuition.
>
> Switching to e-textbooks would save the school district money in the long run, but the initial investment would be costly at a time when the district's budget is already stretched thin.
>
> A national ID card might be an easy way for people to verify their identity for security purposes, but it could also infringe on civil liberties and give the government too much personal information about individuals.

These are significant concerns. Whenever you advocate a new policy, you must be prepared to show that it is workable. No matter how serious a problem may be, listeners usually want some assurance that a speaker's plan will actually solve the problem.[10]

connect

View this excerpt from "The Most Dangerous Habit" in the online Media Library for this chapter (Video 16.3).

One way to provide this assurance is to show that a plan similar to yours has been successfully implemented elsewhere. For example, Video 16.3 in the online Media Library for this chapter shows an excerpt from a student speech calling for tougher measures to reduce smoking in the speaker's state. As you view the video, notice how the speaker points to the success of a similar plan in California as evidence that it will work in her state.

If you oppose a shift in policy, one of your major arguments will be that the change is impractical—that it will create more problems than it can solve. For example, critics of a plan to send astronauts to Mars might say that it is highly risky and requires technology that does not currently exist. Others might argue that the cost of the mission would be better spent on any number of causes here on Earth. If listeners accept these arguments, they will probably decide that NASA should not continue working on sending astronauts to Mars.

How much of your speech should you devote to need, to plan, and to practicality? The answer depends on your topic and your audience. For example, if your audience is not aware of the health and environmental problems caused by antibacterial chemicals in household products, you will have to give much of your time to need before covering plan and practicality. On the other hand, if your listeners already know about the problems caused by antibacterial household products, you can quickly remind them of need and then devote most of your speech to plan and practicality.

ORGANIZING SPEECHES ON QUESTIONS OF POLICY

Effective organization is crucial when you speak on a question of policy. Although any of the basic patterns of organization explained in Chapter 9 can be used, four special patterns are especially valuable for policy speeches. They are problem-solution order, problem-cause-solution order, comparative advantages order, and Monroe's motivated sequence.

Problem-Solution Order

If you advocate a change in policy, your main points often will fall naturally into problem-solution order. In the first main point you demonstrate the need for a new policy by showing the extent and seriousness of the problem. In the second main point you explain your plan for solving the problem and show its practicality. For example:

problem-solution order

A method of organizing persuasive speeches in which the first main point deals with the existence of a problem and the second main point presents a solution to the problem.

Specific Purpose: To persuade my audience that the U.S. Congress should pass legislation curbing the spread of phony pharmaceuticals.

Central Idea: Because phony pharmaceuticals are a serious problem in the United States, Congress should pass legislation ensuring that the medications we buy are safe.

Main Points:

I. The spread of phony pharmaceuticals is a serious problem.
   A. Phony pharmaceuticals are one of the most profitable areas of criminal activity in the world.
   B. The spread of phony pharmaceuticals is producing serious health risks in the United States.

II. Solving the problem of phony pharmaceuticals requires action by the federal government.
   A. Congress should pass legislation targeting the spread of phony pharmaceuticals and imposing strict penalties for violators.
   B. Experts believe that such legislation will go a long way toward solving the problem.

connect

View an excerpt from "Phony Pharmaceuticals" in the online Media Library for this chapter (Video 16.4).

You can use the problem-solution format just as easily to organize a speech opposing a change in policy. In such a speech your job is to defend the current system and to attack your opponents' proposed policy. Thus in the first main point you might argue that there is *not* a need for change. In the second main point you might show that even if there were a serious problem, the suggested new policy would *not* solve it and would create serious problems of its own. For example:

Specific Purpose: To persuade my audience that the city council should not pass legislation merging the police and fire departments.

Central Idea: Merging the police and fire departments is neither necessary nor practical.

Main Points:

I. Merging the police and fire departments is not necessary.
   A. Under the current system, the police department has developed a reputation for excellence that has made it a model for departments in other cities,
   B. The fire department is equally well-respected for doing its job quickly and efficiently.

II. Besides being unnecessary, merging the police and fire departments is highly impractical.
   A. Rather than saving the city money, merging the departments would increase costs.
   B. Merging the departments would also harm morale and reduce the high level of performance we expect from our police force and firefighters.

PROBLEM-CAUSE-SOLUTION ORDER

problem-cause-solution order

A method of organizing persuasive speeches in which the first main point identifies a problem, the second main point analyzes the causes of the problem, and the third main point presents a solution to the problem.

For a variation on problem-solution order, you might arrange your speech in problem-cause-solution order. This produces a speech with three main points—the first identifying a problem, the second analyzing the causes of the problem, and the third presenting a solution to the problem. For example:

Specific Purpose: To persuade my audience that action is required to deal with the problem of childhood obesity.

Central Idea: Childhood obesity is a serious problem that can be controlled by changes in diet and exercise.

Main Points:

I. Childhood obesity is a major problem in the United States.
   A. Childhood obesity continues to grow at a rapid pace.
   B. Obesity is producing serious health problems among children.

II. There are two major causes of the increase in childhood obesity.
   A. The first cause is dietary.
   B. The second cause is physical inactivity.

III. Solving the problem requires dealing with both causes.
   A. Parents and schools must make sure that children are eating healthy foods.
   B. Parents and schools must also make sure that children get enough exercise.

connect

View an excerpt from "The Epidemic of Childhood Obesity" in the online Media Library for this chapter (Video 16.5).

Some teachers prefer this method of organization because it requires a speaker to identify the causes of the problem. This in turn makes it easier to check whether the proposed solution will get at the causes of the problem.

Comparative Advantages Order

comparative advantages order

A method of organizing persuasive speeches in which each main point explains why a speaker's solution to a problem is preferable to other proposed solutions.

When your audience already agrees that a problem exists, you can devote your speech to comparing the advantages and disadvantages of competing solutions. In such a situation, you might put your speech in comparative advantages order, devoting each main point to explaining why your solution is preferable to other proposed solutions.

Suppose you are speaking at a meeting of the city council about ways to alleviate traffic congestion in your city. Some citizens support the construction of a new highway. You, however, support a rapid bus system that can be built on already-existing roads. Using comparative advantages order, you compare the highway proposal with the bus-system proposal and show why the latter is a better choice. Your specific purpose, central idea, and main points might look like this:

Because it follows the process of human thinking, Monroe's motivated sequence is especially useful for persuasive speakers who seek immediate action from their listeners.

Specific Purpose: To persuade my audience that our city should build a rapid bus system instead of a new highway.

Central Idea: A rapid bus system will be cheaper and more effective than a new highway.

Main Points:

I. Research models show that we will save a million dollars if we build a rapid bus system instead of a new highway.

II. Research models also show that a rapid bus system will reduce traffic congestion more than a new highway.

Monroe's Motivated Sequence

Monroe's motivated sequence

A method of organizing persuasive speeches that seek immediate action. The five steps of the motivated sequence are attention, need, satisfaction, visualization, and action.

Developed in the 1930s by Alan Monroe, a professor of speech at Purdue University, the motivated sequence is tailor-made for policy speeches that seek immediate action. The sequence has five steps that follow the psychology of persuasion:

1. *Attention.* First, you gain the attention of your audience by using one or more of the methods described in Chapter 10: relating to the audience, showing the importance of the topic, making a startling statement, arousing curiosity or suspense, posing a question, telling a dramatic story, or using visual aids.
2. *Need.* Next, you make the audience feel a need for change. You show there is a serious problem with the existing situation. It is important to state the need clearly and to illustrate it with strong supporting materials. By the end of this step, listeners should be so concerned about the problem that they are psychologically primed to hear your solution.
3. *Satisfaction.* Having aroused a sense of need, you satisfy it by providing a solution to the problem. You present your plan and show how it will work. Be sure to offer enough details about the plan to give listeners a clear understanding of it.

4. *Visualization.* Having given your plan, you intensify desire for it by visualizing its benefits. The key to this step is using vivid imagery to show your listeners how *they* will profit from your policy. Make them *see* how much better conditions will be once your plan is adopted.
5. *Action.* Once the audience is convinced that your policy is beneficial, you are ready to call for action. Say exactly what you want the audience to do—and how to do it. Then conclude with a final stirring appeal that reinforces their commitment to act.

Many speakers prefer the motivated sequence because it is more detailed than problem-solution order. It follows the process of human thinking and leads the listener step by step to the desired action. One indication of its effectiveness is that it is widely used by people who make their living by persuasion—especially advertisers. The next time you watch television, pay close attention to the commercials. You will find that many of them follow the motivated sequence.

Try using the motivated sequence when you want to spur listeners to action. You should find it easy and effective, as did one student who used it in a speech urging classmates to work for passage of a local tenants' rights bill. Here are the highlights of his speech:

Attention: Have you ever had cockroaches running through the cupboards in your apartment? Have you shivered in the cold because the furnace was broken? Or waited months for the security deposit you never got back even though you left your apartment as clean as when you moved in?

Need: Throughout this city students and other tenants are being victimized by unresponsive and unethical landlords. Just last year more than 200 complaints were filed with the city housing department, but no action has been taken against the landlords.

Satisfaction: These problems could be solved by passing a strong tenants' rights bill that defines the rights of tenants, specifies the obligations of landlords, and imposes strict penalties for violators.

Visualization: Such bills have worked in a number of college communities across the nation. If one were passed here, you would no longer have to worry about substandard conditions in your apartment. Your landlord could not violate the terms of your lease or steal your security deposit.

Action: A tenants' rights bill has been proposed to the city council. You can help get it passed by signing the petition I will pass around after my speech. I also urge you to circulate petitions among your friends and to support the bill when it is debated in the city council next week. If we all work together, we can get this bill through the council.

Monroe's motivated sequence is perfectly compatible with the standard method of outlining discussed in Chapter 11. The following outline shows how one speaker incorporated the sequence into a speech urging her classmates to change the way they use their cell phones (the full text is printed in the appendix that follows Chapter 19):

Specific Purpose: To persuade my audience to use their cell phones in a way that will protect their health.

Central Idea: You can avoid the long-term health risks of cell phone use by making some simple changes.

Introduction

Attention:

I. Your cell phone is your constant companion. You use it everywhere you go, day and night.

II. But what if your constant companion is potentially hazardous to your health?

III. After doing extensive research, I hope to persuade each of you to use your cell phone in a manner that will protect your health.

connect

View an excerpt from "The Dangers of Cell Phones" in the online Media Library for this chapter (Video 16.6).

Body

Need:

I. Although cell phones are safe in the short run, they may pose long-term health risks.

A. Using a cell phone exposes you to radiation that builds up over time.

B. Some scientists warn about the long-term dangers of cell phone use.

C. Even cell phone manufacturers caution against keeping phones too close to the body.

Satisfaction:

II. You can guard against these risks by making simple changes in the way you use your cell phone.

A. Above all, do not press your cell phone against your head while talking.

B. Get in the habit of using ear buds or your phone's internal speaker.

Using public speaking in your CAREER

After earning your teaching certificate, you landed a job in one of the best public school districts in the state. You've excelled in the classroom, and evaluations of your teaching are consistently outstanding.

But the newly announced state budget means drastic cuts for the district. Either 100 teachers will be laid off, or every teacher will have to accept a 10 percent pay cut. Because the newest teachers are the first to be fired, and you have been on the job for only three years, you know that the only way to keep your position is if all teachers agree to the pay cut. What's more, laying off 100 teachers will mean more students in each classroom, which will harm the quality of education.

In one week, the school superintendent will hold an open meeting for teachers to voice their opinions. You plan on arguing for the pay cut, but you're unsure how to organize your speech. Which of the following methods of organization will be most effective, and why: problem-solution, comparative advantages, Monroe's motivated sequence?

Visualization: III. These changes will help protect your health.

A. They are easy changes to make.

B. They will help you use your cell phone without long-term health risks.

Conclusion

Action: I. So I encourage each of you to make these changes starting today.

II. Make sure your constant companion is not endangering your health.

Try using the motivated sequence when you seek immediate action from your listeners. Over the years it has worked for countless speakers—and it can work for you as well.

Sample Speech with Commentary

connect

View "Changing Lives Through the Literacy Network" in the online Media Library for this chapter (Video 16.7).

The following persuasive speech deals with a question of policy and provides an excellent example of Monroe's motivated sequence. As you read the speech, notice how the speaker uses strong, well-chosen supporting materials as she moves through each step of the motivated sequence. The speech also shows how a speaker's delivery can enhance the impact of his or her ideas—as you can see by watching Video 16.7 in the online Media Library for this chapter.

Changing Lives Through the Literacy Network

COMMENTARY	SPEECH
The first step in Monroe's motivated sequence is gaining attention, which the speaker accomplishes with a vivid hypothetical example that she ties directly to her audience through the use of "you" and "your."	Imagine being dropped into a foreign country—a country where you can't read the street signs, can't order food from a menu, can't fill out a job application. You're surrounded by scribbles and squiggles that simply don't make sense. Now imagine that that country isn't a foreign one, but your own.
A real-life example shows that the opening hypothetical scenario is not far-fetched. Poignant and memorable, the example introduces Dwayne MacNamara, who will appear again later in the speech.	That's exactly what people like Dwayne MacNamara experience on a daily basis. A father of two daughters, Dwayne has struggled with reading and writing for years. These struggles made it difficult for him to find a job, to take care of his family, and to develop a positive self-image. "Not being able to read and write as well as other people," Dwayne says, "has taken a life-long toll on my confidence and my ability to make sound decisions."

Here the speaker reveals the topic of her speech and indicates that low literacy is a local, as well as a national, problem.

Dwayne is far from alone in dealing with these problems. Low literacy affects millions of adults throughout the United States, including right here in Madison and Dane County.

The speaker establishes her credibility by citing her personal experience with the Literacy Network. She ends the introduction by stating her central idea and previewing the body of her speech.

For the past year, I've been volunteering at the Literacy Network—a local, Madison-based, nonprofit organization that helps adults and families with reading, writing, and speaking skills. I've seen the problems people face because of low literacy, and I've also seen how improved literacy can change people's lives for the better. Today I'd like to encourage you to join me as a volunteer. But first let's look more closely at low adult literacy and the problems it can cause.

The speaker moves into the need step of Monroe's motivated sequence, in which she explains the problem of low adult literacy.

According to a 2012 report from the U.S. Department of Education and the National Research Council, more than 30 million adults in the United States lack basic literacy skills. Another 60 million have only basic skills, but little beyond that.

A combination of statistics and expert testimony documents the extent of low adult literacy. The speaker uses high-quality evidence and clearly cites her sources.

When you add these two groups together, 90 million people—more than 40 percent of the adult population—have trouble reading the newspaper, understanding instructions from a doctor, registering to vote, or reading a lease for a place to live. As the National Commission on Adult Literacy states, we face an "adult education crisis that permeates every aspect of American life."

This paragraph builds upon the previous one by showing the many challenges facing adults who have low literacy skills.

The problem is even worse when you consider the social consequences of low adult literacy. According to a report from the American Institutes for Research, 42 percent of people with less-than-basic literacy skills live in poverty. Adults with low literacy are less likely to participate in the workforce, to assist with their children's education, and to be involved in their community.

By moving from the national level to the local level, this paragraph shows how low adult literacy affects the immediate community.

Here in Madison we are not immune to these challenges. The Literacy Network estimates that 17,000 people in Dane County lack "the functional literacy skills needed to read a letter from their children's teacher, a label in a grocery store, or instructions from a doctor." Another 38,000 don't know English well enough to perform these tasks.

As in this case, testimony from a personal interview can be an excellent way to reinforce a speaker's ideas.

When I interviewed Jeff Burkhart, Executive Director of the Literacy Network, he told me that "even though we live in a university town, thousands of people still struggle with everyday literacy skills necessary for success."

The question at the start of this paragraph signals that the speaker is moving to the satisfaction section of her speech. Notice how clearly she explains the range of services provided by the Literacy Network.

So what can you and I do to help combat the problem of low adult literacy? One option is to volunteer at the Literacy Network. It offers a range of services that include basic skills of reading and writing, learning English as a second language, even math and health skills. Best of all, all these services are free. Individuals and families pay absolutely nothing to receive help.

The speaker encourages her classmates to join her as a volunteer at the Literacy Network. She provides options for her listeners by noting a number of ways in which they can contribute.

But the Literacy Network can only offer its services for free if it has enough volunteers—and that's where you come in. Whatever your skill set, the Literacy Network has a way for you to help. You can join me as a tutor and help improve people's writing, speaking, and reading skills. If tutoring doesn't sound right for you, you can help with data entry, fundraising, or scheduling. There are also positions for photographers and those with computer skills.

In this paragraph and the next, the speaker addresses the audience's possible hesitations about volunteering. By relating her own experiences as a new volunteer, she personalizes her ideas and gives them added credibility.

If you volunteer as a tutor, you don't need prior experience, teaching certification, or fluency in another language. You'll attend a training seminar at which the staff will show you exactly what to do. I have to admit: I was a little nervous during my first training seminar. But it calmed my nerves and helped me understand exactly what I was doing. Then, when I met my adult learner for the first time, I was ready to get started.

Whenever a speaker asks listeners to donate time to a cause, it is important to show how they can fit the volunteer activities into their schedules.

But, you may be asking, how much time does it take to be a literacy tutor? The usual commitment is two hours a week. It can be before class, after class, during lunch, on the weekends—whatever works best for you. You can even pick the place. I meet my learner in a study room at Memorial Library. It's a convenient spot for both of us.

Having explained her plan and its practicality, the speaker moves into the visualization section. Returning to the example of Dwayne MacNamara gives the speech a sense of unity and shows the concrete benefits provided by the Literacy Network.

Whether you volunteer as a tutor or in some other capacity, you *will* change the lives of people who have suffered for far too long. Remember Dwayne MacNamara, who I mentioned in my introduction? He lives here—in Madison. Because of the Literacy Network, he now works at a home-improvement store, where reading instructions and dealing with customers is essential.

An instance of peer testimony, the quotation from Dwayne MacNamara is particularly effective.

Dwayne is also able for the first time to help his kids with their homework. He even reads to them every night before bed. "The Literacy Network gave me the skills I needed to succeed," Dwayne says. "I have become more confident, and I am more motivated and excited to go forward with life."

As you can see from the video, the sincerity and directness of the speaker's delivery add to her persuasiveness.

Dwayne's experience is matched by many others. Here are some brochures you can take a look at after my speech. They are filled with success stories from people here in Madison whose lives have been changed through literacy.

The speaker moves into the action section. Once again she addresses her classmates directly as "you."

So I hope you will join me as a volunteer. You can help someone's life go from isolation and despair to a life of progress and promise.

The Literacy Network's motto provides a perfect vehicle for the speaker's closing appeal.

"Improving Lives Through Literacy"—that's the motto of the Literacy Network. It's a motto I've seen come to life over the past year. And it's a motto I hope you will see for yourself by becoming a volunteer. Thank you.

Summary

Persuasion is the process of creating, reinforcing, or changing people's beliefs or actions. When you speak to persuade, you act as an advocate. The ability to speak persuasively will benefit you in every part of your life, from personal relations to community activities to career aspirations.

How successful you are in any persuasive speech depends on how well you tailor your message to your listeners' values, attitudes, and beliefs. You should think of your speech as a mental dialogue with your audience. Identify your target audience, anticipate objections they may raise to your point of view, and answer those objections in your speech.

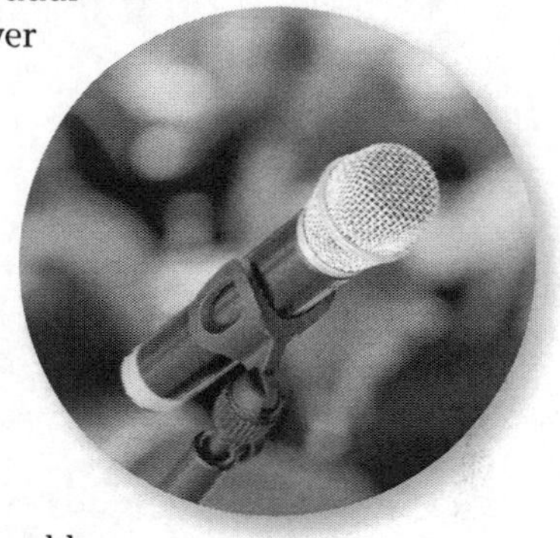

Persuasive speeches may center on questions of fact, value, or policy. When giving a persuasive speech about a question of fact, your role is akin to that of a lawyer in a courtroom trial. You will try to get your listeners to accept your view of the facts.

Questions of value involve a person's beliefs about what is right or wrong, good or bad, moral or immoral, ethical or unethical. When speaking about a question of value, you must justify your opinion by establishing standards for your value judgment. Speeches on questions of value do not argue directly for or against particular courses of action.

Once you go beyond arguing right or wrong to urging that something should or should not be done, you move to a question of policy. When you speak on a question of policy, your goal may be to evoke passive agreement or to spark immediate action. In either case, you will face three basic issues—need, plan, and practicality. How much of your speech you devote to each issue will depend on your topic and your audience.

There are several options for organizing speeches on questions of policy. If you advocate a change in policy, your main points will often fall naturally into problem-solution order or into problem-cause-solution order. If your audience already agrees that a problem exists, you may be able to use comparative advantages order. Whenever you seek immediate action from listeners, you should consider a more specialized organizational pattern known as Monroe's motivated sequence.

Regardless of your topic or method of organization, you need to make sure your goals are ethically sound and that you use ethical methods to persuade your audience.

Key Terms

persuasion (306)
mental dialogue with the audience (310)
target audience (310)
question of fact (311)
question of value (313)
question of policy (315)
speech to gain passive agreement (316)
speech to gain immediate action (316)
need (317)
burden of proof (317)
plan (317)
practicality (318)
problem-solution order (319)
problem-cause-solution order (320)
comparative advantages order (320)
Monroe's motivated sequence (321)

Review Questions

After reading this chapter, you should be able to answer the following questions:

1. What is the difference between an informative speech and a persuasive speech? Why is speaking to persuade more challenging than speaking to inform?
2. What does it mean to say that audiences engage in a mental dialogue with the speaker as they listen to a speech? What implications does this mental give-and-take hold for effective persuasive speaking?
3. What is the target audience for a persuasive speech?
4. What are questions of fact? How does a persuasive speech on a question of fact differ from an informative speech? Give an example of a specific purpose statement for a persuasive speech on a question of fact.
5. What are questions of value? Give an example of a specific purpose statement for a persuasive speech on a question of value.
6. What are questions of policy? Give an example of a specific purpose statement for a persuasive speech on a question of policy.
7. Explain the difference between passive agreement and immediate action as goals for persuasive speeches on questions of policy.
8. What are the three basic issues you must deal with when discussing a question of policy? What will determine the amount of attention you give to each of these issues in any particular speech?
9. What four methods of organization are used most often in persuasive speeches on questions of policy?
10. What are the five steps of Monroe's motivated sequence? Why is the motivated sequence especially useful in speeches that seek immediate action from listeners?

connect

For further review, go to the LearnSmart study module for this chapter.

Exercises for Critical Thinking

1. Look back at the story of Nicolás Navarro at the beginning of this chapter (page 305). Like Nicolás, most people do a certain amount of persuading every day in normal conversation. Keep a journal of your communication activities for an entire day, making special note of all instances in which you tried to persuade someone else to your point of view. Choose one of those instances and prepare a brief analysis of it.

   In your analysis, answer the following questions: (1) Who was the audience for your persuasive effort? (2) What were the "specific purpose" and the "central idea" of your persuasive message? (3) Did you rehearse your persuasive message ahead of time, or did it arise spontaneously from the situation? (4) Were you successful in achieving your specific purpose? (5) If you faced the same situation again, what strategic changes would you make in your persuasive effort?
2. Below are four specific purposes for persuasive speeches. In each case explain whether the speech associated with it concerns a question of fact, a question of value, or a question of policy. Then rewrite the specific purpose statement to

make it appropriate for a speech about one of the other two kinds of questions. For instance, if the original purpose statement is about a question of policy, write a new specific purpose statement that deals with the same topic as either a question of fact or a question of value.

Example:

Original statement: To persuade my audience that it is unfair for judges to favor natural parents over adoptive parents in child custody disputes. (question of value)

Rewritten statement: To persuade my audience that the courts should establish clear guidelines for settling disputes between adoptive parents and natural parents in child custody cases. (question of policy)

a. To persuade my audience that e-cigarettes are harmful to human health.

b. To persuade my audience that a national sales tax should be adopted to help reduce the national debt.

c. To persuade my audience that it is unethical for doctors to receive money from pharmaceutical companies to promote their products.

d. To persuade my audience to join Teach for America.

3. Choose a topic for a persuasive speech on a question of policy. Create two specific purpose statements about that topic—one for a speech to gain passive agreement, another for a speech to motivate immediate action. Once you have the specific purpose statements, explain how the speech seeking immediate action would differ in structure and persuasive appeals from the speech seeking passive agreement. Be specific.
4. Analyze "Phony Pharmaceuticals" in the appendix of sample speeches that follows Chapter 19. Because this is a speech on a question of policy, pay special attention to how the speaker deals with the basic issues of need, plan, and practicality. Does the speaker present a convincing case that a serious problem exists? Does she offer a clear plan to solve the problem? Does she demonstrate that the plan is practical?
5. Select a television commercial that is organized according to Monroe's motivated sequence. Prepare a brief analysis in which you (a) identify the target audience for the commercial and (b) describe each step in the motivated sequence as it appears in the commercial.

YES on 30

17

Methods of Persuasion

Building Credibility

Using Evidence

Reasoning

Appealing to Emotions

Sample Speech with Commentary

Persuasion is big business. Authors and consultants promise to teach you the one key secret to persuading people to do what you want. Dan Lok claims to reveal "forbidden psychological tactics" that will "give you an unfair advantage in dealing with people." Chris St. Hilaire offers "simple strategies to seduce audiences and win allies." Kevin Dutton claims to have discovered "a single, definitive formula" for "a mysterious, previously unidentified, superstrain of persuasion." These people charge thousands of dollars for their seminars and motivational speeches. Companies and individuals flock—and pay—to read and hear what they have to say.

It sounds good, but does anyone really have the "one key secret" to persuasion? Probably not. Persuasion is too complicated for that. Yet, as the number of books, seminars, and videos on the subject shows, there is a perpetual fascination with the strategies and tactics of effective persuasion.

What makes a speaker persuasive? Why do listeners accept one speaker's views and reject those of another? How can a speaker motivate listeners to act in support of a cause, a campaign, or a candidate?

People have been trying to answer these questions for thousands of years—from the ancient Greek philosopher Aristotle to modern-day communication researchers. Although many answers have been given, we can say that listeners will be persuaded by a speaker for one or more of four reasons:

Because they perceive the speaker as having high *credibility.*

Because they are won over by the speaker's *evidence.*

Because they are convinced by the speaker's *reasoning.*

Because their *emotions* are touched by the speaker's ideas or language.

In this chapter we will look at each of these. We will not discover any magical secrets that will make you an irresistible persuasive speaker. But if you learn the principles discussed in this chapter, you will greatly increase your odds of winning the minds and hearts of your listeners.

Building Credibility

Here are two sets of imaginary statements. Which one of each pair would you be more likely to believe?

The U.S. judicial system needs major organizational changes to deal with the growing number of court cases. (Sonia Sotomayor)

The U.S. judicial system can deal with the number of court cases without any organizational changes. (Aaron Rodgers)

Technology is changing professional football in ways that the average fan cannot see. (Aaron Rodgers)

Technology is not having a major impact on professional football. (Sonia Sotomayor)

ethos

The name used by Aristotle for what modern students of communication refer to as credibility.

Most likely you chose the first in each pair of statements. If so, you were probably influenced by your perception of the speaker. You are more likely to respect the judgment of Sotomayor, Associate Justice of the U.S. Supreme Court, when she speaks about the organization of the American judiciary. You are more likely to respect the judgment of Rodgers, quarterback of the Green Bay Packers, when he speaks about technology in professional football. Some instructors call this factor *source credibility.* Others refer to it as *ethos,* the name given by Aristotle.

FACTORS OF CREDIBILITY

Many things affect a speaker's credibility, including sociability, dynamism, physical attractiveness, and perceived similarity between speaker and audience. Above all, though, credibility is affected by two factors:

- *Competence*—how an audience regards a speaker's intelligence, expertise, and knowledge of the subject.
- *Character*—how an audience regards a speaker's sincerity, trustworthiness, and concern for the well-being of the audience.

The more favorably listeners view a speaker's competence and character, the more likely they are to accept what the speaker says. No doubt you are familiar with this from your own experience. Suppose you take a course in economics. The course is taught by a distinguished professor who has published widely in prestigious journals, who sits on a major international commission, and who has won several awards for outstanding research. In class, you hang on this professor's every word. One day the professor is absent; a colleague from the Economics Department—fully qualified but not as well known—comes to lecture instead. Possibly the fill-in instructor gives the same lecture the distinguished professor would have given, but you do not pay nearly as close attention. The other instructor does not have as high credibility as the professor.

credibility

The audience's perception of whether a speaker is qualified to speak on a given topic. The two major factors influencing a speaker's credibility are competence and character.

It is important to remember that credibility is an attitude. It exists not in the speaker, but in the mind of the audience. A speaker may have high credibility for one audience and low credibility for another. A speaker may also have high credibility on one topic and low credibility on another. Looking back to our imaginary statements, most people would more readily believe Aaron Rodgers speaking about professional football than Aaron Rodgers speaking about the organization of the U.S. judiciary.

TYPES OF CREDIBILITY

Not only can a speaker's credibility vary from audience to audience and topic to topic, but it can also change during the course of a speech—so much so that we can identify three types of credibility:

- *Initial credibility*—the credibility of the speaker before she or he starts to speak.
- *Derived credibility*—the credibility of the speaker produced by everything she or he says and does during the speech itself.
- *Terminal credibility*—the credibility of the speaker at the end of the speech.[1]

initial credibility

The credibility of a speaker before she or he starts to speak.

derived credibility

The credibility of a speaker produced by everything she or he says and does during the speech.

terminal credibility

The credibility of a speaker at the end of the speech.

All three are dynamic. High initial credibility is a great advantage for any speaker, but it can be destroyed during a speech, resulting in low terminal credibility. The reverse can also occur, as in the following example:

> Amit Patel is the information technology manager for a nonprofit research foundation. Soon after taking the job, he installed a new content management system for the company's Web site. He assumed there would be some glitches, but they turned out to be much worse than anything he had imagined. It took nine months to get the system working properly.
>
> A year later, the foundation decided to purchase new tablets that would allow employees to interact more efficiently with data on the internal network. When Amit discussed the tablets at a weekly staff meeting, he had low initial credibility. Everyone remembered the content management system, and they did not want to go through the same problems again.
>
> Aware of his low initial credibility, Amit began by reminding everyone that he hoped to make their jobs easier. He then acknowledged that he had told them the same thing about the content management system—an admission that drew a laugh and helped everyone relax. Finally, he explained that he had checked with other nonprofits that had adopted the same tablets he was purchasing, and they had all told him that the tablets worked flawlessly.

By the time Amit finished, most staff members were eager to start using their tablets. He had achieved high terminal credibility.

In every speech you give you will have some degree of initial credibility, which will be strengthened or weakened by your message and how you deliver it. And your terminal credibility from one speech will affect your initial credibility for the next one. If your audience sees you as sincere and competent, they will be much more receptive to your ideas.

ENHANCING YOUR CREDIBILITY

How can you build your credibility in your speeches? At one level, the answer is frustratingly general. Since everything you say and do in a speech will affect your credibility, you should say and do *everything* in a way that will make you appear capable and trustworthy. In other words—give a brilliant speech and you will achieve high credibility!

The advice is sound, but not all that helpful. There are, however, some specific ways you can boost your credibility while speaking. They include explaining your competence, establishing common ground with the audience, and speaking with genuine conviction.

Explain Your Competence

One way to enhance your credibility is to advertise your expertise on the speech topic. Did you investigate the topic thoroughly? Then say so. Do you have experience that gives you special knowledge or insight? Again, say so.

Here is how two students revealed their qualifications. The first stressed her study and research:

connect

View these excerpts from "Bursting the Antibacterial Bubble" and "Keeping the Safety Net for Those Who Need It" in the online Media Library for this chapter (Video 17.1).

> Before I studied antibacterial products in my public-health class, I always used antibacterial soaps and antibacterial all-surface cleaner for my apartment. I also know from my class survey that 70 percent of you use antibacterial soaps, cleaners, or other products. But after learning about the subject in class and reading research studies for this speech, I'm here to tell you that, try as we might, we cannot build a bubble between ourselves and germs with antibacterial products and that these products actually create more problems than they solve.

The second student emphasized her background and personal experience:

> Most of us have no idea what it means to be poor and hungry. But before returning to school last year, I spent three years working at local assistance centers. I can't tell you everything I have seen. But on the basis of what I can tell you, I hope you will agree with me that government help for the poor and needy must be maintained.

Both speakers greatly increased their persuasiveness by establishing their credibility.

Establish Common Ground with Your Audience

Another way to bolster your credibility is to establish common ground with your audience. You do not persuade listeners by assaulting their values and rejecting their opinions. As the old saying goes, "You catch more flies with

A speaker's credibility has a powerful impact on how her or his speech is received. One way to boost your credibility is to deliver your speeches expressively and with strong eye contact.

honey than with vinegar." The same is true of persuasion. Show respect for your listeners. You can make your speech more appealing by identifying your ideas with those of your audience—by showing how your point of view is consistent with what they believe.[2]

Creating common ground is especially important at the start of a persuasive speech. Begin by identifying with your listeners. Show that you share their values, attitudes, and experiences. Get them nodding their heads in agreement, and they will be much more receptive to your ultimate proposal. Here is how a businesswoman from Massachusetts, hoping to sell her product to an audience in Colorado, began her persuasive speech:

creating common ground

A technique in which a speaker connects himself or herself with the values, attitudes, or experiences of the audience.

> I have never been in Colorado before, but I really looked forward to making this trip. A lot of my ancestors left Massachusetts and came to Colorado nearly 150 years ago. Sometimes I have wondered why they did it. They came in covered wagons, carrying all their possessions, and many of them died on the journey. The ones who got through raised their houses and raised their families. Now that I've seen Colorado, I understand why they tried so hard!

The audience laughed and applauded, and the speaker was off to a good start.

Now look at a different approach, used in a classroom speech favoring a tuition increase at the speaker's school—an unpopular point of view with his classmates. He began by saying:

connect

View this excerpt from "Let's Protect the Quality of Our Education" in the online Media Library for this chapter (Video 17.2).

> As we all know, there are many differences among the people in this class. But regardless of age, major, background, or goals, we all share one thing in common—we're all concerned about the quality of education at this school. And that quality is clearly in danger.
>
> The economic crisis has hit every aspect of life, and education is no exception. Budgets are shrinking, faculty salaries are falling, student services are

> disappearing, and we are being crowded out of classes we need to take. Whether we like it or not, we have a problem—a problem that affects each of us.
>
> There are no easy answers, but one thing that will help solve the problem is an increase in tuition. I don't like it any more than you do, but sometimes we have to do what is necessary to protect the quality of our education.

By stressing common perceptions of the problem, the student hoped to get off on the right foot with his audience. Once that was done, he moved gradually to his more controversial ideas.

Deliver Your Speeches Fluently, Expressively, and with Conviction

There is a great deal of research to show that a speaker's credibility is strongly affected by his or her delivery. Moderately fast speakers, for example, are usually seen as more intelligent and confident than slower speakers. So too are speakers who use vocal variety to communicate their ideas in a lively, animated way. On the other hand, speakers who consistently lose their place, hesitate frequently, or pepper their talk with "uh," "er," and "um" are seen as less competent than speakers who are poised and dynamic.[3]

All of this argues for practicing your persuasive speech fully ahead of time so you can deliver it fluently and expressively. In addition to being better prepared, you will take a major step toward enhancing your credibility. (Review Chapter 13 if you have questions about speech delivery.)

Speaking techniques aside, the most important way to strengthen your credibility is to deliver your speeches with genuine conviction. President Harry Truman once said that in speaking, "sincerity, honesty, and a straightforward manner are more important than special talent or polish." If you wish to convince others, you must first convince yourself. If you want others to believe and care about your ideas, you must believe and care about them yourself. Your spirit, enthusiasm, and conviction will carry over to your listeners.

Using Evidence

Evidence consists of supporting materials—examples, statistics, testimony—used to prove or disprove something. As we saw in Chapter 8, most people are skeptical. They are suspicious of unsupported generalizations. They want speakers to justify their claims. If you hope to be persuasive, you must support your views with evidence. Whenever you say something that is open to question, you should give evidence to prove you are right.

evidence

Supporting materials used to prove or disprove something.

Evidence is particularly important in classroom speeches because few students are recognized as experts on their speech topics. Research has shown that speakers with very high initial credibility do not need to use as much evidence as do speakers with lower credibility. For most speakers, though, strong evidence is absolutely necessary. It can enhance your credibility, increase both the immediate and long-term persuasiveness of your message, and help "inoculate" listeners against counterpersuasion.[4]

Evidence is also crucial whenever your target audience opposes your point of view. As we saw in Chapter 16, listeners in such a situation will mentally argue with you—asking questions, raising objections, and creating counterarguments to "answer" what you say. The success of your speech will depend partly on how well you anticipate these internal responses and give evidence to refute them.

You may want to review Chapter 8, which shows how to use supporting materials. The following case study illustrates how they work as evidence in a persuasive speech.

HOW EVIDENCE WORKS: A CASE STUDY

Let's say one of your classmates is talking about shortcomings in the U.S. mental health system. Instead of just telling you what she thinks, the speaker offers strong evidence to prove her point. Notice how she carries on a mental dialogue with her listeners. She imagines what they might be thinking, anticipates their questions and objections, and gives evidence to answer the questions and resolve the objections.

She begins this way:

> Right now in our city, there is a homeless man muttering to himself on a street corner. An elderly woman living with too many cats. A teenager cutting her arms and legs. Some call them crazy. But to me, these are people who need help—help that they're not receiving because of our nation's inadequate mental-health services.

How do you react? If you already know about the deficiencies in mental-health services, you probably nod your head in agreement. But what if you don't know? Or what if you're skeptical? Perhaps you think taxpayer dollars could be better spent elsewhere. If so, a few anecdotes probably won't persuade you. Mentally you say to the speaker, "These are sad stories, but maybe they're isolated cases. Do we really have a national problem?"

Anticipating just such a response, the speaker gives evidence to support her point:

> According to a recent story on *CNN.com*, the number of state-run psychiatric beds across America has decreased by 14 percent during the past five years. More shockingly, since 1960 that number has fallen by a whopping 92 percent.

"Okay, that's a big decline," you may think. "But people with mental-health issues receive care in other ways. The number of psychiatric beds doesn't tell the whole story." The speaker answers:

> What happens to the people who can't receive treatment at a state-run facility? According to Bernard Harcourt, a criminology professor at the University of Chicago, many end up behind bars. Fifty years ago, there were almost 1.1 million people in mental-health facilities, compared with 270,000 people in prison. Today, there are only 150,000 people in mental-health facilities and 2 million in prison. As the mental-health population has declined, the prison population has skyrocketed.

"That's an interesting correlation," you say to yourself. "But is that the extent of the problem?" Keeping one step ahead of you, the speaker continues:

> Nor is the mental-health crisis isolated to our prisons. Consider the following statistics from the National Alliance on Mental Illness. Untreated mental illnesses

> cost the United States almost $200 billion a year in lost productivity. Adults living with serious, but treatable, mental illness die an average of 25 years earlier than the rest of the population. And veterans who experience mental health issues are committing suicide at alarming rates—an average of 22 every single day of the year.

"I didn't know that," you say to yourself. "Is there anything else?"

> One last point. *Time* magazine reports that more and more children are not getting the mental-health care they need. There are currently 7,500 psychiatrists serving children and adolescents. To meet demand, however, we need more than 20,000 psychiatrists. On top of everything else, we are putting our children at risk.

Now are you convinced? Chances are you will at least think about the lack of mental-health care as a serious problem. You may even decide that increasing funding for mental-health services would be a good investment of tax dollars. If so, you will have changed your mind in part because the speaker supported each of her claims with evidence.

TIPS FOR USING EVIDENCE

Any of the supporting materials discussed in Chapter 8—examples, statistics, testimony—can work as evidence in a persuasive speech. As we saw in that chapter, there are guidelines for using each kind of supporting material regardless of the kind of speech you are giving. Here we look at four special tips for using evidence in a persuasive speech.

Use Specific Evidence

No matter what kind of evidence you employ—statistics, examples, or testimony—it will be more persuasive if you state it in specific rather than general terms.[5] In the speech about mental illness, for example, the speaker did not say, "Lack of adequate mental-health care costs the U.S. economy lots of money." That would have left the audience wondering how much "lots" amounts to. By saying, "untreated mental illnesses cost the United States almost $200 billion a year in lost productivity," the speaker made her point much more persuasively. She also enhanced her credibility by showing that she had a firm grasp of the facts.

Use Novel Evidence

Evidence is more likely to be persuasive if it is new to the audience.[6] You will gain little by citing facts and figures that are already well known to your listeners. If they have not persuaded your listeners already, they will not do so now. You must go beyond what the audience already knows and present striking new evidence that will get them to say, "Hmmm, I didn't know *that*. Maybe I should rethink the issue." Finding such evidence usually requires hard digging and resourceful research, but the rewards are worth the effort.

Use Evidence from Credible Sources

Listeners find evidence from competent, credible sources more persuasive than evidence from less qualified sources.[7] Above all, listeners are suspicious of evidence from sources that appear to be biased or self-interested. In assessing

Persuasive speeches need strong evidence to convince skeptical listeners. Research shows that evidence will be most convincing when it is stated in specific rather than general terms.

the current state of airline safety, for example, they are more likely to be persuaded by testimony from impartial aviation experts than from the president of American Airlines. If you wish to be persuasive, rely on evidence from objective, nonpartisan sources.

Make Clear the Point of Your Evidence

When speaking to persuade, you use evidence to prove a point. Yet you would be surprised how many novice speakers present their evidence without making clear the point it is supposed to prove. A number of studies have shown that you cannot count on listeners to draw, on their own, the conclusion you want them to reach.[8] When using evidence, be sure listeners understand the point you are trying to make.

Notice, for example, how the speaker in Video 17.3 in the online Media Library for this chapter drives home the point of his evidence about the rate of motorcycle fatalities in comparison to automobile fatalities:

connect

View this excerpt from "Saving Lives with Motorcycle Helmets" in the online Media Library for this chapter (Video 17.3).

> According to the Governors Highway Safety Association, last year there were more than 5,000 motorcycle deaths in the United States. That's a jump of 9 percent from the previous year. If 5,000 people dead doesn't sound like a lot, consider this: Over the past 15 years, motorcycle deaths have doubled, while automobile deaths have dropped by 23 percent. Here in Wisconsin alone, 114 people died last year. That's a 34 percent increase from the year before.
>
> Clearly, we can do more to solve the problem. Here in Wisconsin, there's an easy solution: We can save lives simply by requiring that all motorcyclists wear a helmet.

Evidence is one element of what Aristotle referred to as *logos*—the logical appeal of a speaker. The other major element of logos is reasoning, which works in combination with evidence to help make a speaker's claims persuasive.

logos

The name used by Aristotle for the logical appeal of a speaker. The two major elements of logos are evidence and reasoning.

checklist

Evidence

YES	NO	
☐	☐	1. Are all my major claims supported by evidence?
☐	☐	2. Do I use sufficient evidence to convince my audience of my claims?
☐	☐	3. Is my evidence stated in specific rather than general terms?
☐	☐	4. Do I use evidence that is new to my audience?
☐	☐	5. Is my evidence from credible, unbiased sources?
☐	☐	6. Do I identify the sources of my evidence?
☐	☐	7. Is my evidence clearly linked to each point that it is meant to prove?
☐	☐	8. Do I provide evidence to answer possible objections the audience may have to my position?

Reasoning

The story is told about Hack Wilson, a hard-hitting outfielder for the Brooklyn Dodgers baseball team in the 1930s.[9] Wilson was a great player, but he had a fondness for the good life. His drinking exploits were legendary. He was known to spend the entire night on the town, stagger into the team's hotel at the break of dawn, grab a couple hours sleep, and get to the ballpark just in time for the afternoon game.

This greatly distressed Max Carey, Wilson's manager. At the next team meeting, Carey spent much time explaining the evils of drink. To prove his point, he stood beside a table on which he had placed two glasses and a plate of live angleworms. One glass was filled with water, the other with gin—Wilson's favorite beverage. With a flourish Carey dropped a worm into the glass of water. It wriggled happily. Next Carey plunged the same worm into the gin. It promptly stiffened and expired.

A murmur ran through the room, and some players were obviously impressed. But not Wilson. He didn't even seem interested. Carey waited a little, hoping for some delayed reaction from his wayward slugger. When none came, he prodded, "Do you follow my reasoning, Wilson?"

"Sure, skipper," answered Wilson. "It proves that if you drink gin, you'll never get worms!"

And what does this story prove? No matter how strong your evidence, you will not be persuasive unless listeners grasp your reasoning.

Reasoning is the process of drawing a conclusion based on evidence. Sometimes we reason well—as when we conclude that ice particles forming

Reasoning is an important part of persuasive speaking. In a legal trial, for example, neither the prosecution nor the defense is likely to sway the jury unless their reasoning is clear and convincing.

on the trees may mean the roads will be slippery. Other times we reason less effectively—as when we conclude that spilling salt will bring bad luck. Most superstitions are actually no more than instances of faulty reasoning.

Reasoning in public speaking is an extension of reasoning in other aspects of life. As a public speaker, you have two major concerns with respect to reasoning. First, you must make sure your own reasoning is sound. Second, you must try to get listeners to agree with your reasoning. Let us look, then, at four basic methods of reasoning and how to use them in your speeches.

reasoning

The process of drawing a conclusion on the basis of evidence.

REASONING FROM SPECIFIC INSTANCES

When you reason from specific instances, you progress from a number of particular facts to a general conclusion.[10] For example:

reasoning from specific instances

Reasoning that moves from particular facts to a general conclusion.

Fact 1: My physical education course last term was easy.

Fact 2: My roommate's physical education course was easy.

Fact 3: My brother's physical education course was easy.

Conclusion: Physical education courses are easy.

As this example suggests, we use reasoning from specific instances daily, although we probably don't realize it. Think for a moment of all the general conclusions that arise in conversation: Politicians are corrupt. Professors are bookish. Dorm food is awful. Where do such conclusions come from? They come from observing particular politicians, professors, dormitories, and so on.

The same thing happens in public speaking. The speaker who concludes that unethical banking practices are common in the United States because several major banks have been guilty of fraud in recent years is reasoning from specific instances. So is the speaker who argues that anti-Semitism is increasing on college campuses because there have been a number of attacks on Jewish students and symbols at schools across the nation.

Such conclusions are never foolproof. No matter how many specific instances you give (and you can give only a few in a speech), it is always possible that an exception exists. Throughout the ages people observed countless white swans in Europe without seeing any of a different color. It seemed an undeniable fact that all swans were white. Then, in the 19th century, black swans were discovered in Australia![11]

When you reason from specific instances, beware of jumping to conclusions on the basis of insufficient evidence. Make sure your sample of specific instances is large enough to justify your conclusion.

Also make sure the instances you present are fair, unbiased, and representative. (Are three physical education courses *enough* to conclude that physical education courses in general are easy? Are the three courses *typical* of most physical education courses?)

Finally, reinforce your argument with statistics or testimony. Because you can never give enough specific instances in a speech to make your conclusion irrefutable, you should supplement them with testimony or statistics demonstrating that the instances are representative.

REASONING FROM PRINCIPLE

Reasoning from principle is the opposite of reasoning from specific instances. It moves from the general to the specific.[12] When you reason from principle, you progress from a general principle to a specific conclusion. We are all familiar with this kind of reasoning from statements such as the following:

1. All people are mortal.
2. Socrates is a person.
3. Therefore, Socrates is mortal.

This is a classic example of reasoning from principle. You begin with a general statement ("All people are mortal"), move to a minor premise ("Socrates is a person"), and end with a specific conclusion ("Socrates is mortal").

reasoning from principle

Reasoning that moves from a general principle to a specific conclusion.

Speakers often use reasoning from principle when trying to persuade an audience. One of the clearest examples from American history is Susan B. Anthony's famous speech "Is It a Crime for a U.S. Citizen to Vote?" Delivered on numerous occasions in 1872 and 1873, at a time when women were legally barred from voting, Anthony's speech reasoned along the following lines:

1. The United States Constitution guarantees all U.S. citizens the right to vote.
2. Women are U.S. citizens.
3. Therefore, the United States Constitution guarantees women the right to vote.

This argument progresses from a general principle ("The United States Constitution guarantees all U.S. citizens the right to vote") through a minor premise ("Women are U.S. citizens") to a conclusion ("Therefore, the United States Constitution guarantees women the right to vote").

When you use reasoning from principle in a speech, pay special attention to your general principle. Will listeners accept it without evidence? If not, give evidence to support it before moving to your minor premise. You may also need to support your minor premise with evidence. When both the general principle and the minor premise are soundly based, your audience will be much more likely to accept your conclusion.

CAUSAL REASONING

There is a patch of ice on the sidewalk. You slip, fall, and break your arm. You reason as follows: "*Because* that patch of ice was there, I fell and broke my arm." This is an example of causal reasoning, in which someone tries to establish the relationship between causes and effects.

causal reasoning

Reasoning that seeks to establish the relationship between causes and effects.

As with reasoning from specific instances, we use causal reasoning daily. Something happens and we ask what caused it to happen. We want to know the causes of chronic fatigue syndrome, of the football team's latest defeat, of our roommate's peculiar habits. We also wonder about effects. We speculate about the consequences of chronic fatigue syndrome, of the star quarterback's leg injury, of telling our roommate that a change is needed.

As any scientist (or detective) will tell you, causal reasoning can be tricky. The relationship between causes and effects is not always clear. For example, the fact that one event happens after another does not mean that the first is the cause of the second. The closeness in time of the two events may be entirely coincidental. If a black cat crosses your path and five minutes later you fall and break your arm, you needn't blame your accident on the poor cat.

You also need to beware of assuming that events have only one cause. In fact, most events have several causes. What causes the economy to boom or bust? Interest rates? Gas prices? Tax policy? Labor costs? Consumer confidence? World affairs? *All* these factors—and others—affect the economy. When you use causal reasoning, be wary of the temptation to attribute complex events to single causes.

ANALOGICAL REASONING

When arguing from analogy, a speaker compares two similar cases and infers that what is true for one case is also true for the other: For example:

analogical reasoning

Reasoning in which a speaker compares two similar cases and infers that what is true for the first case is also true for the second.

> If you're good at tennis, you will probably be good at Ping-Pong.

Although playing Ping-Pong is not exactly the same as playing tennis, the two are close enough that the speaker is on firm ground in concluding that being skilled at one increases the odds of being skilled at the other.

Analogical reasoning is used frequently in persuasive speeches—especially when the speaker is dealing with a question of policy. When arguing for a new policy, you should find out whether it has been tried elsewhere. You may be able to claim that your policy will work because it has worked in like circumstances. Here is how one speaker used reasoning from analogy to support his claim that controlling handguns will reduce violent crime in the United States:

> Will my policy work? The experience of foreign countries suggests it will. In England, guns are tightly regulated; even the police are unarmed, and the murder rate is trivial by American standards. Japan has even fewer guns than England, and its crime rate is lower than England's. On the basis of these comparisons, we can conclude that restricting the ownership of guns will reduce crime and murder rates in America.

By the same token, if you argue against a change in policy, you should check whether the proposed policy—or something like it—has been implemented elsewhere. Here, too, you may be able to support your case by reasoning from analogy—as did one speaker who opposed gun control:

> Advocates of gun control point to foreign countries such as England and Japan to prove their case. But the key to low personal violence in these and other countries is the peaceful character of the people, not gun control laws. Switzerland, for example, has a militia system; more than 1 million automatic rifles and military pistols are sitting at this moment in Swiss homes. Yet Switzerland's murder rate is only 8 percent of ours. In other words, cultural factors are more important than gun control when it comes to violent crime.

As these examples illustrate, argument from analogy can be used on both sides of an issue. You are more likely to persuade your audience if the analogy shows a truly parallel situation.

FALLACIES

fallacy

An error in reasoning.

A fallacy is an error in reasoning. As a speaker, you need to avoid fallacies in your speeches. As a listener, you need to be alert to fallacies in the speeches you hear.

Logicians have identified more than 125 different fallacies. Here we look at 10 that you should guard against.

Hasty Generalization

hasty generalization

A fallacy in which a speaker jumps to a general conclusion on the basis of insufficient evidence.

Hasty generalization is the most common fallacy in reasoning from specific instances. It occurs when a speaker jumps to a conclusion on the basis of too few cases or on the basis of atypical cases. For example:

> Throughout American history, military leaders have always made excellent presidents. Look at the examples of George Washington, Andrew Jackson, and Dwight Eisenhower.

Washington, Jackson, and Eisenhower are widely regarded as outstanding chief executives, but are these examples enough to conclude that military leaders *always* make excellent presidents? In fact, they are not. James Buchanan and Ulysses S. Grant were both highly decorated military leaders during the 19th century, but they are usually rated among the nation's worst presidents. An accurate statement would be:

> Throughout American history, military leaders have sometimes made excellent presidents—as with Washington, Jackson, and Eisenhower.

This statement is factually correct and avoids the fallacy of hasty generalization.

False Cause

false cause

A fallacy in which a speaker mistakenly assumes that because one event follows another, the first event is the cause of the second.

The fallacy of false cause is often known by its Latin name, *post hoc, ergo propter hoc,* which means "after this, therefore because of this." In other words, the fact that one event occurs after another does not mean that the first is the cause of the second. The closeness in time of the two events may be entirely coincidental—as in this case:

In addition to using evidence to support their ideas, effective persuasive speakers rely on research to help them avoid fallacies that may undermine their credibility and persuasiveness.

When a team from the NFC wins the Super Bowl, economic growth during the next year is stronger than when a team from the AFC wins the Super Bowl. Therefore, if we want economic growth, we should root for a team from the NFC to win this year's Super Bowl.

There may be a slight correlation between economic growth and which conference wins the Super Bowl, but there is no *causal* connection between the two events. Whether the American economy rises or falls is not dependent on the outcome of the Super Bowl.

Invalid Analogy

As we saw on 343–344, when reasoning from analogy, a speaker concludes that what is true in one case is also true in another. An invalid analogy occurs when the two cases being compared are not essentially alike. For example:

invalid analogy

An analogy in which the two cases being compared are not essentially alike.

Employees are like nails. Just as nails must be hit on the head to get them to work, so must employees.

This statement is obviously fallacious. No one in his or her right mind can seriously think that employees, which are human beings, can be compared with inanimate objects such as nails.

But what about the following statement:

In Great Britain, the general election campaign for prime minister lasts less than three weeks. Surely we can do the same with the U.S. presidential election.

At first glance, this analogy may seem perfectly sound. But are the British and American political systems enough alike to warrant the conclusion? Not really. The United States is much larger than Great Britain and its party system operates much differently. As a result, the factors that allow Great Britain to conduct campaigns for prime minister in less than three weeks are not present in the United States. The analogy is not valid.

As this example suggests, determining whether an analogy is valid or invalid is not always easy, but doing so is important for speakers and listeners alike.

Bandwagon

bandwagon

A fallacy which assumes that because something is popular, it is therefore good, correct, or desirable.

How often have you heard someone say, "It's a great idea—everyone agrees with it"? This is a classic example of the bandwagon fallacy, which assumes that because something is popular, it is therefore good, correct, or desirable.

Much advertising is based on the bandwagon fallacy. The fact that more people use Tylenol than Advil does not prove that Tylenol is a better painkiller. Tylenol's popularity could be due to clever marketing. The question of which product does a better job reducing pain is a medical issue that has nothing to do with popularity.

The bandwagon fallacy is also evident in political speeches. Consider the following statement:

> The governor must be correct in his approach to social policy; after all, the polls show that 60 percent of the people support him.

This statement is fallacious because popular opinion cannot be taken as proof that an idea is right or wrong. Remember, "everyone" used to believe that the world is flat and that space flight is impossible.

Red Herring

red herring

A fallacy that introduces an irrelevant issue to divert attention from the subject under discussion.

The name of this fallacy comes from an old trick used by farmers in England to keep fox hunters and their hounds from galloping through the crops. By dragging a smoked herring with a strong odor along the edge of their fields, the farmers could throw the dogs off track by destroying the scent of the fox.

A speaker who uses a red herring introduces an irrelevant issue in order to divert attention from the subject under discussion. For instance:

> How dare my opponents accuse me of political corruption at a time when we are working to improve the quality of life for all people in the United States.

What does the speaker's concern about the quality of life in the United States have to do with whether he or she is guilty of political corruption? Nothing! It is a red herring used to divert attention away from the real issue.

Ad Hominem

ad hominem

A fallacy that attacks the person rather than dealing with the real issue in dispute.

Latin for "against the man," *ad hominem* refers to the fallacy of attacking the person rather than dealing with the real issue in dispute. For instance:

> The head of the commerce commission has a number of interesting economic proposals, but let's not forget that she comes from a very wealthy family.

By impugning the commissioner's family background rather than dealing with the substance of her economic proposals, the speaker is engaging in an *ad hominem* attack.

Sometimes, of course, a person's character or integrity can be a legitimate issue—as in the case of a police chief who violates the law or a corporate president who swindles stockholders. In such cases, a speaker might well raise questions about the person without being guilty of the *ad hominem* fallacy.

Either-Or

Sometimes referred to as a false dilemma, the either-or fallacy forces listeners to choose between two alternatives when more than two alternatives exist. For example:

either-or

A fallacy that forces listeners to choose between two alternatives when more than two alternatives exist.

> The government must either raise taxes or eliminate services for the poor.

This statement oversimplifies a complex issue by reducing it to a simple either-or choice. Is it true that the *only* choices are to raise taxes or to eliminate services for the poor? A careful listener might ask, "What about cutting the administrative cost of government or eliminating pork-barrel projects instead?"

You will be more persuasive as a speaker and more perceptive as a listener if you are alert to the either-or fallacy.

Slippery Slope

The slippery slope fallacy takes its name from the image of a boulder rolling uncontrollably down a steep hill. Once the boulder gets started, it can't be stopped until it reaches the bottom.

slippery slope

A fallacy which assumes that taking a first step will lead to subsequent steps that cannot be prevented.

A speaker who commits the slippery slope fallacy assumes that taking a first step will lead inevitably to a second step and so on down the slope to disaster—as in the following example:

> Now that the TSA is allowed to use full body scanners and invasive pat-downs before letting us through security, it's only a matter of time before they strip-search every man, woman, and child who wants to fly on a plane.

If a speaker claims that taking a first step will lead inevitably to a series of disastrous later steps, he or she needs to provide evidence or reasoning to support the claim. To assume that all the later steps will occur without proving that they will is to commit the slippery slope fallacy.

Appeal to Tradition

Appeal to tradition is fallacious when it assumes that something old is *automatically* better than something new. For example:

appeal to tradition

A fallacy which assumes that something old is automatically better than something new.

> I don't see any reason to abolish the electoral college. It has been around since the adoption of the U.S. Constitution in 1787, and we should keep it as long as the United States continues to exist.

There are good arguments on both sides of the debate over abolishing the electoral college. However, to conclude that the electoral college should be kept forever solely because it has always been a part of the U.S. Constitution commits the fallacy of appeal to tradition.

Just because a practice, an institution, or an idea is old does not automatically make it better. Its value should be based on its contributions to society, not on its age. If tradition were the sole measure of value, we would still have slavery, women would not be able to vote, and people would undergo surgery without anesthesia.

Using public speaking in your CAREER

As the service manager for a local home improvement company, you have been pleased to see your company expand its size and scope, but you don't want that growth to come at the expense of customer service. In particular, you're worried about losing touch with one of the company's key demographics—women, who make up 55 percent of your customer base. To prevent this from happening, you have developed a plan for a range of personalized services targeted at women, including one-on-one teaching of do-it-yourself skills and free in-home consultations.

When you present your plan at a meeting of the company's management team, you listen as one executive argues in opposition. Among his points are the following: (1) If your plan is adopted, customers will expect more and more special services and eventually will demand free installation of flooring and carpeting; (2) Because a majority of the management team opposes your plan, it must not be a good idea; (3) One of your competitors tried a customer service plan specifically for women, but it did not succeed; therefore, your plan is doomed to failure.

In your response to the executive, you will point out the fallacy in each of his points. What are those fallacies?

Appeal to Novelty

appeal to novelty

A fallacy which assumes that something new is automatically better than something old.

The fallacy of appeal to novelty is the opposite of appeal to tradition. Appeal to novelty assumes that because something is new, it is therefore superior to something that is older. For example:

> Our church should adopt the 2011 New International Version of the Bible because it is 400 years newer than the King James Version.

The fact that the New International Version of the Bible is newer than the King James Version (completed in 1611), does not *automatically* make it better. There are many reasons why a church might prefer the New International Version, but the speaker should *explain* those reasons, rather than assuming that one version is better than another simply because it is new.

Advertisers often commit the fallacy of appeal to novelty. They tout their latest products as "new and improved," yet we know from experience that new does not always mean improved. As always, we need to look carefully at the claim and make sure it is based on sound reasoning.[13]

Appealing to Emotions

Effective persuasion often requires emotional appeal. As the Roman rhetorician Quintilian stated, "It is feeling and force of imagination that make us eloquent."[14] By adding "feeling" and the "force of imagination" to your logical arguments, you can become a more compelling persuasive speaker.

WHAT ARE EMOTIONAL APPEALS?

Emotional appeals—what Aristotle referred to as *pathos*—are intended to make listeners feel sad, angry, guilty, afraid, happy, proud, sympathetic, reverent, or the like. These are often appropriate reactions when the question is one of value or policy. As George Campbell wrote in his *Philosophy of Rhetoric,* "When persuasion is the end, passion also must be engaged."[15]

pathos

The name used by Aristotle for what modern students of communication refer to as emotional appeal.

Below is a list of some of the emotions evoked most often by public speakers. Following each emotion are a few examples of subjects that might stir that emotion:

- *Fear*—of serious illness, of natural disasters, of sexual assault, of personal rejection, of economic hardship.
- *Compassion*—for war refugees, for battered women, for neglected animals, for starving children, for victims of AIDS.
- *Pride*—in one's country, in one's family, in one's school, in one's ethnic heritage, in one's personal accomplishments.
- *Anger*—at terrorists and their supporters, at business leaders who act unethically, at members of Congress who abuse the public trust, at landlords who exploit student tenants, at vandals and thieves.
- *Guilt*—about not helping people less fortunate than ourselves, about not considering the rights of others, about not doing one's best.
- *Reverence*—for an admired person, for traditions and institutions, for one's deity.

There are many other emotions and many other subjects that might stir them. However, this brief sample should give you an idea of the kinds of emotional appeals you might use to enhance the message of your persuasive speech.

Emotional appeals often make a persuasive speech more compelling. Such appeals should always be used ethically and should not be substituted for facts and logic.

GENERATING EMOTIONAL APPEAL

Use Emotional Language

As we saw in Chapter 12, one way to generate emotional appeal is to use emotion-laden words. Here, for instance, is part of the conclusion from a student speech about the challenges and rewards of working as a volunteer with Teach for America:

> The promise of America sparkles in the eyes of every child. Their dreams are the glittering dreams of America. When those dreams are dashed, when innocent hopes are betrayed, so are the dreams and hopes of the entire nation. It is our duty—to me, it is a sacred duty—to give all children the chance to learn and grow, to share equally in the American dream of freedom, justice, and opportunity.

The underlined words and phrases have strong emotional power, and in this case they produced the desired effect. Be aware, however, that packing too many emotionally charged words into one part of a speech can call attention to the emotional language itself and undermine its impact. The emotion rests in your audience, not in your words. Even the coldest facts can touch off an emotional response if they strike the right chords in a listener.

Develop Vivid Examples

Often a better approach than relying on emotionally charged language is to let emotional appeal grow naturally out of the content of your speech. The most effective way to do this is with vivid, richly textured examples that pull listeners into the speech.

Here is how one speaker used a vivid example for emotional appeal. She was speaking about the malaria epidemic in Africa. Here is what she might have said, stripping the content of emotional appeal:

> Malaria is one of the biggest problems facing Africa. Many die from it every day. If the rest of the world doesn't help, the malaria epidemic will only get worse.

connect

View this excerpt from "The Tragedy of Malaria" in the online Media Library for this chapter (Video 17.4).

What she actually said went something like this:

> Nathan was only five years old when the fever struck him. At first, no one knew what was wrong. No one knew that parasites inside his body had infected his red blood cells. No one knew those cells were clumping together, choking the flow of blood through his body and damaging his vital organs. No one knew his kidneys would soon fail and seizures would begin. No one knew he would wind up in a coma.
>
> The parasites in Nathan's body came from a mosquito bite, a bite that gave him malaria. And Nathan is not alone. The World Health Organization tells us the horrible truth: In Africa, a child dies from malaria every 30 seconds.

People who listen to a speech like that will not soon forget it. They may well be moved to action—as the speaker intends. The first speech, however, is not nearly as compelling. Listeners may well nod their heads, think to themselves "good idea"—and then forget about it. The story of Nathan and his tragic fate gives the second speech emotional impact and brings it home to listeners in personal terms.

Speak with Sincerity and Conviction

Ronald Reagan was one of the most effective speakers in U.S. history. Even people who disagreed with his political views often found him irresistible. Why? Partly because he seemed to speak with great sincerity and conviction.

What was true for Reagan is true for you as well. The strongest source of emotional power is your conviction and sincerity. All your emotion-laden words and examples are but empty trappings unless *you* feel the emotion yourself. And if you do, your emotion will communicate itself to the audience through everything you say and do—not only through your words, but also through your tone of voice, rate of speech, gestures, and facial expressions.

ETHICS AND EMOTIONAL APPEAL

Much has been written about the ethics of emotional appeal in speechmaking. Some people have taken the extreme position that ethical speakers should avoid emotional appeal entirely. To support this view, they point to speakers who have used emotional appeal to fan the flames of hatred, bigotry, and fanaticism.

There is no question that emotional appeals can be abused by unscrupulous speakers for detestable causes. But emotional appeals can also be wielded by honorable speakers for noble causes—by Winston Churchill to rouse the world against Adolf Hitler and the forces of Nazism, by Martin Luther King to call for racial justice. Few people would question the ethics of emotional appeal in these instances.

Nor is it always possible to draw a sharp line between reason and emotional appeal. Think back to the story of Nathan, the five-year-old boy who was infected with malaria. The story certainly has strong emotional appeal. But is there anything unreasonable about it? Or is it irrational for listeners to respond to it by donating to anti-malarial causes? By the same token, is it illogical to be compassionate for victims of natural disasters? Angered by corporate wrongdoing? Fearful about cutbacks in student aid? Reason and emotion often work hand in hand.

Emotional language and vivid examples can help generate emotional appeal, but neither will be effective unless the speaker talks with genuine sincerity and conviction.

One key to using emotional appeal ethically is to make sure it is appropriate to the speech topic. If you want to move listeners to act on a question of policy, emotional appeals are not only legitimate but perhaps necessary. If you want listeners to do something as a result of your speech, you will probably need to appeal to their hearts as well as to their heads.

On the other hand, emotional appeals are usually inappropriate in a persuasive speech on a question of fact. Here you should deal only in specific information and logic. Suppose someone charges your state governor with illegal campaign activities. If you respond by saying "I'm sure the charge is false because I have always admired the governor," or "I'm sure the charge is true because I have always disliked the governor," then you are guilty of applying emotional criteria to a purely factual question.

Even when trying to move listeners to action, you should never substitute emotional appeals for evidence and reasoning. You should *always* build your persuasive speech on a firm foundation of facts and logic. This is important not just for ethical reasons, but for practical ones as well. Unless you prove your case, careful listeners will not be stirred by your emotional appeals. You need to build a good case based on reason *and* kindle the emotions of your audience.[16]

When you use emotional appeal, keep in mind the guidelines for ethical speechmaking discussed in Chapter 2. Make sure your goals are ethically sound, that you are honest in what you say, and that you avoid name-calling and other forms of abusive language. In using emotional appeal, as in other respects, your classroom speeches will offer a good testing ground for questions of ethical responsibility.

Sample Speech with Commentary

connect

View "The Living-Wage Solution" in the online Media Library for this chapter (Video 17.5).

The following persuasive speech on a question of policy is organized in problem-solution order. As you read the speech, notice how it employs the methods of persuasion discussed in this chapter. Pay special attention to the speaker's evidence, which she uses not only to establish the existence of a serious problem but also to explain her plan and to document its practicality.

In addition, the speech shows how visual aids can be used in a persuasive presentation to help an audience keep track of complex data and arguments. You can view it in the online Media Library for this chapter.

The Living-Wage Solution

COMMENTARY

The speaker opens with an extended example that gains attention and draws the audience into the speech.

SPEECH

José Morales was sleeping on cardboard boxes in a garage in Compton, California. Before the sun came up, he would walk to a nearby bus stop, where he would ride the bus for two hours to Los Angeles International Airport, where he worked as a janitor. On two occasions, he was mugged while waiting for the bus. Working 40 hours a week for minimum wage, this was the best he could do.

The speaker completes her opening story and identifies the topic of her speech.

But then José's situation improved drastically. As Robert Pollin, an economist at the University of Massachusetts, reports, José received health insurance and a 36 percent raise. He had enough money to rent his own apartment and to buy a car. It all happened because José started to receive the living wage.

In this paragraph, the speaker defines the living wage and contrasts it with the minimum wage. As you can see on the video, she uses PowerPoint to help clarify her points.

What is the living wage, you ask? Well, it's not the same as the minimum wage. The minimum wage is set by Congress and is the same in every part of the country. The living wage goes beyond the minimum wage. As the *Wall Street Journal* reported in August 2013, the living wage is tied to the local cost of living and can vary from location to location. Its purpose is to help workers and their families meet the most basic standard of living, even when that standard of living is higher than the minimum wage.

Here the speaker establishes her credibility by noting that her conclusions are supported by "numerous economists and public-policy researchers."

I first heard about the living wage last semester in my econ class. After researching it for this speech, I've come to the same conclusion as numerous economists and public-policy researchers. The living wage can help the working poor without adversely affecting businesses or the health of the economy.

The speaker ends her introduction with a concise statement of her central idea and a preview of the main points she will discuss in the body.

That's why we need to pass federal legislation mandating a living wage—a wage that can help people secure the basic necessities of life. So let's first look at the difficulties faced by the working poor, and then we'll look at the living-wage solution.

This speech is organized in problem-solution order. Here the speaker starts the problem main point by documenting the number of working poor in the United States. She cites a combination of statistics and uses PowerPoint to help listeners follow along as she moves from figure to figure.

Poverty remains a significant problem in the United States in part because wages have not kept up with the cost of living. According to a recent study by the Bureau of Labor Statistics, more than 46 million Americans live in poverty. Of these 46 million, 10 million are referred to as the "working poor": people who are employed at least 27 weeks a year and who are still stuck in poverty. Of these 10 million people, half—5 million—are employed full time. They work 40 hours a week, 52 weeks a year, but they still can't make ends meet.

The speaker explains why the current minimum wage is inadequate to keep a family above the poverty line.

How can that be? It happens in part because of the federal minimum wage. Since 2009, the minimum wage has been $7.25 an hour. If you calculate that, someone working full time would earn just over $15,000 a year. For an individual, that's just above the poverty line. The problem comes when there are two-, three-, or four-person households—as with a single mother trying to squeak by. It's almost impossible to raise a family on $15,000 a year.

Pointing to the ineptitude of Congress helps the audience understand why the minimum wage lags behind the cost of living.

Another problem is that the federal minimum wage doesn't change until Congress changes it—and we all know how long it can take for Congress to do anything. In fact, it took Congress more than 10 years to raise the minimum wage from its previous $5.25 to its current rate of $7.25. As a result, millions of workers were still earning in 2008 what they had earned in 1998.

The speaker ends her first main point with expert testimony that sums up the problem and emphasizes the need for action.

The result was "a lost decade for wage growth," according to *The State of Working America*, published in 2012 by Cornell University Press. The same book predicts another lost decade if we don't take action soon.

A question leads into the solution main point, in which the speaker lays out a plan, shows its practicality, and responds to potential objections.

So what can we do? How can we help make sure that people who work full time earn enough money to lift themselves and their families above the poverty level? One way is to implement a federally mandated living wage.

The speaker provides background on living wage plans in the United States. Such plans, she notes, currently cover only 1 percent of workers—which is why a national living wage law is needed to cover everyone who works full time.

The first city in America to institute a living wage was Baltimore, in 1994. Since then, the living-wage movement has spread to more than 140 jurisdictions. However, as David Neumark, Matthew Thompson, and Leslie Koyle reported in a 2012 issue of the *Journal of Labor Policy*, most living-wage laws cover only people who work for companies with government contracts. At best only 1 percent of workers in a city receive the living wage. It's time to cover everyone who works full time—and to do so with a national living-wage law.

The speaker's plan consists of two parts. Here she discusses the living-wage calculator.

Here's how such a law would work. First, we would calculate the living wage for every county in the United States. To do that, we'd use the living-wage calculator created by Amy Glasmeier, a professor of Urban Studies and Planning at MIT.

The speaker does an excellent job of explaining complex ideas clearly and concisely. Once again, she uses visual aids to highlight key points.

Based on this calculator, the living wage in Chicago, my hometown, for this year would be $10.48 per hour. In Dallas, it would be $9.29. In New York, it would be $12.75. As you can see, there is large variation in the cost of living across different parts of the country. A national living wage would account for these variations.

The second part of the speaker's plan ties the living wage to the cost of living.

Second, we would tie the living wage to the Consumer Price Index. The Consumer Price Index tracks the price of goods and services in different parts of the country. As the Consumer Price Index increases, the living wage would increase at the same rate.

As you can see from the video, the speaker communicates with excellent vocal variety and strong eye contact.

In Chicago, the Consumer Price Index rose by 2 percent last year. The living wage in that city would then go from $10.48 an hour to $10.69 an hour. And it would cover everyone who works full time, whether they work for the government or in the private sector. In this way, we can ensure that wages for everyone keep up with the cost of living.

Responding to potential objections, which the speaker does in this and the following paragraph, is a crucial part of persuasive speaking. Like the rest of the speech, this section is crisply organized and uses signposts to help the audience keep track of the speaker's ideas.

As you might expect, there is opposition to instituting a living-wage policy. Those who oppose the living wage offer two main arguments. First, they argue that the living wage would be too costly for businesses. But that's not what Jeff Thompson and Jeff Chapman, researchers at the Economic Policy Institute, found. After surveying existing living-wage laws, they found that the increased cost of wages is offset by higher productivity and lower employee turnover. Happier workers mean stronger businesses.

Here, as elsewhere, the speaker supports her argument with expert testimony. Notice how clearly she identifies her source and states his qualifications. This is a fine example of how to work oral citations into a speech.

The second argument of critics is that the living wage will lead to fewer jobs. But again the research doesn't bear this out. A 2011 study in *Economic Development Quarterly* by T. William Lester, a professor at the University of North Carolina, found that living-wage laws do not have a large negative impact on employment. In a 2012 study, Lester, who specializes in labor economics, found that living-wage laws can actually "create jobs of higher quality." In addition to being good for workers, a living-wage law can benefit businesses and the economy in general.

The speaker signals the beginning of her conclusion and restates her central idea.

In conclusion, the time has come to pay American workers a wage that will keep up with the cost of living. We need a federally mandated living wage. In a time of massive corporate profits and skyrocketing executive pay, those at the bottom of society deserve to advance along with those at the top.

Returning to the example cited in the introduction gives the speech a sense of psychological unity. The quotation from José Morales adds emotional appeal and leads into the strong closing line.

Those like José Morales, who I mentioned at the start of my speech, deserve a better future. "Everyone thinks that working here at the airport we must earn a lot of money," Morales says. "It's not true, but at least now with the living wage we can hold our heads up high." And that's something everyone working a full-time job should be able to say.

Summary

Listeners accept a speaker's ideas for one or more of four reasons—because they perceive the speaker as having high credibility, because they are won over by the speaker's evidence, because they are convinced by the speaker's reasoning, or because they are moved by the speaker's emotional appeals.

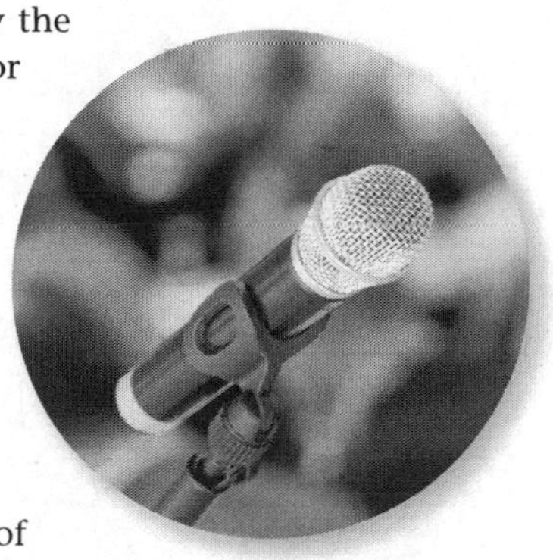

Credibility is affected by many factors, but the two most important are competence and character. The more favorably listeners view a speaker's competence and character, the more likely they are to accept her or his ideas. Although credibility is partly a matter of reputation, you can enhance your credibility during a speech by establishing common ground with your listeners, by letting them know why you are qualified to speak on the topic, and by presenting your ideas fluently and expressively.

If you hope to be persuasive, you must also support your views with evidence—examples, statistics, and testimony. Regardless of what kind of evidence you use, it will be more persuasive if it is new to the audience, stated in specific rather than general terms, and from credible sources. Your evidence will also be more persuasive if you state explicitly the point it is supposed to prove.

No matter how strong your evidence, you will not be persuasive unless listeners agree with your reasoning. In reasoning from specific instances, you move from a number of particular facts to a general conclusion. Reasoning from principle is the reverse—you move from a general principle to a particular conclusion. When you use causal reasoning, you try to establish a relationship between causes and effects. In analogical reasoning, you compare two cases and infer that what is true for one is also true for the other.

Whatever kind of reasoning you use, avoid fallacies such as hasty generalization, false cause, invalid analogy, appeal to tradition, and appeal to novelty. You should also be on guard against the red herring, slippery slope, bandwagon, *ad hominem,* and either-or fallacies.

Finally, you can persuade your listeners by appealing to their emotions. One way to generate emotional appeal is by using emotion-laden language. Another is to develop vivid, richly textured examples. Neither, however, will be effective unless you feel the emotion yourself and communicate it by speaking with sincerity and conviction.

As with other methods of persuasion, your use of emotional appeal should be guided by a firm ethical rudder. Although emotional appeals are usually inappropriate in speeches on questions of fact, they are legitimate—and often necessary—in speeches that seek immediate action on questions of policy. Even when trying to move listeners to action, however, you should never substitute emotional appeals for evidence and reasoning.

Key Terms

ethos (332)
credibility (333)
initial credibility (333)
derived credibility (333)
terminal credibility (333)
creating common ground (335)
evidence (336)
logos (339)
reasoning (341)
reasoning from specific instances (341)
reasoning from principle (342)
causal reasoning (343)
analogical reasoning (343)
fallacy (344)
hasty generalization (344)
false cause (344)
invalid analogy (345)
bandwagon (346)
red herring (346)
ad hominem (346)
either-or (347)
slippery slope (347)
appeal to tradition (347)
appeal to novelty (348)
pathos (349)

Review Questions

After reading this chapter, you should be able to answer the following questions:

1. What is credibility? What two factors exert the most influence on an audience's perception of a speaker's credibility?
2. What are the differences among initial credibility, derived credibility, and terminal credibility?
3. What are three ways you can enhance your credibility during your speeches?
4. What is evidence? Why do persuasive speakers need to use evidence?
5. What are four tips for using evidence effectively in a persuasive speech?
6. What is reasoning from specific instances? Why is it important to supplement reasoning from specific instances with testimony or statistics?
7. What is reasoning from principle? How is it different from reasoning from specific instances?
8. What is causal reasoning? Why is the relationship between causes and effects not always clear?
9. What is analogical reasoning? Why is analogical reasoning frequently used in persuasive speeches on questions of policy?
10. What are the ten logical fallacies discussed in this chapter?
11. What is the role of emotional appeal in persuasive speaking? Identify three methods you can use to generate emotional appeal in your speeches.

connect

For further review, go to the LearnSmart study module for this chapter.

Exercises for Critical Thinking

1. Research has shown that a speaker's initial credibility can have great impact on how the speaker's ideas are received by listeners. Research has also shown that a speaker's credibility will vary from topic to topic and audience to audience. In the left-hand column below is a list of well-known public figures. In the right-hand column is a list of potential speech topics. Assume that each speaker will be addressing your speech class.

   For each speaker, identify the topic in the right-hand column on which she or he would have the highest initial credibility for your class. Then explain how the speaker's initial credibility might be affected if the speaker were discussing the topic in the right-hand column directly across from her or his name.

Speaker	**Topic**
Mark Zuckerberg	The Art of Making Movies
Carrie Underwood	Life in the White House
Louis C. K.	The Future of Social Media
Michelle Obama	Trends in Country Music
Quentin Tarantino	The Challenges of Stand-Up Comedy

2. Identify the kind of reasoning used in each of the following statements. What weaknesses, if any, can you find in the reasoning of each?
   a. The U.S. Constitution prohibits cruel and unusual punishment. Life sentencing for juvenile offenders is cruel and unusual punishment. Therefore, life sentencing for juvenile offenders is contrary to the U.S. Constitution.
   b. We can see from its work all around the world that Women for Women International is a worthy charitable organization. It has helped women in Rwanda operate sewing machines and make clothing. It has given women in Kosovo the skills to operate businesses in their communities. It has shown women in the Democratic Republic of Congo how to create and market ceramics.
   c. According to a study by the National Institutes of Health, children with gluten sensitivity have a three times greater risk of developing scoliosis than do children without gluten sensitivity. We can see, then, that gluten sensitivity is the cause of scoliosis.
   d. Almost every industrialized nation in the world except for the United States has a national curriculum and national tests to help ensure that schools throughout the country are meeting high standards of education. If such a system can work elsewhere, it can work in the United States.
3. Over the years there has been much debate about the role of emotional appeal in public speaking. Do you believe it is ethical for public speakers to use emotional appeals when seeking to persuade an audience? Do you feel there are certain kinds of emotions to which an ethical speaker should not appeal? Why or why not? Be prepared to explain your ideas in class.
4. Analyze the sample speech with commentary at the end of this chapter ("The Living-Wage Solution," pages 352–355). Pay special attention to the speaker's credibility, evidence, reasoning, and emotional appeal. View the video of the speech in the online Media Library for this chapter so you can also assess the speaker's delivery and use of visual aids.

Speeches for Analysis and Discussion
Appendix

Medical Robots: From Science Fiction to Science Fact

Ramadan

The Dangers of Cell Phones

Phony Pharmaceuticals

The Wonderful World of Dr. Seuss

Elie Wiesel

connect

View "Medical Robots: From Science Fiction to Science Fact" in the online Media Library for this appendix (Video A.1).

MEDICAL ROBOTS: FROM SCIENCE FICTION TO SCIENCE FACT

One of the toughest tasks for an informative speaker, inside the classroom or out, is exploring a technical topic with a general audience. The speaker must find a way to communicate complex ideas so they will be clear and meaningful to people who are not specialists in the subject—and who may know very little about it in advance of the speech. Like many things, this looks easy when done well. But in fact it takes a great deal of thought, planning, and creativity.

All of these elements can be seen in the following classroom speech on medical robots. It is skillfully organized, contains well-chosen supporting materials, and is expressed in everyday language that is appropriate for a non-technical audience. The speaker's communication is also enhanced by his dynamic delivery and superb visual aids. Most notable is his creative use of PowerPoint in paragraph 5 to visualize for his audience the otherwise invisible "light whiskers" that help orderly robots navigate their way around hospital corridors. You can view the speech in the online Media Library for this appendix.

1 Maureen Schrader lay on the operating table at Saint Barnabas Medical Center in Livingston, New Jersey. Four mechanical arms moved with precision over her abdomen. In one arm was a high-definition camera. The other three contained small surgical instruments that made a five-centimeter incision just below her ribcage. It was a tiny opening, but it was big enough to put a new kidney into Maureen's body.

2 At no point during the surgery did the surgeon actually touch Maureen. In fact, he sat several feet away peering into a monitor and holding what looked like video game controls. But the work of his hands was digitally recorded and sent to the robotic arms, which mimicked his every movement. The robot became an extension of the surgeon, and together they transplanted the kidney.

3 Robots in the operating room are now a reality, and the next operation you or a family member undergoes may well involve a robot. But surgery is just one of the areas in which robots are changing modern medicine. As a pre-med student interested in becoming a surgeon, I've long been fascinated with medical robots. After researching the topic for this speech, I'd like to introduce you to the world of medical robots. We'll take a look at three kinds of robots in particular—orderly robots, remote-presence robots, and surgical robots. Let's begin with orderly robots.

4 Orderly robots help hospital staff accomplish routine tasks. Their primary function is to transport medicine, food, and lab supplies—and to do so without a human by their side. Here is one of the most popular orderly robots—the TUG, or tug robot—which, according to its manufacturer, can be found in more than 100 hospitals in the United States alone.

5 A September 2010 story in *Discovery News* explains how the robot works. Relying on a digital map of the hospital, the robot moves from room to room picking up and dropping off supplies. It senses people and obstacles by what are called "light whiskers"—invisible beams of sonar, infrared, and laser. These light whiskers are represented by the colored lines you see in this drawing. They constantly scan the environment to avoid collisions.

6 TUG robots can also communicate with one another about the most efficient route to a location given current hallway conditions. They are highly efficient and make fewer delivery errors than people. Mark Weigel, director of food services at Bethesda Memorial Hospital in Maryland, notes that the TUG robot "never argues with patients, takes no breaks, is always polite and always on time."

7 But orderly robots are not the only robots transforming modern medicine. Remote-presence robots allow a doctor to visit with a patient even when the doctor is not in the same room. "Remote presence" means that the doctor can be present with the patient even when the doctor is in a remote location.

8 Imagine you're sitting in a hospital room when in comes this—the RP-7. A 2009 story in *U.S. News & World Report* explains that physicians can pilot these robots from a laptop located anywhere in the hospital or in the world. A screen, camera, microphone, and speaker system—like the ones you see in this photograph—allow the doctor to interview the patient. Hospital staff can even attach medical devices such as electronic stethoscopes to the robot so the doctor can review a patient's vital signs.

9 According to a 2010 article in *Hospital Management*, the RP-7 is used in more than 250 U.S. hospitals and has performed more than 100,000 clinic sessions. They are particularly useful in hospitals with a high patient-to-doctor ratio.

10 In addition to orderly robots and remote-presence robots, a third kind of robot is transforming modern medicine. Surgical robots, like the kind I mentioned at the start of my speech, are increasingly being used in operating rooms around the world. Most popular is the one you see here—the da Vinci. According to a 2010 article in the *Miami Herald*, there are more than 1,400 da Vinci robots in hospitals worldwide, and they're used in more than 200,000 operations every year.

11 How does da Vinci work? Intuitive Surgical, maker of da Vinci, explains that the surgeon controls the robot from a remote terminal. You can see the terminal in this photograph. Usually, the terminal is a few feet away, as in the photograph. But it can be as far as thousands of miles away, so a surgeon in San Francisco can operate on a patient in Miami. The surgeon controls the robot's arms utilizing an interactive 3-D imaging system. But make no mistake: Even though the robot is touching the patient, the surgeon is always in control.

12 Doctors love da Vinci because it dramatically improves the quality of surgical procedures. Dr. Jeffrey Wolf, a head-and-neck surgeon at the University of Maryland Medical Center, states that da Vinci "gives us unprecedented access with really good 3-D visualization. . . . We're now able to perform intricate surgeries in a very small space with great dexterity." Da Vinci also reduces the risk of postsurgery complications, allows for faster healing, and helps patients leave the hospital sooner.

13 In conclusion, we've seen that medical robots are playing an increasingly important role in modern medicine. Whether they're running errands for hospital employees, helping physicians connect with their patients, or acting as a surgeon's eyes and hands, medical robots have brought the future into the present.

14 So the next time you find yourself at the hospital, keep your eyes peeled for the kind of technological marvels that used to exist only in science fiction. Medical robots are now a matter of science fact.

connect

View "Ramadan" in the online Media Library for this appendix (Video A.2).

RAMADAN

Choosing a topic based on one's personal experience can be an excellent decision, especially when the speaker supplements her or his existing knowledge with additional research—as in the following informative presentation on the Muslim holy month of Ramadan. As you read, notice how crisply the speech is organized, how the speaker relates her topic to the audience, and how she explains each aspect of Ramadan clearly and engagingly.

The speech also provides an instructive example of extemporaneous delivery, which you can see by watching the video in the online Media Library for this appendix. The speaker maintains strong eye contact with the audience and refers to her notes only as needed. Despite her nerves, she comes across as poised and confident. Her gestures are natural and spontaneous, and her voice conveys a strong sense of communication.

1 This past month, more than one billion people around the world skipped lunch every day. They ate no food of any kind and drank no liquid of any kind from sunup to sunset. They did this every day during the month, and they do the same thing every year. I myself did it. Why? Last month was a time for tending to the mind, the body, and the spirit. Last month was the Muslim holy month of Ramadan.

2 I'm sure most of you have heard of Ramadan, but you may not know a lot about it. Ramadan refers to the ninth month in the Islamic calendar, when Muslims fast from sunrise to sunset. But Ramadan is much more than a time of fasting. As Tariq Ramadan, author of *Western Muslims and the Future of Islam,* explains, Ramadan is a time when "believers strengthen their faith and spirituality while developing their sense of social justice."

3 As a practicing Muslim, I have observed Ramadan my entire life. My parents moved to the United States from Pakistan shortly before I was born, and I remember going to the mosque as a child and breaking my fast at the end of the day with my family and friends. Nowadays, I get together with other students here on campus.

4 The goal of my speech today is to inform you about Ramadan—specifically its history and practices. In the end, I hope you'll have a better understanding of this sacred time for Muslims in the United States and around the globe. Let's begin by exploring the history of Ramadan.

5 Ramadan can be traced back 1,400 years to the Middle East and the beginnings of the Quran. As explained in Karen Armstrong's *Islam: A Short History,* in 610 A.D. the Prophet Mohammed embarked on a spiritual journey through the desert in what is now Saudi Arabia. At one point in this journey, Muslims believe, Allah spoke to Mohammed through the archangel Gabriel—the same Gabriel of the Jewish and Christian scriptures.

6 This is when the Prophet Mohammed received the first verses of the Quran. Gabriel told Mohammed to remember the revelation by observing a holy time every year. In the years after this journey, the Prophet Mohammed and his followers made the ninth month of the Muslim year the month of Ramadan.

7 The word "Ramadan" literally means "scorcher" in Arabic, because it was in the intense heat of the summer that the Prophet Mohammed encountered Gabriel. But unlike the Western calendar, the Islamic calendar follows the cycles of the moon and contains only 354 days. As a result, Ramadan always begins approximately ten days before it began the previous year. So, for example, this year Ramadan came on August 11th. Next year, it will come on August 1st.

8 Now let's take a look at what Muslims do during this holy month. The practices of Ramadan center on fasting, prayer, and charity.

9 Fasting is one of the five pillars of Islam, and it becomes especially important during Ramadan. The Ramadan fast, known as the *Sawm,* begins at sunrise and ends at sunset. Seyyed Nasr, author of *Islam: Religion, History, and Civilization,* explains that "the fast is required of all Muslims, male and female, from the age of adolescence until one no longer possesses the physical strength to undertake it." The only exceptions are for the sick, the elderly, travelers, and pregnant women.

10 At the end of daylight hours, Muslims break the fast with *Iftar*—the evening meal, during which families, friends, and communities gather. As Donna Bowen and Evelyn Early explain in their book *Everyday Life in the Muslim Middle East, Iftar* usually begins with eating a date, which is what the Prophet Mohammed is said to have done. After eating a date and drinking water, my family would eat the *Iftar* dinner my mother cooked for us. We would always marvel that even though she was fasting and couldn't taste what she was cooking, she still somehow got the spices just right.

11 Prayer is also central to Ramadan. Muslims traditionally pray five times a day, but during Ramadan prayer is encouraged even more. Ramadan prayers are often tied to oral readings of the Quran—a practice known as *Tarawih.* The goal is to read and recite the entire Quran over the course of the month.

12 In addition to fasting and prayer, charity plays a key role in Ramadan. *Iftars* are often organized and funded by the wealthy as a way of feeding the poor and the needy. Also, many Muslims increase their charitable giving during the month. At the end of Ramadan, my family donates to charity and we also exchange gifts like Christians do on Christmas.

13 If you think about it, the main purpose of Ramadan is the same as most religious holidays—spiritual development. Christians and Jews gather regularly to commemorate their histories, to enact certain rituals, and to feel closer to God. Muslims do the same thing during Ramadan.

14 Today, we've explored the history of Ramadan and its practices—fasting, prayer, and charity. I'd like to leave you with the traditional greeting that Muslims utter during this holy month: "Ramadan Kareem," which means "Ramadan is generous." Less than a year from now, when the next Ramadan comes around, I hope you'll have a better understanding of why it is so sacred for one billion people around the world.

THE DANGERS OF CELL PHONES

It is widely known that using cell phones while driving can be dangerous. But what about simply holding a cell phone up to your ear? In recent years, researchers have begun to study the health risks of prolonged cell-phone use. The following persuasive speech examines those risks and their implications. Rather than taking the unrealistic position of urging her classmates to give up their cell phones entirely, the speaker asks them to make one simple—but important—change in the way they use their phones.

The speech is organized in Monroe's motivated sequence. As you read, notice how the speaker builds her case as she moves through each step of the sequence. Also pay attention to her delivery and to her use of the methods of persuasion

connect

View "The Dangers of Cell Phones" in the online Media Library for this appendix (Video A.3).

discussed in Chapter 17. How does she establish credibility and goodwill, both at the beginning of the speech and as it proceeds? Does she present strong evidence in support of her arguments? Is her reasoning clear and convincing? How does she appeal to the emotions of her audience? You can view the speech in the online Media Library for this appendix.

1 It's your constant companion. It's in your pocket, in your bag, in your hands, or against your head. You use it at home, in class, at the gym, before you go to sleep at night and first thing when you wake up in the morning. I'm talking, of course, about your cell phone. According to my class survey, everyone in this room has a cell phone, and all of us use it dozens of times every day.

2 But what if your constant companion is dangerous? What if it's hazardous to your health? Evidence is piling up that long-term use of cell phones can lead to tissue damage, tumors, and even brain cancer. Given that there are well over 4 billion people worldwide using cell phones, we're looking at a problem of potentially staggering magnitude. According to Devra Davis, epidemiologist and author of the 2010 book *Disconnect: The Truth About Cell Phone Radiation*, we may be watching "an epidemic in slow motion."

3 I'd never thought much about the possible perils of cell phones before I saw a *CBS News* report on the subject earlier this year. But doing extensive research for this speech made me realize that cell phones do in fact pose a danger to our health.

4 Now, don't worry, I'm not going to try to persuade you to abandon your constant companion. I still use mine on a regular basis, and I probably always will. But I do hope to persuade you to make one simple change in the way you use your cell phone—a change that will protect your health and could even make the difference between a long life and premature death. But first, let's look more closely at the health risks posed by cell phones.

5 Those risks stem from the fact that cell phones emit small amounts of radiation that, over time, can damage tissue. Every time you use your cell phone, you expose yourself to that radiation. The amount is minuscule in comparison to that given off by x-ray machines—about one one-billionth of the intensity. However, Ronald Herberman of the University of Pittsburgh Cancer Institute explains that the problem with cell phone radiation is not how much is emitted at a single time, but how much we are exposed to with repeated use day after day, year after year.

6 It's this long-term use of cell phones that has led researchers to warn about their danger. In one study, for example, the World Health Organization tracked 10,000 cell phone users over the course of 10 years. As reported in the *New York Times* on November 13, 2010, the data in this study indicated that subjects who used a cell phone 10 or more years doubled the risk of developing brain tumors.

7 Other studies have reached the same conclusion. Perhaps most important is a study in the *Journal of Occupational and Environmental Medicine* that surveyed all the previous research on cell phone use. It found "a consistent pattern of increased risk" for developing brain tumors among people who used cell phones for more than 10 years.

8 Alan Marks is one of those people. A 58-year-old real estate developer and father of three, he talked on his cell phone an hour a day for 23 years. Two years ago, doctors found a golf-ball-sized tumor in his brain. "There's no question what caused it," he says. "It was my cell phone."

9 And Alan Marks isn't the only person to conclude that he's sick because of his cell phone. Ann Gittleman's 2010 book *Zapped*, which deals at length with the health problems of cell phones, catalogues people who developed blinding headaches, dizziness, circulatory problems, nausea, and cancer from the kind of radiation emitted by cell phones.

10 Still not convinced about the potential dangers posed by your constant companion? Take a look, then, inside the thick manual that comes with your phone. You'll see that all cell phone manufacturers warn against keeping the phone right next to your body. Apple, for example, recommends keeping the iPhone five-eighths of an inch away from your body. Makers of the BlackBerry recommend that you keep their phone a full inch away. Cell phone manufacturers don't publicize this information widely, but they clearly recognize that their products are potentially hazardous.

11 So what's the solution? As I said earlier, it's not to stop using cell phones altogether. I still use mine on a regular basis, and I can't imagine being without it—and I'm sure you can't imagine being without yours. You can, however, take seriously the risks of cell phones and find a way to minimize those risks. Time and again, experts point out that the single most effective way to reduce the risk is not to press your cell phone against your head while using it. Since the phone emits radiation, the closer you put it to your head, the more radiation you expose yourself to.

12 At the very least, you should hold the phone one-half an inch to one full inch away from your ear. But ideally, you should get in the habit of not putting it up to your head at all. I now use my earbuds almost every time I use my phone. Another option is to use your speakerphone.

13 As with breaking any habit, changing the way you talk on your cell phone may be slightly inconvenient at first but will soon become second nature. You'll be able to enjoy all the benefits of your constant companion without suffering the fate of Alan Marks. If Marks had known the dangers of prolonged cell phone use, he would have done things a lot differently. "I wouldn't have held it to my head," he says. "I would have used the headset. I would have used the speakerphone. . . . And I would not have had the problems I had."

14 So please get in the habit of keeping your cell phone away from your ear when talking, and encourage your friends and family to do the same. Start today, with your next phone call, and continue every day in the future.

15 We can avoid the slow-motion epidemic that doctors and scientists are warning us about—as long as we remember to keep this away from this.

PHONY PHARMACEUTICALS

According to the U.S. Food and Drug Administration, the market for counterfeit prescription drugs is close to $75 billion a year. One expert, cited in the following speech, states that criminals "can make more money in counterfeit drugs than they can in heroin." This is an arresting fact, one of many that the speaker presents in documenting the problem of phony pharmaceuticals.

connect

View "Phony Pharmaceuticals" in the online Media Library for this appendix (Video A.4).

The speaker does not stop with the problem, however. As is necessary in a persuasive speech on a question of policy, she goes on to present a plan for solving the problem. She outlines the plan in four distinct steps that, taken together, advance a practical course of action. The speech as a whole is concise and uncluttered; there are

few wasted words and the ideas progress cleanly and briskly. As you can see from the video in the online Media Library for this appendix, the speaker's persuasiveness was further strengthened by her energetic delivery and inventive visual aids.

1 Take a look at these two pills. Do you notice a difference between them? How about these two? Do you see a difference here? How about these?

2 To the naked eye, these pills are indistinguishable. But at a chemical level, they are very, very different. In each case, the pill on the left is real; it will help you get better. The pill on the right is counterfeit; it will not help you get better. In some cases, it may even kill you.

3 Katherine Eban, author of *Dangerous Doses: How Counterfeiters Are Contaminating America's Drug Supply,* explains that phony pharmaceuticals are drugs that have been diluted, drugs in which the active ingredient has been replaced with something else, or drugs that have been relabeled to appear stronger than they truly are. Taking a phony pharmaceutical means that you do not receive the medicine you need to get better, and the results can be deadly.

4 I first became aware of this issue after my younger sister received a phony drug for her asthma last summer. Fortunately, the error was discovered before it caused her any lasting harm. But I've been concerned about the issue ever since, and I did a great deal of research on it for this speech. As a result, I am convinced that we need to take action now to combat the problem of phony pharmaceuticals. Later in my speech, I'll share with you my plan for curbing the spread of these dangerous drugs. But let's start by taking a closer look at the problem.

5 Phony pharmaceuticals are dangerous because of the health risks they pose. According to Graham Jackson, editor of the *International Journal of Clinical Practice*, counterfeit drugs include ingredients such as boric acid, leaded road paint, floor polish, shoe polish, talcum powder, and cement powder. But that's not all. There's also brick dust, chalk, nickel, and arsenic. Ingesting too much boric acid or floor polish can make you sick; leaded road paint and arsenic can kill you.

6 In one highly publicized case, 81 people in the United States died in 2008 because they took a counterfeit version of the blood thinner heparin. As reported by *CNN*, the phony heparin was originally manufactured outside the United States using a cheap sulfate that proved deadly. After slipping past all regulatory checks, it ended up in the United States, with tragic results.

7 The U.S. government's Bureau of International Information Programs estimates that 700,000 people around the world will die this year from phony pharmaceuticals—almost three times the number of people who live here in Madison. In fact, Roger Bate, of the American Enterprise Institute, reports that "trafficking in counterfeit drugs has become one of the world's fastest-growing criminal enterprises."

8 Phony pharmaceuticals are so widespread that they have become big business. The FDA estimates that they will bring in close to $75 billion in revenue this year alone—up from $40 billion only a few years ago. Tom Kubic, head of the Pharmaceutical Security Institute, told *USA Today* in September 2010 that criminals "can make more money in counterfeit drugs than they can in heroin."

9 Given the rewards of the counterfeit drug trade, the problem will only get worse in the coming years unless we take steps to bring it under control. The solution I propose is similar to House Resolution 2726, which is under consideration by the U.S. Congress. There are four steps to this solution.

10 First, criminal penalties for drug counterfeiters should be increased from three years in prison, which is the current limit, to no limit at all. If a drug peddler kills someone with phony pharmaceuticals, the punishment should fit the crime.

11 Second, the Food and Drug Administration should have the authority to recall prescription drugs. Right now, the FDA can encourage drug manufacturers to issue a recall, but it has no power to issue a recall on its own. To get phony pharmaceuticals off the street, recall authority needs to rest with a central agency that will act quickly and uniformly.

12 Third, the FDA should be given the resources for spot-checking the chemical makeup of prescription medication. We have health inspectors for food, why not have inspectors for prescription drugs?

13 Fourth, legitimate drug manufacturers should be required to implement track-and-trace technology. As explained in the *New York Times*, this technology stamps each bottle and pill with a unique code tied to a secure, centralized database. The code allows pharmacies and distributors to determine whether drugs are legitimate or phony, plus the route the drugs took to get to store shelves.

14 Representative Steve Israel of New York, sponsor of House Resolution 2726, says these four steps will "ensure that the domestic drug supply chain is secure for every American." It "will crack down on counterfeiting and increase the penalties for the outlaws who are compromising our health." The time has come for Congress to pass this vital legislation.

15 In conclusion, phony pharmaceuticals are pervasive and dangerous. By implementing the solution I have outlined, we will be able to control this public-health menace.

16 You have the right to know that the medication you're taking is real. You have the right to know that your next trip to the drugstore will be a safe one. And you have the right to know that what you see is what you get.

THE WONDERFUL WORLD OF DR. SEUSS

The aim of a commemorative speech is to pay tribute to a person, a group of people, an institution, or an idea. The following talk commemorates Theodor Seuss Geisel, author of the Dr. Seuss books. Unlike an informative presentation, which would provide biographical details about Geisel's life, this speech focuses on his activist spirit, focused determination, and creative genius. The speaker says enough to illustrate these traits, but his ultimate purpose is to inspire the audience rather than to inform it.

By blending his own words with memorable passages from Dr. Seuss, the speaker captures both the linguistic whimsy for which Seuss was so beloved and the serious lessons he sought to teach children and adults alike. As you can see from the video in the online Media Library for this appendix, the speaker's delivery strikes the right tone for his subject.

connect

View "The Wonderful World of Dr. Seuss" in the online Media Library for this appendix (Video A.5).

1 His words echoed through our childhoods: "I do so like green eggs and ham! Thank you! Thank you, Sam-I-Am!" His characters played in our imaginations: Horton the elephant, Yertle the turtle, the Cat in the Hat, the Lorax. And his books connected us to a whimsical world of color and creativity. He is the great doctor, whom you know as Seuss.

2 At the time of his death in 1991, Dr. Seuss had published 44 children's books. Perhaps more than any other author, he captured our childlike wonder and inspired the imagination of generations. Today, let us return to some of his stories—not to remember them, but to honor the man behind them—Theodor Seuss Geisel, whose activist spirit, focused determination, and creative genius made him the one and only Dr. Seuss.

3 From working on student newspapers to creating advertisements to crafting humorous essays, Geisel possessed an activist spirit long before he became famous as Dr. Seuss. During World War II, he illustrated training videos to help inspire the troops in the field. He also drew political cartoons that featured the same rhythmic cadence that readers have long admired—a cadence much like the march of soldiers overseas.

4 Eventually, Geisel would bring the same cadence and spirit to his books. *The Lorax*—my personal favorite—was so controversial because of its negative portrayal of the logging industry that some towns tried to ban it. But Geisel knew he needed to make a statement for the environment:

> *"I repeat," cried the Lorax,*
> *"I speak for the trees!" . . .*
> *"which you seem to be chopping as fast as you please!"*

5 Coupled with Geisel's activist spirit was a focused determination. His first published work, *And to Think That I Saw It on Mulberry Street*, was rejected by publishers more than twenty times. But Geisel pressed on, and the book appeared in 1937 to critical acclaim.

6 Determination was also central in the creation of *The Cat in the Hat*. Geisel's publisher challenged him to create a story that would introduce young readers to more than 200 new vocabulary words. Geisel met the challenge, and he put the words together in the story of a boy, a girl, a fish, a cat, a hat, Thing 1, and Thing 2:

> *We looked!*
> *Then we saw him step in on the mat!*
> *We looked!*
> *And we saw him!*
> *The Cat in the Hat!*

7 Ultimately, what stands out most about Geisel is his creative genius. With pleasing rhyme schemes, memorable characters, and instantly recognizable art, he created not just brilliant books but new realities.

8 He created the Grinch, the green menace who stole Christmas. He created Horton, the elephant who helped hatch an egg. And he created Yertle, the turtle king who took a long fall. Geisel's creative genius turned story time into a time of imagination, play, and possibility:

> *And today the great Yertle, that Marvelous he,*
> *Is King of the Mud. That is all he can see.*
> *And the turtles, of course . . . all the turtles are free*
> *As turtles and, maybe, all creatures should be.*

9 From Seuss's activist spirit, focused determination, and creative genius came the words, characters, and books that shaped our youth. No less important, it was Seuss who gave us a sense of optimism and possibility when facing the world. As he told us in *Oh, the Places You'll Go*:

You have brains in your head.
You have feet in your shoes.
You can steer yourself any direction you choose.

ELIE WIESEL

Few people are more universally admired than Elie Wiesel. A survivor of the Nazi death camps during World War II, he went on to become a prolific author, an esteemed teacher, and a powerful voice for marginalized people the world over. When Wiesel received the 1986 Nobel Peace Prize, he was described as "a messenger to mankind" on behalf of "peace, atonement, and human dignity."

The following commemorative speech praises Wiesel as an eloquent, fearless, and selfless leader. It provides sufficient information to make clear why Wiesel is commendable without getting bogged down in biographical details. The language is vivid and uplifting. Of special note is the repetition of "A-7713," Wiesel's prisoner number at Auschwitz. The speaker uses that number to dramatic effect in the introduction and then again in the conclusion to provide artistic unity.

In addition to reading this speech, you can view it in the online Media Library for this appendix.

connect
View "Elie Wiesel" in the online Media Library for this appendix (Video A.6).

1 A-7713. His new name, the graffiti stamped on his skin. A-7713, a concentration camp tattoo. At age fifteen, A-7713 was taken from his home by the Nazis and sent to Auschwitz, one of the twentieth century's most potent symbols of evil. Here A-7713 witnessed the deaths of thousands of human beings, including his mother and younger sister.

2 Somehow, A-7713 survived, and when World War II ended, he put his pain and grief to work making sure the world did not forget the Holocaust and making sure another Holocaust did not take place.

3 Today, the world knows A-7713 as Elie Wiesel, noted speaker and lecturer, author of more than 40 books, and recipient of the Presidential Medal of Freedom, the Congressional Gold Medal, and the Nobel Peace Prize, among others. Elie Wiesel is an eloquent, fearless, selfless leader who took the evils of Auschwitz as motivation to improve the world.

4 An eloquent leader, Elie Wiesel uses the power of language to confront the problems of humanity. Through compelling prose and brutal honesty, he explains that we cannot root out evil unless we recognize it and battle it wherever it exists. In his classic book, *Night*, he says of Auschwitz: "Never shall I forget that night, the first night in camp, which turned my life into one long night, seven times cursed and seven times sealed. Never shall I forget that smoke. Never shall I forget the little faces of the children, whose bodies I saw turned into wreaths of smoke beneath a silent blue sky." Haunting words that remind us of the reality of evil.

5 A fearless leader no less than an eloquent one, Elie Wiesel has spent 40 years battling the evils that continue to plague our planet. To the Miskito Indians of Nicaragua, displaced from their homeland, he brought inspiring words of strength and compassion. To men and women facing apartheid in South Africa, he brought a powerful denunciation of racial segregation and violence. To Cambodian refugees suffering from starvation and disease, he brought food and the promise of a new beginning. And to those of us who follow his work, he continues to provide inspiration.

6 A selfless leader as much as an eloquent and fearless one, Elie Wiesel has consistently put the needs of others before his own. With every award, his modesty stands side by side with his achievements. As he stated in his Nobel Prize acceptance speech, "Neutrality helps the oppressor, never the victim. Silence encourages the tormentor, never the tormented. . . . Wherever men and women are persecuted because of their race, religion, or political views, that place must—at that moment—become the center of the universe."

7 Today, at more than 80 years of age, Elie Wiesel continues to fight against the night. Through all his trials and all his triumphs, the tattoo remains: A-7713, a constant reminder of evil, injustice, and indifference. In battling these forces, Elie Wiesel has shown the kind of moral leadership too often lacking in today's world.

8 There is no better way to end than to quote his own words: "There may be times when we are powerless to prevent injustice, but there must never be a time when we fail to protest. . . . What these victims need above all is to know that they are not alone, that we are not forgetting them, that while their freedom depends on ours, the quality of our freedom depends on theirs."

Notes

Chapter 1 Speaking in Public

[1]Pericles, quoted in Richard Whately, *Elements of Rhetoric,* 7th ed. (London: John W. Parker, 1846), p. 10.

[2]*It Takes More Than a Major: Employer Priorities for College Learning and Student Success* (Washington, D.C.: Hart Research Associates, 2013); American Management Association, *AMA 2012 Critical Skills Survey* (New York: American Management Association, 2013).

[3]Dave McGinn, "Me? Public Speaking?" *Globe and Mail,* December 1, 2009, p. L1.

[4]Quoted in Emily Driscoll, "Um, Like, Whatever: College Grads Lack Verbal Skills," Foxbusiness.com, March 4, 2011. April 6, 2011.

[5]George A. Kennedy, *Comparative Rhetoric: An Historical and Cross-Cultural Introduction* (New York: Oxford University Press, 1998).

[6]Geoffrey Brewer, "Snakes Top List of Americans' Fears," Gallup News Service, February 2001; Alex Blyth, "How to Get the Most Out of Public Speaking Training," *Training Magazine* (June 14, 2006), p. 7.

[7]A. M. Ruscio, T. A. Brown, W. T. Chiu, J. Sareen, M. B. Steain, and R. C. Kessler, "Social Fears and Social Phobia in the USA: Results from the National Comorbidity Survey Replication," *Psychological Medicine* (January 2008), pp. 15–28.

[8]Cicero, *De Oratore,* trans. E. W. Sutton (Cambridge, MA: Harvard University Press, 1942), p. xxvi.

[9]Digby Jones, "Public Speaking Tests the Nerves of Most Directors," *Birmingham Post,* August 25, 2003.

[10]Elayne Synder, *Speak for Yourself—With Confidence* (New York: New American Library, 1983), p. 113.

[11]Sharon Aschaiek, "Conquer Your Fear of Public Speaking," *Toronto Sun,* March 16, 2005.

[12]A number of studies have shown that taking a public speaking course is effective in reducing stage fright. For an excellent review of the research, consult Graham D. Bodie, "A Racing Heart, Rattling Knees, and Ruminative Thoughts: Defining, Explaining, and Treating Public Speaking Anxiety," *Communication Education,* 59 (2010), pp. 70–105.

[13]Lilly Walters, *Secrets of Successful Speakers* (New York: McGraw-Hill, 1993), pp. 32–36.

[14]See Steven Ungerleider, *Mental Training for Peak Performance,* rev. ed. (Emmaus, PA: Rodale Books, 2005).

[15]Joe Ayres, Tim Hopf, Michael T. Hazel, Debbie M. A. Sonandre, and Tanichya K. Wongprasert, "Visualization and Performance Visualization: Applications, Evidence, and Speculation," in John A. Daly et al. (eds.), *Avoiding Communication: Shyness, Reticence, and Communication Apprehension,* 3rd ed. (Cresskill, NJ: Hampton Press, 2009), pp. 375–394.

[16]Dick Cavett, quoted in Steve Allen, *How to Make a Speech* (New York: McGraw-Hill, 1986), p. 10.

[17]For more detail on the ideas in this paragraph, see Michael T. Motley, *Overcoming Your Fear of Public Speaking: A Proven Method* (Boston, MA: Houghton Mifflin, 1998).

[18]Chris R. Sawyer and Ralph R. Behnke, "Reduction in Public Speaking State Anxiety During Performance as a Function of Sensitization Processes," *Communication Quarterly,* 50 (2002), pp. 110–121.

[19]For more detail on the dimensions of critical thinking, see M. Neil Browne and Stuart M. Keeley, *Asking the Right Questions: A Guide to Critical Thinking,* 9th ed. (Upper Saddle River, NJ: Pearson Education, 2012).

[20]For other models of the speech communication process, see Em Griffin, Andrew Ledbetter, and Glenn Sparks, *A First Look at Communication Theory,* 9th ed. (New York: McGraw-Hill, 2015); Stephen W. Littlejohn and Karen A. Foss, *Theories of Human Communication,* 8th ed. (Long Grove, IL: Waveland Press, 2011).

[21]Herman Melville, *Redburn: His First Voyage* (New York: Harper and Brothers, 1850), p. 214.

[22]William B. Gudykunst and Young Yun Kim, *Communicating with Strangers: An Approach to Intercultural Communication,* 4th ed. (New York: McGraw-Hill, 2003), p. 4.

[23]For more detail on gestures and other aspects of intercultural communication, see Judith N. Martin and Thomas K. Nakayama, *Intercultural Communication in Contexts,* 6th ed. (New York: McGraw-Hill, 2013); Larry A. Samovar, Richard E. Porter, Edwin R. McDaniel, and Carolyn S. Roy, *Communication Between Cultures,* 8th ed. (Boston, MA: Wadsworth, 2013).

[24]Adapted from Roger E. Axtell (ed.), *Do's and Taboos Around the World,* 3rd ed. (New York: John Wiley and Sons, 1993), p. 41.

[25]Myron W. Lustig and Jolene Koester, *Intercultural Competence: Interpersonal Communication Across Cultures,* 6th ed. (Boston, MA: Allyn and Bacon, 2013), pp. 137–139.

[26]For more on multiculturalism and communication, see Shang Liu, Zala Volčič, and Cindy Gallois, *Introducing Intercultural Communication: Global Cultures and Contexts* (Thousand Oaks, CA: Sage, 2011).

Chapter 2 Ethics and Public Speaking

[1]Richard L. Johannesen, Kathleen S. Valde, and Karen E. Whedbee, *Ethics in Human Communication,* 6th ed. (Prospect Heights, IL: Waveland Press, 2008), p. 14.

[2]Johannesen, Valde, and Whedbee, *Ethics in Human Communication,* p. 13.

[3]See, for example, Vincent Ryan Ruggiero, *Thinking Critically About Ethical Issues,* 9th ed. (New York: McGraw-Hill, 2015).

[4]Haig A. Bosmajian, *The Language of Oppression* (Lanham, MD: University Press of America, 1983), p. 5.

[5]See Steven J. Heyman, *Free Speech and Human Dignity* (New Haven, CT: Yale University Press, 2008).

[6]Thomas L. Tedford and Dale A. Herbeck, *Freedom of Speech in the United States,* 7th ed. (State College, PA: Strata Publishing, 2013), pp. 196–203.

[7]Kenneth Blanchard and Norman Vincent Peale, *The Power of Ethical Management* (New York: Ballantine Books, 1988), p. 64.

[8]For two excellent guides to ethical decision making, see Peter Singer, *Practical Ethics*, 3rd ed. (New York: Cambridge University Press, 2011); Ronald A. Howard and Clinton D. Korver, *Ethics for the Real World* (Boston, MA: Harvard Business Press, 2008).

[9]*MLA Handbook for Writers of Research Papers,* 7th ed. (New York: Modern Language Association of America, 2009), p. 52.

[10]Michele Mandel, "Felled TDSB Director Chris Spence's Mistakes Were Not Innocent," *Toronto Sun*, January 11, 2013; Kristin Rushowy and Louise Brown, "Chris Spence Breaks Silence on Plagiarism Scandal," *Toronto Star,* July 25, 2013. Also see Kristin Rushowy, "TDSB's Chris Spence Resigns Amid Growing Plagiarism Scandal," *Toronto Star,* January 10, 2013; Oliver Moore and Simona Chiose, "DSB Director Resigns Over Plagiarism, PhD Dissertation Includes Unattributed Passages," *Globe and Mail*, January 10, 2013; Megan O'Toole, "Publisher to Investigate 'Troubling' Plagiarism Allegations Against TDSB Director Chris Spence," *National Post*, January 20, 2013.

[11]Bruce Perry, *Malcolm: The Life of the Man Who Changed Black America* (Tarrytown, NY: Station Hill, 1991), p. 380.

[12]The credo can be accessed at http://www.natcom.org/Tertiary.aspx?id=2119&terms=credo on ethical.

[13]See http://www.natcom.org/Tertiary.aspx?id=2119&terms=credo on ethical.

Chapter 3 Listening

[1]Larry Barker and Kittie Watson, *Listen Up: What You've Never Heard About the Other Half of Every Conversation* (New York: St. Martin's, 2001), p. 5.

[2]Michael P. Nichols, *The Lost Art of Listening,* 2nd ed. (New York: Guilford, 2009).

[3]See Lyman K. Steil and Richard K. Bommelje, *Listening Leaders: The Ten Golden Rules to Listen, Lead, and Succeed* (Edina, MN: Beaver's Pond Press, 2004).

[4]Judi Brownell, *Listening: Attitudes, Principles, and Skills,* 5th ed. (Boston, MA: Allyn and Bacon, 2013), p. 8.

[5]Jan Flynn, Tuula-Ritta Valikoski, and Jennie Grau, "Listening in the Business Context: Reviewing the State of Research," *International Journal of Listening*, 22 (2008), pp. 141–151; Laura A. Janusik, "Listening Pedagogy: Where Do We Go From Here?" in Andrew D. Wolvin (ed.), *Listening and Human Communication in the 21st Century* (West Sussex: Blackwell, 2010), pp. 193–194.

[6]See, for example, Melissa L. Beall, Jennifer Gill-Rosier, Jeanine Tate, and Amy Matten, "State of the Context: Listening in Education," *International Journal of Listening,* 22 (2008), pp. 123–132; Graham D. Bodie and Margaret Fitch-Hauser, "Quantitative Research in Listening: Explication and Overview," in Wolvin, *Listening and Human Communication in the 21st Century,* pp. 46–93.

[7]Andrew W. Wolvin and Carolyn Gwynn Coakley, *Listening,* 5th ed. (Dubuque, IA: Brown and Benchmark, 1995), pp. 223–396.

[8]Brownell, *Listening: Attitudes, Principles, and Skills,* p. 81.

[9]Louis Nizer, *My Life in Court,* rpnt. ed. (Whitefish, MT: 2010), pp. 297–298.

[10]Adapted from Lyman K. Steil, Larry L. Barker, and Kittie W. Watson, *Effective Listening* (Reading, MA: Addison-Wesley, 1983).

[11]Two excellent guides to the premises and methods of active listening are Bernard T. Ferrari, *Power Listening: Mastering the Most Critical Business Skill of All* (New York: Penguin, 2012), and Tim Hast, *Powerful Listening. Powerful Influence* (North Charleston, NC: CreateSpace Independent Publishing, 2013).

[12]George H. Putnam, *Abraham Lincoln* (New York: Putnam, 1909), pp. 44–45.

[13]M. Scott Peck, *The Road Less Traveled: A New Psychology of Love, Traditional Values, and Spiritual Growth,* 25th anniversary ed. (New York: Touchstone Books, 2003), p. 127.

[14]Jack Hayes, "Fifty Years of Meteorological Advances," *Vital Speeches,* 77 (2011), pp. 27–30.

[15]See Ralph G. Nichols and Leonard A. Stevens, *Are You Listening?* (New York: McGraw-Hill, 1957), pp. 113–114. This classic work still has much of value to say about its subject.

[16]On some of the other challenges involved in note taking, see Dung C. Bui, Joel Myerson, and Sandra Hale, "Note-Taking with Computers: Exploring Alternative Strategies for Improved Recall," *Journal of Educational Psychology,* 105 (2013), pp. 299–309; Annie Piolat, Thierry Olive, and Ronald T. Kellogg, "Cognitive Effort During Note Taking," *Applied Cognitive Psychology,* 19 (2005), pp. 291–312.

[17]See, for example, Tamas Makany, Jonathan Kemp, and Itiel E. Dror, "Optimizing the Use of Note-Taking as an External Cognitive Aid for Increasing Learning," *British Journal of Educational Technology,* 40 (2009), pp. 619–635.

Chapter 6 Analyzing the Audience

[1]Seeing the speech classroom as a real audience is also important because it engages students in a form of rhetorical activity that is vital to participatory democracy. See Rosa A. Eberly, "Rhetoric and the Anti-Logos Doughball: Teaching Deliberating Bodies the Practices of Participatory Democracy," *Rhetoric and Public Affairs,* 5 (2002), 296.

[2]Saul Alinsky, *Rules for Radicals* (New York: Random House, 1971), p. 81.

[3]For a broader discussion of gender issues in communication, see Julia T. Wood, *Gendered Lives: Communication, Gender, and Culture,* 11th ed. (Boston, MA: Wadsworth, 2015).

[4]Diana L. Eck, *A New Religious America* (New York: HarperCollins, 2001), p. 4.

[5]Research shows that speakers are usually more persuasive when they attempt to refute opposing arguments rather than ignoring them. See Richard M. Perloff, *The Dynamics of Persuasion: Communication and Attitudes in the 21st Century,* 5th ed. (New York: Routledge, 2014), p. 265.

Chapter 7 Gathering Materials

[1]For more detail on Internet research, see Randolph Hock, *The Extreme Searcher's Internet Handbook: A Guide for the Serious Searcher,* 4th ed. (Medford, NJ: CyberAge Books, 2013).

[2]See, for example, Imogen Casebourne, Chris Davies, Michelle Fernandes, and Naomi Norman, *Assessing the Accuracy and Quality of Wikipedia Entries Compared to Popular Online Encyclopedias: A Comparative Preliminary Study Across Disciplines in English, Spanish, and Arabic* (Brighton, UK: Epic, 2012); N. J. Reavley et al., "Quality of Information Sources About Mental Disorders: A Comparison of Wikipedia with Centrally Controlled Web and Printed Sources," *Psychological Medicine,* 42 (2012), pp. 1753–1762; Don Fallis, "Toward an Epistemology of Wikipedia," *Journal of the American Society for Information Science and Technology,* 59 (2008), pp. 1662–1674.

[3]These criteria are adapted from Sheridan Libraries, "Evaluating Information Found on the Internet," *Johns Hopkins University.* Web. April 20, 2014.

[4]For more information on various interview types and situations, see Charles J. Stewart and William B. Cash Jr., *Interviewing: Principles and Practices,* 14th ed. (New York: McGraw-Hill, 2014).

[5]For an interesting study that confirms the extent to which the process of researching and developing speeches can affect the beliefs and attitudes of student speakers, see Barbara Mae Gayle, "Transformations in a Civil Discourse Public Speaking Class: Speakers' and Listeners' Attitude Change," *Communication Education,* 53 (2004), 174–184.

Chapter 8 Supporting Your Ideas

[1]See, for example, Kathryn Greene, Shelly Campo, and Smita C. Banerjee, "Comparing Normative, Anecdotal, and Statistical Risk Evidence to Discourage Tanning Bed Use," *Communication Quarterly,* 58 (2010), pp. 111–132.

[2]I would like to thank *21st Century* and *China Daily* for permission to include this excerpt from Sun Yan's speech in the online Media Library for *The Art of Public Speaking.*

[3]Elliot Aronson, *The Social Animal,* 11th ed. (New York: Worth, 2011), pp. 92–93.

[4]This point was made by James A. Winans in his classic *Speech-Making* (New York: Appleton-Century-Crofts, 1922), p. 141.

[5]Over the years, there has been much debate over whether statistics or examples have more impact on listeners. For a recent study that addresses this subject, see Bing Han and Edward L. Fink, "How Do Statistical and Narrative Evidence Affect Persuasion? The Role of Evidentiary Features," *Argumentation and Advocacy,* 49 (2012), 39–58.

[6]One implication of Han and Fink, "How Do Statistical and Narrative Evidence Affect Persuasion," is that multiple statistics tend to be more persuasive than single statistics.

[7]Joel Best, *Stat-Spotting: A Guide to Identifying Dubious Data* (Berkeley, CA: University of California Press, 2008), provides a fascinating look at the use and misuse of statistics. For a more technical approach, see Neil J. Salkind, *Statistics for People Who (Think They) Hate Statistics,* 5th ed. (Thousand Oaks, CA: Sage, 2014).

[8]Bob Papper, "TV Salaries Fall, Radio Stagnant," Radio Television Digital News Association (RTDNA). Web. April 23, 2014.

[9]Mike Allen et al., "Testing the Persuasiveness of Evidence: Combining Narrative and Statistical Forms," *Communication Research Reports,* 17 (2000), pp. 331–336.

[10]For research confirming the importance of citing sources when presenting evidence, see Rodney A. Reynolds and J. Lynn Reynolds, "Evidence," in James Price Dillard and Michael Pfau (eds.), *The Persuasion Handbook: Developments in Theory and Practice* (Thousand Oaks, CA: Sage, 2002), pp. 429–430.

[11]Richard M. Perloff, *The Dynamics of Persuasion: Communication and Attitudes in the 21st Century,* 5th ed. (New York: Routledge, 2014), pp. 267–269.

Chapter 9 Organizing the Body of the Speech

[1]Ernest C. Thompson, "An Experimental Investigation of the Relative Effectiveness of Organizational Structure in Oral Communication," *Southern Speech Journal,* 26 (1960), pp. 59–69.

[2]Harry Sharp Jr., and Thomas McClung, "Effects of Organization on the Speaker's Ethos," *Speech Monographs,* 33 (1966), pp. 182–183.

[3]See, for example, B. Scott Titsworth and Joseph P. Mazer, "Clarity in Teaching and Learning: Conundrums, Consequences, and Opportunities," in Deanna L. Fassett and John T. Warren (eds.), *Sage Handbook of Communication and Instruction* (Thousand Oaks, CA: Sage, 2010), pp. 241–261; Amber L. Finn and Paul Schrodt, "Students' Perceived Understanding Mediates the Effects of Teacher Clarity and Nonverbal Immediacy on Learner Environment," *Communication Education,* 61 (2012), 111–130.

Chapter 10 Beginning and Ending the Speech

[1]Shaun Donovan, "We All Work for Terrell," *Vital Speeches of the Day,* 79 (2013), pp. 381–382.

[2]Robert M. Gates, "About the Institution You Will Someday Lead," *Vital Speeches of the Day,* 77 (2011), pp. 138–142.

[3]Dorothy Sarnoff, *Speech Can Change Your Life* (Garden City, NY: Doubleday, 1970), p. 189.

[4]Sarnoff, *Speech Can Change Your Life,* p. 190.

Chapter 11 Outlining the Speech

[1]Robert T. Oliver, *History of Public Speaking in America* (Boston, MA: Allyn and Bacon, 1965), p. 143.

[2]Oliver, *History of Public Speaking,* p. 145.

Chapter 12 Using Language

[1]For a valuable collection of essays on language, meaning, and culture, see Susan D. Blum (ed.), *Making Sense of Language,* 2nd ed. (New York: Oxford University Press, 2013).

[2]Dorothy Sarnoff, *Speech Can Change Your Life* (New York: Doubleday, 1970), p. 71.

[3]Annmarie Mungo, "A Child Is Born," *Winning Orations, 1980* (Mankato, MN: Interstate Oratorical Association, 1980), pp. 49–50.

[4]See Joseph M. Williams and Joseph Bizup, *Style: Lessons in Clarity and Grace,* 11th ed. (New York: Longman, 2013), for more on the principles of verbal clarity.

[5]James Geary, *I Is an Other: The Secret Life of Metaphor and How It Shapes the Way We See the World* (New York: Harper, 2011), provides a highly readable exploration of the role of metaphor in human expression.

[6]Edward Bliss Jr. (ed.), *In Search of Light: The Broadcasts of Edward R. Murrow, 1938–1961* (New York: Knopf, 1967), p. 276.

[7]Rosalie Maggio, *Talking About People: A Guide to Fair and Accurate Language* (Phoenix, AZ: Oryx Press, 1997), p. 26.

Chapter 13 Delivering the Speech

[1]Irving Bartlett, *Wendell Phillips: Boston Brahmin* (Boston, MA: Beacon Press, 1961), p. 192.

[2]A. Craig Baird, *Rhetoric: A Philosophical Inquiry* (New York: Ronald Press, 1965), p. 207.

[3]Daniel J. O'Keefe, *Persuasion: Theory and Research,* 2nd ed. (Thousand Oaks, CA: Sage, 2002), p. 185.

[4]Dorothy Sarnoff, *Speech Can Change Your Life* (Garden City, NY: Doubleday, 1970), p. 73.

[5]See William Labov, *Dialect Diversity in America: The Politics of Language Change* (Charlottesville, VA: University of Virginia Press, 2012), for a provocative examination of regional dialects in the United States.

[6]For more detail on all aspects of voice production, consult Kenneth C. Crannell, *Voice and Articulation,* 5th ed. (Boston, MA: Wadsworth, 2012).

[7]Mark L. Knapp, Judith A. Hall, and Terrence G. Horgan, *Nonverbal Communication in Human Interaction,* 8th ed. (Boston, MA: Wadsworth, 2014), pp. 17–18.

[8]Richard M. Perloff, *The Dynamics of Persuasion: Communication and Attitudes in the 21st Century,* 5th ed. (New York: Routledge, 2014), pp. 253–259.

[9]For more on delivery, plus other aspects of public speaking, see Carmine Gallo, *Talk Like TED: The 9 Public Speaking Secrets of the World's Top Minds* (New York: St. Martin's, 2014); Garr Reynolds, *The Naked Presenter* (Berkeley, CA: New Riders, 2011).

[10]Thomas F. Calcagni, *Tough Questions—Good Answers: Taking Control of Any Interview* (Sterling, VA: Capital Books, 2008), provides many practical tips on managing question-and-answer sessions.

[11]Adapted from Timothy J. Koegel, *The Exceptional Presenter Goes Virtual* (Austin, TX: Greenleaf Book Group, 2010), p. 117.

[12]Koegel, *The Exceptional Presenter Goes Virtual,* p. 100.

[13]Cynthia Clay, *Great Webinars: How to Create Interactive Learning That Is Captivating, Informative, and Fun* (San Francisco, CA: Pfeiffer, 2012), p. 5.

Chapter 14 Using Visual Aids

[1]For a review of research on these subjects, see Richard E. Mayer, "Instruction Based on Visualizations," in Richard E. Mayer and Patricia A. Alexander (eds.), *Handbook of Research on Learning and Instruction* (New York: Routledge, 2011), pp. 427–445.

[2]See Stephen Few, *Now You See It: Simple Visualization Techniques for Quantitative Analysis* (Oakland, CA: Analytics Press, 2009), for a revealing look at the art of statistical graphics.

[3]Garr Reynolds, *Presentation Zen: Simple Ideas on Presentation and Delivery,* 2nd ed. (Berkeley, CA: New Riders, 2012), p. 11.

[4]See, for example, Eunmo Sung and Richard E. Mayer, "When Graphics Improve Liking but Not Learning from Online Lessons," *Computers in Human Behavior,* 28 (2012), pp. 1618–1625.

[5]Garr Reynolds, *Presentation Zen Design: A Simple Visual Approach to Presenting in Today's World*, 2nd ed. (Berkeley, CA: New Riders, 2014), provides a wealth of insight about designing high-impact visual aids.

[6]Bert E. Bradley, *Fundamentals of Speech Communication: The Credibility of Ideas*, 6th ed. (Dubuque, IA: William C. Brown, 1991), p. 280.

[7]For a fascinating look at the principles of information graphics in general, consult Albert Cairo, *The Functional Art: An Introduction to Information Graphics and Visualization* (Berkeley, CA: New Riders, 2013).

Chapter 15 Speaking to Inform

[1]John R. Johnson and Nancy Szczupakiewicz, "The Public Speaking Course: Is It Preparing Students with Work-Related Public Speaking Skills?" *Communication Education*, 36 (1987), pp. 131–137; Andrew D. Wolvin and Diana Corley, "The Technical Speech Communication Course: A View from the Field," *Association for Communication Administration Bulletin*, 49 (1984), pp. 83–91.

[2]Richard E. Mayer, Sherry Fennell, Lindsay Farmer, and Julie Campbell, "A Personalization Effect in Multimedia Learning: Students Learn Better When Words Are in Conversational Style Rather Than Formal Style," *Journal of Educational Psychology*, 96 (2004), pp. 389–395.

[3]Joseph Conrad, "Youth: A Narrative," in Samuel Hynes (ed.), *Collected Stories of Joseph Conrad* (Hopewell, NJ: Ecco Press, 1991), p. 166.

[4]James Humes, *Roles Speakers Play* (New York: Harper and Row, 1976), p. 25.

Chapter 16 Speaking to Persuade

[1]There are many competing definitions of persuasion. Mine is drawn from Gerald R. Miller, "On Being Persuaded: Some Basic Distinctions," in James Price Dillard and Lijiang Shen (eds.), *The SAGE Handbook of Persuasion: Developments in Theory and Practice*, 2nd ed. (Thousand Oaks, CA: Sage, 2013), pp. 70–82.

[2]Amanda Bennett, "Economics + Meeting = A Zillion Causes and Effects," *Wall Street Journal*, January 10, 1995, B1.

[3]See Richard L. Johannesen, Kathleen S. Valde, and Karen E. Whedbee, *Ethics in Human Communication*, 6th ed. (Prospect Heights, IL: Waveland Press, 2008), for a full look at communication ethics.

[4]Adapted from Herbert W. Simons and Jean G. Jones, *Persuasion in Society*, 2nd ed. (New York: Routledge, 2011), p. 46.

[5]This view of the interaction between speaker and listener reflects cognitive processing models of persuasion and attitude change in general and the elaboration likelihood model in particular. For a concise explanation of the latter, see Em Griffin, Andrew Ledbetter, and Glenn Sparks, *A First Look at Communication Theory*, 9th ed. (New York: McGraw-Hill, 2015), pp. 188–199.

[6]There is a great deal of research confirming the need for persuasive speakers to answer potential objections to their arguments. See John A. Banas and Stephen A. Rains, "A Meta-Analysis of Research on Inoculation Theory," *Communication Monographs*, 77 (2010), pp. 282–311.

[7]For an insightful look at the research on courtroom persuasion, see John C. Reinard, "Persuasion in the Legal Setting," in Dillard and Shen, *SAGE Handbook of Persuasion*, pp. 331–353.

[8]Richard M. Perloff, *The Dynamics of Persuasion: Communication and Attitudes in the 21st Century*, 5th ed. (New York: Routledge, 2014), pp. 351–352.

[9]Daniel J. O'Keefe, *Persuasion: Theory and Research*, 2nd ed. (Thousand Oaks, CA: Sage, 2002), pp. 218–219.

[10]See, for example, Amber Marie Reinhart, Heather M. Marshall, Thomas Hugh Feeley, and Frank Tutzauer, "The Persuasive Effects of Message Framing in Organ Donation: The Mediating Role of Psychological Reactance," *Communication Monographs*, 74 (2007), pp. 229–255.

Chapter 17 Methods of Persuasion

[1]James C. McCroskey, *An Introduction to Rhetorical Communication*, 9th ed. (Boston, MA: Allyn and Bacon, 2006), pp. 84–96.

[2]Rachel A. Smith and Edward L. Fink, "Compliance Dynamics within a Simulated Friendship Network I: The Effects of Agency, Tactic, and Node Centrality," *Human Communication Research*, 36 (2010), pp. 232–260.

[3]Richard M. Perloff, *The Dynamics of Persuasion: Communication and Attitudes in the 21st Century*, 5th ed. (New York: Routledge, 2014), pp. 281–283.

[4]See John A. Banas and Stephen A. Rains, "A Meta-Analysis of Research on Inoculation Theory," *Communication Monographs*, 77 (2010), pp. 282–311.

[5]John C. Reinard, "The Empirical Study of the Persuasive Effects of Evidence: The Status after Fifty Years of Research," *Human Communication Research*, 15 (1988), pp. 37–38.

[6]See, for example, Michael T. Stephenson, "Examining Adolescents' Responses to Antimarijuana PSAs," *Human Communication Research*, 29 (2003), pp. 343–369.

[7]Rodney A. Reynolds and J. Lynn Reynolds, "Evidence," in James Price Dillard and Michael Pfau (eds.), *The Persuasion Handbook: Developments in Theory and Practice* (Thousand Oaks, CA: Sage, 2002), pp. 429–430.

[8]Daniel J. O'Keefe, *Persuasion: Theory and Research*, 2nd ed. (Thousand Oaks, CA: Sage, 2002), pp. 216–218.

[9]Adapted from James C. Humes, *A Speaker's Treasury of Anecdotes about the Famous* (New York: Harper and Row, 1978), p. 131.

[10]In classical systems of logic, reasoning from particular facts to a general conclusion was known as induction. Contemporary logicians, however, have redefined induction as any instance of reasoning in which the conclusion follows from its premises with probability, regardless of whether the reasoning moves from specific instances to a general conclusion or from a general premise to a specific conclusion. In this scheme, reasoning from specific instances is one kind of inductive argument—as are causal reasoning and analogical reasoning. See, for example, Nancy M. Cavender and Howard Kahane, *Logic and Contemporary Rhetoric: The Use of Reason in Everyday Life*, 12th ed. (Boston, MA: Wadsworth, 2014).

[11]Lionel Ruby, *The Art of Making Sense* (Philadelphia: Lippincott, 1954), p. 261.

[12]In classical systems of logic, reasoning from a general premise to a specific conclusion was known as deduction. But just as contemporary logicians have redefined induction (see note 10 above), they have redefined deduction as any instance of reasoning in which the conclusion follows from its premises with certainty. Some deductive arguments move from general premises to a specific conclusion, but others move from specific premises to a general conclusion. Many speech textbooks confuse reasoning from principle, which is one form of deduction, with deductive reasoning in general.

[13]For more on fallacies and argumentation in general, see Douglas Walton, *Methods of Argumentation* (New York: Cambridge University Press, 2013).

[14]H. E. Butler (trans.), *The Institutio Oratoria of Quintilian* (Cambridge, MA: Harvard University Press, 1961), IV, p. 141.

[15]George Campbell, *The Philosophy of Rhetoric*, ed. Lloyd F. Bitzer (Carbondale, IL: Southern Illinois University Press, 1988), p. 77.

[16]Research on fear appeals, for example, has demonstrated that messages devoted exclusively to arousing fear in the audience are usually less effective than messages that combine fear appeals with reasonable explanations of how to eliminate or cope with the source of fear. For an excellent review of that research, see Paul A. Mongeau, "Fear Appeals," in James Price Dillard and Lijiang Shen (eds.), *The SAGE Handbook of Persuasion: Developments in Theory and Practice*, 2nd ed. (Thousand Oaks, CA: Sage, 2013), pp. 184–199.

Chapter 18 Speaking on Special Occasions

[1]James C. Humes, *Roles Speakers Play* (New York: Harper and Row, 1976), p. 8.

[2]For both speeches, see "President Obama Welcomes the Teacher of the Year," April 24, 2012 (http://www.whitehouse.gov/blog/2012/04/24/president-obama-welcomes-teacher-year), May 13, 2014.

[3]Humes, *Roles Speakers Play*, pp. 33–34, 36.

Chapter 19 Speaking in Small Groups

[1]Gloria J. Galanes and Katherine Adams, *Effective Group Discussion: Theory and Practice*, 14th ed. (New York: McGraw-Hill, 2013), pp. 233–244.

[2]See Kyle R. Andrews, Franklin J. Boster, and Christopher J. Carpenter, "Persuading in the Small Group Context," in James Price Dillard and Lijiang Shen (eds.), *The SAGE Handbook of Persuasion: Developments in Theory and Practice*, 2nd ed. (Thousand Oaks, CA: Sage, 2013), pp. 354–370, for a review of scholarship on this subject.

[3] For more on the many dimensions of group leadership, see John W. Gastil, *The Group in Society* (Thousand Oaks, CA: Sage 2010), pp. 139–166.

[4] Consult Scott A. Myers and Carolyn Anderson, *Fundamentals of Small Group Communication* (Thousand Oaks, CA: Sage, 2008), pp. 199–215, for more detail on dealing with conflict in small groups.

[5] Charles Pavitt and Kelly K. Johnson, "Scheidel and Crowell Revisited: A Descriptive Study of Group Proposal Sequencing," *Communication Monographs,* 69 (2002), pp. 19–32.

[6] For research on this subject, see Michele H. Jackson and Marshall Scott Poole, "Idea-Generation in Naturally Occurring Contexts: Complex Appropriation of Simple Group Procedure," *Human Communication Research,* 29 (2003), pp. 560–591.

[7] For more on small-group oral presentations, see Katherine Adams and Gloria J. Galanes, *Communicating in Groups: Applications and Skills,* 9th ed. (New York: McGraw-Hill, 2015).

Index

D

Q

R